THE LONG WAR OF IDEAS

THE LONG WAR OF IDEAS

AMERICAN PUBLIC DIPLOMACY
IN ARABIC AFTER 9/11

NATHANIEL GREENBERG

Columbia University Press
New York

Columbia University Press
Publishers Since 1893
New York   Chichester, West Sussex
cup.columbia.edu

Copyright © 2026 Columbia University Press
All rights reserved

Cataloging-in-Publication Data available from the Library of Congress.
ISBN 9780231215978 (hardback)
ISBN 9780231215961 (trade paperback)
ISBN 9780231561068 (epub)

LCCN 202503332

Cover design: Elliott S. Cairns
Cover image: Courtesy of the Barack Obama Presidential Library

GPSR Authorized Representative: Easy Access System Europe,
Mustamäe tee 50, 10621 Tallinn, Estonia, gpsr.requests@easproject.com

For my children

CONTENTS

Preface ix
Acknowledgments xiii

Introduction   1

1. Public Diplomacy and the Arab World   33
2. Free Play   73
3. Iraq and the World   101
4. Gray Is the New Black   123
5. Silicon Armies   147
6. Endgames   179

    Conclusion   206

   Notes   219
   Bibliography   275
   Index   299

   Image gallery begins after page 146

PREFACE

"With the attack of the World Trade Center," wrote Jean Baudrillard, "we have now witnessed the ultimate event, the mother of all events, an event so pure it contains within it all the events that never took place." Twenty years on, with the century's first pandemic in hindsight, climate crises ever-present, and new global wars on the horizon, it seems strange, almost quaint, to think of September 11 as the ultimate reckoning with globalization. But for many at the time—my generation at least—it was indeed just that. Then, like now, we framed the experience in clinical terms. "Terrorists, like viruses, are everywhere," wrote Baudrillard. The world seemed smaller but its peoples somehow more distant.[1]

In the months following 9/11, empathy toward the United States was eerily ubiquitous, including in the pages of Le Monde, where Baudrillard's essay first appeared. This certainly was my impression before leaving France, in the winter of 2001, where I had spent the semester on exchange from the City University of New York, Hunter College, to the University of Paris VIII, St-Denis.

Crowded into the common room of an international student dormitory near Stalingrad station, I watched as the attacks unfolded live on TV. The other students in the room, mostly young men from Chad, Mauritania, and other parts of Francophone Africa, took note of my presence. One student embraced me. *"J'ai de famille en New York,"* he said. "I have family in New York." *"Nous sommes avec vous,"* said another. "We are with you."

Who was this "us," this "you"? The sight of American flags hanging from balconies and adorning store windows along the Champs-Élysées made clear to me their sentiment. Wherever you went, people asked about your family's safety and in the same breath expressed admiration for the United States. Such abstractions were surreal, at first, but then cut like a bitter chill.

Returning to New York that winter, in January 2002, meant the cold hard truths of our new reality: the "see something, say something" New York; the grieving New York; the mobilizing New York. I became news editor of *The Hunter Envoy*, one of the largest student newspapers in the city, and we covered stories like the Muslim families protesting in front of City Hall because their loved ones had gone missing and were being detained as a result of the Patriot Act; the debates on campus around the push to war; and the cleanup efforts at Ground Zero. A guy I worked with at a bakery near Hunter College, John, committed suicide by jumping off the roof of the school. My boss said John had been suffering a mental health crisis and had sent him a note saying that he was quitting his job and dropping out of school to travel to Jerusalem. That shook me because I worked with John and never knew about his struggles. But everyone, it seemed, was battling with the times. These were heady days, and it was clear to me that 9/11 and its aftereffects would dominate the next part of my life.

In February 2003, I marched in the streets as the city shut down for the largest antiwar protests since Vietnam. A lot of kids I went to school with—in Colorado where I grew up and at Hunter College—were enlisting in the military. Some of my closest friends at Hunter were Muslims, and their worlds were being flipped upside down by anti-Muslim hate and suspicion. I knew I would become involved in the conflict. I sensed I was already. But my compulsion was to learn, not to fight. There were no City University of New York schools that regularly offered Arabic at that time, but I found an adjunct professor at Queens College who agreed to tutor me at her Flushing home. I learned the basics, and after I had saved enough money by working odd jobs around the city, I moved to Cairo. There I worked as an English tutor and began the long, maddening, and enlightening journey of learning Arabic.

This book began as an attempt to recall those days. It seeks to understand how information and the exchange of people and ideas can serve the foreign-policy objectives of government but how government in turn has struggled to connect the right information with the right publics at the right time. In piecing together a genealogy to the so-called "second front in the War on Terror," this book hopes to reconsider the essential goods of public diplomacy to understand what was lost that September morning. Who waged the battle for hearts and minds? On whose behalf and to what end? Where did the reboot of American public diplomacy lead us? And what steps have we taken, on a national level, to regain some semblance of peace?

ACKNOWLEDGMENTS

My thanks to the US-Spain Binational Fulbright Commission and the Fulbright Scholar Program that awarded me a Senior Fulbright Scholar award to complete this project. A special thanks as well to Yvonne Haddad, Waleed Mahdi, and Nadia Oweidat, who helped point me in the right direction. At George Mason University, my thanks to the College of Humanities and Social Sciences and to the AbuSulayman Center for Global Islamic Studies. My thanks as well to Mohammad Salama, Rei Berroa, and Sam Lebovic, who became key readers of the project at various stages. I am deeply grateful to the hardworking and brilliant individuals who granted me an interview for this book. In particular, Leon Shahabian deserves a special shout-out. His unique experience in the gray space of American propaganda gave clarity to the book's full-spectrum scope. The book and the speed with which it accelerated reflect the clear-eyed commitment of my editors at Columbia University Press. As with all else, the singular thought partner for this book has been my wife, Elizabeth. This book could not have happened without her.

THE LONG WAR
OF IDEAS

INTRODUCTION

"Before 9/11 it was all about making peace," Larry Schwartz, the State Department's deputy assistant secretary for public diplomacy, said to me in 2020 on the anniversary of the attacks. "After 9/11 it was all about making war." A career Foreign Service Officer (FSO) who was the State Department's press spokesperson in Tel Aviv immediately prior to 9/11, Schwartz was among those FSOs pulled from the work of globalization and repurposed for the work of war. Watching the attacks unfold on TV before senior-level meetings at Foggy Bottom on the morning of 9/11, he could not anticipate the scale of changes ahead.[1] Twenty years on, with approximately eight trillion dollars in federal spending exhausted and some nine hundred thousand lives lost, the changes that affected Schwartz's realm of operations have been among the most enduring but also among the most difficult to measure.[2]

A tsunami of funding flowed toward public diplomacy following 9/11, an enterprise that, prior to the mid-1960s, was known interchangeably as the "information and educational exchange program," "psychological warfare," or, more simply, "American propaganda."[3] Soft power dollars in the war on terror slushed into the Beltway and across industries. The money bled over borders and inundated creative entrepreneurs far and wide. At the center of these efforts was the reconstruction of American public diplomacy proper, which, in the years before 9/11, had been laid waste by a Washington consensus that saw little need for compelling hearts and minds in the absence of the Berlin Wall. Piecemeal at times and often drawn from a motley combination of enterprising media types, FSOs, and foreign-based reporters, no single vision, philosophy, or policy emerged to explain the country's vast and jumbled mass of Arabic-language communications. Yet there the body lay. Discerning the threads of continuity—first through aesthetics and then through the technological, strategic, and logistical models that have persisted across this brief but dense chapter in American history—is the primary aim of this book. Shedding light on the hardworking and unsung voices that have contributed to the American government's peculiar songbook in Arabic is another. This book represents an attempt to better understand who shaped the United States' propaganda apparatus in Arabic following 9/11, what their legacy is within the annals of American public diplomacy, and how their vision has contributed to the amelioration or escalation of conflict in the Middle East and North Africa.

As I discuss throughout the book, the continuity of major tropes within the canon of American public diplomacy toward the Arab and Muslim world speaks to the ingenuity of America's Cold War information warriors but also the relative paucity of US information strategy in the years since. At its core, the history of American propaganda in Arabic raises fundamental questions about the ideological prerogatives of State Department officials, the relationship between public and private actors in the sphere of foreign communications, and the extent to which propaganda, in any form, can be an effective tool for influencing public opinion, especially, if not exclusively, on foreign soil. Through vast resources and with the participation of some of the country's biggest players in the realm of information and communications technology, innovations in American public diplomacy helped set the stage for what Evan Osnos, David Remnick, and Joshua Yaffa have described as the "New Cold War."[4] In addition to the showcasing of advanced technologies, the narratives born of the battle for hearts and minds became paradigmatic of a new class of information warfare. As I describe in the book's final chapter, the Middle East remains at the crossroads of this conflict, the origins of which are that vivid September day.

PUBLICS BEYOND POLITICS

As described in the first annual report of the United States Advisory Commission on Information in 1949, the "Near and Middle East" has long represented a vanguard space for American propagandists. Distinct from the hegemonies of "old Europe," the Arab world—as a site in which "traditional patterns" were seen as rapidly dissolving and the gap between "the ruling class and the masses of the people" steadily narrowing—became a staging ground for some of the most audacious information ploys of the Cold War era.[5] Within the context of the newly created Information and Educational Exchange Act of 1948 (Public Law 402), the United States' "mass media program"—which encapsulated a host of new media technologies, strategic partnerships, and budgetary prerogatives—served the objective of reaching a vastly disparate and largely illiterate population. Newly minted academic and cultural exchange programs such as the Fulbright Award were an ideal vehicle for maintaining ties with a cosmopolitan elite whose allegiance to the capitalist model was already established. Embassy and consulate reading rooms, publication ventures, and academic exchanges sought to engage the "younger, progressive-minded, foreign-educated officials" whose contact with the United States was "relatively" limited but whose attention was hotly contested by the Soviet Union.[6]

Thematically, American propaganda in Arabic worked to integrate each of these threads by highlighting the achievements of Arab Americans and visiting Fulbright scholars, the collaborative work of Arabs and Americans in the realms of science, medicine, agriculture, and education, and the work of American beneficence overseas. As I discuss in chapter 1, the inaugural August 6, 1952, edition of the United States' largest Cold War publication in Arabic, *Al-Sadaqah*, spelled out many of the core elements of American public diplomacy toward the Middle East. Beneath a lavish spread of images showing "Egyptian teachers" in the United States and "medical experts" boarding a plane en route to Washington, a guest essay by one of the United States' key collaborators—Abd al-Rahman Azzam, the first secretary general of the Arab League—made the case for "democracy in the Arab world." Articles on Islam in the United States and more explicitly still on the role of Islam as "an Impenetrable Spiritual Wall that Communism Cannot Penetrate" proliferated across two decades of *Al-Sadaqah*.[7] Where Soviet propaganda regularly featured exposés on the negative treatment of African Americans in the United States, US propaganda in Arabic countered by highlighting the participation of Black Americans in sports, culture, and education. Of the available audience surveys conducted on US publications in Arabic, the results were unsurprising. Readers appreciated the number of photographs in publications such as *Al-Sadaqah*, *Al-Akhbar/News*, *Al-Majal*, and *Al-Hayat fi Amrika*. Less impressive was the written content they contained, which, as one survey found, focused too much on the United States and not enough on the Arab world. Another survey noted that readers viewed the material as overtly propagandistic, which, of course, it was.[8]

These "white" or overt examples of American public diplomacy in Arabic have rightly commanded the bulk of a very limited body of scholarship on the subject.[9] But the "gray" or "black" operations—those with questionable attribution or no attribution at all to the US government—were equally vital to US information strategy during the Cold War. Legislation protecting the use of covert information operations, NSC 4-A, emerged "only minutes" after the National Security Council codified the country's overt propaganda, on December 9, 1947. Drawing on guidance that the government supplement its overt propaganda (including Voice of

America, academic exchanges, and English-language teaching initiatives such as America House) with "covert psychological operations" as initiated and conducted by the CIA, it was the Office of Policy Coordination, later the Directorate of Operations, that was charged with managing the country's covert propaganda.[10] Following decades of speculation and at times violent scandal in the form of assassinations, secret wars, and "subversion against hostile states," many of the CIA's covert operations were exposed by the Church Committee of 1976. But as the historians Christopher Simpson, John Prados, and others have observed, the "mechanism of presidential approval" as embodied in NSC 4-A remained in place and the CIA's underlying strategies in the realm of influence continued to thrive.[11]

The postwar Middle East was equally seminal to the development of American covert information operations. By definition the legacy of this aspect of US public diplomacy remains more difficult to trace. To help situate it, in chapter 1, I look to one particular case, in post-1952 Cairo, which exemplified the CIA's influence strategy toward the Arab and Muslim world. NSC 4-A prescribed that "activities sponsored or conducted by the United States either in support of friendly governments or against hostile ones, be 'so planned and executed that any US Government responsibility for them is not evident to unauthorized persons and that if uncovered the US Government can plausibly disclaim any responsibility,'" so supplementary information operations toward the Arab world included a heavy degree of deniability.[12] The use of proxied sources for the purpose of tipping the scale on Arab perspectives in the Cold War became a common tactic in US strategy toward the Middle East. Some operations—including an elaborate CIA-led "crypto-diplomacy" campaign to lure the Nasserite regime away from Soviet entreaties—imploded beneath the weight of their own design. As I discuss in the conclusion of chapter 1, blowback to the CIA's Cairo project could be harnessed for a time—insofar as it turbocharged Islamist opposition—but its long-term impact entailed a range of unintended consequences.

More importantly, many of the strategies developed during the Cold War proved useful in the wake of 9/11. The deliberate generation of creative entrepreneurialism—a tactic observed by the scholars Frances Stonor Saunders, Amanda Laugesen, Hugh Wilford, and others who have examined the use of literary patronage by the CIA during the Cold War—reemerged with distinction following 9/11.[13] Reborn amid the auspices of USAID-backed initiatives such as "Injaz," a "best student company competition" that launched in coordination with the Jordanian Ministry of Education and was distributed in narrative form across the Arabic-language media sphere, cultural and scientific patronage has continued to drive American public diplomacy toward the Arab world.[14] As I discuss with Leon Shahabian, a cofounder of Layalina Productions, Arabic-language reality shows such as "Generation Entrepreneur," which included the Injaz competitions, piggybacked on patronage initiatives and in doing so became information operations in the classical sense: compelling narrative shells for the delivery of a particular package to a specifically intended audience.

In the shadow of historians such as Nicholas J. Cull, Jason C. Parker, Philip Seib, and Justin Hart, I am also concerned in this book with what Cull described as the "default message of US Cold War propaganda in the Middle East," the overwhelming focus of the country's overt propaganda on the shared religiosity of the Muslim and Western world.[15] The Holy Land has always loomed large in American influence operations. A prolific stream of churches and mosques flows across eight decades of US-stamped Arabic-language media, giving flesh to the critique, long-standing within and outside the diplomatic corps, that the "international perception of Christian bias in American advocacy" had become a point of debilitation in America's efforts at public diplomacy.[16] From the myriad Arabic-language broadsheets distributed across the region, to the programming of Voice of America (VOA) Arabic, or the unattributed and massive book translation campaigns that sent to libraries and booksellers across the region thousands of volumes on topics ranging from US history and society to child-rearing and biochemistry, US public diplomacy in Arabic has frequently been oriented around a narrow, if not myopic, set of principally white, Protestant, and pro-business values.[17] Public diplomacy leaders such as Edward W. Barrett, founder of the *Columbia Journalism Review* and assistant secretary of state for public affairs under President Truman, returned time and again to the notion, as Steven Rockefeller wrote of John Dewey's "industrial democracy," that "social institutions should exist first and foremost, not as a means of producing things," but of "*creating* individuals" (original emphasis). Rockefeller's volume from 1991 titled *John Dewey: Religious Faith and Democratic Humanism*, represented in itself a testament to the historical nexus of American capitalism, "religious faith," and "democratic humanism" that, like the Rockefeller family, had been integral to American public diplomacy for nearly a century. Through waxing elegy for the great "congregationalist liberal" of American pluralism, the fourth-generation Rockefeller tycoon and former dean of Middlebury College signaled what had been lost amid the so-called "disaggregation" of the United States Information Agency (USIA) in the early 1990s.[18] The retraction of American public diplomacy represented not simply a "unilateral disarmament in the weapons of advocacy," as one influential report described it, but the dismantling of the country's principal mechanism for the control and exportation of American values.[19] Still, the ideological North Star of American public diplomacy was never far gone; as this book shows, much of the substance behind the public diplomacy reboot following 9/11 looked and sounded eerily familiar to that which emerged after Pearl Harbor.

CHATTER ON THE NILE

American public diplomacy toward the Middle East and North Africa—a practice I distinguish from propaganda in the abstract sense to include intercultural exchange programs (from state-led art exhibitions to the Fulbright Program), foreign public opinion research, and the fast media operations of radio, print, film, and

TV—has long been burdened by geopolitics, broadly, and the proverbial "clash of civilizations," more specifically. The Office of War Information (OWI) began its battle for the hearts and minds of Arab peoples amid the North African campaign of 1942. Less than a decade later, the first Arabic broadcast of the VOA was established with the aim of rebuffing Soviet influence among the newly independent nations of the global South. Much like in the aftermath of 9/11, the Cold War battle for hearts and minds relied heavily on the centrality of mass communications technology; here it was not simply for the purpose of reaching beyond the region's relatively small enclaves of educated elites but for the creation of new publics, which, to the eyes of American officials, were nowhere to be found. The asynchronous development of public opinion polling and public diplomacy in the Arab world illustrated a disconnect between native interlocutors such as Isa Khalil Sabbagh and Ahmed Zaki Abu Shadi—the first broadcasters for the VOA's Arabic division in the 1950s—and the audiences they sought to influence. Their position as a mouthpiece of the American government exposed them at times to vitriol from the communities whose politics they knew best. To overcome their reliance on independent Arab sources, the United States Information Service (USIS) (the overseas product of the USIA) and the CIA moved to create a hub of operations in the heart of the region's greatest capital, Cairo.

Part of the impetus behind the Americans' focus on Egypt, the Arab world's largest media hub at the time, was the recognition that the United States' existing organs of mass media in Arabic were lagging. At the outset of the Eisenhower administration, it seemed hardly anyone was listening to VOA in Arabic. Its reception was poor and, in any case, the United States had no viable tool for measuring audience engagement.[20] Combined with an understanding that with the onset of revolution Egypt was in the midst of unprecedented historical change, American information officials saw in the country an opening through which US public diplomacy could be reimagined for the region as a whole. By 1955, just 13 percent of the USIA's budget supported Near East operations (for context, Latin America fared even worse, receiving just 8 percent); this compared to the 36 percent of the seventy-million-dollar budget that had been appropriated by the USIA for European operations that year.[21] American information strategy, post-WWII, adapted to such restraints by utilizing and developing human capital on the ground; incorporating the voices and talents of Radio Cairo, a Wafdist-centric operation in the heart of downtown Cairo; and building inroads with the new Revolutionary Regime Council through an elaborate CIA-front operation that would include, among other things, the construction of a powerful new radio tower in Cairo that, as one former CIA officer described it, "worked so well that we later found it necessary to finance stations in other locations to counter a gift that had been turned against our interests."[22]

THE HARD SCIENCE OF SOFT POWER

Well before the phrase "public diplomacy" was coined, the political volatility of mass media—its creation, distribution, and consumption—posed an unprecedented set of foreign policy challenges. As the sociologist Mark May wrote in his remarks before the first semiannual review of the US Advisory Commission on Information in 1949, the ultimate purpose of American propaganda had never been to simply connect publics but to "create public opinion."[23] In the wake of WWII, recognizing that much of the world's decolonized spaces had become the frontline in the perceived struggle against communism, the Eisenhower administration moved to do just that.

In 1953, Congress consolidated the work of the USIS, the VOA, and the myriad information and cultural exchange initiatives then under the auspices of the International Information Administration (IIA) within the Department of State into a separate organization known as the USIA. The hope was that the same mechanisms of influence used to shape the theater of war could be deployed to create peace. The rationale used to support this theory, as articulated before the House Foreign Affairs Subcommittee on International Organizations and Movements by the pioneering public relations expert Edward L. Bernays, was that "the attitudes of foreign peoples towards us affects the attitudes of their governments towards us, and in this shapes our foreign policy to some extent."[24]

Public opinion polling, a feature of American politics from at least the Reconstruction era, became a central tool of America's new propaganda strategy. Edward W. Barrett observed of the postwar European landscape, "The Italian Government dares not take a step which it knows is vital because it fears Italian mass opinion."[25] Propagandists, it was understood, neglected the input side of their enterprise at their own peril. The utilization of polling, moreover, offered a consumer-centric counterpoint to the totalitarian leanings of Soviet propaganda, which, Barrett suggested, was thought to have a budget of one billion dollars a year by the end of the second Truman administration, nearly ten times the amount allocated toward information activities by the United States.[26]

Speaking before Congress and the Committee on Foreign Affairs in July 1968, George Gallup made note of the demands newly placed on his industry during the Cold War, describing the work of his survey company's affiliates around the world as a response to the Johnson administration's call for an evaluation of the "reputation of the United States" as it existed in terms of " 'images'—or 'mental pictures' . . . and in terms of 'best friend.' "[27] Gallup's American Institute on Public Opinion was one of many enterprises to employ Walter Lippman's compelling concept of the "stereotype" to capture the spoils of the administration's "voracious" appetite for polls both "foreign and domestic."[28] As the historians Christopher Simpson, J. Michael Sproule, David H. Price, and Daniel Bessner have shown, many of the early pioneers of public opinion polling including such scholars as the Columbia University professor Daniel Lerner; Hans Speier, the first director of RAND Corporation's social science wing; Harold Laswell, a Yale Law professor and former president of the American Political Science Association; and Wilbur Schramm, the founder of the Iowa Writers' Workshop, cut their teeth during WWII with the OWI and continued to orient a large percentage of their work toward federally sponsored public diplomacy and covert influence research. Hadley Cantril, an expert consultant to the OWI during WWII who later served as editor of *Public Opinion Quarterly* from 1935 to 1946 and as longtime director of Princeton University's Institute for International Social Research (IISR), told the *New York Times* in 1977 that his office derived "nearly all" of its funding from surveying projects for the CIA and that he and his colleague, former USIA officer Lloyd Free, effectively "ran" the institute on behalf of the spy agency.[29]

As examined in chapters 1 and 2, State Department and Department of Defense (DoD) officials again began looking to the academic and private sectors for guidance in the discernment of foreign "attitudes" following 9/11. However, the degree to which such outside expertise impacted the programming side of American public diplomacy remains uncertain. Scott Atran, an anthropologist and lead researcher on numerous federal contracts following 9/11, described the relationship thusly: "We were giving the State Dept. feedback, and they would nod their heads and agree, but really do nothing about it. But that's pretty much the case with gov't policy: It's only when everything goes south and all the hunches, gut feelings, biases, and a priori beliefs have led to nothing or worse that one begins to look into the science, which is by then often out of date."[30]

Through a vast system of grants and cooperative agreements, the State Department along with defense management bureaus such as the Air Force Office of Scientific Research (AFOSR), the Army Research Office (ARO), and the Office of Naval Research (ONR) received white papers, while university and industry outfits—primarily within the orbit of DoD-sponsored University Affiliated Research Centers—received funding and at times guidance for the deciphering of an emergent set of problems that had been largely dormant since the Cold War.[31] Questions pertaining to the "dynamics," "dimensions," and above all "deterrence" of "terrorist ideologies," "terrorist organizations," and "authoritarian regimes" in the service of "national security" populated the dossiers of a rapidly expanding defense intelligence industry.[32]

Among the earliest and most contentious public diplomacy programs—or what the DoD referred to as "strategic communications"—from the 2003 Iraq War was the Human Terrain System (HTS), a short-lived initiative that involved "direct social-science support in the form of ethnographic and social research, cultural information research, and social data analysis" for "deployed brigade commanders and their staffs."[33] The program, which was administered by the Foreign Military Studies Office of the US Army's Training and Doctrine Command and cost an approximate $726 million between 2007 to 2014, envisioned a scenario in which social science research occurred synchronously and in real time with psychological operations in the theater of war.[34] In practice the program witnessed a handful of recent PhDs from the humanities and social sciences embedded within forward operating units with little to no instruction as to their perceived contribution or output. Few of the HTS participants spoke Arabic or the dialect of their assigned target populations and most had no previous military experience. The initiative was widely assailed in the press and in academia and was ultimately discontinued.

But the HTS was just part of a vast suite of research that included funding for an unprecedented range of inquiry across the human and social sciences. Through initiatives such as the multilingual research program at the Army Research Laboratory, the DoD's Language and Speech Exploitation Resources (LASER) project, and the Translingual Information Detection, Extraction, and Summarization (TIDES) initiative led by the Defense Advanced Research Projects Agency (DARPA), defense-funded academics and private industry experts delved into issues of natural language processing, text analysis and identification, and open-source intelligence gathering to a degree that had never before been attempted. Much of the pioneering research during this time helped lay the groundwork for the century's forthcoming boom in artificial intelligence. But as Secretary of Defense Robert M. Gates exclaimed on the fiftieth anniversary of the National Defense Education Act in 2008, such undertaking formed part of a long and complicated tradition of cooperation between the American military and academia. In almost cynical fashion, Gates introduced the DoD's Minerva initiative by invoking the extraordinarily unsuccessful Office of Special Plans, the controversial TALON Reporting System, and the Orwellian Total Information Awareness Program.[35] He pointed out that "understanding the traditions, motivations, and languages of other parts of the world has not always been a strong suit of the United States." The peoples of Afghanistan and Iraq, in his words, were "organized by networks of kin and tribe" and "ancient codes of shame and honor." These characteristics, he proffered, "often mean a good deal more." And it was for this reason, he explained, that expertise in the disciplines of history, anthropology, sociology, and "evolutionary psychology" would be critical to the US invasions insofar as "the heroic efforts and best intentions of our men and women in uniform have at times been undercut by a lack of knowledge of the culture and people they are dealing with every day."[36] The rationale, a paradigmatic testament to American neo-orientalism, unleashed an unprecedented bounty of research dollars and set the stage for the creation of a new generation of "defense intellectuals" in the war of ideas.[37]

With the aim of providing "some structure in understanding why foreign audiences believe stories that, from an American perspective, may appear surprising, contradictory, or outlandish," the CIA's Open Source Center collaborated with academics on the creation of a "master narrative" reports series to "capture historically-grounded stories reflecting a foreign community's identity and experiences as well as explain its hopes, aspirations, and concerns." Minerva-funded research focused on topics ranging from "Studies of Terrorist Organizations and Ideologies" (2008–2011) and "Belief Formation and Movements for Change" (2012–2013) to "Models of Societal Resilience and Change" (2012–2013), "Identity, Influence, and Mobilization" (2013–2014), and much more.[38] Such initiatives required an unprecedented degree of funding (twenty million dollars per year on average from the Minerva initiative alone) and demanded extensive collaboration with experts outside of government. But nowhere was the government's shortage in matters of human and social intelligence more pronounced than in the realm of foreign languages, the very backbone of public diplomacy.[39]

As identified by the influential "Djerejian Report" of the Advisory Group on Public Diplomacy for the Arab and Muslim World, the US-led Coalition Provisional Authority in Iraq needed "'a thousand Arabic speakers' to create an effective press operation and interact with the Iraqi media."[40] The 2003 invasion had involved, among other things, the dismantling of the Iraqi state media apparatus, which in turn generated a tsunami of new media, including some "160 new newspapers, 20 television stations, and 80 radio stations."[41] In the absence of Arabic speakers within its military ranks, and in contrast to the explosion of new media, the Coalition Provisional Authority faced the prospect of becoming indiscernible to the very public that its guns had helped to liberate. As part of its wide-ranging Quadrennial Defense Review, the Pentagon recognized this conundrum and in turn adopted the position that, as Robert Kaplan wrote, with "an unpredictable enemy—and one that was easy to kill but hard to locate" the military would need to develop expertise in "local language and culture and to bond with the indigenous inhabitants."[42] Language training programs, including Project Global Officer, a university-led critical language training initiative for ROTC cadets; the Language Flagship program, designed to enhance critical language skills among undergraduates in general; and National Training Centers, which were geared toward fostering language acquisition among active duty officers, soon followed suit.

With an endemic dearth of foreign-language investment across the country (the 9/11 Commission report pointed out, for example, that in 2002 American colleges and universities produced a total of just six undergraduates with a degree in Arabic), the State Department was unprepared for a new war of ideas.[43] At the time of 9/11, the government's principal body for overseas engagement maintained no "language designated" positions for South Asia, indicating the State Department expected English to be a sufficient mechanism for engaging with the vitally strategic and linguistically diverse part of Asia. As detailed in a September 2003 report by the Government Accounting Office in December 31, 2002, 21 percent of the 352 FSOs filling "'language-designated' public diplomacy positions" did not satisfy the requirements of their position. The report noted that, based on speaking proficiencies alone, the "highest percentages not meeting requirements were in the Near East" where 30 percent of the officers scored below sufficient levels. By 2007, the problem had grown only worse, with just 64 percent of the State Department's Arabic-language posts being filled by FSOs who were able to speak the language at the "designated level." Opposite findings applied for those FSOs in French- and Spanish-speaking countries where the language requirements were overwhelmingly met.[44]

Despite demands for improvement, enhanced foreign-language training and cultural intelligence research faced the additional hurdle of an engrained skepticism in Washington where lawmakers routinely, if unconsciously, embraced the notion, as Hans Speier described in the 1950s, that "since in modern societies the mass of the population cannot overthrow, or actively influence the policies of despotic regimes . . . the population at large is no rewarding target of conversion propaganda from abroad."[45] Change across the Islamic world, it was held, could emerge only through the coercion of ruling elites or the threat of military force. As Shibley Telhami observed in his influential study of Arab public opinion, *The Stakes* (2002), this attitude directly shaped the Camp David Accords, in 1978, which sought an Arab-Israeli peace agreement without the participation of the Palestinians, and it became all the more stark following the first Gulf War, wherein multiple Arab regimes were enlisted into the US war effort at the expense of their credibility with an Arab public whose input took the form of mass protests.[46] Mitigating the presumption of chaos—the so-called "democratic fallacy"—among foreign policy hawks regarding the Middle East required appositionally rigid metrics of input. To "justify federal agency budgets before a suspicious Congress," public diplomacy polling was obligated to embrace an artificially quantitative, or "'hard' science," approach to the inherently ambiguous questions of human persuasion and ideology.[47] It was a departure from the more nuanced assessments of the Cold War. "We cannot judge our successes by sales," Edward R. Murrow famously said of US information operations. "No cash register rings when a man changes his mind."[48] Yet by the late 1990s, and with the passage of the Government Performance and Results Act (GPRA), the predominance of hard science in the measurement of US influence operations had grown endemic. Promises to "Marry the Mission to the Market" and to measure success predominantly, if not exclusively, by the size of the audience, conquered the day. Metrics of engagement along with rhetorically biased queries such as whether respondents believed "objective and independent media are important" provided necessary fodder for budgetary requests and programming directives alike.[49] As late as 2021, the Advisory Commission on Public Diplomacy was still identifying as a top priority for both the Global Engagement Center and the United States Agency for Global Media an increased emphasis on "data-driven decision-making."[50]

THE MARKET AND THE MISSION

Shortcomings in the realm of public opinion research haunted the work of American public diplomacy during the first decade following 9/11. Joseph Nye observed just five million dollars a year had been allocated toward public diplomacy research three years out from the attacks. Still, the production side of the enterprise was booming and there was no shortage of experts in Washington waiting to sell the American brand to "fence sitters" and hostiles around the globe.[51]

Within two years of the 9/11 attacks, a billion dollars had reportedly been allocated toward nonmilitary public diplomacy efforts with the largest increases going toward Muslim-majority countries, including a 63 percent bump for public diplomacy spending in South Asia and a 58 percent increase for the Near East. While spending on public diplomacy would remain a fraction of the government's total discretionary spending (.14 percent in 2021) and just 4 percent of the budget for international affairs, public diplomacy spending increased steadily over the first two decades following 9/11, reaching over $2.23 billion by 2021.[52]

Despite the emergence of several new bureaucracies, the main channels of activity remained much as they were before 9/11. The State Department, via the office of the under secretary for public diplomacy and public affairs, and the US Agency for Global Media (USAGM), formerly the Broadcasting Board of Governors (BBG), jointly commanded the largest percentages of the overall public diplomacy budget. The State Department's Bureau of Educational and Cultural Affairs (ECA) controlled the largest share of the department's portion ($736 million in 2021). By 2021, the USAGM's budget of approximately eight hundred million dollars was distributed broadly across its three major broadcasting platforms, including the Voice of America, the semi-independent Radio Free Europe/Radio Liberty (RFE/RL), Radio Free Asia (RFA), and the Middle East Broadcasting Networks (MBN).[53]

In light of the above-mentioned linguistic deficiencies—and driven by an ardent belief within the Bush administration that creative expertise existed primarily, if not exclusively, outside of government—major contributions to the reboot of the country's information strategy during the first decade following 9/11 flowed from both private and nonprofit sectors.

Bush's first pick for under secretary for public diplomacy and public affairs, a job that included oversight of the country's foreign propaganda regimen, proved controversial. Charlotte Beers was a recognized expert in the world of marketing, having built her career in the Madison Avenue offices of J. Walter Thompson, a giant in the advertising field and a long-standing partner in American public diplomacy. She brought to the job a clear-sighted methodology for persuading people, but it seemed at odds with the function of the federal government. "The members of the BBG [the Board of Broadcasting Governors] were not the only neophytes directing America's outreach to the world's one billion Muslims," wrote the former CBS

News Middle East correspondent and academic Lawrence Pintak in his scathing indictment of public diplomacy during the Bush years. "Enter Charlotte Beers, a former Madison Avenue advertising executive hired weeks after 9/11 to repackage Brand America."[54] After barely seventeen months, Beers stepped down. And while her office succeeded in generating a handful of highly visible, if much-maligned campaigns—including the magazine *Hi* and a television commercial campaign called "Shared Values," which was derided as an attempt to depict "Happy Muslims" in the United States—the job was an uphill battle from the start.

As the Congressman Henry Hyde noted in the first congressional hearing devoted to 9/11 in October 2001, Beers was just the second person to hold the broadly conceived position. Her predecessor, Evelyn Lieberman, who was appointed at the end of Bill Clinton's second term, had been responsible for overseeing the disaggregation of the USIA. The storied agency's star had been waning on Capitol Hill since the George H. Bush administration, but the USIA was ultimately dissolved following passage of the Foreign Affairs Reform and Restructuring Act of 1998. As the public diplomacy historian Nicholas J. Cull has argued, the disaggregation of the USIA—an entity that, by the end of the Reagan administration, included some ten thousand employees across 150 countries and was operating on a budget of nearly $820 million a year—was in essence political, the result of a quid pro quo between the Clinton administration and a recalcitrant Senate Republican bloc unwilling to support a vote on the Chemical Weapons Convention.[55] The USIA, and its constellation of area offices around the globe, had served for decades as "custodians of the long-range public diplomacy effort to create better understanding by foreign audiences of American culture, institutions and values."[56] But this was also what contributed to the targeting of the agency by Republicans who saw its work as an extension of Clintonian internationalism.

Concurrent, however, with the collapse of the USIA, government assistance to independent foreign media was booming. As Krishna Kumar has shown, USAID alone spent more than $260 million on independent media assistance between 1985 and 2001, most of it targeting the Balkans and countries of the Eastern bloc. The effort was augmented by the simultaneous explosion of investment in free media from a range of international organizations such as the United Nations and the World Bank as well as private foundations such as the Ford Foundation, the Independent Media Foundation, the John S. and James L. Knight Foundation, the Rockefeller Foundation, and the Soros Foundation.[57] This new flow of investment gave rise to a global network of nongovernmental agencies, which, in the tradition of organizations like the International Institute of Education, capitalized on their independence from both the private and public sector to serve as go-betweens for the implementation of information-orientated projects. As the public diplomacy scholar and former FSO Wilson P. Dizard pointed out, this "new kind of internationalism" distinguished above all by the centrality of "global electronic networks and the digital information that flows through them" was integral to Nye's famous description of "soft power" as a public diplomacy model for the twenty-first century.[58] Yet, as I argue, the differentials in thinking between the "new" internationalism and that which characterized the information strategies of the post-WWII period, while dissimilar in tone and structure, were almost indistinguishable in practice.

By 1953, Edward R. Barrett was already noting that a "nongovernmental organization could achieve substantial results if it would undertake the large job of inducing American corporations and other organizations to mobilize their overseas representatives in the national effort." The objective then was to elevate the "American business representative . . . as an effective explainer of modern-day American capitalism—American industrial democracy."[59] Less than a decade after its creation, Congress directed the VOA to "farm out" 75 percent of its programming to private networks.[60] By the mid-1950s, following the recommendations of the Jackson Commission, a key advisory body led by Eisenhower's close adviser and former *Time* magazine editor C.D. Jackson, a marked uptick in funding for the Office of Private Cooperation solidified the practice of not only private-sector collaboration but also the state-sponsored patronage of wholly private actors in the public diplomacy realm.[61] By 1955, the United States Advisory Commission on Information was reporting that 1,169 private organizations were cooperating with the USIA, particularly in the realm of cultural activities such as "radio symphony exchanges" and book distribution programs.[62] The USIA's Motion Picture Service, which by the early 1980s had become fully developed, was producing about a hundred films annually (primarily documentaries and short features), but an additional three hundred films, estimated the public diplomacy veteran Allen C. Hansen, were "acquired from private US sources."[63]

Such state-private initiatives became a calling card of US information programs. The notion of "cooperation" before "conflict" was seminal to the US Objectives and Programs for National Security, better known as NSC 68, in which the confrontation with communism was framed as a constitutional imperative to "create conditions" under which America's "free and democratic system can live and prosper."[64] And the staggering of the two approaches empowered the USIA and its overseas satellites while creating a new modus operandi in which collaboration—or the outsourcing of information operations to private entities, including foreign actors—emerged as a new "total culture" approach in the war of ideas.[65]

Thomas C. Sorensen, who served as a public affairs officer (PAO) in Beirut, Baghdad, and Cairo and later became deputy director of the USIA, in 1961, captured the lived dimensions of NSC 68 in his pseudo-memoir *The Word War* (1974). His richly descriptive voice merits revisiting.

> Like most of his counterparts in other capitals, the Beirut PAO is on call around the clock. His workday begins at breakfast in [a] pleasant, airy apartment, which probably affords a view of the blue Mediterranean or the snowcapped Lebanon Mountains. But at this point the PAO is concentrating not on postcard horizons but on those of Beirut's plethora of morning newspapers that he is able to read himself, the several dailies in English and French. . . . Having scanned

the press, the PAO carefully reads the ten-thousand-word Wireless File which the Agency's Press Service in Washington has radio-teletyped to all USIS posts in the Middle East and South Asia during the night.... The Wireless File contains texts of major policy pronouncements plus news, features, and editorials supporting U.S. objectives. The most useful of the material will be adapted for local use by USIS's Press Officer and staff, translated in Arabic, French, and Armenian, and distributed to local newspapers and government officials.[66]

Sorensen goes on to recount discussions surrounding a commissioned translation into Arabic of a memoir by Stalin's daughter (presumably Svetlana Alliluyeva's controversial *Twenty Letters to a Friend*), the promotion of a visiting US scholar, and "a conversation" with the editor of *Al-Nahar*, the paper of record in Lebanon. He describes the efforts made to place on Lebanese television the "kinescope" of an interview with President Nixon as he outlined his position on Vietnam for *Meet the Press* and to organize for the president of Lebanon and his staff a screening of a USIA color documentary.[67] While deliberately hypothetical—and set after his own retirement—Sorensen's narrative set between lunchtime Martinis and a quick shave before dinner illustrated some of the cultural peculiarities behind American public diplomacy at the time. It also gave flesh to the inherent dependency of information operatives on allies within their host environments. Sorensen's PAO makes no attempt to read the dominant Arabic papers himself. "Translators, writers, librarians, projectionists, drivers, artists, secretaries, printers" are all accepted as mandatory facets of the job, which, at its core, is performed as a kind of "Track Two diplomacy," one that engages ministers' wives as well as editors of newspapers, film producers, and businessmen.[68]

The scramble for foreign and private content creators became paramount to the post-9/11 reboot of public diplomacy. As outlined in chapters 3 and 4, the near total reliance of US media operations in Arabic on foreign and private collaborators generated major backlash within Washington but nonetheless set in motion the creation of an otherwise nonexistent presence for the United States on the Arabic media stage. Within the country, the Bush administration's reliance on the private sector touched virtually all corners of the domestic media market. As reported by the *New York Times*, the administration famously dispatched Karl Rove and other White House staff to discuss with Hollywood producers and studio executives how they might "cooperate in the war on terrorism and begin setting up a structure to make it happen."[69] As the *Times* reported, Rove was careful to emphasize that the government did not have a role in directing or managing Hollywood's contribution. But the trip inevitably raised questions. If there was no intention of coordinating output, why was the government reaching out at all? Were money and resources flowing toward contributors? Whose vision underscored the "suggestions" Rove was advancing?

Not at issue was the willingness of Hollywood to participate. As one participant observed, the meeting with Rove "was the first time in his 35 years" that "representatives from every major studio, network and union" got together in a show "of seamless unity."[70] Nonetheless, the outreach to Hollywood was poorly received in Washington not least because the State Department and the BBG already had in place several high-powered communications entrepreneurs who were poised to redirect the existent structure of American public diplomacy toward a more commercial, if less nimble, Cold War model.

Among the most visible members of the BBG was Norman J. Pattiz, the Los Angeles–based founder of the largest radio network in the country, Westwood One. Pattiz's relationship with American propaganda efforts dated back decades. In the mid-1980s, as a part of a deal between Charlie Wick, then the head of USIA, and his Soviet counterpart Alexandre Yakovlev to stop jamming VOA broadcasts in exchange for giving airtime to Radio Moscow in the United States, Pattiz volunteered the use of the Westwood One network, which then encompassed the stations of the Mutual Broadcasting System and the former NBC radio network.[71] As part of his background research for the BBG position, Pattiz led a "fact-finding" trip to the Middle East in February 2001 that included, as he later wrote, meetings with senior Arab officials, "radio and TV broadcasters, journalists, media executives, academics and others," all of whom, in his words, affirmed the belief that the BBG and its networks, including VOA, needed an "overhaul." The push to deliver on this call first centered on the VOA—the country's oldest bastion of public diplomacy—where a newly created division under the moniker of the Middle East Radio Network (MERN), now Radio Sawa, sought to target young adults of the Middle East through a format-driven approach that used "Arabic-Western" popular music interspersed with short segments of news and information.[72] Broadcasting, at first, from the same transmission towers on the Greek island of Rhodes once used by the USIA, Radio Sawa echoed early innovations of VOA Arabic, which regularly incorporated the talents of musical stars but pursued in essence an inverse strategy from its Cold War predecessor of primarily using music to build audiences regardless of their disposition toward American values or policy. Soon after its creation, the BBG separated Radio Sawa from the VOA by propping it up as a nonprofit organization similar to the VOA's clandestine Cold War counterparts Radio Free Europe and Radio Liberty (RFE/RL). The MBN, which, like RFE/RL, operates today as a grantee within the budget of the USAGM (the new iteration of the BBG), signaled the end of an era in VOA programming. As Carnes Lord wrote in his 2006 study *Losing Hearts and Minds?*, the creation of MBN, which included shutting down the Arabic service of the VOA and propping up Radio Sawa as well as Radio Farda, in Persian, and the television broadcasting network Al-Hurra, triggered an "open revolt" within the VOA, where employees argued that the MBN would not be held to the same "journalistic standards and monitoring" as the VOA.[73] Simultaneously, MBN was repeating a timeworn pattern in American public diplomacy toward the Arab world wherein extra-official or private actors like Pattiz became the de facto visionaries of the government's messaging strategy and enterprising foreign counterparts, the messenger.

GRAY IS THE NEW BLACK

The "state-private network," as the historian James R. Vaughn and others have described it, extended from the use of Coca-Cola promotional videos within the widely distributed newsreels of the USIS to the collaborative work of the nonprofit and private universities responsible for hosting and publicizing the work of the Fulbright Commission.[74] Proxied news sources, including citizen-journalists as well as corporations willing to promote shared objectives, have long been central to US propagation efforts, and like any mode of communication the digital age enhanced and streamlined existent strategy. But while many collaborative initiatives functioned in a largely hands-off manner, at times capitalizing on little more than the convening power of officials, collaboration in the realm of content creation required a more engaged, if covert, approach to deliberation.

As I discuss in chapter 4, collaborative content creation in the battle for hearts and minds was particularly sensitive for American public diplomats in the Middle East because the region's perceived "reservoir of default anti-Americanism" was thought to compromise the viability of the kind of overt communication vehicles once used during the Cold War.[75] The perception of US-backed funding not only challenged the authenticity of a product but, in some instances, created an opening for political violence toward its producers.[76] This latter dynamic was on vivid display in the early months of the US invasion of Iraq where media projects funded by the DoD and the State Department, including the Iraq Media Network Al-Iraqiyya, the newspaper *Al-Sabah*, Diyala TV and Radio (later the Independent Radio and Television Network), the VOA, Al-Hurra, and Radio Free Iraq (an offshoot of RFE/RL), fell under regular attack. According to the Committee to Protect Journalists, some twenty-seven indigenous reporters associated with US-backed media outlets were killed or murdered in Iraq between 2003 and 2007. The numbers far outpaced the losses absorbed by other media organizations, and the deaths were at times leveraged through social media or the oppositional press for their symbolic value.[77] American leadership seemed at times indifferent to this dynamic. (Charlotte Beers remarked openly on PBS's *Newshour* that between 2002 and 2003 the US government was actively purchasing overseas newspapers and media outlets including those in Malaysia, Indonesia, Pakistan, Egypt, Kuwait, and Lebanon).[78] But to offset the impact of such negative associations with US-backed content, a small group of Washington insiders with deep expertise in American foreign policy, public diplomacy, and influence operations quietly launched a subtler approach.

Initially formed as a charitable organization under Section 170(c) of the Internal Revenue Code, little is known about the origins of *Al-Haqiqah* ("the truth"). Led by the ambassador Richard Fairbanks and supported by a board that included some of the country's most illustrious figures in the realm of information statecraft, including former President George H. W. Bush, Henry Kissinger, James Baker, Brent Scowcroft, George Schultz, Sam Nunn, Lloyd Cutler, and Sandy Berger, *Al-Haqiqah* was explicitly designed from the outset to create "foreign-language TV programs to be broadcast in Muslim countries."[79] In 2003, leadership of the initiative was handed over to the young Lebanese-born interlocutor Leon Shahabian, who began as an intern at the Center for Strategic and International Studies, where Fairbanks was president and CEO. A self-described "information operative" with a background in French literature, Shahabian reports rebranding *Al-Haqiqah* as "Layalina" (meaning "our nights") in reference to the organization's core strategy: the placement of original content on the prime-time slot of major Arab-owned satellite channels. Layalina became one of two 501(c)(3), or tax-exempt, organizations that emerged as a creative vehicle for the production and distribution of public diplomacy content in the global war on terror. The other, America Abroad Media (AAM), which focused on documentary-style town halls and news and information, was geared principally, though not exclusively, toward Afghanistan with the Department of Defense–backed Tolo TV being its primary channel of distribution. Through conversations with Shahabian and Aaron Lobel, the founder of AAM, I explore the work of the two media organizations and discuss the efficacy of the groups' central strategy: the placement of public diplomacy media content on mainstream Arab and Asian satellite channels. Although fire-charged by the creative networking strategy of operatives like Shahabian and the use of twenty-first-century genres like reality TV, the substance of the nonprofit productions—shows like *Generation Entrepreneur* or the most well-known example of a Layalina production, *'Ala tariq fi Amrika* (On the Road in America, 2007–2009)—signaled more an aesthetic continuity than timely innovation. Centered around the lives of nonprofessional or "public" actors from the Arab world as they engaged with and enacted ostensibly common Western activities and debates, such shows closely resembled USIA productions from the 1950s and 1960s. By attempting to aestheticize universality such manufactured narratives, I argue, naturally sharpened the divide. The extra-official productions of Layalina and AAM, while loosely attributable to US resources, epitomized America's long war of ideas, a pluralist-centered paradigm that tragically delineated a seemingly irreparable dichotomy of "us" and "you."

DIGITAL HEARTS, PIXELATED MINDS

Although sparked by the hard reality of the attacks, "in the war of ideas," wrote Antony Blinken, "facts have been losing ground to fiction." As the future secretary of state observed just three months after 9/11, the world seemed indifferent to the argument that the "United States saved tens of thousands of Muslims in the Gulf, Somalia, Bosnia, and Kosovo"; that "U.S. troops were deployed to Saudi Arabia at that country's request to protect its people and Islam's holy sites from Iraq"; or that the Taliban were killing "far more Muslims intentionally than the U.S. bombing campaign did accidentally."[80] Instead, it was clear that the empathy once expressed toward the victims of 9/11 had descended into a battle for influence or, more precisely, a war of perspectives with a series of running battles for the truth.

In December 2001, for example, the Pentagon released a grainy, hour-long video—reportedly found in Afghanistan—of Osama bin Laden eating, speaking, and socializing at length with several of his deputies, including Sulaiman Abu Ghaith and Aymin al-Zawahiri. The video, which lacked reliable audio but was subtitled by the Department of Defense, begins with bin Laden, Abu Gaith, and the camera operator discussing instances in which the attack on the towers and the battle between America and al-Qaeda had been revealed to them in dreams before and without knowledge of the attack. Bin Laden expounds on the secrecy of the mission, noting that the pilots—who were unaware of one another—did not know the precise targets of their attack before departing.[81] Within hours of being released, the tape—which was broadcast around the world as evidence of bin Laden's role in the attack—was dismissed by commentators on Al-Jazeera as a fabrication. Speaking from London, the Salafist commentator Hani al-Sebai exclaimed on Al-Jazeera that the congratulatory tenor of the conversation between bin Laden and al-Zawahiri was in regards to the marriage of bin Laden's son and al-Zawahiri's daughter. It is unbelievable, al-Sebai said, that "an organization like Al-Qaeda would record a video as blatant as that and leave it lying around a house."[82]

In Washington, the dispute surrounding the authenticity of the video was as much a problem as the material itself. The incident prompted the creation of the Office of Global Communications, the "brainchild" of the senior Bush adviser Karen P. Hughes, according to the *Washington Post*.[83] And it made vivid a more complex phenomenon of the 9/11 era wherein digitization and the rapid distribution of information were thought to be eroding the authority of lived experience. President Barack Obama's special council, Rashad Hussain, who was one of just two advisers to join the president in advance of his historic address in Cairo, alluded to the problem in a speech to the Countering Violent Extremism Summit in Australia in 2015. While the enemy (read "ISIS") appeared to disseminate "tens of thousands of tweets daily," most were sent through automata, he noted, "bots without followers."[84]

This ostensible disconnect between the actual might of al-Qaeda or ISIS and the image that preceded them was met, first, with cynicism and, second, a reluctant recalculation on the part of lawmakers to embrace the "phantom" space of the dark web as both a legitimate threat and an opportunity for innovation. Funded primarily through DoD initiatives and drawing on the resources of the CIA's Open Source Center, early AI warfare in the new war of ideas deployed rudimentary algorithms across a small percentage of Twitter feeds or known chat rooms to capture keywords and narratives that, theoretically, could be mobilized in the service of counternarratives to be deployed across said chat rooms and threads. Among the first fully formed iterations of this new approach was the Center for Strategic Counterterrorism Communications (CSCC) and within that the Digital Outreach Team (DOT) (*Fariq al-Tawwasul al-Elektruni*). With a budget of just $6.8 million in 2011, the CSCC was arguably doomed to failure. An infamous campaign launched by the DOT—"Think Again, Turn Away," which highlighted the brutality of ISIS but simultaneously gave air to its propaganda—sealed the fate of the short-lived agency.

Still, as I discuss in chapter 5, the creation of the CSCC marked an important point of evolution in the space of American public diplomacy, more broadly, and information operations, more specifically. As articulated by Alberto Fernandez, the second director of the CSCC, the office helped lay the groundwork for a new generation of stealth public diplomacy, one for which the information sphere was imagined no longer as auxiliary to policy but, like during WWII, a theater of engagement. The perceived aptitude of ISIS in the realm of digital persuasion compelled multiple reconfigurations of the CSCC and ultimately resulted in the creation of the country's first fully-fledged digital information hub in the Global Engagement Center (GEC). Before it was dismantled in the wake of Kamala Harris's loss to Donald Trump in 2024, the multimillion-dollar interagency powerhouse, as articulated by Richard Stengel, a former under secretary for public diplomacy and public affairs, was charged with amplifying "credible voices" in a "coordinated way" while empowering "a global network of partners—from NGOs to foreign governments to religious leaders—who could act as more credible messengers to target audiences."[85] Formalized through legislation in 2016, the GEC appeared, for a brief span of time, as a third and major player in the federal government's nonmilitary suite of public diplomacy media. Its distinction was driven by its public-facing posture, its focus on Russian and Chinese propaganda, media literacy, and disinformation. I look at the work of the GEC alongside other similar experiments, including the Dubai-based and (formerly) US-backed Sawab Center, in chapters 5 and 6.

HORIZONS OF CONFLICT

Much of the early strategy behind American public diplomacy in the post-WWII period centered on countering the Soviet presence in those regions of the world where, as described in the first report of the United States Advisory Commission on Information in 1949, governments were perceived as "weak, or narrowly based and the vast masses of people are underprivileged."[86] American information statecraft evolved throughout the Cold War in relative proximity to the idea that the battle for hearts and minds was at once a competition—with the Soviets—and an opportunity for what another, influential treatise from the period described as the "reconstituting of the human community."[87] The narrative strategy underpinning US influence operations then was both interventionist and introspective, flowing from conflict abroad and recycled through solutions at home or, in some instances, vice versa: projecting abroad those values discerned as universal. Of USIA short films from the 1960s, Nicholas Cull observed that producers were compelled to capture the "human side of one of the issues then central to the USIA."[88] Coverage of the civil rights movement was broadcast through newsreels across Africa; a short film depicting the death of a refugee at the site of the Berlin Wall invoked support for the free flow of people and information. Quoting Theodore Streibert, the first director of the USIA, the film critic Richard Dyer MacCann took note of a similar dynamic. USIA movies in their earliest iteration were limited to "subjects which support our foreign policy and to those which refute communist lies." By the 1960s, however, a more measured tact was emergent. As expressed by George V. Allen before the House Appropriations Committee in 1960, USIA officials had understood that "we cannot restrict ourselves solely to the exposition of the fallacy of communism" but "rather, we devote most of our energies to setting out what the United States *is*."[89]

Following 9/11, US influence operations tracked a similar course. Major news organizations like the MBN or less visible mechanisms like the CSCC sought to meet jihadist propaganda in its own space by refuting perceived lies and exposing any fallacies. Similarly, in line with the USIA's human-centered aesthetic—an approach made visible by films such as *Nine from Little Rock* (1964) *Let Poland Be Poland* (1982), or the short documentary *Afghanistan: Caught in the Struggle* (1983)—federal grantee media projects like those from Layalina or AAM focused their sights on the public subject with ideological bylines only loosely drawn to US policy. The genres today are as diverse as they were in the past—from animation and satire to long-form fiction, neorealism, and documentary. But while there exists in American influence operations toward the Middle East a continuity and eclecticism of form that, natural to the lifespan of a FSO, transcends administrations, the same properties have enabled a host of imitators, laying the groundwork for a new century of contestation.

As I describe in chapter 6, Russian state media in Arabic today resemble a parallax view of American public diplomacy. Where the United States steadfastly built an Arabic-language empire through outsourced talent and contracted resources, the Russian state media behemoth RT Arabic, as with its Chinese counterpart CGTN Arabic, is built largely on the shoulders of domestic foreign-language programs whose rigor and sophistication far outstrip those of the United States. Similar to US-style CVE initiatives such as the Dubai-based Sawab Center or the Washington-based Digital Outreach Team but distinct in their lack of attribution,

Russian-backed narrowcast campaigns—from Libya, Sudan, Egypt, and the Democratic Republic of the Congo—use culturally charged narratives to divide and animate their target audiences. Similar to US efforts to embed American media within foreign outlets, Russian-state media in Arabic actively syndicate their programming and, increasingly, translocate broadcasting to undisclosed networks within their target language communities. Most notable, however, is the extent to which Russian and increasingly Chinese state media attempt to mirror the kind of public diplomacy once advocated by George V. Allen, namely, a communicative strategy based not simply on overt acts of refutation or propagation but a more nuanced mode of cultural expressionism.

That Russian propagandists in Arabic are just as likely today to frame their messaging in the shape of a Hollywood-style action movie as pamphleteering or proselytizing lends credence to the notion, as Baudrillard wrote, that the attack on 9/11 was simultaneously the image of an attack and a digital product made global by the "system's" (read America's) own "worldwide distribution."[90] The 9/11 attacks and the soft power offensive that accompanied America's response precipitated tremendous innovation in the form of persuasion technology (see chapter 2), institutional reform (chapter 3), collaborative content design (chapter 4), and new media production (chapter 5). But with each iteration there appeared, in W. J. T. Mitchell's terms, the risk of "indefinite duplication."[91] The Middle East and North Africa, as a global center of media adventurism, weathered the storm of America's longest wars, I argue, and the region continues to draw the resources of information operators far and wide. This is not to suggest the American soft power model has prevailed but rather the US footprint helped widen the playing field for foreign media production in the region by creating a normative aesthetic divide, one in which foreign mercenaries and religious zealots—like those seen in the Russian state-backed movies *Shugalei* or the Chinese-funded blockbuster *Wolf Pack*—compete for the soul of a seemingly faceless humanity. While derivative of certain Hollywood-style war-on-terror fantasies, these media operations directly complement the strategic communications of their respective backers. In chapter 6, I unpack some of the differences between US and Russian-state influence operations in the Middle East by concentrating on the narrative trends that distinguish them. The aim of this concluding chapter is to interrogate the legacy of American influence operations in Arabic, the counter-communications campaigns that emerged in response, and the future of public diplomacy, as an aspirational tool, for navigating conflict and sustaining the "human community" in the hyperdigitized realm of the twenty-first century.

1
PUBLIC DIPLOMACY AND THE ARAB WORLD

Stick to appeals at the grassroots level which will cause pressures on the leaders to stay away from independent deals with the Great Powers, and make such appeals exclusively by Radio Cairo or by other means, if any can be found, that do not involve personal contact between Egyptian officials of the target countries. If fanatics of these countries provide the best material for operations built on such appeals, so be it.

—MILES COPELAND, *THE GAME OF NATIONS*

In 1945, just weeks before the Allied invasion of Germany and with barely a month remaining in his presidency, President Roosevelt and First Lady Eleanor Roosevelt held a meeting with the president's former Yale classmate and Office of Strategic Services (OSS) official Colonel Harold Hoskins. Intending to discuss the state of US outreach in the Near East, Roosevelt wanted to know if American "moving pictures" were being screened or if there existed the possibility of "taking over at least one small theater in various cities where American films of various kinds might be shown." Hoskins, a Lebanese-born Arabist cut from the ilk of Protestant missionaries, proposed using the outside wall of a building in

Baghdad (as he had seen the British do before), to which Roosevelt responded favorably, adding that an outside wall was better than a theater as it could reach "women as well as men." The First Lady, the cable tells us, noted, "To be effective, such films would have to be specially prepared, having in mind the specific areas where they would be shown."[1]

Beyond the fog of war and with images of Nazi brutality in full resolution, the United States would eventually devise the capacity for "specially prepared" films capable of resonating within specific "areas." In the mid-1960s, President Lyndon Johnson directed the United States Information Agency (USIA) and other agencies to integrate the Planning, Programming, Budgeting System, the principle aim of which was to create "mission-oriented" programming through "quantitative measures."[2] But in 1945, Hoskins and the Roosevelts had to settle for an alternate approach. "Baghdad at night," wrote a British observer several years later, "resounds to swing and wild west shootings from the various open-air cinemas."[3] The aesthetics of Hollywood, the officials knew, were well suited for capturing hearts and minds; American propagandists needed only to set up the projector.

The Baghdad cinema proposal ultimately landed on the desk of Archibald MacLeish, the newly appointed assistant secretary of state for public and cultural relations and a renowned poet who until recently had served as the librarian of Congress. MacLeish, whose film credits included a seat at the writers' table on Ernest Hemingway's 1937 pro-Loyalist film *The Spanish Earth*, had articulated the need for just such an operation a few months before during an address before the Senate Committee on Foreign Relations.[4] "Today, whole peoples are in direct and continuing contact with each other through day-to-day and even hour-by-hour exchanges of ideas, news dispatches, magazine articles, books, broadcasts, persons, works of art—all the innumerable instruments of modern communication," MacLeish exclaimed. "The result is that the attitudes of entire peoples, and particularly their attitudes toward each other, become major influences in foreign relations. It would not be too much to say that the foreign relations of a modern state are conducted quite as much through the instruments of public international communication as through diplomatic representatives and missions."[5]

MacLeish's observations were rooted in the experience of war. The quiet success of the Office of War Information (OWI), the Voice of America (VOA), and other parallel outfits born amid strife had made clear for advocates like MacLeish the value of information operations in dissolving conflict and even, possibly, preventing it. Simultaneously, by 1945, American officials were looking beyond Europe to the perceived frontline of an emergent competition for foreign resources and the publics that surrounded them. Distinct from the hegemonies of "old Europe" cities such as Baghdad, where the press, while booming, was still hampered by the tight regulations of British colonialism, became exemplary spaces for innovation in the foreign information space. It was here that "traditional patterns" of communication were dissolving and the gap between "the ruling class and the masses of the people" quickly narrowing.[6] The Educational Exchange Act (Public Law 80–402), or Smith-Mundt Act of 1948, succinctly captured this American vision of the postwar world and laid the groundwork for a new, multipronged strategy in the war of ideas.

Speaking to the public and over the heads of other governments became integral to the "Campaign of Truth" in the early 1950s, which in turn helped to galvanize and fund a vast array of new programs. Embassy and consulate reading rooms, English-language instruction, and new print media ventures were created to engage "younger, progressive-minded" individuals whose contact with the United States was limited but whose attention was paramount to Soviet interests. A high-speed "mass media program" capable of reaching beyond the capitals of the global South sought to engage audiences through radio, television, and film; those people were seen as distant from the bastions of power but especially vulnerable to the allure of communism. And a revamped Bureau of Educational and Cultural Affairs (CU) within the State Department envisioned the empowerment of future foreign leaders through study abroad and professional exchanges in the United States. Public diplomacy, as an umbrella concept for all of these activities, did not replace the old practice of government-to-government engagement but there too relationships with foreign leaders were being reimagined as a ground-up effort, especially, if not exclusively in the postcolonial global South.[7]

At their core, each of these new initiatives centered on an imperfect and politically expedient notion of the "public." Led by scholars such as William James and John Dewey, the pluralistic turn in American philosophical thought had already presaged the rationale for a publicly minded politics that was distinct from the perceived totalitarianism of Marxist ideology. Yet, as the journalist and scholar Lester Markel observed in a study for the Council on Foreign Relations in 1949, "Public Opinion and Foreign Policy," the integration of public opinion into American foreign policy was a hard-won sell, especially to those charged with its implementation: "There are still too many career diplomats who look upon themselves as Brahmins and upon fact-seekers as Untouchables; too many officials in high position who feel public opinion has no place in the frock-coated world in which both their bodies and their minds move." Despite the prognostics of people such as MacLeish or Markel, public opinion, and in turn public diplomacy, developed in US foreign policy as more of a recognition of fact than moral aspiration. The State Department's Division of Cultural Relations, a predecessor to the CU, only began sponsoring exchange programs after revelations that the Nazi Party was already doing as much in Latin America. The VOA, the United States' most storied institution of public diplomacy, similarly grew out of hindsight. As the long-time USIA officer and journalist Alan Heil observed, the VOA "went on air seventy-nine days after the attack on Pearl Harbor"; its appearance, as he put it, made America "the last major power to broadcast internationally."[8]

Prior to WWII, there was no US equivalent to the British Broadcasting Corporation (BBC) or, for that matter, the *Volksempfänger* (the people's radio) of Nazi Germany. According to Wilson P. Dizard, the United States' absence on the international broadcasting scene had resulted in part from the reluctance of lawmakers in Washington to cooperate with the emerging protocols of interwar Europe. The relative lack of short-wave radio demands in the private market similarly provided little incentive for commercial enterprises. But with the vitriolic discourse of Joseph Goebbels resounding across German radio stations amid the push to war, the Roosevelt administration appropriately reversed course. The WWII experience dramatically shaped the contours of American public diplomacy, and while unpacking the full scope of what Hugh Wilford described—quoting a key player in this Cold War history—as a "massive campaign 'of political warfare and of propaganda'" is beyond the scope of this chapter, a brief history is nonetheless needed to appreciate the legacy inherited by information operatives after 9/11, both the limitations it imposed on them and the possibilities it contained.[9]

FINDING VOICE

Established as a branch of Roosevelt's New York-based Foreign Information Service (FIS)—itself a wing of the OSS—the Voice of America was devised initially as a weapon of deterrence; many of its earliest pioneers, including artists and playwrights like Robert Sherwood, saw the opportunity as a cri de coeur in the face of barbarity. "We are living in an age when communication has achieved fabulous importance," Sherwood wrote in 1939. "There is a new decisive force in the human race, more powerful than all the tyrants. It is the force of massed thought—thought which has been provoked by words, strongly spoken."[10] Capitalizing on the use of existing British transmitters, the VOA launched its first broadcasts in German (followed by French, Italian, and English) for the explicit purpose of refuting Third Reich propaganda. Soon after its creation, in February 1942, the VOA was taken over by the OWI, which worked to forge a worldwide network. As the *New York Times* reported in November 1942, VOA broadcasts were reaching Europe, Africa, and Latin America, and from San Francisco, Asian-language programming beamed toward Oceania and into Asia. Its expansion, according to the *Times*, signaled that "the battle was in progress in the war of ideas."[11]

Roosevelt's "total war" strategy drew heavily on the VOA, which in turn was thought to offer a kind "grapeshot" tactic in the so-called "war of ideas."[12] But it was not long before questions appeared as to whether the VOA, which included news, commentary, and cultural programming, was to serve a strictly auxiliary function or to stand alone as an American version of the BBC. According to Edward W. Barrett—who helped to establish the OWI's overseas network, the United States Information Service (USIS), the VOA, and the first United Nations radio system—early VOA programming was part of the OWI's "sykewar" or "psychological warfare" strategy.[13] Under the aegis of the Political Warfare Division and based out of Algiers, "radio teams" commandeered local transmitters and used "artillery-fired leaflets," loudspeaker messages, and rumor dissemination to shape the theater of war.[14] Leafleteers papered the walls of busy intersections while "local newspapers, radio stations, cinemas, and magazines" were gutted of their staff and repurposed for the work of propaganda.[15] The *New York Times* and other newspapers covered the operations extensively, and for an American public deeply skeptical of any form of propaganda, such tactics did not go unnoticed. The Roosevelt administration dissolved the OWI soon after its mission was completed, in 1945, and many of its overseas posts were recalled. Its members, however, now primed for success in the realm of information operations, went on to fill the ranks of the United States' postwar bureaucracy; many joined the nascent Central Intelligence Agency and the USIA, which were created in 1947 and 1953, respectively. As the two major hubs for the institutional memory of the OWI, these two agencies would become the principal vehicles for the propagation of American public diplomacy throughout the Cold War.[16]

In addition to personnel, many of the OWI's wartime operations outlived the war, the VOA being the most prominent survivor. But with the bulk of attention concentrated on Europe and the Mediterranean during the war years, America's mass media programs faced major challenges during the second term of the Truman administration. In 1949, the United States Advisory Commission on Information estimated there were fewer than half a million radio and short-wave receivers for all of the Middle East and Africa. That number reached just 6 percent of the population; in comparison, in the countries of the "Iron Curtain," the Far East, and Latin America, it was believed radio transmissions were reaching close to 30 and 20 percent, respectively. In Western Europe, an estimated seventy million radio and short-wave receivers were capable of reaching well over half the population.[17] The absence of US information about Africa and the Middle East could be understood as a reflection of the starkly uneven distribution of communications technology during the twilight years of European colonialism. Commercial news agencies and publishing distributors were simply uninterested in wide swaths of the world. Countries like "Afghanistan, the Belgian Congo, Congo, Ethiopia, Iran, Iraq, Jordan, Libya, Morocco, Nigeria, Syria, Gold Coast [Ivory Coast], Kenya, and Tunisia" were not commercially serviced by American agencies. Others, like "Ceylon [Sri Lanks], Egypt, India, Israel, Lebanon, Pakistan, and Turkey" received only limited distribution. In most of these countries, USIS activities provided the only source for American-made information, printed or otherwise. It was a vital but precarious effort, not least of which because the Soviets, through their principal state-news agency TASS, were active across all of the above-mentioned countries and in multiple media.[18]

Archives of US information operations toward the Arab and Islamic world speak to an esprit de corps within the USIA that favored local independence and entrepreneurialism while struggling nonetheless with the preconditions of the broader US-Soviet conflict.

In the Maghreb, where OWI operatives once occupied former Italian outposts, USIS personnel directed Arabic, French, and English broadcasts over Army transmitters to far-flung "tribal chieftains" of the greater Sahara and Sahel.[19] Speaking from Tehran, in contrast, the ambassador Henry F. Grady expressed trepidation about creating a VOA relay in Bahrain because, as he wrote in a cable from 1950, the station would likely be "exploited with Soviet assistance by Iranian Nationalists and other oppositionist elements to embarrass the present Iranian Government"—a serious risk for an allied regime that was seen in Washington as a bulwark to Soviet advances in the greater caucuses.[20]

Embassies and consulates in Beirut, Damascus, Amman, Baghdad, Tel Aviv, Jidda, and Cairo navigated similar challenges. Public affairs officers (PAOs) coordinated messages to counter perceived stories of anti-Americanism by placing corrective articles in local newspapers; creating partnerships between Voice of America and local radio stations; and displaying "anti-Soviet posters" in prominent areas of the capital cities.[21]

Amid the outbreak of war on the Korean peninsula, public diplomacy efforts and the VOA received a surge of attention from Washington. The Advisory Commission on Public Diplomacy recommended increasing the number of PAOs based in Seoul from just one in 1949 to twenty-seven the following year, and Congress appropriated more than $130 million for overseas programming. The VOA itself saw an increase in its budget for the 1951 fiscal year from nine million dollars to thirteen million, the largest single increase in its history.[22] Similar to the early efforts of the OWI, new emphasis on non-European spheres of interest emerged—arguably as a reactionary development. In 1945, the Soviet Union launched an overseas broadcast in Arabic, adding to the already diverse linguistic portfolio of Radio Moscow and its affiliate stations. That same year, the Turkish Straits conflict erupted, exposing the reach of Soviet influence and the centrality of the region to the economic interests of the emerging superpowers. Some, like Barrett, held that the "Moslem lands" of the former Ottoman Empire had been integral to American overseas strategy for decades.[23] But it was not until 1948, with the appointment of George V. Allen, a former ambassador to Iran and chief of the Middle Eastern Division of the State Department as assistant secretary of state for public affairs, that the VOA began regular operations in the languages of Asia and the Near East.

In 1949, Turkish and Persian services, which had broadcast only intermittently for three years beginning in 1942, were restaffed and assigned regular programming. The first Arabic broadcast launched on January 1, 1950; Hebrew programming followed a year later. Following the creation of Reorganization Plan No. 8, in 1953, in which the International Information Administration (IIA) along with the information services of the Mutual Security Agency were merged together to create the USIA, a host of new languages were established, including Urdu, Hindi, Thai, Vietnamese, Burmese, Russian, Indonesian, Malayan, Korean, and four dialects of Chinese. Many of these services functioned with little more than one or two editors, receiving, translating, and often reading the news from their shared booths at the VOA's headquarters in Manhattan.[24]

Despite their small size, the foreign-language broadcasts punched well above their weight. In the years following WWII, the New York offices of the VOA became a hub of artistic and political energy, bringing together some of the most electric minds of the postwar period. In 1951, as observed by a reporter for the Puerto Rican daily *El Mundo*, the VOA's Russian-language service was running five different thirty-minute segments of news and commentary twenty-four hours a day and transmitting via four points in Europe and the Mediterranean—including Woofferton (England), Salónica (Greece), Munich (Germany), and Tangiers (Morocco). Featuring major postwar intellectuals, such as Claude Lévi-Strauss and André Breton on the French service, and led by prominent experts, including the acclaimed writer and Communist Party dissident Bertram Wolfe, who headed the VOA's "department of ideology" in the early 1950s, the efficacy of its broadcasting, as the journalist Julio Antonio observed, could be gauged by the extent to which the Soviet Union attempted to block the VOA signal while routinely denouncing its programming through state-media organs such as *Pravda* and *Izvestia*.[25] The VOA made inroads in key nonaligned countries slike Argentina, where the BBC was banned, and it became a major tactical tool in the first major conflict of the Cold War period in Korea. While the Senate subcommittee hearings led by Joseph McCarthy in the early 1950s accused broad swaths of the VOA of "Red leanings," new talent from across many sectors continued to gravitate toward the Voice.[26] As described by Heil and other veterans of the organization, John F. Kennedy's appointment of the famed CBS News broadcaster Edward R. Murrow as the director of the USIA represented a high note in the VOA's history, helping set in motion a veritable boom in top-shelf programming that included well-known voices from the worlds of art and music, people like Walter Abel, Martha Scott, or Willis Conover, whose jazz specials were broadcast around the world.[27]

SAWT AMRIKA

Although broadcasts were frequently marred by poor reception, listeners to VOA Arabic could on occasion hear big names, too. Musicians such as Fayrouz of Lebanon or Abdel Halim al-Hafiz and Mohammed Abdel Wahab of Egypt, held live performances from their respective studios in Beirut and Cairo. Legendary figures of film and literature—including Salah Abu Seif, Youssef Idris, Nawaal Sadaawi, and Naguib Mahfouz—were frequent guests at the Cairo studios of *Sawt Amrika* well into the 1980s.[28]

The broadcasters on VOA Arabic also drew popular name recognition. Yet, similar to Radio Free Europe/Radio Liberty (RFE/RL), nonprofit organizations whose funding, coordination, and infrastructure were later attributed to the CIA, the VOA's Arabic-language broadcasters hailed from an émigré community that set itself apart from its respective native audiences. VOA employees—then and now—faced a daunting task in this regard. And while audience surveys from the time remain sparse, it is clear that some of the attention garnered through the use of well-known figures did not always achieve the intended effect.

The first major luminary of the VOA's Arabic-language broadcast was the BBC's Arabic personality Isa Khalil Sabbagh. A towering figure in the world of international Arabic broadcasting, Sabbagh moved to the United States from England in 1948, where he helped to establish the first VOA Arabic broadcast in 1950. The opening broadcast led by Sabbagh featured a reading by the New York–based poet Ilya Abu Madi and a message from Abd al-Rahman Azzam, the first secretary general of the Arab League. Arriving amid the Arab-Israeli War, Sabbagh, a Palestinian by origin, was thrust into the heart of the United States' burgeoning Near East policy, which, as he later described in a blistering indictment, seemed to orient itself almost exclusively around support for the nascent Jewish state. "Israel, and before it the Jewish Agency, and before that the global Zionist movement succeeded in consolidating within American society an illustrious image of the Jewish state," he wrote.

> It [Israel] presents the image of a newborn country, one that has been oppressed but does not accept oppression; a natural partner to America in the Third World; a natural extension of Western values and of all those constituent parts that combine to form a global civilization. It presents the image of a depleted country, one that is in need of intervention, of new, healthy blood to sustain it and to empower it to shoulder the burden of America's needs in the Middle East, or indeed the needs of the entire Western world! So robust was this image that as aid and supplies began to flow the recipients held high their noses—proud owners of their new gifts as if to say: "What's so strange about it? We provide them strategic, cultural, and technological advantage. We provide them with intelligence and craft their propaganda. America owes Israel."[29]

Sabbagh worked at the VOA for just over two years before gaining American citizenship and becoming a foreign service officer. Upon the request of Allen, then the head of the USIA, Sabbagh went to the American embassy in Saudi Arabia, where he established the country's first USIS post. He gained favor with his Saudi hosts for the spoken eloquence of his broadcasts on VOA. He later recalled a tearful reception by the Crown Prince Mohammad bin Abd al-Aziz after Sabbagh eulogized his father, King Abd al-Aziz Al Saud, in 1953. Sabbagh ultimately remained in the country for nearly two decades, establishing himself as a pivotal interlocutor and translator for five administrations from Kennedy to Carter. Although he may have functioned, as one Saudi commentator noted, as a "representative of [Palestinian] Jerusalem to Saudi Arabia," his utility to American diplomats was untarnished. Kissinger in particular noted his diplomatic and linguistic versatility, which was frequently praised by the Saudis. In addition to his continued airtime on the VOA, Sabbagh became editor of the USIA journal *Al-Majal*, the journal *Al-Mustaqbal*, and the Jidda-based journal *'Akadh*. He also appeared regularly on Saudi Arabian television where he could be seen reporting on topics ranging from politics in Washington to US diplomatic maneuvers or the launch of the Discovery Space Shuttle.[30]

Sabbagh's position, as a propagandist for a government whose policies directly challenged his own political stance, epitomized the emerging trend within US information strategy to outsource production to willing collaborators, regardless of the ethical, moral, or physical blowback they faced within their target language communities.

Another early Arabic-language broadcaster was the Egyptian romantic poet Ahmed Zaki Abu Shadi. Abu Shadi had been a luminary of the Egyptian New School (*al-madrasah al-hadithah*) in the 1920s and 1930s, publishing multiple volumes of well-known poetry and cofounding the influential literary journal *Apollo* (1932).[31] After arriving in New York, in 1946, he became a fixture in the then-burgeoning New York Arab literary scene, continuing to publish poetry and essays, as well as plays and radio operas for the United Nations and Voice of America. He launched a new literary journal—*Rabatat Minerfah* (The Minerva Association), was an active painter, and taught Arabic at the Asia Institute of New York. It is not difficult to imagine why Abu Shadi was compelled to join the VOA's New York broadcasting booth. As evidenced in his 1954 testimonial or "creed" for Edward R. Murrow's famous *This I Believe* program on CBS Radio, Abu Shadi expressed deep admiration for the United States' unparalleled support for the freedom of expression. "Gradually," he wrote, "freedom became for me not only a synonym for life, but even for the Almighty. For the sake of freedom, I preferred to leave my country when tyranny was throwing independent thinkers into chains. In order to speak my mind and gain intellectual and spiritual liberty, I suffered the material and moral hardships of voluntary exile."[32]

Resulting in part from an apparent literary dispute with the prominent Egyptian intellectual 'Abbas Mahmud al-'Aqqad, Abu Shadi broke with the cultural establishment in Egypt soon after *Apollo* gained prominence. His rapid ascent within the New York literary scene was also not without controversy.

Described as a "humanist" with a trusting and sincere demeanor, Abu Shadi was already enmeshed in New York's Arab intellectual scene when he joined the VOA. But within a matter of months local Arab newspapers, including the influential *Al-Islah*, had begun to challenge his involvement. Run out of a modest brick building in the West Chelsea neighborhood of Manhattan and seldom printing more than a thousand copies of its four-page spread, the weekly transnational newspaper *Al-Islah*, established in Allepo by the Syrian poet and activist Hassan 'Abd al-'Aal in 1941 and edited in New York by Alphonse Djamil Chaurize, had become, by 1955, a hub for political and social debate within the New York City *mahjar* crowd. Described as a "friend" of the paper and an individual in possession of great "sincerity of conscience," Abu Shadi appeared not infrequently in its pages. But his employment with the VOA, and his reported presence in that capacity as a guest of honor at a gathering of the Presbyterian Labor Temple on Fourteenth Street and Madison, drew heavy fire from the editors: "May our dear friend, Dr. Abu Shadi, explain to us his relationship with this Zionist Center [Labor Temple] that, disguised as Christian or 'Humanist,' exploits Christian sentiment to serve the cause of Israel."[33]

If Abu Shadi fostered any political sentiment, it was hard to discern from the thrust of his broadcasts. With the content largely proscribed from USIA headquarters, VOA programming in Arabic was quite formulaic during its first half decade. The broadcasts opened with Abu Shadi's signature segment "*Hadith 'an al-adab al-'Arabi* (thoughts on Arabic literature) and followed with a summary of "Western newspapers"; "dramatic or poetic readings"; a segment on "Quran, Hadith, and Islamic affairs" (*al-shu'un al-islamiyya*); segments on modern agriculture and industry; health and science; Arab affairs; child-rearing; Arabs in America; a segment titled "women's world" (*dunya al-mar'ah*); and an interview with an Arab or American "personality" (*shaksiyat*). Relatively narrow in scope and with programming that also reflected, presumably, the rarified interests of its leading broadcaster (literature and drama), VOA Arabic did not attract much fire from the McCarthy hearings. Its pioneers, however, as seen in the pages of *Al-Islah*, faced other, perhaps fiercer critics.[34]

SACRED PUBLICS

In one of the earliest, major tests of the United States' new global information strategy, a sudden crisis opened the doors for communicative action abroad and popular support at home. The so-called "Magic Carpet" or "Hajji Airlift" operation epitomized the might of US logistics and the peculiarity of America's information strategy toward the greater Islamic world.

It was August 27, 1952, and nearly ten thousand Muslim pilgrims en route to Mecca had become stranded outside Beirut. "State and Defense Department officials accomplished near-miracles by slashing red tape and arranging emergency Air Force transport for 3,138 aging Arabs stranded tragically," wrote Edward Barrett.

While the airlift could take pilgrims only to the border of the Saudi Kingdom "because infidels . . . the air crews—are forbidden entry," wrote the *New York Times*, the operation, which included about half of those in the holding camps, was praised as a success and gained traction around the globe. According to the *Times*, an Iranian religious leader and president of the Chamber of Deputies, Ayatollah Kashani, was among those airlifted to his destination. The Mufti of Lebanon "ordered" worshippers to thank the United States in their prayers. A Lebanese editorial wrote, "Has America at last found its way?"[35]

Framing the event as a moral victory, USIS posts disseminated the news widely. Officials quickly produced several hundred thousand copies of a pamphlet that described the operation in Arabic, English, and Turkish as an act of religious solidarity. The near simultaneity of the coining of the phrase "magic carpet" and the airlift itself signaled, as Colonel James T. Currie wrote for the Air Force Historical Foundation, that American officials in the region were keenly aware of the political damage inflicted by a better known "Operation Magic Carpet" that the United States had participated in just four years earlier. That maneuver, in 1949, involved the airlift of some thirty thousand Yemenite Jews to Israel by US and British forces. As Esther Meir-Glitzenstein showed, the "myth" that emerged around the operation in the Western press as "a religious craving to come to the Holy Land" hardly reflected the actual, convoluted process of Jewish Yemeni migration that occurred over three years. But the championing of Zionism as a predominately religious act had effectively cornered US officials into a narrative that was held by some but not all.[36]

The tension over Zionism and the United States' support of the Jewish state was quickly becoming an insurmountable public relations challenge for US officials. Key officers, including Kermit ("Kim") Roosevelt Jr., a renowned CIA Arabist and the grandson of President Theodore Roosevelt, were working covertly through front organizations such as the American Friends of the Middle East (AFME) to counter support for Zionism in the United States and to bolster the country's standing with the newly independent nations of the Middle East.[37] The Mecca airlift operation coincided with the establishment of a new influence hub in Cairo that was created in part to expedite that effort.

In 1952, amid the chaos of the Free Officers' coup that effectively ended half a century of British rule in Egypt, the USIS struck an arrangement with Egyptian State Broadcasting and Radio Cairo, then stalwarts of the quickly fading Wafd Party, to create a large operations hub next to the American embassy in the Garden City neighborhood of Cairo. Referred to as the Cairo Packaging Center (later the Cairo Programming Center), the USIS station soon grew to be the largest in the region and the USIA's major point of access for the Middle East and North Africa. As described by the USIA officer John Hogan, the Center's second director, in 1956, the station ran fifteen-minute news relays from Washington that then traveled via shortwave from the *Courier*, a Coast Guard ship that had been repurposed as a relay station and docked off the island of Rhodes. News broadcast through the Radio Cairo tower at the top of the hour every evening and in the morning and was followed by forty-five minutes of original programming from the employees of Radio Cairo. The latter were under contract by the USIS. Some 80 percent of the broadcasts were distributed beyond the shores of Egypt to other Arab countries, making Cairo the center of the Americans' information strategy for the region.[38]

The narrative dynamics underpinning the media products of the new Cairo hub were diverse, often featuring pieces on racial integration in the United States, progress in science and engineering, and the lives of Arabs and Muslims in the United States. The Near East offices at times trailed other posts in circulating major themes as identified by the US Advisory Commission on Information. "People's Capitalism, the Family of Man, Free Elections, Atoms for Peace, and United States culture," along with the teaching of "American English," were identified as global areas for improvement in the group's 1957 annual report.[39]

But the most well-defined scripts for the Near East offices could be discerned by the formula engrained in the Mecca airlift campaign. As Nicholas J. Cull observed, religious causes became the "default message of US Cold War propaganda in the Middle East." The tendency colored both the "slow" and "fast" portfolios of America's propagandists.[40]

During the first decade of the Cold War, for example, the USIA's sister bureaucracy, the CU, began funding a series of leadership grants, intending to create allegiances between the US and foreign representatives from the political, cultural, and, above all, religious spheres, who were thought to represent "a wider range of public opinion than those persons already collaborating closely with the United States." The deployment of leadership grants was hardly a straightforward exercise in public diplomacy, as one PAO observed in a cable from Baghdad to the Division of the Exchange of Persons in Washington. In Iraq, many of the most appealing candidates were unlikely to be granted visas by the governing monarchy because their political sympathies with the left had already exposed them to police persecution.[41] But in Egypt, where the USIA and Fulbright recruited the majority of exchange students from the Arab world, there was less resistance, and the CU could tailor its efforts to those cultural arenas viewed as most relevant to the United States' greater Cold War strategy. In 1953, for example, the United States International Information and Educational Exchange Program (USIE) sponsored the visit to Washington, DC, of Said Ramadan, the editor-in-chief of the influential magazine *El-Muslim* and grandson of the founder of the Muslim Brotherhood, Hassan Banna. Ramadan was just one of forty Muslim scholars and political leaders invited to participate in a covertly funded "Colloquium on Islamic Culture" at Princeton University, which, as described in a State Department memo from that year, was intended to "look like an exercise in pure learning" while also "serving both short-term and long-term United States political objectives in the Moslem area." The USIA's Policy and Planning Staff initiated the event and arranged for the Library of Congress to cosponsor it. Princeton's Philip K. Hitti led the effort, and in advance of the meeting he conducted a tour of the region, presumably to make arrangements for the colloquium and to help recruit participants. A description of his activity appeared in the June 4, 1953, edition of *Al-Sadaqah*.[42]

As the CIA historian Brent Geary observed, the main reservoir of talent during this time was the student body at Al-Azhar University, the oldest and most prestigious institute of Islamic learning in Egypt. USIA staff conducted ESL classes for a number of Al-Azhar students in the early and mid-1950s and subsequently recruited from the same group of students for the Fulbright exchange. The students featured prominently in USIA print material and, as Geary notes, many were later employed across different branches of the US-Arabic language propaganda portfolio as English-language instructors or translators for the government's myriad Arabic-language book programs.[43]

The religious focus of the Americans' strategy in the Middle East was spelled out in a letter from Aramco's William A. Eddy, a former OSS officer then based in Saudi Arabia, to Dorothy Thompson, a celebrated public intellectual and figurehead of Roosevelt's AFME scheme. "In the fifth paragraph of my letter to you of April 25, I referred to the possible strategy of the Christian democratic West joining with the Muslim world in a common moral front against communism," wrote Eddy.

> Since then my secretary in Washington has sent to you some extracts from my correspondence from others who showed a genuine interest in this possibility, the value of which would be not only to strengthen support for the democratic West in the Muslim world, but also to constitute a recognition by the West of the moral strength and historical significance of Islam. As you know, there have been very few signs that the Western Powers place any value upon Muslims and from the point of view of psychological warfare alone, we need desperately some common ground to which we welcome the Muslims and the Arabs as respected and valued friends.[44]

CCing Brigadier General Robert A. McClure, the Director of Psychological Warfare within the Department of Defense, the "Bishop of Delaware" Arthur McKinstry, and other officials from Aramco, Eddy identified several prominent figures in the Arab and Islamic world who he imagined to be well positioned, ideologically and politically, to join in the "moral front" against communism. Eddy was keenly aware of the utility of proxied communicators in advancing US interests in the region, a dynamic epitomized by the United States emerging relationship with Saudi leaders. In an August 8, 1945, memo to then Secretary of State Francis Byrnes, Eddy observed that King Abd al-Aziz Al Saud was insisting that the "Saudi flag should fly over the inland posts." However, in Eddy's view, as the historian Irene Gendzier wrote, "such arrangements were advantageous" in that they worked to protect "the U.S. military from 'untamed tribesmen' who might otherwise think the foreigners represented an invading force."[45] In marshalling a religious front against Soviet advances, his hope was that prominent Arab influencers—including the likes of Hajji Amin al-Husseini, the Grand Mufti of Jerusalem and a well-known Nazi sympathizer—could be mobilized to generate "support for the democratic West in the Muslim world." With no sign of irony, Eddy noted that al-Husseini was of the belief that his "actions" during the War were "vindicated" by the Allies' arming of West Germany and that the Allies should have joined him in supporting the Nazis against Russia. Eddy wrote that el-Husseini "spoke cordially of the cooperation which would be offered by Muslims to promote a joint propaganda with Christians" and wished to make clear the danger of Russia, which, el-Husseini said, would destroy "all historic religion" should it "conquer the world." In his memo to Dorothy Thomson, he goes on to single out the King of Saudi Arabia, Abd al-Aziz Al Saud who, he says, "addressed himself strongly to the same point," and attaches the translation of a talk by Muhammad 'Ali 'Alluba, the Minister of Education in Farouk's Egypt who, he says, wrote "reverently of Jesus" in a way that previously would have been "inconceivable" for a "Muslim prominent in public life."[46]

Eddy's principal target of interest for Arab collaboration, however, was Abd al-Rahman Azzam. Apart from being easy to find as the secretary general of the Arab League with its occasional offices in New York, Azzam was a former member of the liberal opposition Wafd party in Egypt that for decades had lobbied the British for Egyptian independence, a position the United States had defended since the end of WWI with Wilson's Fourteen Points and the promise of "absolutely unmolested opportunity of autonomous development" for the "other nationalities" previously under Ottoman rule.[47] Azzam Pasha, Eddie notes, had expressed solidarity with the notion of a Christian-Muslim front in the battle against communism before a group of US Army and Navy officials in Washington the past

December. Azzam had also taken the message with him to a "private audience with the Pope." The Pope, Eddy reports, had told Azzam he "may make some official pronouncement in this field," and had followed up on the meeting by welcoming "Muslim diplomatic representatives" to the Vatican.[48]

THE CIRCLE OF FRIENDSHIP

While the historical records are incomplete, it is clear that Eddy's recommendations carried some weight. In just over a year, the center of the Arab Muslim world was in turmoil and the Near East division of the USIA was setting up shop for its biggest information operation to date: a lavishly illustrated and tightly edited weekly broadsheet by the name of *Al-Sadaqah*—meaning "friendship." On the front page of its inaugural edition beneath a snappy byline by the legendary Ambassador to Egypt, Jefferson Caffery, appeared a richly spun essay by Azzam titled "The Arabs and Democracy" (*Al-'arab wa al-dimuqratiyya*). It remains a vivid testament to the centrality of indigenous collaboration in the war of ideas.

> "Our examples of democracy fell prey to the systems that proceeded them," Azzam writes. "As an example of the Arab social and psychological situation consider the story of the Caliph Umar, (may God be pleased with him). When the Persians sent a messenger to Medina, they opened the gates to him and he was astonished by their power—not that which was wielded by the sword, as some people think, but rather the Arabs' powerful democratic system which Islam had called for and which was propagated among its followers."[49]

Azzam's "The Arabs and Democracy" presaged a major refrain among some Arab nationalists that argued Arab society, from its tribal origin, reflected a spirit of democracy that much of the outside world had failed to understand. "If democracy is based on the doctrine of equality," wrote Azzam, "and the notion that all people are born equal, they must live equally, and there is no distinction between them excepting that which has been earned through wealth or prestige, then the Arabs, who do not disdain such distinctions, have always and throughout generations been democrats."[50]

Appearing just a month after the Free Officers' revolution and issuing its last publication before the Six Day War of 1967, *Al-Sadaqah* was not simply an organ for the distribution of news and information but a locus for the consolidation of most every aspect of American public diplomacy toward the Middle East. From the weekly programming schedule of Voice of America Arabic, to news about book publications, updates on student and professional exchanges, and Islam in America, *Al-Sadaqah*'s coverage ran the gamut of Cold War propaganda. At its height, the paper was thought to reach a total circulation of nearly fifty-five thousand copies a year.[51] Along with the monthly *Al-Hayat fi Amrika*, special interest magazines and newsletters like *Amrika tukafihu al-marad* and the bilingual *Al-Akhbar* which targeted the Levant and Iraq, *Al-Sadaqah* was part of a bouquet of USIA publications that, by 1960, included "fifty-seven magazines in twenty languages" and "twenty-two newspapers in fourteen languages." As Wilson P. Dizard observed by the late 1950s, the USIA/S, had become the "largest international periodical publisher in the world."[52]

TARGET AUDIENCE

Integral to the USIA's foreign-language expansion was increased emphasis on the opinions of the proverbial publics it sought to influence. On one hand, print material like *Al-Sadaqah* or *Al-Hayat fi Amrika* provided opportunities for counter-communications through the exposure of certain Soviet restrictions in regards to religion, or the celebratory dissemination of US cultural practices—from summer-time swimming clubs, to culinary practices, or innovations in science and medicine. On the other hand, the publications became vehicles for the measurement of attitudes and purchasing behaviors that were thought to illuminate what CIA propagandist Miles Copeland, quoting Nasser, described as the "emotional environment" of the postcolonial target audience. Following closely on the heels of the products themselves, audience surveys provided insight into the behavioral patterns and preferences of certain subsets within a given society which, in turn, became the seeds of further articulation in the form of student or professional exchange opportunities, short-wave broadcasting, or even human intelligence gathering.[53]

Such was the spirit of a proposal put forward by a young William R. Polk conducting research in Iraq with a Rockefeller Foundation fellowship, in 1951. The future University of Chicago and Harvard historian envisioned a project that, through "mass observation" and "informal interview techniques," would delineate the "attitudes" of "young middle class" Iraqi "intellectuals" and "endeavor to discover how subjects arrive at opinions." As conveyed by the Ambassador to Iraq, Edward S. Crocker II, in a memo to Secretary of State Dean Acheson, Polk's surveys would unfold in "coffee houses" and "important centers for young middle class intellectuals." He would attribute funding to potential magazine editors, Polk told the Embassy, where he may publish some of the research. But in actuality all findings would be delivered to the Embassy and moreover a public affairs officer could direct the survey "from behind [the] scenes."[54]

The embassy's openness to the young scholar's pitch, which included a sum contribution "not to exceed $2,500 from the State Department," spoke to the dearth of early USIS research operations in the Middle East. As expressed by Crocker's successor, Burton Berry, Iraq stood out in the postwar years as a country where there was "not a single Arab language pro-West newspaper" and that "therefor those who hold pro-West views are shy while others who hold anti-Western views shout them out."[55] Slightly better conditions prevailed in other regional hubs; Beirut, Riyadh and Cairo, especially. But as evidenced by the work of people like Daniel Lerner, a pioneer in public opinion research whose most famous book, *The Passing of Traditional Society* (1958), derived from a classified survey for the near east division of the VOA in the 1940s, the US had no answer for the breadth and ferocity of the region's domestic media operations. Nasser's Radio Cairo and its most famous program, *Sawt al-Arab* (or Voice of the Arabs), for example, was broadcasting a staunchly anti-Western message across virtually the entirety of the Middle East by the mid-1950s. Like the US and Russia, Lerner found that Egypt was also supporting proxy stations throughout the region and was distributing content in a dozen languages, including Indonesian and Swahili.[56]

Rather than dissuade officials, such findings intensified calls for additional funding, which, in turn, elevated the role of outside experts like Lerner. Among the so-called "defense intellectuals" tapped with discerning foreign views of the United States and its operations were some of the giants of American public opinion research, many of whom now looked to public diplomacy as a key source of funding and debate.[57]

"The absence of such a systematic summary of psychological warfare research may be explained partly in terms of widely varying types of problems which were posed for research," wrote John W. Riley and Leonard S. Cottrell on the use of propaganda during WWII. Their influential 1957 article "Research for Psychological Warfare" posited that foreign public opinion was an indispensable piece to the production of propaganda but that standard practices of measurement remained stubbornly insufficient.

> At one extreme were the simple operational problems of the nose-counting variety: "What proportion of prisoners carried leaflets?", "Were the French civilians warned to move?" Such questions as these could usually be dealt with successfully, since appropriate research techniques were at hand. At the other extreme, global and far-reaching questions of psychological warfare strategy were asked. These questions led directly to the bases of human motivation, communication, and social structure. Not only were the research techniques inadequate; the necessary theory was lacking as well. Research on these broad questions, with a few exceptions ... did not thrive.[58]

Despite such concerns, "the necessity to justify federal agency budgets before a suspicious Congress" propelled those studies most focused on quantitative and abstract approaches to questions of human persuasion and ideology.[59] Hadley Cantril, the editor of the journal *Public Opinion Quarterly* where Riley and Cottrell published their analysis, lamented the problem in his 1965 work *The Pattern of Human Concerns*, a study itself commissioned by the CIA. "There is the very great danger," he wrote, "that the psychologist, as well as others who study different aspects of human behavior, will confuse the level of experience with which he is dealing and begin to think that the abstractions he has created actually are reality."[60]

As it were, USIA surveys took nearly a decade to mature but quickly became one of the agency's signature activities. Whereas CIA-backed studies, including those which established the agency's World Fact Book, tended toward broad social psychologies, USIA surveys, often led by Madison-avenue marketing experts, ultimately embraced a more granular approach, focusing on the distribution and reception of certain media products within particular social environments. Credibility among local audiences became critical for accuracy, but also funding from additional sources. The surveys also worked to solidify the networking capacity of the agency whose reliance on local opinion and local opinion researchers was paramount.

This was especially true for the USIS officers of the Cairo Packaging Center in Egypt where, by the summer of 1966, the government had dramatically tightened its hold on foreign and independent media voices and where the Johnson administration was hastening its promise to maintain the previous administration's commitment to the mission of public diplomacy. It was in this context that USIS Cairo commissioned one of its largest audience surveys to date; a detailed report titled simply: "Demographic Characteristics of Readers of Al-Hayat fi Amrica in the UAR."

THE NUMBERS GAME

Conducted by the Cairo-based Arab Research & Advertising Centre (ARAC) and commissioned by the USIA, the survey, "Demographic

Characteristics of Readers of Al-Hayat fi Amrica in the UAR [sic],"
aimed to measure readers' attitudes toward the agency's lavishly
illustrated lifestyle magazine *Al-Hayat fi Amrika* and to paint a
general picture of reading habits and opinions in mid-twentieth
century Cairo. Despite the vendor's domestic expertise, the sponsors at USIA showed an exacting set of standards. As detailed
in the report's introduction, the methodology deployed in the
collection of information was "pre-planned," leaving the Centre
"little freedom to introduce changes it felt would be helpful." Chief
among the demands was that the audience be kept unaware of the
survey's sponsor.[61]

As a monthly magazine the distribution of *Al-Hayat fi Amrika*,
or *Life in America* was more limited than *Al-Sadaqah*. Of the total
supply in Cairo and Alexandria in 1966, 3,105 copies were distributed to kiosks and stalls across the two metropolitan centers. An
additional 684 were provided to street vendors and dispatched for
home delivery. Apart from providing a fascinating panoply of the
city's literary topography ("Mohamed Madbouli," of the soon-to-be
Madbouli Bookstore on Midaan Talat Harb, received 100 copies of
the propaganda magazine; a certain "Mahfouz" received 10 copies
in front of the Grand Hotel on the corner of Tawfik Street) the ARAC
report reflected the precision with which the USIS sought to track
its products.

Integral to the agency's method was the obfuscation of the
USIA as the primary sponsor of the survey. ARAC researchers
were instructed to embed their questions within a mix of twelve
other publications ("Sabah El Kher," "Akher Sa'a," "Rosealuousef,"
"El Ethad Al Sovietti," or "Al Magalla Al Almaniah" [sic]). Surveys
were conducted "on the spot" at the point of purchase, and the
interviewers, postgraduates of local business programs throughout
Cairo, served as interlocutors. Along with recording what readers
"liked" and "didn't like" about each journal, the surveyors recorded
a host of demographic and professional information about each
buyer even ranking the order in which they selected their magazines. The majority of purchases were made by male university
graduates between the ages of twenty-one and twenty-nine, the

survey found. The qualities buyers appreciated most about *Al-Hayat fi Amrika* were its "excellent printing" and "coloured pictures." The great majority found "nothing they didn't like" about the journal, but ninety-five people reported disagreeable feelings about the magazine's role as a "tool of propaganda for the West and the United States."[62]

Data from audience surveys could be used to "furnish guidance," as the CBS News executive and former head of RFE/RL, Sig Mickelson, wrote. The notion was that through a statistical readout of listening or reading patterns of men versus women, or urban versus rural audiences, producers could calibrate more target specific products thereby increasing audience share and ultimately influencing more 'hearts and minds.' "We must begin with the existing curiosities and desires for specific kinds of knowledge by asking: '*Who wants to know what about us?*' " wrote Mark A. May, a social scientist with the Yale Institute of Human Relations in his conclusionary remarks before the US Advisory Commission on Public Diplomacy.

> The answer to this question is that doctors, nurses, health officers, dentists, etc., want to know about American medicine and health measures; manufacturers want to know about our production methods; road builders want to know how we build roads; musicians want to hear American music; labor leaders want to know how American labor is organized; and in Sweden rat exterminators want to know how we control rodents in the U. S. A. I believe that more attention should be given to this each-to-each *type* of communication without diminishing the more general and over-all dissemination by radio and press.[63]

Locally outsourced expertise was a natural building block for targeted programming, but conformity to strict protocol in design and execution as well as heavy vetting of the principal investigators helped pre-determine the parameters to some of the USIA's largest surveys. For example, a 1963 poll of Tehran University Students Attitudes, part of a multi-national "world-wide survey" that spanned over a decade and involved among other things costly methods of data input with the use of IBM punch cards, noted that the "Director and other staff members" of the administrating contractor in Iran—The National Institute of Psychology—were "American trained and hold advance degrees from American universities."[64] A declassified media survey in Lebanon conducted for the USIA by the Institute for International Market and Public Opinion Research (EMNID) in West Germany and the Middle East Marketing Research Institute (MEMRI) in Beirut, notes that the USIA delivered the questionnaire and that Professor Charles Churchill from the Economic Research Institute of the American University in Beirut was responsible for the sample design.[65] And while such dynamics appeared indicative of the kind of "feedback cycle" Christopher Simpson and others have described of government-funded research surveys, other declassified documents from the archives of the USIA's Research Data Collection Project show growing awareness of such problems on the part of the Washington-based USIA officials.

Declassified survey notes from a commissioned study of media habits in Tunisia, for example, included annotations expressing skepticism toward questions like "Do you feel foreign cultural centers benefit your community or are they of no concern, or are they harmful to the community," because, as one official wrote, they risked "putting ideas into their minds" and held no programmatic value.[66] As described by former deputy director of the USIA, Thomas C. Sorensen, many US career diplomats were of the position that public opinion polling distracted from their principal charge of dealing with governments, "not with the public."[67] Still, the focus on variation was a hard-won principle. Early specialists, from Walter Lippman to Daniel Lerner, sought to inform foreign policy through broad insight into the rhetorical biases of different population clusters. Practitioners and specialists like May and Sorensen in contrast lobbied for more limited and product-specific audience-based feedback. And by 1966, under the directorship of Leonard Marks, the USIA effectively "discontinued" many of the general country surveys to concentrate on polls pertaining to specific USIA products.[68]

But no degree of testing could guarantee absolute insight nor predict the success of any given operation. "Audience research," as Mickelson wrote regarding RFE and RL, could demonstrate that people were listening, but it gave "no clue" as to whether the information was influencing people's perspectives or simply "passing through the mind."[69] Testing at times revealed contradictory patterns. Nicholas J. Cull points to a 1952 survey of German engagement with US public diplomacy that found "Germans consider the most reliable source of information about America" to be "other Germans who have visited [the United States]" by a margin of 50 percent, nearly forty points higher than "fast" operations like print, radio and film which scored the lowest for reliability at just 2 percent.[70] Similar surveys from Egypt in the mid-1950s found high favorability of cultural exchange programs over those of the information broadcasts.[71] And, ironically, some surveys reinforced the need for less, not more, public diplomacy.[72] Writing from Baghdad in 1952, Chargé d'affaires Philip Ireland pointed to audience surveys to spell out the irony of certain experiments in public diplomacy. Following the screening of a Metro-Goldwyn-Mayer film, *Ninotchka*, in which a young Soviet operator played by Greta Garbo defects for Paris, the audiences reacted in dismay to the character's decision, Ireland wrote, because they found "Ninotchka's somber existence in Russia preferable to her gay and immoral life in Paris."[73]

In *The Game of Nations*, Miles Copeland described similar points of irony in the research conducted by the CIA on the behalf of a young Nasserite government. Drawing on a network of informants, the agency's lead officer in Cairo in the 1950s (presumably James Eichelberger), set out to examine the "Susceptibility of the Egyptian People to Soviet Communism" by attempting to "identify specific attitudes of the people—by occupational classification (farmer, workers, professionals, intelligentsia)—that the Communists would be able to play upon." The findings were later handed over to Colonel Muhammad Abd al-Kader Hatem, Nasser's Deputy Prime Minister for Culture and National Guidance and to Nasser himself, who, according to Copeland, put the material "under lock and key in his own desk drawer." Additional research from the Bureau of Applied Social Research at Columbia, Copeland claimed, provided the "basic propositions" to Nasser's widescale campaign to "wake up the Egyptian people."[74]

BOOKENDS

Supporting the cause of Arab nationalism had been the original aim of US operations in Egypt but, ironically, as the tides shifted following the Suez crisis and the Americans sought to shore up influence via the Baghdad Pact, Nasser's nonalignment policies including what Muhammad Abd al-Kader Hatem described as the regime's "mastery of the techniques of opinion formation," became an ultimate thorn in the side of the Americans.[75]

In the 1950s, the challenge facing the Truman administration was not whether the US should incorporate public opinion polling for the work of propaganda or why propaganda matters but how to bridge the divide between the newly established channels of information input and output. With the President's "Reorganization Plan 9" which consolidated the information operations of the OWI, the Voice of America and other parallel services such as the State Department's Embassies' library program, and the VOA's motion picture service into a single bureaucracy, the chain of command for American propaganda shifted from the State Department to the National Security Agency and the White House itself. Simultaneously, much of the covert work that had been conducted by the OWI—including its Research and Analysis Unit (RAU) as well as its listening and translation services—were rerouted to the auspices of the Central Intelligence Agency (CIA) in the form of the CIA's Foreign Broadcasting Information Service (later the Open Source Center).[76]

Bridging the divide between the input and output side of public diplomacy consequently helped to generate one of the Cold War's most storied organizations, the Psychological Strategy Board (PSB). As Nicholas J. Cull writes, the PSB addressed as one of its first matters of business the disparate efficacies of US influence operations targeting the Arab world. At a conference organized in Istanbul soon after the board's formation, members fielded input from station chiefs regarding the relative success of USIS mobile film units and the failures of VOA programming. As described below the gathering precipitated an uptick in US outreach toward the Middle East, including through new publication ventures like *Al-Sadaqah* and *Al-Akhbar* and the creation of Franklin Publications, in 1952. But pushback toward the PSB arrived quickly. State Department officials in charge of the VOA expressed dismay about a pending turf war and PSB members were assailed for swerving out of their lane. As observed by William E. Daugherty, a senior researcher for the DoD's Operations Research Division during WWII, "'announcing Chinese Communist Intervention in Korea'—how three different broadcast outlets, subjects to American jurisdiction, handled the news stories of Chinese intervention in the war in Korea in November 1950—suggests an almost total lack of central guidance, unified control, or operational coordination."[77] VOA short-wave broadcasts from New York, he wrote, competed with the Voice of UN Command (VUNC), then under General MacArthur, which competed with the Broadcast Corporation of Japan, also under command of MacArthur as Supreme Commander of the Allied Powers. Three organs of American propaganda each beaming toward the conflict in Korea and each with a different message.

Underlying the need for coherence in messaging was the more primitive demand for understanding just who the audience was and how best to influence their perspectives. Deliberate listening was not simply a co-requisite of success in public diplomacy but, arguably, the very essence of the enterprise.

USIA publications like *Al-Sadaqah* or *Al-Hayat fi Amrika* provided a valuable template for the open engagement and quiet discernment of Arab audiences. Editors at *Al-Sadaqah* first attributed its creation obliquely to "Americans living in Cairo," but subsequent issues included front matter that disclosed the hand of the USIA. The recruitment of contributors and the news and features pieces that ran on its pages, however, advanced a more clandestine agenda.

News of book publications epitomized this trend and effectively served to direct readers toward an entire intellectual universe that had been covertly supported by US propagandists.

One such enterprise was detailed in a declassified exchange between the State Department and Victor Weybright, founder of The New American Library of World Literature, then the parent company of Penguin Books. "As you have probably noted, our representatives have been working closely with your staff in Washington who are concerned with books, and inexpensive books in particular overseas," wrote Victor Weybright to Edward Barrett in November, 1951.

> I worked very hard in London on my way home to secure distribution rights for certain of our basic titles in India where such distribution is controlled contractually through British book publishers. This required a great deal of diplomacy, since it was confidential matter that the Department of State was interested; and I had to reveal our purpose as largely a commercial one. Actually, however, we do not regard the overseas circulation of our books as an entirely commercial one. Indeed, we are now working on a number of forthcoming books at the suggestion of Messrs. Hodge and Fanget of your staff in which the primary motivation is to be of service to the international aims of the country.[78]

While some mass media initiatives like the Voice of America or later the Motion Picture and Television Division of the USIA could rely on a pool of easily motivated émigrés, book publishing and distribution required a network of private collaborators. Soon following the exposures of the Church Committee in 1975, there appeared a string of revelations concerning covert CIA funding for some 800-strong "news and public information organizations" which, as John M. Crewdson and Joseph R. Treaster wrote for the *New York Times* in 1977, at times consisted of little more than "a third-string guy in Quito who could get something in the local paper."[79] Major publishing houses like Praeger brokered a diffuse range of CIA-backed publications and numerous academics, journalists, and fly-by-night reporters built their careers by channeling covert agendas.[80] But the most storied such operation was the Franklin Book program, which, by an order of magnitude, focused its attention on the Arabic speaking world.

Established first by the OSS and developed in collaboration with the USIA, local support of publishing houses like Al-Karnak in Egypt, and private collaborators such as Victor Weybright who became a "founding trustee" of the enterprise, the Franklin publishing program set a new standard for American propaganda in the developing world.[81] Based out of New York, Franklin Books, which also received covert funding from the CIA via the Asia Foundation and other small non-profit organizations targeting the global South, published and had translated some 2,428 titles through their Cairo bureau alone, between 1953 and 1978. As recounted by the famed Egyptian writer Gamal al-Ghitany who was a college student at the height of the book program, his was a generation that "that grew up with a tradition of hostility toward the United States and anything it offers on the political and sometimes the cultural levels," but, yet, like others, al-Ghitany remained intimately bound to the writers and citizens of the US through the volumes that populated his environment.

"In the 1950s we used to criticize US-funded cultural institutions such as the Franklin Publishing Institute and al-Karnack Publishing House," he wrote, "before realizing their significant contribution to the translation of important works. For example, the Franklin Institute published the only book available in Arabic by the brilliant French architect Le Corbusier, and al-Karnak published some of the best translations of short stories, which still adorn my personal library."[82]

Discerning the intent behind the selection of titles that were translated and distributed through the Franklin Book program—from John Steinbeck's *Of Mice and Men* to Richard M. Nixon's *The Art of Growing*; Allen Koenig's *The Farther Vision*, and Tocqueville's *Democracy in America*—seems a fool's errand. But emphasis appears to have been placed on topics concerning science, engineering, and agriculture—all prominent features in *Al-Sadaqah*; as well as seminal textbooks in secondary-school pedagogy, history, and politics. As reported by the *New York Times* and others, Franklin books was just one of many US publishing houses to receive covert CIA funding. Some, including Putnam, Scribner's, and Doubleday even published volumes that included unattributed CIA intelligence. In terms of foreign-language publications, however, it was evident that no other operation approximated the extent of material distributed by the Franklin Book Program. In addition to Arabic, which commanded the lion's share of publications, there appeared some 850 translations in Persian; Urdu, Bengali and Indonesian followed in third, fourth, and fifth place with 448, 331, and 221 titles, respectively. Malay, Chinese, Spanish, Portuguese, and Turkish audiences each received approximately 100 translated titles. Pashto and Dari readers in Afghanistan, 20.

The USIA's book programs were thought to be especially effective in those areas where American media operations were sparse. As the chairman to the United States Advisory Commission on Information, Mark May, wrote of his field visits to USIS offices in Lebanon, Syria and Jordan the posts were small and in the case of Jordan "inadequately staffed," but the translation of "many books into the Arabic language" had helped greatly in "getting the American viewpoint across."[83]

Significant interest from across agencies flowed into the book programs in part because the Soviets were known to be highly active in the same space. In 1957, for example, the Soviet Union launched a partnership with Al-Sharq bookstore in Cairo. This followed a landmark translation by the Soviet Publishing House of a collection of nineteen translated stories by Arab authors, including works by Mahmud Taymur, 'Abd al-Rahman al-Sharqawi, and Mahmud Tahir Lashin for the volume *Egipetskie Novelly*. The Kremlin sponsored the translation of V.I. Pudovkin's *Film Technique and Film Acting* (1954), and funded a delegation of "Egyptian cinema specialists" to travel to Moscow.[84] The USIA countered by expanding their collaborative outreach to include as many as twenty-six different publishers in the Arab world and concentrating nearly a fourth of its new publications on religious topics. USIA reading rooms, which housed many of the titles, welcomed hundreds of visitors, including from the ranks of Egypt's national high-school system that had written into their curriculum a visit to the American Reading Room.

BLOWBACK

Egyptian authorities were not unaware of its country's information deluge. As early as 1950, the influential newspaper *Al-Misri* was reporting that USIA operations in North Africa, which included "leaflets as well as radio broadcasts," signaled yet further evidence that the United States was stepping into the role once occupied by England. The Voice of America, the newspaper reported, made evident that the Arab world was in the crosshairs of a joint Anglo-American "propaganda front in the struggle against Russia."[85] Writing of the Franklin Book program in the influential state newspaper *Al-Gomohuriyya*, the Egyptian cineaste and occasional critic Samy Daoud described a kind of "intellectual invasion" and an attempt to "Americanize Egyptian culture."[86] But it was the question of intent surrounding the American information campaigns that generated the most widespread concern. What were the ultimate objectives of the two superpowers in the Near East? Ambiguity surrounding the intentions of the information campaigns as well as the sharp dichotomy that had emerged between the two competing spheres of influence created an opening that both sides sought to exploit.

"The political blunders of the Western powers are continually used as a base for creating discontent," wrote American University of Beirut President Stephen Penrose in a telegram to the State Department in June, 1951.

> Arab bitterness toward Israel and particularly toward the powers which brought it into being is being played upon continuously.

The frightful condition of the Arab refugees from Palestine is played up as being the result of the action of Western imperialism. Active efforts are being made among the refugees themselves to create the belief that in Soviet Russia alone lies any hope of a restoration of their property and their human rights. American efforts to provide funds for the economic development of underdeveloped countries and American loans to Europe and to Middle East countries are labeled as efforts of the Western imperialists to buy friendship, which of course cannot be bought. Finally, the Soviets emphasize ad nauseam the fear of economic and political exploitation which is endemic in the Arab world.[87]

Much of the Arab skepticism toward the Americans' posture, as observed by Penrose and others, stemmed from the situation in Palestine. The Voice of Israel, which inherited the technology and some of the personnel of the British Palestine Broadcasting Station was derided in the Arab press, already by 1946, as a "colonial plot" in favor of the Jewish cause.[88] Clandestine radio stations, attributed alternately to the British, the French, and the US, became a topic of scorn but also pride for those like Muhammad Abdel-Kader Hatem, the Deputy Prime Minister of Egypt under Sadat, who helped fashion the country's communications infrastructure in response to the perceived machinations of Western propaganda. "Such broadcasts aimed to confuse Egyptian public opinion," Hatem wrote of The Voice of Egypt, an unattributed broadcast he believed to have been operated from Cyprus by the French. "But, by refuting the lies perpetrated by these means, the Egyptian information media succeeded in destroying their credibility in the eyes of opinion at home and throughout the Arab World."[89] Nasser's powerful beacon of anti-imperialism, Voice of the Arabs, provided the most evident counterpoint to American and foreign propaganda. Yet, ironically, as alleged in the memoirs of two CIA agents charged with managing the country's covert operations in Cairo, *Sawt al-Arab* may never have existed without the Americans' own itinerate agenda.

Centered around the residency of CBS foreign correspondent Frank Kearns at number 8 Salah Ayoub Street in Zamalek (today the site of the Argentine Embassy), the CIA agent and propagandist Miles Copeland, then working undercover with Booze, Allen & Hamilton, had set up shop as a management consultant for the Free-Officers' government. As described in his 1969 memoir *The Game of Nations*, Copeland's team formed part of a newly created Information Planning Staff within the CIA's Directorate of Plans for the Near East that worked next door (literally) to the office of Kim Roosevelt who had previously advised Husni al-Za'im, the Syrian-Kurdish military officer who briefly seized power in Damascus following a coup d'état in March, 1949. According to multiple Cold War historians, as well as his own accounts, Copeland and his team, which included Kearns and James Eichelberger the CIA station chief in Cairo, worked to affect the policies of the new regime through a kind of "crypto-diplomacy," in Copeland's terms. The effort, he said, was imagined as a way to "fill the gap" of *Pax Britannica* and to stymie the spread of communism.[90] His wife later described the operation as the "old glue factory," a two-part allusion to the bonds that formed among the agents and their spouses who kept their secrets, and the indelible preference within the CIA for betting on its own horses to win.[91]

Because little is known about this group, apart from the memoirs by Copeland and Wilbur Eveland, also a CIA agent who worked alongside Copeland and Kearns, it is unclear to what extent the revelations—appearing after the collapse of US-Arab relations following the Six Day war—served a subterfuge purpose. While it is likely that the agents' cover—Copeland as an advisor for Booze, Allen & Hamilton, and Eichelberger an advertising specialist with J. Walter Thompson—indeed allowed the Nasserite regime to receive assistance and planning from the CIA without the stigma of direct association, the 'unmasked' memoirs written in the post-1967 era risked the opposite effect, namely, undermining Nasser's legitimacy by dint of his connection to the Americans.[92] In *The Game of Nations*, Copeland claimed the CIA had directly contributed to the construction of Nasser's "repressive base," including the regime's intelligence and propaganda apparatus. In addition to paying for the radio tower that helped launch Nasser's illustrious broadcast, Copeland claimed the CIA team provided policy documents that were translated and used by Nasser at Bandung.[93] He writes that the CIA recruited former German officers for Nasser's government, and that Eichelberger and Paul Linebarger, a CIA expert in propaganda, helped create a major policy paper "Power problems of a revolutionary government" (*Mushakil al-sultah f-il-al-hakumat al-thawra*) attributed to the first Director of the *Mukhabarat* or General Intelligence Service, Zakaria Muhieddin.[94] Eichelberger, Copeland notes, was adept at instructing press liaisons within Nasser's circle on how to disparage rivals (including then President Mohammad Naguib) by "seeming to praise them"—something that nearby *Al-Sadaqah* did on more than one occasion.[95]

With few points of verification beyond the agents' own memoirs (or the accounts of their spouses), it is difficult to measure the true extent or aim of CIA involvement in Cairo. It was not without some irony that Copeland prefaced his account of the Zamalek operation with a description of the so-called "Games Center," an exercise held on the twelfth floor of the State Department wherein a group of "super experts" assumed the role of various world leaders to "game out" the choices they were likely to make.[96] Copeland of course played the role of Nasser, a compelling assignment, he tells the reader, not least because Nasser himself had described the same sensation, in *Pirandellian* terms, as embodying the end result of a "role in search of an actor."[97]

Copeland's descriptions of Nasser effectively repeat this motif throughout; Nasser the vessel, the role in search of an actor. Regardless their veracity, in whole or part, the illocutionary effect of such utterances (to borrow a notion from J.L. Austin) mirrored the kind of "psychological warfare" Copeland claimed the OSS had deployed since WWII—"it served the purposes of the Allies to exaggerate the omniscience of the German intelligence services," he writes, "and to pretend that one could not have a friendly discussion in a Piccadilly coffee shop without some German agent's overhearing it and cabling a brief summary to Berlin."[98] Here, in contrast, it is the CIA whose presence is imagined as omnipresent in the streets of Nasser's Cairo. Beginning with Husni al-Za'im the leader of the Syrian coup d'état of 1949 and ending with Nasser, Copeland's narrative is one in which the CIA sought to fill the vacuum left by the Europeans by delivering an Arab leader who "would have more power in his hands than any Arab leader had ever had before."[99] In between is acknowledgement that the Americans' intentions were disparate.

In 1951, Copeland writes, Dean Acheson, then secretary of state, assembled a committee—with experts from Defense, State, the business community, and academia—to "study the Arab world, with particular reference to the Arab-Israeli conflict, to identify the problems and assign priorities to them and to work out solutions." He acknowledges and dismisses the information that "someone advanced the idea of promoting a 'Moslem Billy Graham'" in the sort of Messianic mindset that fills the pages of now declassified cables of that era held in the National Archives.[100] Of the Egyptian revolution he acknowledges and then dismisses information that Kermit Roosevelt had conspired with King Farouk to stay in power, of which the evidence is clear, before alleging Roosevelt had met with the Free-Officers in advance of the Coup—the evidence of which is scant. More notably still, Copeland's memoir acknowledges but quickly tip-toes past the so-called operation "Ajax" in which Roosevelt "almost single-handedly called pro-Shah forces on to the streets of Tehran and supervised their riots so as to oust Mossadegh and restore the Shah, who had fled to Rome."[101]

By championing Nasser as a master "game player," Copeland's account, post '67, ascribed to the icon of Arab nationalism a fatefully coöpted position. The translation of his book into Arabic just a year later compounded this effect, becoming not only a source of great speculation within certain Western circles but powerful fodder for the opposition within Egypt, including notably the Islamists.

In 1985, Muhammad Jalal Kishk, a well-known public intellectual and proponent of political Islam, was among the first to absorb

Copeland's account and to fashion by way of a near verbatim reprinting of the Arabic-language translation a monumental polemic on the relationship between Nasser and the CIA in *Kalimati lil-mughaffalin* (My Words for the Fools, 1985). To the extent that the memoir and its rapid translation served to undermine the Nasserite regime following the 1967 fallout, Kishk is largely unconcerned. Mohammad Hassanein Heikal, Nasser's chief communications operator and one of the country's most influential figures had engaged Copeland's account a decade prior with the *Cairo Documents* (1973), noting that while the CIA indeed operated in Cairo and had attempted to buy influence among Nasser and his men, the aim of the memoir had been to compromise the regime.[102] Kishk, in contrast, challenges Heikal's account as sheer hypocrisy, maintaining without variance Copeland's "Game of Nations" formula that

> The American intelligence men who contacted the Free Officers Organization and cooperated with Abdel Nasser's group were motivated by three goals: to prevent a true radical revolution in Egypt; to protect Israel; and to liquidate (*tasfiyya*) the two empires in the Arab world—British and the French—while replacing them with American—instead of Russian—influence.[103]

While early Cold War records of US influence operations in Cairo and the Arab world evade singular explanation, Copeland's account, and in turn, Kishk's rationalization of it, has stood the test of time. In 2017, Al-Jazeera produced a detailed documentary on Kishk's book featuring multiple self-described Islamist writers and intellectuals championing the presumed revelations as evidence of a secret origin story in the history of the postcolonial Arab states; one that, not surprisingly, diminishes the accomplishments of secular republicanism and lionizes the 'true revolutionary' goals of political Islam.

While Copeland's memoir may well have been designed to disinform readers by exaggerating the relationship between Nasser and the CIA, the synergy that emerged in consequence, between the revolutionary narrative of political Islam and American support for religious movements in the Middle East, was in place well before the revelations took hold. Attempts to break this cycle, through direct investment in domestic language training and increased foreign public opinion polling, for example, represented alternative directions in the evolution of American information statecraft. But these approaches too—costly and time consuming—soon gave ground to more well-worn techniques (i.e. outsourcing and deference to foreign-based actors). As discussed in the following chapters, the post 9/11 period ultimately rekindled many of the strategies behind the United States' first great communicative foray into the Arab world. The early Cold War experiments revealed that while the technologies of mass media—their production, distribution, and consumption—may well serve the goal of "creating individuals" in the spirit of democracy, there exists no prescribed ideology to the tools of communication and the fallout of even modest operations remains difficult to anticipate.[104] Similarly, as veteran and novice operators alike looked to the accomplishments of the Cold War period for inspiration and guidance amidst the great reboot of American public diplomacy, there was no way to know that the headiest days were still ahead.

2
FREE PLAY

I find it ridiculous that the world's greatest superpower is printing cheap stuff in Kuwait and dumping it over Iraq.
—MOHAMMED SAEED AL-SAHHAF, IRAQ'S MINISTER OF INFORMATION

The march to war after 9/11 seemed inevitable.

By mid-September 2001, Congress had passed a bipartisan resolution supporting President George W. Bush's constitutional right to respond to the attacks on 9/11 "under international law." Lengthy deliberations over the extent of the president's powers, the role of the United Nations, and the authority of Congress followed suit. By October 7, Operation Enduring Freedom (OEF) was underway with US and British forces launching a heavy bombing campaign over parts of eastern Afghanistan.[1]

It was nighttime in Paris when I learned about the development. President Jacques Chirac appeared live on television shortly before 9 P.M. saying that *"la lutte contre le terrorisme est un combat complexe et sans merci"* (the struggle against terrorism is a complex and merciless battle) and that the French had deployed naval vessels to assist. The announcement was a blip on the screen for the Parisians in the bar where I stood, but it struck me still as the beginning of a seismic shift in mood.²

The next day, the conservative-leaning newspaper *Le Figaro* described the Afghanistan campaign as "Bush's war." Bush and Chirac had refused to utter bin Laden's name, but the statements of al-Qaeda's leader—prerecorded and broadcast on Al-Jazeera shortly after the bombs began to fall—found space on the cover of the October 8 morning edition. Al-Qaeda had touched the United States' "vital nerve center," bin Laden said. "Americans would never again know a sense of security just as the Palestinians have never known security."³

Focusing on the Americans' use of air bases in Uzbekistan and Tajikistan, the leading quotidian, *Le Monde*, spelled out the irony of what the editors described as "*La nouvelle amitié russo-américaine*" (the new Russo-American friendship), which included calls of solidarity between Putin and his US counterpart and new lines of cooperation on matters of intelligence and counterterrorism. The Russians' overtures and the Americans' embrace had inspired new confidence in a Russian leader who was otherwise burdened on the world stage by domestic "instability" and the perception of being "vindictive and stubborn in the face of democratic norms."⁴ A more stinging indictment came from the left-leaning pages of the weekly *Le Monde diplomatique*. Its October 11 cover included an essay by the editor-in-chief Ignacio Ramonet; citing the 1973 CIA-backed coup in Chile, he asserted, "The most common public reaction to the attacks in New York and Washington [among 'countries of the South'] has been: what happened in New York was sad, but the US deserved it."⁵

Support for the American campaign in Afghanistan became tenuous at best. For a country like France with a large Arab population and plenty of skepticism toward American leadership, the battle for hearts and minds occupied the core of public debate.

Along with the headline on October 9, "*La guerre contre Al-Qaida a commencé*" (the war against al-Qaeda has begun), *Le Monde* reprinted on page two a short *AP* article on the Americans' use of "psychological warfare airplanes." The United States had deployed two EC-130

Commando Solo aircraft designed for "airborne information operations broadcasts" and "electronic warfare" almost two weeks prior to the official commencement of OEF. While little was reported about the mission at the time, the arrival of the hundred-million-dollar aircraft, in advance of the American bombers, helped illustrate an important aspect of the struggle. The so-called "second front" in the global war on terror was often on the frontline; in its infancy, it was forged through AM/FM radio broadcasts emanating from the skies and dispersed across thousands of leaflets littering the mountains of Afghanistan.[6]

Psychological operations specialists had long been in the practice of empowering local and credible voices in the dissemination of American propaganda. But collaborative networks were nonexistent in Afghanistan at the outset of the incursion and so both the thematic and messaging components of the American missives were created stateside primarily on the Army bases of Fort Bragg in North Carolina and Fort Belvoir in Maryland. Arturo Muñoz, a CIA officer in the Directorate of Operations and a long-time specialist in covert influence operations who had worked for years in Central America and other parts of the global South but spoke no Arabic, Farsi, Dari, or Pashto, was tasked with approving some of the early leaflets. He later wrote about several successful and unsuccessful examples in his RAND study *U.S. Military Information Operations in Afghanistan* (2012). As an example of the latter variety, Muñoz described how an image of the Twin Towers in flames with text written in small print describing the numbers of the dead was met with confusion by the people whose land it appeared on. The theme behind the message was that the US invasion was justified based on the attacks of 9/11. The remote villagers who found the leaflets, however, were mostly illiterate; they had not seen a skyscraper nor could they grasp the implied correlation between the structures ablaze, the lives lost, and the need for revenge on their soil. Another flyer attempted to display all twenty-six flags of the member NATO states in a dizzying collage of symbolism and color. Still worse, a leaflet that was never pretested and distributed in violation of the Army's own field manual for information operations featured an image of a dog with the words of the *Shahada*, the Islamic proclamation of faith, superimposed onto its body. Insignia of the Afghan security forces adorned an adjacent image of a lion. The leaflet was designed to champion the security forces while degrading the Taliban. But, of course, the intended effect was the opposite. Blasphemy was understood by all to be the greatest sign of ignorance.[7]

SEGMENTARY LINEAGE SYSTEM

Within months of the bombs falling in Afghanistan the drum of war was sounding anew as the Bush administration turned its sights on Iraq. The popular animus toward the prospect of war had reached a fever pitch by the beginning of the year, and on February 15, 2003, millions of people took to the streets in capitals around the world in what the *New York Times* and others described as "the largest, most diverse peace protest since the Vietnam War."[8] But circling above Baghdad a more concerted campaign was already underway. In October 2002, the US military had reportedly dropped some 120,000 leaflets "warning Iraqi forces not to fire on US and UK aircraft in the no-fly zones"; to stay in their homes; to choose "family" over the "regime"; and to not be afraid of the leaflets.[9] Radio broadcasts from Commando Solo aircraft, advertised on the leaflets as *Radio Muʿalamat* (information radio), had also begun by December of that year. Based out of Fort Bragg, and with the assistance of Iraqi exiles along with scores of translators from across the intelligence and defense community, US military personnel from the 4th Psychological Operations Group crafted messages that denounced the regime while promising a new day for the "People of Iraq."[10]

> Throughout the history of the world, mankind has shown a desire to progress and expand. Great leaders have built vast civilizations and empires that spanned continents. These leaders have sponsored

education programs, paved vast roads, and built housing for the less fortunate. The leaders of the past have turned deserts into arable land, and created innovations which made life easier for their people. The great leaders of the past are known for their generosity and charity towards their own people, as well as their neighboring lands. In Afghanistan, once the Taliban was removed from power, the standard of living drastically improved. Relief aid is pouring into Afghanistan and is appropriately distributed. Schools are open and people all across Afghanistan are better off.[11]

Psychological warfare was a well-worn tactic for the US military in Iraq. As part of the first Gulf War, American forces disseminated over twenty million leaflets and broadcast messages warning Iraqi forces against advancing on Kuwait. Multiple radio streams broadcast AM/FM programming from EC-130Js and across ally transmission towers in Saudi Arabia and Turkey.[12] Gray and black (semicovert and covert) propaganda also peppered the early battlefields in Iraq. As described in an Air Force commissioned report from 1996, a broadcast known as the "Voice of the Gulf" (*Sawt al-Khaleej*) "maintained the fiction" that it was an Iraqi station throughout the course of the war.[13] In 1998, *Idha'at al-'Iraq al-hurr*, or Radio Free Iraq, was established under the auspices of RFE/RL, based in Prague. The broadcast, which purported to be "free of any political party, ruling or opposition group, or exilic organization" (*munazimat al-muhajireen*), operated for nearly two decades before being folded into Radio Sawa in 2015.[14] At its height it was thought the station reached 12 percent of the Iraqi population, 73 percent of whom found the broadcast to be "very" or "somewhat" trustworthy, which was a higher credibility score than any other radio news broadcast polled by the Broadcasting Board of Governors (BBG), including BBC Arabic and the state news channel, Radio Baghdad.[15] In late February 2003, the *Guardian* reported on a covert operation similar to "Voice of the Gulf" called Radio Tikrit, which, ostensibly based in Saddam Hussein's hometown, purported a patriotic line before abruptly shifting its tone toward incitement. The *Guardian* claimed the station broadcast from Kuwait and was likely coordinated with two opposition broadcasters, Radio Mustaqbal and Radio Nahrain, which, as described in a report by the House of Commons, were created in coordination with local residents outside Basra for the UK's Psychological Operations in advance of the invasion.[16]

In addition to radio, American and British intelligence agencies worked together to create an Arabic-language news and information television station, *Nahwa al-huriyya* (Towards Freedom TV), which was also disseminated from EC-130Js. As noted in a C-SPAN rebroadcast of programming in April 2003, the United States was recording approximately four hours of content per day and their UK counterparts an additional hour.[17] The episodes lasted a little over 30 minutes and drew on the animation and sound-editing style of *PBS NewsHour*. Featuring stories of looting and chaos in the streets of Baghdad and Basra, the aim of the show was more tactical than strategic, with citizens calling for the return of the police and coalition forces patrolling the streets in a show of force. One British-produced episode featured a summary of the Coalition forces' notorious "deck of cards" of Iraq's "most wanted," followed by a lengthy interview with the expatriate soccer star Sharar Haidar calling for calm. Baroness Emma Nicholson describes a scheme led by her foundation, Ammar, to repatriate Iraqi experts to lead the country. And, in another segment, the anchor repeats a call from General Robin Brims of the UK's 1st Armoured Division for "one of the sheiks of Basra" to "prepare a list of people whom he believes to be trustworthy and capable of controlling the area" (*al-mantaqa*). Their authority, he explains, would be "temporary, not permanent."[18]

Similar to the Voice of America (VOA) and other media from the Cold War era, Towards Freedom TV included information about other, parallel operations. Interspersed within a segment featuring a Kurdish leader detailing his vision for a Federation-style government in Iraq and another warning that former regime elements are committing violence disguised as Coalition forces, the anchor describes the arrival of a "free newspaper" to be published six times per week under the name *Al-Zaman*. The paper will include the "activities of the allied forces and other news," he explains. "Look forward to it."[19]

Working in concert with the CIA, the military conducted psychological warfare in Iraq under its own mandate. In addition to the Army's field manual for information operations, which had been in place since the 1990s, the Department of Defense (DoD) adopted, in 2003, the *Information Operations Roadmap*, which emerged as part of the Quadrennial Defense Review from two years earlier. The roadmap, which was declassified through the Freedom of Information Act, described an approximate $383 million budget allocation toward information operations with the aim of positioning the practice as "a core military competency on a par with air, ground, maritime, and special operations."[20] Concentrated under the auspices of US Strategic Command, the document envisioned a "full-spectrum" overhaul of information operations to include kinetic activities such as improving "Network and Electro-Magnetic Attack Capability" and ratifying the importance of "PSYOP products based on in-depth knowledge of the audience's decision-making processes and the factors influencing [their] decisions."[21]

The roadmap spelled out the use of PSYOP products for the purpose of "discouraging, dissuading and directing an adversary" ("military deception"); protecting "plans" and misdirecting the enemies' response ("operational security"); controlling "adversarial communications and networks" ("electronic warfare"); and, "when executed to maximum effect, seizing control of adversary communications and networks" ("computer network operations").[22] Many of the practices illustrated in the roadmap had been in use since WWII when Office of War Information (OWI) operatives in North Africa commandeered local transmission towers, disseminated strategic messages in the form of flyers and posters, and blocked Axis maneuvers to similar effect. But while the roadmap highlighted the importance of "peacetime preparation" in psychological warfare, including "intelligence, surveillance and reconnaissance," the events of 9/11 had triggered a full-scale and virtually simultaneous activation of all the above. The result, as Muñoz described, created something akin to a "segmentary lineage system." With no central coordination, US information operations in Afghanistan and Iraq replicated and competed with another. "The VOA set up a radio station in Kabul and then the DoD did the same," Larry Schwartz explained. The two institutions had to share resources and ended up competing for the same pool of talent. In the end, however, the military commanded the bulk of the work. Schwartz explained, "We have a military industrial complex so well-funded that they can do anything they want and no one will tell them not to."[23]

"COLLECTIVE SECURITY IS YOUR DEFENSE"

The year 2003 was not the first time Americans had tried to launch a mass media operation in Iraq. That ignominious distinction fell to the United States Information Service (USIS). The formal establishment of the United States Information Agency (USIA) was still two years out, in February 1951, when some "twenty important United States diplomats" gathered in a "secluded huddle" in the "ancient city" of Istanbul to discuss the future of US defense and information strategy for the Near and Middle East. As reported by the *New York Times*, the week-long gathering of "chiefs of diplomatic missions" laid the groundwork for Turkey's ascension to a "system of common defense"—a prelude to its admission to NATO in 1952—and the formulation of the administration's new "eastern Mediterranean" containment strategy.[24] A lengthy, classified memo summarizing the findings and recommendations of the "Conference of Middle East Chiefs" emphasized the perceived import of Greece as well as Turkey; dispelled the idea of admitting Egypt to NATO (for fear of raising the "question of association by other southwestern Mediterranean nations"); and highlighted the value of a "'grass roots' approach" to the State Department's information and exchange programs in the region. Mission chiefs, it was thought, should "limit intervention to the most vital issues" while focusing on the cultivation of "indigenous political leadership"—a strategy that had proven effective in Syria in 1949 and would shortly play out in Egypt and Iran.²⁵ Among the major recommendations to emerge from the conference was "stepped up work" in virtually all facets of the government's information strategy for the Near East, from improvements in VOA programming to more selective personnel hirings and increased publication activity for "literate elements" in the region.²⁶ The Franklin Book program began its first set of translations into Arabic on the heels of the Istanbul conference. Edward R. Murrow's *This I Believe*, a collection of essays from his legendary radio program, was the first commissioned volume.²⁷

Also prominent in the discussions was the place of Israel and the perceived challenge of the Palestinian refugee crisis for stability in the region. "Israel needs peace more than the Arabs do," the memo stated. "It is now completely dependent upon air and sea communications which can be completely severed in time of war. Consequently, Israel must in some way, through unilateral, partial, or overall negotiations, make substantial concessions in the fields of territorial adjustments or refugee repatriation."²⁸

Truman's Psychological Strategy Board (PSB) had drafted a major policy paper for the National Security Council the year before outlining the need for a new information strategy as a result of Israel's founding. In Iraq—the country with the largest Jewish population in the region outside of Palestine—the Arab-Israeli dynamic had grown volatile. Iraqis, "like other Arabs," wrote the former CIA officer Wilbur Eveland, were "convinced that the state of Israel would not have been created without American assistance."²⁹

Arab trust in the new Western superpower plummeted after the creation of the Jewish State in 1948. Meanwhile, Jews in Baghdad, numbering some 130,000 at the time of Israel's creation, were being pulled into the crosshairs. Many, including the founders of the international public relations firm Saatchi & Saatchi, which would become the Americans' principal creative vehicle in the region following 9/11, were abandoning the country for Israel and Europe. Threats of violence in part precipitated the exodus. "A bomb had exploded harmlessly outside a Passover gathering," Eveland wrote, "causing nearly 10,000 Jews to queue up to take advantage of the Iraqi government's policy of not restricting legal emigration to Israel."[30] The seizures of arms caches held by Zionist groups and subsequent small-scale attacks on synagogues further accelerated the phenomenon.[31]

Concurrent with the hostilities generated by the Arab-Israeli conflict, another equally pressing challenge was outlined by the mission chiefs in Istanbul.

> The low royalty pattern followed in the past by the Iraq Petroleum Company and the Anglo-Iranian Oil Company, the failure in the past of the former company to develop adequate production rates, and the continuation by both companies of colonial methods in dealing with local governments have led to increasing hatred of foreign oil operations. While on the one hand the British Government has agreed with the United States on the necessity for stability of the area, on the other hand, agencies of the British Government have not in fact been able to assure that British oil companies are acting in conformity with that policy.[32]

"Soviet and communist influence," the chiefs recognized, were "kept under fairly effective control through police action in the various states of the Middle East"—a "virtual propaganda monopoly of the Soviets in northern Iran" being the sole exception. Rather, as outlined in the report, more damaging to American interests were the actions of the United States' primary ally in the region, the United Kingdom.

The UK, Eveland observed, still considered Iraq its colony and the fifteen-year-old monarch, King Faisal II, whom they had brought from Saudi Arabia after WWI, to be a vassal of British authority.[33] The exploitation of royalties by oil companies went unchecked and the vast poverty unfolding across the country was addressed by policing those opposition voices that took issue with the inequality. Strict rules of censorship—a practice known as the "Faruq Code" named for the British-backed monarch of

Egypt—targeted the publication of images depicting "social revolutions, demonstrations, or squalidness"; "dirt lanes"; the "homes of poor peasants"; "workers on strike"; and "attacks" by workers against their employers and "vice versa."[34] Opposition papers like *Al-Ahali*, run by the founder of Iraq's *Hizb al-Watani al-Dimuqrati* (the National Democratic Party or NDP), were frequently shut down. And journalists such as Kamil al-Chadriji, the liberal democratic cofounder of the NDP who was also editor-in-chief of *Al-Ahali*, gained elevated political stature. As described by the historian Hana Batutu in his monumental study of the pre-Republican era, *The Old Social Classes and the Revolutionary Movements of Iraq* (1978), al-Chadriji's influence on Iraqi politics became especially visible during a massive uprising in 1952 that nearly brought down the government. Demonstrators chanted in the streets for "a democratic government under Kamil al-Chadirji," Batutu wrote. Al-Chadriji was subsequently arrested and remained in prison until the Iraqi revolution, or so-called "Free Officers' coup," in reference to the influence of Egypt's Revolutionary Command Council, in 1958.[35]

All of this translated into direct action against Western powers and in particular their perceived organs of political communication. The USIS library on Al-Rashid Street was targeted with grenades in March 1951. Eight months later it was burned to the ground. The British embassy in Baghdad was stoned. Rather than address those root causes of hostility as laid out at the Istanbul conference, the United States' information strategy for Iraq was built around the prospect of deflection. It is not clear if this tactic was deliberate. According to Eveland, none among the small coterie of State Department officials in Baghdad spoke Arabic at this time, and along with their wives the Americans were almost wholly reliant on the expertise of their British counterparts. Nonetheless, it was a tactic harmonious with the United States' broader Cold War strategy.[36]

Focusing on the perils of communism, the Iraqi mission's information strategy was twofold. First, as articulated by Edward S. Crocker II, the State Department's ambassador in Baghdad who also attended the Istanbul conference, the United States wished to "change the general prevailing public attitude in Iraq which is either unaware of or apathetic toward the dangers of Soviet imperialism and, therefore, is generally opposed to measures of collective security with the West." Second, the government hoped to "maintain the continuing interest of those already oriented to America through travel and education in the United States."[37]

The two-phased campaign included the creation of a weekly Arabic-language magazine, *Al-'Urwa*, which was designed to "emphasize the interest of the United States in the development and prosperity of Iraq" and "stress the mutuality of interests between the two countries." (The name "*al-'urwa*" referred to a "bond," as in a "bond of friendship." The Americans were perhaps unaware that it also translated as "the noose"). And it featured the creation of an "English language bulletin" that was to serve as the primary vehicle for maintaining and promoting "interest in the United States among American-trained Iraqi students." The campaign, Crocker noted, should cost $2,150 upfront, and it could be replicated across other Middle East outposts: "Karachi, Tehran, Ankara, Beirut, Damascus, Cairo and Tripoli."

Phase two, in Crocker's information strategy for Iraq and the greater Middle East, was to exploit the inroads created by the publications to "make Iraqis aware of the dangers of Soviet imperialism and to change existing deep-seated concepts and attitudes opposing Iraq's participation in cooperative Western defense calls for a specialized propaganda effort." To do so the information needed to be presented in such a way that it evoked "an emotional response," one that could overwhelm the Iraqi people's "present antagonism and suspicion toward the West." In a cable to the Department of State, Crocker wrote, "Is there such a theme? There is—the same self-interest that forced the United States into Korea; the same self-interest that formulated our policy of Soviet containment; the same self-interest that quickened the desire for collective security in Western Europe. A realization of a common, global foe can forge a common, global bond between Iraq and the Western defense powers."[38] Crocker believed simple abstractions were the best way to accomplish the goal of forging the common enemy. "Can this realization be brought home swiftly to Iraq?" he asked with rhetorical flare. "It can—with a single picture... the map" (original emphasis). Phase two, as Crocker imagined, would see the distribution far and wide of a carefully crafted map of Soviet communism with its ominous spread across western Asia depicted in " 'hot' red for maximum impact" and with an "intense thick red line at each boundary with light pink areas on either side which gradually darken to the overall red color." A "white arrow" slicing through the Caucuses and bearing down on the Middle East was added for additional effect. "The size of lettering in Arabic, Kurdish and English should correspond to the lettering as shown in the photograph," he wrote. " 'COLLECTIVE SECURITY IS YOUR DEFENSE' " (original emphasis). The map would accompany a host of other white and gray propaganda—radio segments offering free giveaways of the map, cardboard cutouts in store windows, purchased ads in the domestic newspapers, and a short, animated movie depicting the rise of humans from an isolated Neanderthal to a member of a collective army—NATO—that would confront an angry horde in the self-interest of his tribe.[39]

Crocker's plan came to fruition over the course of the following summer. But it required yet further reliance on the existent infrastructure of the Americans' singular ally in the long war of ideas: the United Kingdom.

The British, who had built the country's principal radio tower and largely controlled its main broadcast, Radio Baghdad, had established by the end of WWII a robust propaganda strategy for the country. Its main utility, as the historian James R. Vaughan wrote, was that of a "stick with which to beat Nasser."[40] The Americans, apart from the floundering VOA Arabic broadcast emanating from a retrofitted fishing vessel off the Greek island of Rhodes, relied on local access to maintain a steady presence on Egyptian airwaves through Radio Cairo and also, in Jordan, through the Hashemite Broadcasting station, which replayed script from the Cairo Packaging Center and the USIA's Wireless File. But in Iraq, as Vaughan observed, "US officials were frustrated by their inability to develop closer links."[41]

Meanwhile, the signing of the Baghdad Pact in 1955 and the Americans' sharp abandonment of Nasser following the Czech arms deal of that same year, further elevated the centrality of Iraq to the Anglophones' collective Cold War posture. The Americans had facilitated already new telecommunications ventures, including a radiotelegraph circuit, with RCA in New York.[42] In October 1954, via a British trade fair arranged by the colonial authorities, television sets were introduced to the country. "King Faisal appeared in front of a television for the first time," reported the Syrian-based newspaper *Alif Baa*. "He learned that Baghdadis will soon have their own station."[43] As reported by Sam Pope Brewer—the CIA's principal contact at the *New York Times*—the Americans "had a hand in organizing program work" for the new station, "but the idea and the financing came entirely from the Iraqi government." The new station broadcast two hours per day with "sports events, documentary films and drama." Programs on home economics also distributed from the United States were rejected on the grounds that "there would be too big a gap between the demonstration and the experience of the Iraqi housewife." To compensate for that lack of content, "short plays" performed in the studio were "produced and acted by local talent."[44]

The activities of the Coalition Provisional Authority and the Iraq Media Network somewhat resembled their Cold War predecessors. In other ways, the two histories were radically dissimilar. There was the US/UK fraternity; the newspaper and the bulletins; the fertilization of propaganda across parallel platforms; and the distribution of information in the form of purchased and manufactured news items in the fledgling local press. Distinct from previous conflicts, however, "theater media and psychological operations" were not run through the USIA or State Department. Rather, like during the first Gulf War, the Defense Department controlled the flow of information in Iraq.[45]

Of course, this too was not a new phenomenon. The American military had been implementing cultural outreach policies for over a century.[46] But defense-led information operations had their roots in the Middle East, the first instance of record being from July 1958 in response to a perceived Egyptian-backed Palestinian uprising in Lebanon. Approximately seventy Palestinians had crossed into the US-allied country from Syria in an attempt to forestall Parliamentary elections and to challenge the government of Chamille Chamoun, one of the last reliable cogs in Eisenhower's so-called "Middle East Doctrine". The VOA was the administration's main vehicle for selling the narrative of the adventure. Its Arabic broadcast increased threefold and programming converted to a news-only format.[47] But the experience made vivid for the military commanders the need to control their own narrative. "When we arrived we generated no photo happenings," recalled Major General David W. Gray. "So some enterprising reporter got one of our soldiers to pose in his company area, sitting backward on a donkey, drinking a bottle of soda. The picture by itself was bad enough, but the *Washington Post* printed it alongside a grim-faced Marine in full battle regalia, with bayonet fixed, charging across the beach."[48] Commanding officers reacted to the incident by dispatching a film crew. But it was too late to rectify the initial impression. "More important is that a commander understand the awesome power of the Press," wrote Gray. "His only defense is to ensure that he has a good PIO, keep him fully informed and ensure that he is capable of establishing good working relationships with all the media, press, TV, and radio."[49]

INFORMATION WARFARE, UNRESTRICTED

By 2003, the military had internalized the experience of 1958, as well as the "horrible press-military breakdown" that characterized popular resentment toward the war in Vietnam, the black-box stigma attached by the press to adventures in Granada and Panama, and the tightly controlled victory of the first Gulf War. The embedded press system, as it became known, capitalized on the placement of more than seven hundred American and one hundred foreign journalists within forward operating units of the Army, Air Force, Marines, and Navy across Iraq and Afghanistan. The idea, as illustrated in the definitive 2004 RAND study *Reporters on the Battlefield: The Embedded Press System in Historical Context*, was to mitigate the aura of secrecy and political fallout that surrounded previous operations. Simultaneously, however, the system enshrined Eisenhower's idea, as quoted by the Office of the Secretary of Defense in its final report on Operation Desert Storm, that "the first essential in military operations is that no information of value should be given to the enemy."[50] Straddling the government's myriad channels of pscyhological warfare was an amorphous new braichild of the defense-intelligence enterprise known loosely as "strategic communications." Born amid the ashes of 9/11 and on the doorstep of the twenty-first century's first global war, the broadly conceived interagency discipline was in essence an exercise in public diplomacy. The United States was failing to understand its enemies, so went the rationale, and much of the world, in turn, struggled to find meaning in the actions of the world's greatest superpower. Misunderstanding was at the core of the emergent crisis, making communications both the ends and the means of victory in the war on terror.

Few officials in Washington understood this dynamic better than Robert M. Gates, a former director of the CIA and president of Texas A&M University, who was appointed secretary of defense under George W. Bush in 2006; he remained in the position under the administration of Barack Obama, from 2008 to 2011. He was the first secretary of defense in history to serve two consecutive administrations, let alone two administrations from different political parties. During his tenure Gates oversaw a massive increase in military funding for basic "peer reviewed" research—$1.7 billion in 2009 and an additional $1 billion increase over the subsequent five years. Much of the funding centered on issues of soft power, or as Gates described in a 2009 article for *Foreign Affairs*, "measures aimed at promoting better governance, economic programs that spur development, and efforts to address the grievances among the discontented, from whom the terrorists recruit."[51] Gates was part of a defense-military establishment that just several years before had begun circulating a pirated translation of an obscure Chinese military treatise known as *Unrestricted Warfare* (1999). Attributed to two colonels in the People's Liberation Army and featuring on the cover an image of the Twin Towers in flames beneath the subtitle "China's Master Plan to Destroy America," the text, which was distributed in 2002 by an unknown Panama-based publisher, compounded the fear among certain defense and intelligence hawks that Beijing had anticipated 9/11, perhaps even providing training and intelligence to al-Qaeda in advance of the attacks. The *Financial Times* and other media outlets later interviewed the authors of the work, Colonel Qiao Liang and Colonel Wang Xiangsui, who denounced the translation as "copyright infringement" and rejected the implied association with al-Qaeda.[52] But the effect of the Panama copy had run its course. John Hopkins University, through the Applied Physics Laboratory and the School of Advanced International Studies, hosted four consecutive annual symposia on the book. And officials like Gates now fully embraced the kind of asymmetric warfare the Chinese document appeared to anticipate. In 2008, along with a slew of defense-oriented research initiatives, Gates announced a major new funding line known as the Minerva Project. Distributing some twenty million dollars a year in funding over a ten-year period, the Minerva Project launched a new generation of psychological warfare research on topics ranging from "the Strategic Impact of Religious and Cultural Changes within the Islamic World" to the "Iraqi Perspective Project," "Terrorist Organizations and Ideologies," and "New Approaches to Understanding Dimensions of National Security, Conflict, and Cooperation." The first Minerva Broad Agency Announcement as issued by the DoD's Army Research Office, however, concerned not terrorism but "Chinese Military and Technology." As Gates described, there was an outstanding need to catalog the "tremendous amount of information about military and technological developments" that the Chinese government was regularly publishing on an "open-source basis."[53] How this project connected to the ongoing wars in Afghanistan and Iraq remained mysterious to the lay public. But the initiative aligned with the government's general interest in fueling a new, global era of "cultural intelligence" within the defense establishment. Regardless of the accuracy of claims surrounding the document—that China had "predicted" the attacks or, as suggested by an unattributed article in the *Washington Times*, that the country was supplying arms to Taliban and al-Qaeda forces after 9/11—the *Unrestricted Warfare* phenomenon compelled investment in a whole range of activity that went well beyond the traditional scope of military dominance and beyond the war on terror.[54] Culture, economics, and information were being positioned as national security domains with implications on and off the battlefield. One of the first, concrete responses to this new dynamic was also one of the Army's most controversial.

HUMANS, TERRAINS, SYSTEMS

Modeled on the Johnson administration's Civil Operations and Revolutionary Development Support (CORDS) initiative, which, through the auspices of "intelligence collection," aimed to win the hearts and minds of the South Vietnamese, the Human Terrain System (HTS) sought to place social scientists and other culturally astute private citizens within forward operating units of the Army and across myriad remote locales in Afghanistan and Iraq. In essence little more than another experiment in public diplomacy lane-swerving, the HTS crystalized key elements of the DoD's strategic communications dossier for an era of "unrestricted warfare." Small units of the Special Forces and paramilitary officers from the CIA had already made considerable headway locating hard-to-find al-Qaeda cells using the "human terrain" and the "information terrain" of eastern Afghanistan. But, as the Unrestricted Warfare Symposium convener Thomas Mahnken described in 2006, more was needed to "export" skills "currently resident in Special Forces—particularly cultural awareness and language proficiency . . . to the general-purpose forces."[55] Imagined in the spirit of network clusters, five "Human Terrain Teams" each consisting of a "leader," a "cultural analyst," a "regional studies analyst," a "human terrain research manager," and "a human terrain analyst"—the HTS, like the embedded press system, served the dual purpose of partially co-opting an influential nongovernmental sector (i.e., academia) while ostensibly exposing US military operations to greater civilian oversight. What was unexpected, however, was the hard reality that academics were no more qualified to understand the human and information terrain of Afghanistan and Iraq than the general-purpose forces. Few of the enlistees—mostly recent graduates from the disciplines of anthropology, sociology, and international studies—had any viable field experience in the parts of the world they had nominally studied. Most were functionally illiterate in their target language environments, and none spoke the dialect of their appointed terrain. More damagingly, popular awareness of the program grew rapidly, and the focus among academic organizations and the American press corps alike was the cost of the project—$41 million for the first year—and the "ethical and procedural concerns" that surrounded "engagement with US security and intelligence communities." In particular, the American Anthropological Association (AAA) issued a statement in 2007 on the heels of its annual meeting in Washington that outlined "the ways that the HTS project violates the AAA Code of Ethics"—the imperative that "anthropologists do no harm to their research subjects"—and the problem of secrecy with regards to the replicability of any scientific output. Not included among mainstream critiques was the fact that the majority of those who participated in the program were only loosely affiliated with academia. The people best positioned to navigate the linguistic and cultural complexities of the war, namely Afghan and Iraqi Americans, did not make it past the training program in Fort Leavenworth, Kansas. Unfortunately, no small number of "fantasists and fraudsters who routinely and obviously embellished their experience," on occasion, did. As described by Ryan Evans, the founder of the influential online journal *War on the Rocks* and a participant in the project, Human Terrain Teams "were never going to 'fix' counterinsurgency or make it work, but at their best, a functioning team could provide a sharper lens through which their brigades could see their area of operations."[56] Academic integrity and the concerns represented by groups such as the AAA, on the other hand, were hardly part of the equation. That doesn't mean that some of the academic research engendered by programs like Minerva did not cut through the cold expediency of wartime operations. But for the most part, unlike during the Cold War, anthropologists and most other qualified civilian experts remained eerily absent from the deliberation of America's longest war. In their stead emerged a new class of "defense intellectuals" drawn mostly from the distant shores of the scientific community: the proverbial Beltway bandits including self-funded Think Tank practitioners and private defense contractor employees with the occasional PhD or university lecturing credit appended to their name. That the HTS imagined a neat solution to the otherwise vast challenges of human connection, persuasion, and influence was hardly the fault of the underemployed individuals that leapt at the opportunity (the HTS paid nearly $250,000 per year). With or without the approval of academia proper, the military needed answers to "China's Master Plan," "Iraqi and Terrorist Perspectives," and the "religious and the ideological" dimensions of the conflict. "The government and the Department of Defense," Gates exclaimed, needed "intellectual disciplines" like "history, anthropology, sociology, and evolutionary psychology."[57] But, despite their best efforts and despite the money, the government and the DoD were not going to get what they needed. Rather, in most instances, they got what they were given. For the most part, outside contributions to the military's battle for hearts and minds flowed from no-bid or single-bid contracts that were solicited and executed at the highest levels of government. One of the first and most prominent such contracts fell squarely on the information side of the Americans' offensive: a dimension of the first Gulf War that most alarmed Qiao and Wang but that now, under George W. Bush, would look very different.

IRAQ, MEDIA, NETWORK

At the center of the military's communications front in Iraq was the rapidly established *Shabakat al-'Ilam al-'Iraqi* (Iraq Media Network or IMN). Created by the Northern Virginia–based Science Applications International Corporation (SAIC) with a no-bid contract for $82 million, the IMN was the brainchild of Paul Bremer III, the director of Bush's Coalition Provisional Authority (CPA), and a fantastical exercise in neocolonial state-making.

The idea of an Iraq-centered American information hub in the spirit of the USIS posts of old had been percolating among public diplomacy strategists for over a decade by the time the Iraq War came along. Compelled by "worldwide attention to events in the Gulf," and with the aim of countering "misperceptions and Iraqi disinformation," the USIA convened, amid the first Gulf War, an Inter-Agency Working Group on Iraq Public Diplomacy "to coordinate media and other public diplomacy activities."[58] In 2001, the Defense Science Board Task Force proposed a similar role for the DoD's Strategic Command.[59] The idea was to create a mechanism for the refutation of the regime's propaganda apparatus while generating new narratives surrounding the ongoing conflict. Saddam Hussein's unchecked and increasingly transregional propaganda machine, which routinely painted Saddam as a "direct descendant from Ali the fourth caliph of Baghdad" and depicted Americans as "crusaders" bent on the "desecration of Mecca," was in many respects the essence of his regime.[60] As Pierre Darle wrote in his 2003 study of Saddam-era propaganda and Hikmat Studio in Baghdad, "it was thanks to television that the regime existed," not just as an extemporaneous force but within "the spirit of the people."[61] Despite recognition of the profundity of the regime's ideological grip and the need to generate a coordinated response to the problem, the Bush administration's solution involved a smattering of private American contractors who in turn hired scores of Arab businessmen, marketers, journalists, and media entrepreneurs, most from culturally remote locations such as Egypt and Lebanon, to fill the airtime the military had cleared. Not surprisingly, blowback to this approach came fast and furious.

In 2005, news broke of some three hundred million dollars that had been allocated by the Pentagon's short-lived Office of Strategic Influence (OSI) to several Washington-based firms for the purpose of improving "public opinion abroad" and assisting "coalition forces" with communications services in Iraq.[62] While just a small piece of the pie in a massive private contracting schema that, by 2011, had ballooned to an estimated $206 billion, the media projects were especially visible and quickly attracted an unparalleled degree of scrutiny.[63]

Among the three companies awarded the money, the Washington-based Lincoln Group was the first to be exposed for its egregious campaign of planting false and misleading stories in the Iraqi press. It had also proposed an "anti-terrorist" comedy show based on *The Three Stooges* as a way of broadening the reach of the military's "stealth persuasion" campaign.[64] The company ultimately lost its contract but the comedy show idea remained. In 2014, an Iraqi production team for *Al-Iraqiyya*—the IMN's renamed television station—released a bizarre, made-for-TV miniseries, *Dawlat al-Khurafa* (The State of Myth), that mocked the Islamic State with a Three Stooges–like motif at the center of the plot. Part of a wave of partially state-sponsored satirical missives against the war on terror, the show, which was featured as part of an Al-Hurra documentary in 2017 and advertised on Radio Sawa, lasted for just one season and received mostly negative reviews from audience surveys.[65]

The defense contractor that won the bid to create the IMN, SAIC, also came under heavy scrutiny. Known principally as an engineering and technology firm, the company had effectively been created for the purpose of fielding multimillion-dollar contracts from the federal government. The wars in Iraq and Afghanistan represented its golden age. SAIC held some "9,000 active federal contracts" by 2007, "more than a hundred" worth "upwards of $10 million apiece" and at least two worth more than $1 billion each.[66] The IMN quickly became one of the company's most promising contracts, but SAIC managed to control the portfolio for barely a year before problems emerged. As reported by *Vanity Fair* and other media outlets, the principal qualification of the company appeared to be its involvement with the OSI.[67] Composed mainly of former Baathist television anchors, now singing the praises of Iraq's "new found freedom," the IMN instantly gained the reputation of being the "Pentagon's Pravda."[68] The contract was switched to the Harris Corporation, a Florida-based "international communications and information technology company" that subsequently outsourced its work to a smattering of local and regional operators, including the Lebanese Broadcasting Corporation International (LBCI), and the Kuwaiti-Iraqi company Al-Fawares. According to the bipartisan congressional commission on wartime contracting, the DoD, State Department, and USAID collectively racked up "at least $31 billion, and possibly as much as $60 billion" in waste and fraud by 2011.[69]

With less stringent security clearance requirements than the federal government, private defense contractors such as SAIC had tremendous latitude in their hiring practices. More than 80 percent of those employed through Defense, State, and USAID contracts were "local or third-country nationals," according to the commission.[70] The phenomenon was especially vivid in the realm of media and communications. As described in Edward P. Djerejian's 2003 report of the Advisory Group on Public Diplomacy for the Arab and Muslim World, the CPA required over a thousand Arabic speakers to "create an effective press operation and interact with the Iraqi media."[71] Some of those Arabic speakers would come from the disbanded offices of the Iraq News Agency. Others, including a core group of media operators hired by the BBG, had about as much experience in Iraq as the Americans.

Under the discretion of Iraq's newly created Communications and Media Commission (CMC)—an invention that included a "Board of Commissioners," a "Director General," a "Hearings Panel," an "Appeals Board," and an "Inspector General"—the CPA set itself to manage "communications and media licensing processes in Iraq" and to ensure that the "radio frequency spectrum" was "used in a manner that recognizes the value and scarcity of this resource."[72] The IMN, along with its newspaper, *Al-Sabah*, and other unknown "publications," became incorporated under the CMC as the Iraq Public Service Broadcaster on March 20, 2004.[73] In addition to this renaming, the CPA hired the marketing firm J. Walter Thompson to "convince Iraqis that IMN or al-Iraqia [sic] was credible."[74] That company, of course, had a long history of massaging the mishaps of American public diplomacy. In addition to Charlotte Beers, Bush's first pick for under secretary of public diplomacy, the company's vice president and top creative advertiser Robert T. Colwell served as a long-time member of the USIA's Broadcast Advisory Committee; James Eichelberger, the CIA station chief in Cairo, used his position with J. Walter Thompson as a cover for his contribution to the CIA's "crypto diplomacy" campaign toward the early Nasserite regime; and in the 1970s and 1980s, the company created the Marines' advertising campaign "The Few. The Proud. The Marines." Despite all this, the company could do little to allay the concerns of even those working for the IMN. By the second year of operations, most of the editorial staff for the newspaper *Al-Sabah* (The Morning Edition) had resigned and started a new iteration of the paper called *Al-Sabah al-Jadid* (The New Morning Edition). Bremer's office imagined the media hub as becoming independent, just like the Public Broadcasting System in the United States, and its innovation in this regard was to distribute the cost of operations across workers' salaries, thereby limiting reliance on state authorities.[75] But the network was still widely derided in the international press as being the CIA's mouthpiece. This was not an entirely fair assessment.

Iraqis oversaw all of the reporting for *Al-Sabah* (before resigning) and the offices were staffed by local employees. Nonetheless, local consternation persisted over the basic incompetence of the operation compared to the ironclad Iraqi News Agency (*Wakalat al-anba' al-Iraqiyya*), which for decades held a near monopoly on news reporting in the country. As part of a comprehensive study of broadcasting between January 1 and December 31, 2024, the University of Baghdad scholar R'ad Jassim Hamza took note of the crude economics driving programming at IMN. Over 70 percent of the company's employees, including its broadcast and production staff, were part-time workers, and a quarter of the people contracted to do radio and television programming had no previous experience in those fields.[76] The editorial slant of *Al-Sabah* also raised questions over the independence of the newspaper, not from Iraqi or

American authorities per se, but rather Western expectations. In one quantitative study of the newspaper's editorial pieces over the first six months of publication under the CPA, the researcher Wathaq Abbas Abd al-Razzaq argued similarly that the predominate focus on broad "value-based" and societal themes such as "women's issues," "human rights," "humanitarian aid," "democracy and governance," "economic development," and so forth, reflected a desire on the part of the newspaper's opinion writers to "consolidate the organizational concepts of civil society institutions" (*al-mu'sasat al- majtam'a al-madani*) so as to "establish common links with organizations, especially institutions representing state authorities, located beyond the borders of Iraq."[77] This internationalist dimension of the newspaper, along with its invariable association with the CPA, took its toll on journalists. The IMN, including *al-Sabah*, had the highest death toll among any news organization in the country. At least fourteen journalists affiliated with the network were killed in the first half decade alone.[78] By the end of the second Bush administration, the US government officially needed to cut ties with the network entirely. The multimillion-dollar communications hub that was intended to counter and recreate Iraq's state-media structure was handed over to the ruling authorities in Baghdad. Today, *Al- Iraqiyya* and *Al-Sabah* are both organs of the Iraqi state.

The Iraq War brought into focus a new kind of synergy in Washington, one in which foreign contractors became the de facto conduits of American propaganda and private American contracting firms the intermediaries. The Cold War model of Washington-based Foreign Service Officers disseminating content via relays and proxy actors on the ground was not entirely abandoned, but this model now competed with myriad forms of information operations flowing from the DoD, the CIA, and other government departments. In the scramble to reconstitute America's public diplomacy apparatus following 9/11, the myriad pieces of the mosaic that once constituted the USIA emerged asynchronously and often without clear purpose. Working alongside established open source media translation programs such as the CIA's Foreign Broadcast Information Service (later the Open Source Center), as well as Vietnam-era social science endeavors such as HTS, defense initiatives such as the Multilingual Research Program from the Army Research Laboratory, Language and Speech Exploitation Resources (LASER), or the Translingual Information Detection, Extraction and Summarization (TIDES) program from DARPA, crystallized what had become a veritable arms race in the war of ideas. Automated language-processing software capable of locating, translating, and explicating keywords and colloquial speech from languages as varied as Arabic, Somali, Dari, and Pashto for the average soldier-analyst sitting in a cubicle in Tampa Bay, Florida, became the Pentagon's answer to the much-coveted and fundamental input side of information warfare. And while critics cautioned that popular models such as the Linguistic Inquiry and Word Count (LIWC) tool for natural language processing inspired a certain "Orientalist pedigree" through its inherent indifference to the "cultural, social and historical dimensions of language," the defense-intelligence community's thirst for quantifiable metrics of human behavior, including language and ideology formation, superseded the slow work of foreign-language learning and intercultural communication training, which, nonetheless, also saw advancements through programs such as Project Global Officer (Project GO), begun in 2007, and the State Department's Critical Language Scholarship (CLS), launched in 2006.[79]

Despite extraordinary investment in technological solutions to the war of ideas, blundered executions routinely overshadowed any gains. As one piercing exposé found, translators for WebOps, a "vast psychological operation" for Central Command that had been outsourced to an Alabama-based "information and engineering services and solutions company"—Colsa—were so underqualified for the job that they even "repeatedly" mixed up the Arabic words for "salad" [*salata*] and "authority" [*sulta*], which led to "open ridicule on social media about references to the 'Palestinian salad.'"[80] The stunning incompetence of the US contractor and its employee base, which, in addition to poorly trained Americans included a majority staff from Morocco (for an operation targeting speakers in Iraq, Syria, and Yemen), ultimately provoked a congressional inquiry as well as an investigation by the Naval Criminal Investigative Service.[81] The contractor meanwhile conducted its own evaluation of the program, which it deemed successful based on the amount of engagements that posts generated on Twitter and other social media platforms. Undisclosed to CentComm officials, as one whistleblower later described, was that "engagements" included automated tweets programmed to target a listserv "every five minutes . . . from now until tomorrow." The Islamic State, ironically, was accused of using a similar tactic.[82]

But the DoD was hardly alone in seeking short-term answers to long-term problems. The tendency to outsource culturally sensitive, psychological missions to corporate-driven actors touting "scientific abstractions," in Hadley Cantril's words, was omnipresent across government.[83] Outside observers cautioned against the trend. In the 2003 report of the Advisory Group on Public Diplomacy for the Arab and Muslim World, researchers found among civilian practitioners of public diplomacy a near relentless predilection toward corporate-style metrics in the measurement of their output. "The BBG's nearly single-minded objective for Sawa is audience building," the authors remarked of the BBG's first major Arabic-language initiative following 9/11. "The view of the Advisory Group is that Sawa needs a clearer objective than building a large audience."[84]

Where leading artists and philosophers remained divided on the premise, as Slavoj Žižek and Frank Wynne wrote, that "human acts are rationally intentional and accountable in terms of the beliefs and desires of the agent," government funding into the research dimensions of public influence and persuasion staked only one position: Quantifiable solutions to enumerated problems dominated the full scope of the United States' response to the battle for hearts and minds.[85] The refining of information research to address not just audience size but, in the State Department's terms, "influence," required more deliberate investment in the front end of a campaign.⁸⁶ Defense initiatives such as the Minerva program sought to generate such anticipatory intelligence, but the grants were designed for nonapplicable research, and classification prerogatives often prevented the integration of defense-funded social psychology into mainstream US media operations. Similarly, turning to large private marketing firms to conduct key surveys, such as the disbanding of VOA Arabic for the pop-radio alternative Radio Sawa, was a decision fueled by a market-driven commitment to the influencing of complex foreign networks and behaviors. The mass contracting of foreign-born Arabic speakers, many of whom had never stepped foot in the United States, to work as the new voice of the United States to the Arabic-speaking world, also mirrored this approach. But as discussed in the following chapter, the country's most costly innovation in the new battle for hearts and minds was made stark by a sharp miscalculation between the evident lack of demand for American broadcasting in Arabic and its emergent supply. Born amid the rubble of the Iraq invasion, the origin of the Middle East Broadcasting Networks looked something like that of the *VOA*. But as Marx famously wrote of history and its tendency to repeat itself, such phenomena occurred "most often in the form of farce."⁸⁷ The Voice of America Al-Hurra was not.

3
IRAQ AND THE WORLD

Someone asked me one time; do you bet on your horses? And I said I rarely do because I invested it in the farm. If I could find someone who would give me odds, I'd bet this is going to be a tremendous, tremendous success because our competitive advantage is truth and free debate and reaching where media is dominated by sensationalism and distortion. And I think that the variability to stage these debates and have this flow of ideas will be what will mark us in the end because in the end we want people in that region to ask the basic question, what went wrong?

—KENNETH TOMLINSON, BBG CHAIRMAN (2002–2007)

Where the military led, Washington followed.

Within months of the bombs falling in Iraq, including on the offices of Al-Jazeera and Saddam Hussein's Iraq News Agency, American-made Arabic-language news content was still broadcasting from the skies. But by late April much of the content's supply chain had shifted from Fort Bragg, NC, to Washington, DC

Similar to the first Gulf War, which featured the involvement of Cold War vehicles like the Voice of Free Iraq and a heavy increase in VOA Arabic programming, Radio Sawa in its early iterations complemented the Department of Defense (DoD), whose psychological operations dominated the theater of war and whose role it was to "support to theater public diplomacy."[1] The Broadcasting Board of Governors (BBG) installed additional transmitters across the country, and from a large investment by USAID and the Office of Transition Initiatives, sought to grow its network of stringers and increase programming, particularly as it pertained to reporting on the United States' humanitarian efforts in the country. As reported by the Office of Inspector General (OIG), USAID officials later said "they were generally not pleased with the BBG's implementation of the Iraq transfer agreement." The funding helped to create a six-minute program dedicated to the topic of humanitarian assistance, *The World Cares*, and a second program, *Challenges*, which, in the OIG's words, contained "elements of news and non-news information about humanitarian and reconstruction issues." By spring 2004, audience surveys contracted by the BBG showed that Radio Sawa had a "dominate audience share in Iraq" but that just 28 percent of listeners considered the news and information portions of its broadcast to be "somewhat reliable."[2]

BBG-made television also followed shortly in the wake of the invasion. Launched with a grant from the US Office of Management and Budget for "about $165,000 a week" and filmed in DC, the show "Iraq and the World" (*Al-'Iraq wa-l-'alam*) became a prototype for Al- Hurra and a harbinger of the nascent broadcast's peculiar worldview. Disseminated from the skies above Iraq and pumping out content in "six-hour blocks," the maximum length of time the Commander Solo aircraft could remain aloft, the show featured news about coalition activities "cobbled together" with clips from other news outlets and the occasional report by a contracted stringer. The BBG official Norm Pattiz, the creator of Radio Sawa and the principal architect of the United States' Arabic-language media reboot, had reportedly wrangled several major New York studios into donating content for the show. Several major American news personalities, including Dan Rather of CBS, Tom Brokaw of NBC, and

Peter Jennings of ABC—none of whom were especially familiar to Iraqi audiences—contributed to the effort by creating segments that were subsequently subtitled in Arabic.³

Using the model of live debate, the discourse of "Iraq and the World" amplified strategic themes in US public diplomacy: to hasten the overthrow of Saddam Hussein, denounce human rights violations, and proselytize democracy. One emblematic segment, from August 5, 2003, featured testimony and conversation with a dozen Arab personalities from around the region; they included the well-known Jordanian-American author Shaker Al-Nabulsi; the dissident Iraqi journalist and founder of the People's Party for Reform (*Hizb al-Sha'ab l-il-Islah*), al-Faeq al-Sheikh Ali; the editor-in-chief of the liberal Bahraini newspaper *Akhbar Al-Khaleej*, Anwar Abdul Rahman; the president of Al-Quds University in Jerusalem, Sari Nusseibeh; and Saad Eddin Ibrahim, a prominent political scientist and human rights activist from Egypt.⁴ Several Kuwaiti intellectuals, politicians, and activists such as Ahmed al-Rab'ee, Shamlan al-Issa, and Ghanem al-Najjar were featured on the show, as was the most visible and enduring aspect of the American propaganda enterprise in Arabic following 9/11: a small but well-connected minority of Lebanese journalists and media entrepreneurs in the near or immediate orbit of Mouafac Harb, a little-known journalist within the Washington, DC, circuit who had recently skyrocketed within the ranks of American public diplomacy to become the newly appointed director of the Middle East Radio Network—forerunner to Radio Sawa. No other individual would have a greater impact on shaping America's message to the Middle East than Harb.

INSIDERS' GAME

Dedicated to the "fall of the Saddam Hussein regime and its impact on the future of Arab democracy," the August 5 segment of "Iraq and the World" included no less than nine Lebanese commentators and political figures, some of whom would go on to become permanent features of early Radio Sawa and Al-Hurra programming. Among them was Gebran Tueni—the editor-in-chief of *Al-Nahar* and an outspoken supporter of Michel Aoun, the former president and prime minister of Lebanon who had been exiled to France by Syrian forces in 1989. Along with the journalists Abdul Wahhab Badrakhan, Hazem Saghieh, Ali Al-Raz, Jamil Mroueh, and Farid Salman, Tueni—who was assassinated in 2005—shared cautious optimism about the prospects for democracy in Iraq. "There is no doubt that the fall of Saddam Hussein's regime, which is a dictatorial regime, will positively affect the future of the region," he exclaimed. "The fall of this regime sets a basic precedent in the Middle East. He is perhaps the first dictator to fall and to not be replaced by another dictator. I consider it an historical event; an event which will compel all countries in the region to understand the message and to reconfigure themselves through a process of development, not a Coup. Or to understand that change from within will be their inevitable fate."[5] In addition to journalists, "Iraq and the World" featured commentary from religio-political figures such as Walid Jumblatt, leader of the Lebanese Druze sect and the Progressive Socialist Party, and Sayyid Hani Fahs, a prominent Shiite cleric and seminal figure in the establishment of Lebanon's Association of Muslim 'Ulama' (*Tajammuʿ al-ʿUlamaʾ al-Muslimin fi Lubnan*), the predecessor to Hizballah and a pseudo-offshoot of the Iranian revolution of 1979.[6]

While Jumblatt would ultimately join with Tueni and other opposition voices in organizing against the Syrian occupation of Lebanon—a movement that resulted in an alliance between the primarily Christian Maronite camp of the so-called "Aounistas" and the largest Islamist party in Lebanon, Hizballah—he did not, in 2003, interpret the US invasion of Iraq as the inevitable fate of a dictatorial regime. "It is [a] positive [thing] that Saddam's regime fell, but not through the American invasion. The theory that America came to the Arabs to build democracy and to preserve human rights is the biggest heresy in history. America came to seize oil and spread chaos in Iraq. It is the institutionalization of chaos, nothing more, nothing less. [The United States] must bear the chaos as it came from the excuse of weapons of mass destruction ... the biggest lie in history."[7] Fahs—a staunch critic of the Syrian Baathist regime—struck a more conciliatory tone. "The people of the region understand civic participation, progress, and democracy to be the only civilizational foundation on which to build their future and their unity," he said.

> Democracy is a basic condition for life and death, but the obstacles to its progress have spread over the years. One of the most significant such obstacles is the Iraqi model [under Saddam]. The model of Iraq, which is predicated on the destruction of democracy, of nationalism, of patriotism and of unity, is a backward system and its tyranny offered a veil of protection for such backwardness. So the fall of the Iraqi regime is the beginning of the fall of the modern authoritarian project in the Arab world. The people did not understand tyranny even if its pretext was religious, even if its pretext was religious and national. There are models for Iraq—from Turkey and Iran—that indicate democracy is a viable destiny. The march of democracy in the region has begun. It was not dependent on the regime's demise, but the fact that it has collapsed will now mobilize the internal will of the Islamic structure (*iradat al-bina'al-dakhli al-islami*) in order to support democracy. The current of moderation that will build our region democratically must expand, take root, and become stronger. Moderation is not necessarily a solution to the problem, but rather a means for the achievement of this goal that is democracy.[8]

Aligned on the surface with US messaging, Fahs' rhetoric, like Jumblatt's, illustrated a dominant trend in American broadcasting in Arabic, post-9/11. Not unlike the early VOA reports of 'Isa Khalil Sabbagh in the 1950s, Al-Hurra reporters were often grounded in the politics of their respective native countries. During the first three years of programming, the voices of America's first twenty-four-hour satellite TV news station were particularly entrenched in the heady dynamics of postwar Lebanon, the presence of Syrian forces on the ground there, and Aoun's uncertain fate. Al-Hurra's focus on the tiny Mediterranean country became part of a hearing by the Subcommittee on Oversight and Investigations of the Committee on International Relations in 2005, but the delegates, led by the Republican Dana Rohrabacher, who had refused hearings on the Iraq War along with any other item challenging White House policy under the Bush administration, appeared just vaguely interested in the station's political disposition, which, in any case, was protected by the grantee structure of Middle East Broadcasting Networks (MBN) programming. When pressed about Al-Hurra's use of overseas stringers, for example, Harb, then its news director, responded simply that "editorial control of the content is solely that of Al-Hurra."[9]

The governing statute of the BBG, unlike during the 1950s, assured near-total independence of the American broadcasting enterprise. Moreover, with its executive leadership composed exclusively of non-Arabic-speaking appointees from the business and media sectors, oversight fell almost entirely to the upper-tier management of the organization's many bureaus and production centers throughout the world—at least fifty existed in more than forty countries, twenty years on from 9/11. The primary information wing of American propaganda following 9/11 was most often not American in this way; rather, it was propagandistic media empowered by the US government's stamp of approval and made possible by congressionally allocated funds ($26 million at first through the 2003 Emergency Wartime Supplemental Appropriations Act and an average of $100 million per year over the decade to follow).[10] Still, not unlike the country's Cold War vehicles of public diplomacy, the nascent satellite broadcaster—along with a second, Iraq-focused iteration known simply as Al-Hurra Iraq—became a major venue for educational and cultural patronage, the amplification of US government policies, and the dissemination of other white, grey, and covert forms of American propaganda.[11]

Programming during the first year at Al-Hurra's Baghdad station included coverage of the 2004 US presidential elections, as well as elections in Afghanistan, Iraq, Tunisia, and Ukraine. Along with news and information, the channel regularly featured interviews with Iraqis in exile and prominent cultural figures such as the renowned actor Rasim al-Jumaili and Fuad Tikerly, one of the country's most celebrated novelists. In conjunction with the last Eid of Ramadan in October 2007, Al-Hurra staff in Baghdad organized a concert featuring the Iraqi National Symphony Orchestra—a sixty-member group composed of an "ethnic and religious cross-section of Iraqi society."[12] The event, which was filmed and broadcast live on Al-Hurra Iraq, marked a high point in American public diplomacy following 9/11, in no small part because the orchestra—in existence since 1959—was on the brink of collapse following incidents of violence and looting in the wake of the US invasion. Saad Mohan Dukan, a Baghdad-based journalist who was hired in 2006 as the bureau chief for Al-Hurra Iraq, described the effort in a letter of resignation he drafted just over a year later. "During the last Eid of Ramadan, in mid-October 2007, I managed to organize a concert over three days on the Banks of the Tigris," he explained. The event was "the first of its kind in Iraq," he wrote, and it helped people to feel "there is more to Iraq than violence and bombs." The event was attended by "government ministers, MPs, politicians, academics, poets, musicians, singers, sportsmen, and many others" and even included the "famous, popular, and hugely influential Iraqi singer, Fadhil Awad," who, according to Mohan, had not been seen on Iraqi television for fifteen years. "He sang and talked about his life and finally commended Al Hurra on camera for defying terrorism and for raising the morale of Iraqis by organizing such an outdoor concert."[13] Despite the targeting of Al-Hurra journalists by insurgent groups and the inherent chaos of a country at war, the station made positive inroads over its first several years of operation. By 2010, BBG commissioned polling was showing some 62 percent of Iraq's population turned on Al-Hurra weekly and an estimated 28 percent were listening to Radio Sawa. Amid a veritable boom in independent media as well as increased availability of major international broadcasters like Al-Jazeera, Al-Arabiya, and the BBC, American media in Iraq, through Al-Hurra, Radio Sawa, Al-Hurra Iraq, and VOA Kurdish had become the most common source of news and information in the country.[14] Strong numbers prevailed for the next several years, but by 2014, according to a BBG-commissioned Gallup survey, US-stamped media in the country, while still the most common source of news and information, was on the decline with some 35 percent of those polled watching Al-Hurra on a weekly basis and just 12 percent listening to Radio Sawa. By 2017, the number of weekly Al-Hurra viewers had dipped to 20 percent.[15]

Alongside some early successes, by the end of the first Obama administration, the signs of trouble ahead had become more apparent. As expressed in his letter to Brian Conniff, then the president of MBN, Mohan wrote, "Employees only turned up once a week just to show up and go. . . . Most people worked on their own with no guidance or work patterns and certainly with the minimum adherence to journalistic rules."[16] Four years later, in 2004, a report by the OIG, which became public as part of a joint *ProPublica/60 Minutes* investigation of Al-Hurra, spelled out some of the indiscretions. At Radio Sawa in Iraq—the predecessor to Al-Hurra—journalists were appropriating content without attribution or notice from other media outlets, including the VOA and Al-Jazeera. Stringers and reporters with no previous experience were being put on air. Basic standards of employment spelled out by the Office of Personnel Management and strictly enforced by other BBG entities including the VOA seemed wholly unfamiliar to Radio Sawa and Al-Hurra officials. In the case of contract employees hired to staff the Middle East Programming Center—the Dubai offices of the two Arabic broadcasts—decisions were made at the sole discretion of Harb, who, as described by one interviewee in the OIG report, hired people after a "five-minute" interview. Another said some people "walked in from the street and were hired."[17]

More serious indiscretions plagued the staffing of Al-Hurra's headquarters in Springfield, Virginia, which Harb set up soon after assuming his position as the station's first news director. Under pressure to begin operations quickly, Harb hired 150 employees for the new location, eighty of whom came from abroad. To house the new employees, he hired a private firm—Capital Communications Group—whose CEO, also a Lebanese national and past Grand Master of the Washington, DC, Masonic lodge, was later exposed as having "traveled to Damascus with a discreet proposal to burnish the image of the Syrian regime in Washington."[18]

The new employees of Al-Hurra were fast-tracked for green cards and put to work as the face of American public diplomacy toward the Middle East. But most of them had never been to the United States, and many were unable to communicate with the office's non-Arabic-speaking staff.[19] Such was the case with Salem Mashkour, who Harb hired to run the Al-Hurra Iraq office. An Iraqi national and practicing Shiite, Mashkour fit a peculiar pattern in Al-Hurra's early hiring practices. Like Harb (who has been described as a "secular Shiite"), Mashkour was deeply entrenched in the world of Lebanese journalism, having previously worked as a columnist for the country's major daily newspaper *Al-Nahar* for a decade. He spent years in exile in Iran, where he worked as a reporter within that country's heavily monitored state-media industry, gaining a name for himself as an astute insider of political Islam. Mashkour was especially enamored by the rise of Hassan Nassrallah, a figure he profiled on several occasions, including shortly after the United States' designation of Nasrallah's group, Hizballah, as a terrorist organization, in October 2001. For Mashkour, Nasrallah was cut from the ilk of Imam Musa al-Sadr, the charismatic Iranian-Lebanese leader of the powerful Amal Movement, who disappeared without a trace in Libya three decades before.

"Eighteen years after the founding of the party (Hizballah), Hassan Nasrallah stood in front of the largest public gathering ever witnessed in the newly liberated South," Mashkour wrote. "Relishing his victory, but with no sign of pride, this now illustrious figure humbly invoked the role of his mentor, al-Sadr, and his enduring place in the history of the revolution. Victory in battle does not lead to appeasement but rather there are other non-military battles ahead. This is the message of Islam as he [Sadr] always made clear."[20] Although criticism of his management style was mounting, including from counterparts in the Baghdad offices, Mashkour maintained close allies in Springfield. Daniel Nassif, an acolyte of Harb's and his successor as the head of Radio Sawa, emerged as one of Mashkour's staunchest supporters. Also a Lebanese national, Nassif's previous work as reported by *ProPublica* had focused on lobbying for a "Lebanese Christian former general" against what he described as "Syrian controlled corrupt government agencies" within Lebanon.[21] His support of Mashkour—who was relegated to hosting a show on Al-Hurra Iraq after dancing for joy on-air following the announcement of Saddam Hussein's execution but who Nassif later reappointed as executive editor—compounded the impression among critics such as the Egyptian journalist Magdi Khalil that Al-Hurra was effectively a "Lebanese business" with policy-making decisions "in the hands of the Shiites."[22] The first part of the characterization was not especially surprising. Lebanese journalists and entertainment specialists had dominated the Arab satellite news industry since the enterprise first began in the 1990s.[23] The second part of Khalil's accusation was more striking and had also caught the attention of key leadership within the State Department.

OUR MAN IN BEIRUT

Among those watching developments at Al-Hurra under Harb's tenure was Alberto Fernandez, then director for Iraq public diplomacy and the future head of public diplomacy for the Near East Bureau at the State Department. As he described in a declassified memo to Karen Hughes, the under secretary of state for public diplomacy who had recently completed a much derided "listening tour" of the region, Al-Hurra's Baghdad bureau was led by "radical Shiite Islamists who favored their political brethren and discriminated against and intimidated members of other parties." The station's leadership in Springfield, he claimed, "had stocked much of its Washington and Lebanon staff with partisans of the former Lebanese general Michel Aoun who is now closely allied to the terrorist group Hezbollah."[24] His comments came as a prelude to the 2005 hearing by the Subcommittee on Oversight and Investigations where lawmakers scrutinized the nature of Harb's hiring practices, including questions surrounding conflicts of interest, and the "Lebanese tilt to the style of reporting" at Al-Hurra.[25] Of particular focus for the group was Harb's relationship with Eli Khoury, a Beirut-based "strat comm specialist" who, until that point, had played an outsized role in the United States' post-9/11 propaganda industry.

Described by one of Al-Hurra's Dubai-based editors as Harb's "best friend in the region," Khoury was a self-made mogul. His influence on the region's media ecosystem extended well beyond Al-Hurra.[26] A former political cartoonist during the Lebanese civil war, Khoury moved to Los Angeles where he studied "communication arts" before returning to Beirut in 1990.[27] By his own account, Khoury was in Iraq "a couple of weeks after the tanks rolled in." Under the auspice of his two companies, Saatchi & Saatchi Levant (created in 1992) and Quantum Communications (2000), he claimed to have fielded contracts for nearly "every western government in Iraq." His most notable contribution to the early war effort, he told journalist Nadia Michel nearly two decades later, was helping the Coalition Provisional Authority "sell" the Iraqi people on a new constitution—a document which, like Lebanon's sect-based system of government—"hoped to achieve national unity by having all sects participate in government and public life." In actuality it created quite the opposite effect. By most accounts the hastily generated document engendered a "climate of nepotism and clientelism," one in which "uneducated, unqualified and corruption-prone individuals" were allowed to "take key posts" and to affect the lives of "millions of Iraqis."[28]

Still, in their effort to brand the constitution, Khoury's company, which boasted contracts from the UK and Jordan as well as the United States, showed how American tax dollars could indeed project democracy. "We used advertising, used posters, films, the things people use," Khoury said. The objective was to "tell people the benefit of drafting a constitution and later on, actually voting." He added, "If you want to change regimes, if you want a majority keeping its majority or a minority becoming a majority or if you want to communicate to your own people about advancement in policy and in social conduct such as democracy. [That's what we do]. We help pacify and practify [sic]. . . . We do what is usually called in that field 'Strat Comms.' "[29]

As identified by the 2005 House hearing, Khoury was also an integral player in the launch of Al-Hurra. By 2004, all three of his firms, the third being Brand Central, held contracts with the MBN. Norm Pattiz described Saatchi & Saatchi under Khoury as the BBG's "primary adviser culturally throughout the region."[30]

Run out of his multistory residential villa in Beirut, Khoury's operations included some three hundred employees, many of whom Harb recruited during the first wave of hiring for Al-Hurra.[31] Saatchi & Saatchi's contribution to American public diplomacy featured an expensive portfolio of generic, mostly kitsch content. Among the most prominent items created by the advertising firm was material for the short-lived US Arabic-language magazine *Hi*. Also included was the robotic music of Al-Hurra's opening credits (showing windswept horses running across a white backdrop); "Alhurra windows" (2004), which featured a montage of men in business suits and women in hijabs gazing onto open windows; and, more recently: "I AM ALHURRA," a marketing campaign that features a two-part slogan: "Freedom is a fundamental human right. Truth always comes first" and the image of a light-skinned woman wearing heavy makeup and a paint-splashed blouse while staring blankly into the camera. A male dancer with a pony tail also appears leaping into the air, and a woman with a loose-fitting hijab (the photographer of the woman with the paint-splashed blouse) holds a camera while gazing pleasantly ahead.[32] Vaguely "Western" and auspiciously decadent, Khoury's American propaganda closely replicated what the Saatchi & Saatchi executive Kevin Roberts described as the company's "lovemark" branding style: a combination of "mystery, sensuality, and intimacy" designed, in the European context, to create an "aspiration lifestyle," or, as Peter van Ham described, "a kind of ersatz for ideologies and political programmes that have lost their relevance."[33]

The preeminence of "lovemark" branding to American public diplomacy extended beyond the studios of Al-Hurra to infuse the media battlefields of Lebanon and Iraq. In Lebanon, Khoury was receiving BBG funding while waging a PSYOPS campaign—alongside a coalition of activists that included "Iraq and the World" guests Tueni and Jumblatt—to expel Syrian forces from the country following the assassination of Prime Minister Rafik Hariri on February 14, 2005. Described by the *New York Times* and other outlets as "an influential organizer of the March 14 Movement," Khoury and the Quantum Group became a "key hub" of activity in the heavily mediated environment of the so-called "Cedar Revolution."[34] Khoury personally claimed credit for "the most effective 'messages'" in Martyr Square and pointed to the experience as a prelude to his highly visible "I love life" campaign: a massive public relations stunt that was designed to counter Hizballah's claim that it had "won" the 2006 war.[35]

FALLOUT

The Saatchi & Saatchi–inflected magazine *Hi* was discontinued just one month after the 2005 congressional hearing. Harb resigned in early 2006 and Pattiz soon thereafter. But controversy at the multimillion-dollar American tax-funded news behemoth Al-Hurra continued unabated. In December 2006, under the direction of Harb's successor, Larry Register, a former CNN executive, the station gave voice to the leader of the Palestinian Islamist group Hamas. It also featured more than sixty minutes of airtime with Nasrallah as he delivered a firebrand sermon to loyalists inside the Lebanese capital.[36] That same month the channel featured "extensive and deferential coverage" of the so-called "Holocaust denial" conference in Tehran.[37] The Al-Hurra journalist Ahmad Amin concluded his report live from Tehran with a declaration that the conference had determined that "Jews had provided no scientific evidence of the Holocaust."[38]

As examples of the channel's politically tone-deaf tendencies, *ProPublica* and other outlets also pointed to an interview with Mishan Jabouri, one of the Defense Department's "most wanted" Iraqi officials, who was on the run in Syria, and highlighted the channel's description of an anti-US demonstration in Iraq organized by the Shiite movement loyal to Muqtada al-Sadr as a birthday celebration for al-Sadr.[39] More damaging still, allegations of nepotism and graft surrounding the network proliferated. Writing in the *American Prospect*, Art Levine noted that the "annual salaries of top network executives," none of whom spoke Arabic, reached $250,000, which was more than the annual salary of the "vice president of the United States."[40] As was revealed by the 2005 congressional hearings, Harb awarded an unprecedented $150 million contract to Capital Communications, the firm that also received payments for relocating employees to an apartment block in Crystal City, Virginia (thirty minutes from Al-Hurra's Springfield office), for translation services.[41] Saatchi & Saatchi was paid $125,000 "per spot" for its "'branding commercials'"; Brand Central, meanwhile, received an additional $250,000 for a website that remained nonfunctional; and Quantum Communications received $500,000 for providing what Levine described in conversation with employees as a "vaguely defined job of 'production coordination' for six programs based in Lebanon and other countries."[42] Harb reportedly hired one of his wife's friends to be a hairdresser for Al-Hurra. He also hired his wife, a television personality in Lebanon, to be the host of a "cultural affairs" program.[43]

Within the Arab press such stories reinforced the impression that Al-Hurra, like the Defense Department's Iraq Media Network, was simply a "third-rate news organization."[44] Anecdotes of blunders in Arabic speech and the mispronunciation of American officials' names multiplied.⁴⁵ Apart from legacy shows such as *Dakhil Washington*, which was hosted by the executive director of Harb's onetime employer—the AIPAC-funded Washington Institute of Near East Studies—the channel's ideology was largely indiscernible and its programming a confused jumble of stereotypical Americana combined with poorly sourced reporting from mainly amateur journalists. As one well-known Arab commentator wrote at the time, Al-Hurra was dominated by "a bunch of remnants of the [Lebanese] Civil War." Its identity and mission seemed as convoluted as the Lebanese parliament.⁴⁶ Complaints of pro-Israeli bias were as frequent as complaints of antisemitism. Al-Hurra and Radio Sawa were accused of being both anti-American and tools of American propaganda. Despite the criticism, however, diehard supporters such as Pattiz or Kenneth Y. Tomlinson, a director of the VOA under Reagan and a disgraced Bush appointee who oversaw Harb's tenure at Al-Hurra as the chairman of the BBG and was later exposed by the State Department's inspector general for hiring "ghost employees" and using public funds to operate a stable of racehorses, continued to cite reports of increased viewership across a handful of locations, particularly Iraq, Jordan, and Lebanon. Al-Hurra's ascension, Pattiz argued, had drawn detractors among competing parties, a problem that in itself was also a mark of distinction.⁴⁷

Nonetheless, with the Bush administration nearing its end, Al-Hurra and the MBN soldiered on. In 2006, the BBG launched a European iteration of the station aimed at Arabic speakers on the Continent. It increased the reach of Al-Hurra Iraq through the construction of a new transmitter near Mosul, and it continued to feature reporting on elections, including in Egypt, Iraq, Israel, Kuwait, and the Palestinian territories. In 2006, in a nod to the enduring strength of the company's Beirut connections, Al-Hurra covered the 2006 Hizballah-Israeli crisis with daily, three-hour live reports.⁴⁸ In 2008, through a supplemental funding request of $11.1 million and 150 new positions, the channel launched its new "signature" show "*Al-Youm*" (Today); built on the model of ABC's *Good Morning America*, it featured a three-hour panoply of news and conversation from around the Arab world.⁴⁹ "*Al-Youm*," along with the program "Eye on Democracy" ('*Ayn 'ala dimuqratiyya*), hosted by the longtime Al-Hurra journalist Mohammad Alyahyai, became the channel's principal vehicles for coverage of the Arab uprisings in 2011. Under the administration of Barack Obama—a president whose overture to the Arab world with his "A New Beginning" speech in Cairo in June 2009 was itself an act of public diplomacy—Al-Hurra attempted to fashion a more publicly engaged political aesthetic. In its 2013 fiscal report, the BBG claimed Al-Hurra was "the sole news entity" to report live from Egypt during the first few days of the uprising as the government had shut down cell-phone and satellite systems, effectively creating an information blackout. The International Broadcasting Board's Office of Technology, Services, and Information was able to capitalize on what it described as a "completely independent" satellite system to broadcast "live reports during the first tumultuous days of the civilian uprising."⁵⁰

The station's renewed focus on the Arab public during the Obama administration included the creation of shows dedicated to highlighting "the simple Egyptian whose story was lost in the crowd."⁵¹ In 2012, the channel launched "Street Pulse" (*Nabdh al-Sha'arah*) and "Where Are You Going?" (*Rayheen 'ala Feen*), two Egypt-based documentary series that, however clumsily produced, featured "ordinary" Egyptians and for the most part were filmed in the streets of Cairo and Upper Egypt. Alyahyai, the host of *Eye on Democracy*, became especially prominent during the Obama years, producing a series of reports and feature-length documentaries on revolutionary topics du jour including the origins of the Tunisian revolution, the role of youth activists and the Internet, oppression in Syria, and the relationship of political Islam with the historic events of the day.⁵² His tenure with the station, and in the United States, lasted just over a decade before unceremoniously evaporating. Like most reporters for Al-Hurra, he ultimately returned to his home country, in his case, Oman.

THE GULF PIVOT

In April 2014, *Eye on Democracy*, then hosted by Haidar El-Mehrabi, featured an "exclusive interview" with two daughters of King Abdullah of Saudi Arabia, the Princesses Sahar and Jawaher, who claimed to have been locked up for thirteen years in one of their father's palaces.[53] Al-Hurra boasted that it was the first Arabic news site to interview the two sisters, whose plight had been made public just two weeks before in an interview with the British station Channel 4. Not surprisingly, the episode began a precipitous decline in the percentage of Saudis who viewed Al-Hurra as "trustworthy," according to the BBG's "credibility score" report of MBN broadcasting from 2016.[54] Positive audience metrics for MBN, in general, saw a decline from their 2013 levels, but as noted by the BBG the drop in the percentage of weekly viewers who considered Al-Hurra "to be very or somewhat trustworthy" (from 84 percent in 2013 to 76 percent in 2017) was largely a reflection of the sharply negative reaction among Saudi Arabian respondents (95 percent found the station "trustworthy" in 2013 and just 74 percent felt the same in 2017).[55] While drastic underfunding has continued to plague BBG reporting (the organization's research budget plummeted from eleven million dollars in the mid-2000s to just two million in 2012), the Saudi numbers also appeared to contrast with findings by the OIG, which noted, unlike in previous reports (in 2004 and 2010), that Al-Hurra had met the objectives of the BBG's strategic plan for the years 2013–2018 and was producing "journalism of exceptional value."[56] Nonetheless, change was afoot.

In 2016, the Trump administration swept to power amid a sea of allegations of misinformation, foreign interference, and race bating. "Eye on Democracy" was discontinued along with most of the programs once associated with the Arab Spring. Fernandez, one of the earliest and sharpest critics of US broadcasting in Arabic, was hired as the president of MBN. The so-called "reboot" of Al-Hurra was underway.

As the previous head of public diplomacy in the Near East Bureau and a fluent speaker of Arabic, Fernandez was a known entity on media circuits in the region. On election day 2017, he was live on-air in Arabic for over two hours, a feat unmatched by any other American official, past or present. His contribution to informing Arabic audiences about the historic events of the day occurred not with Al-Hurra, however, but on Sky News Arabia, the satellite news giant based in the United Arab Emirates (UAE) that launched in 2012 as a competitor, in part, to Al-Hurra.

During Fernandez's tenure, MBN moved squarely into the orbit of Gulf Arab media, Sky News in particular. As one of his first acts, Fernandez appointed as the news director of Al-Hurra Nart Bouran, the long-time editor-in-chief of Sky News Arabia and a major power broker within the UAE's ascendant media empire. Many of Bouran's top deputies at Sky News followed him to Al-Hurra. An accomplished entrepreneur within the world of satellite broadcasting, Bouran fit the bill for his new position. Although he had no formal connection with the United States, he spoke English fluently, was a pioneer in the development of state-sponsored social media operations, and was familiar to both Western and Arab journalists. Also, like other news directors, Bouran's ticket to Al-Hurra was a round-trip fare. Bouran remained on the job for just two years before returning to the UAE, leaving much of his staff in place. In 2020, he assumed the role of chief executive officer of International Media Investments, the parent company of Sky News, and one of the predominant bodies of media development in the booming Arabian Gulf media sector.[57]

As part of the overhaul, nearly half of the staff at Al-Hurra were ultimately replaced. The channel opened a fully operational bureau in Dubai, and the Springfield offices were overhauled to resemble the slickly designed studios of Sky News. At this time, as well, another close competitor in the world of satellite news media in Arabic caught the eyes of Fernandez and MBN officials: Russia Today, or RT.

As just the second foreign-language broadcast created after English as part of the Russian state-media conglomerate's multilingual bouquet of channels, RT Arabic's rise in the Middle East and North Africa was steady and aggressive. As Fernandez said in a 2018 interview, "RT Arabic is just one example of where content is awful but it looks good."[58] As part of the reboot, Al-Hurra was reimagined to not only resemble RT, but, as Fernandez later said, to reflect the ideological candor of the Russian-state organ, including its capacity for generating viral content. "We wanted our reporting to be edgy," he noted. The days of staid journalism at Al-Hurra were over.[59]

Paralleling the Trump administration's courtship of Saudi Arabia, Fernandez and Bouran also made overtures to the UAE's powerful Gulf neighbors. Under his direction, Bouran told the Saudi English-language mouthpiece *Arab News*, Al-Hurra would "boost its presence across the Arab world, and especially in Saudi Arabia."[60] Gone were the myriad Iraqi programs, especially those with an historically Shi'a bent, and in were shows such as *"Hadith al-Khaleej"* (Gulf Talks), *"Islam Hurr"* (Free Islam), and *"Al-Hurra tatahara"* (Investigative Reports), which promised a "weekly no-holds-barred show . . . produced by Alhurra's new investigative news unit" and hosted by none other than MBN's new president, Alberto Fernandez.

Well-coiffed, "moderate," and with a hundred-million-dollar budget in tow, Al-Hurra's new slate of programming was oriented around "known quantities."[61] Ibrahim Eisa, who had risen to fame amid the 2011 uprising in Egypt as an aggressive, on-the-ground voice for Al-Tahrir, an upstart television channel he founded amid the heady days of protest, was given his own show. Others included a former editor for the Lebanese newspaper *Al—Nahar*, Joumana Haddad. Samuel Tadros, an Egyptian Copt and a prolific commentator for the conservative Hoover Institute, and Ammar Abdulhamid, a Syrian opposition leader and blogger who had become a staple within Washington's Near East policy circles, launched a political talk show focused on addressing taboo topics in the Arab world.⁶² Another show, "*Islam Hurr*," built around the personality of Islam al-Behairy, a controversial Egyptian cleric who was jailed in 2015 on charges of "blasphemy" resulting from comments he made on his Egyptian show "*Ma' Islam al-Behairy*," was considered "too dull" and "static," Fernandez explained, and so was ultimately discontinued.⁶³

The new ensemble of personalities and subjects arguably reflected Fernandez's worldview. A Cuban exile and an ardent conservative, Fernandez became a signatory, in 2020, of the *Carta Madrid*— a manifesto of the ultraright Spanish Vox party whose political identity was fashioned in the spirit of a "new Inquisition."⁶⁴ Before, during, and after his position at the helm of MBN, he provided regular commentary and interviews for the "Christian realism" magazine *Providence*, whose byline reads "We believe American Christians have a special duty to interpret America's vocation in the world today."⁶⁵ And after completing his brief tenure at MBN, Fernandez returned to his leadership role at the Middle East Media Research Institute (MEMRI), a website focused on highlighting sectarianism in the Middle East through the translation and distribution of incendiary content as found within the Arabic media sphere.⁶⁶ He also maintained his ties to the UAE as a nonresident fellow with TRENDS Research and Advisory, a state-sponsored think tank based in Abu Dhabi.

By 2021, two decades after 9/11, America's signature tool in the war of ideas had run the gamut of Middle Eastern politics. Al-Hurra cycled through the intercultural complexities of the Lebanese Civil War. It doubled down on the popular protests of the Arab Spring. And it drifted squarely into the orbit of the Gulf monarchies, the UAE in particular. As the Trump administration brokered a new accord between Israel and the UAE, the so-called "Abraham Accords," Al-Hurra seemed to be emblematic of the ideological synergy to come. While still ranked below most competitors, it now resembled, at least aesthetically, its Gulf counterparts and could compete with the Middle East news cycle from its hub in Dubai. Similarly, Washington's preeminent, pro-Israeli think tank, the Washington Institute for Near East Studies, still maintained its heavy ideological footprint on the station. Its executive director, Robert Satloff, kept his program *Dakhil Washington* (now infused with an occasional monologue in a newly acquired if awkwardly formed Arabic), and the institute provided, not infrequently, stock content for Al-Hurra's website and publications. The emergence of the UAE as a one-stop shop for all things regarding US public diplomacy in Arabic (a phenomenon I explore in chapter 5) created both opportunities and challenges for the country's information strategy. Although the UAE had signed on with the Abraham Accords—a diplomatic milestone in the Near East peace process that aimed at normalizing relations between Israel and its Arab neighbors—it was also building ties with Washington's emergent nemesis at the time, Russia. Bilateral trade between the two countries rose 68 percent in 2022; this was after Washington tried to shut down trade with Russia following the Kremlin's invasion of Ukraine in February of that year.[67] According to Alexa Analytics, Skynewsarabia.com (the principal website of Sky News Arabia) had become, by 2021, Alhurra.com's primary point of "audience overlap," meaning visitors to Al-Hurra's website also visited Sky News more than any other website. Simultaneously, however, Sky News Arabia had moved thoroughly into the orbit of RT, an association Bouran had no qualms about highlighting as he oversaw the studio upgrades in Springfield. Sky News Arabia replayed reporting found on Russian state media, and the UAE was called out by Meta and other online watch groups for having fueled campaigns of coordinated inauthentic behavior' in places such as Libya and Sudan.[68] For some in the Trump administration, including the president himself, who expressed support for the UAE and Russia's strongman ally in Libya, Khalifa Hifter (in contrast to the recommendations of his own State Department), none of this was cause for concern. The triumph of the Abraham Accords overshadowed any doubts for the Trump administration, and in the twilight of Trump's troubled term in office, the State Department, led by Mike Pompeo, approved the sale of "advanced capabilities" worth $23.37 billion to the UAE, including F-35s and armed drones, a first for an Arab country.[69] That deal ultimately stalled under the Biden administration. The marriage of the United States' information strategy with the state-media systems of the UAE, however, did not. Like the gleaming towers of Abu Dhabi and Dubai, American public diplomacy in Arabic had undergone a facelift of historic proportions; its occupancy and purpose, however, were anyone's guess.

4
GRAY IS THE NEW BLACK

In this town, if you want to be read you have to write fiction.
—LEON SHAHABIAN, "INNOVATION AND NATIONAL SECURITY"

It was 2007, and a little-known media company was making the rounds on the cable news networks to promote its new reality TV show, "*'Ala tariq fi Amrika*" (On the Road in America). The director of the series, Jerome Gary, a minor Hollywood figure who made a name for himself with *Pumping Iron* (1977), the award-winning documentary about professional bodybuilding featuring Arnold Schwarzenegger, appeared on the *Glenn Beck Program*. "What if you were a group of Arab students whose only impression of America came from newspapers and sit-coms in the Middle East?" exclaimed the conservative pundit Beck in his opening monologue. "What would you take from a cross-country road trip here in America? A new Middle Eastern reality TV series decided to find out."[1]

The executive producer of *On the Road in America*, Leon Shahabian, and the assistant director Lara Abou Saifan appeared on CNN's *Good Morning America*. Shahabian and Gary, along with Saifan and two other participants from the show, also went on the Al-Jazeera talk show "*Min Washington*" (From Washington) to discuss the series, beginning the segment with a recap of the fighting between Israel and Hizballah in what had become known as "*Harb Tammuz*" (The July War). The clip Al-Jazeera selected featured Lara Saifan, also a subject on the show, as she defended her support for Hizballah in front of a pair of American talk-radio hosts. "Does Israel have a right to exist?" one of the hosts asked her.

"We do not discuss whether it has a right to exist or not," she replies. "Because it exists already. It's not going to just disappear."

It was a poignant selection by Al-Jazeera and an eerie reminder of an ageless trope in American propaganda. Israel and the subsequent precarity of those interlocutors charged with mitigating its relationship with the US for Arab audiences back home could not escape even the best-laid script. The participants' diplomatic journey across the United States was a quixotic one. The producers knew what they were looking for, yet, as one unwitting journalist for the *Associated Press* wrote of the snippets provided to him through the Sundance Channel, the show "leaves us perplexed as to what the point of all of this is even supposed to be."[2] Biking through parks, or gazing out the windows of their tour bus—the participants' banal expedition was somehow, at once, imbued with meaning and peppered throughout with a grand discourse on Americana and the happy destination of Western civilization.

Built for entertainment in the model of the hit reality show *Road Rules* (1995–2007), *On the Road in America* replicated past iterations of public diplomacy and served to illustrate, in the end, a critical, third-way approach to the war of ideas. Unhinged from the formal apparatus of traditional public diplomacy yet impossible without its support, Layalina's state-side screenings and domestic promotional tours were a testament to the company's ostensible independence. The show avoided the stigma of official propaganda while still accomplishing what many hoped public diplomacy might someday achieve: the seemingly organic interchange of foreign and domestic publics that, in the end, and through the magic of cinema, could redeem the story of America, not as an omnipotent force in the world but as an open society where the First Amendment, in the end, prevails.

ON THE ROAD . . . TO HOLLYWOOD

Layalina productions had been in existence for nearly half a decade by the time *On the Road in America* first broadcast. The company was one of two, including America Abroad Media (AAM), that emerged as a key supplier of foreign-language content in the battle for hearts and minds. In addition to *On the Road in America*, Layalina produced nearly a dozen feature-length documentaries and TV series, most of which found airtime on major Arab satellite channels. Originally titled *Al-Haqiqah* (The Truth), in reference to the Soviet Union's propaganda organ *Pravda*, and envisioned, at first, by its founder Richard M. Fairbanks as a stand-alone TV station, Layalina made little secret of its ties to the greater mission of the United States' public diplomacy reboot.[3] Former ambassador to Morocco and American Israel Public Affairs Committee (AIPAC) stalwart Marc Ginsberg, president of Layalina from 2002 to 2012, has described the company as "America's most successful producer of cross cultural Arabic language television diplomacy."[4] In 2003, when the influential Djerejian report of the Advisory Group on Public Diplomacy for the Arab and Muslim World called for the development of "a less costly alternative or supplement to METN [Middle East Television Network/Al-Hurra]" in the form of content produced through partnerships "with private firms, nonprofit institutions, and government agencies" and "distributed through existing channels in the region," Layalina was no doubt a model.[5] With an approximate $1.5 million in funding for its first year, the mission of the nonprofit organization was to "develop and produce Arabic language television programming for the Middle East that forthrightly addresses even the most controversial issues affecting US-Arab relations."[6] Its primary investor, via his family's foundation, was Fairbanks, a former special negotiator for Middle East peace under the Reagan administration and the president and CEO of the Center for Strategic and International Studies. Grants from the State Department followed the first season of programming as other smaller donors jumped in.[7] Along with Ginsberg and Shahabian, Fairbanks envisioned Layalina as an alternative content provider for a region that was otherwise inundated with lowbrow American programming—from *The Jerry Springer Show* to "reruns of *Dallas* and shoot-'em-up movies."[8] While audience surveys remain hard to come by, one Ipsos poll commissioned by the Middle East Broadcasting Company (MBC) in March 2010 showed that *On the Road in America* had an estimated viewership of 1,503,000 in Saudi Arabia for its 10 P.M. time slot, making it the second-most-watched show in the Kingdom of Saudi Arabia at that time, following the spin-off *Star Academy*, which was broadcast by the Lebanese Broadcasting Corporation. Numbers for Kuwait and the UAE, where the poll was conducted, were smaller relative to those countries' population size but still showed large audiences.[9]

Although not explicit in their outlook, Fairbanks and others at Layalina were well aware that the history of American public diplomacy was littered with attempts at redirecting the country's major engines of creativity toward the national cause. As far back as the 1930s, when the Office of International Information and Cultural Affairs (OICA) struck an agreement with Hollywood to express more "sensitivity" on international topics in exchange for access to the archives of the Rockefeller Bureau (a predecessor to the OICA that contained a rich collection of data and information on Latin America, in particular), American propagandists have sought coordination with their Hollywood counterparts. During WWII, the Office of War Information was quietly pretesting films in Germany to gauge the efficacy of the medium in shaping public opinion. The United States Information Agency (USIA) enlisted major Hollywood talent such as George Stevens Jr. and Cecil B. DeMille to produce films or consult on productions. The Pentagon maintained its film and TV liaison office for the purpose of advising on and supporting Hollywood productions. And the CIA funded artists and filmmakers, foreign and domestic, through mechanisms like the Congress for Cultural Freedom.[10]

Part of the impetus for such negotiations, as well as the full-fledged creation of a film unit within the Voice of America (VOA) in 1953 (in 1963, it became a unit within the USIA), was recognition on the part of State Department officials that while film was undeniably paramount to the United States' psychological warfare strategy, the country's primary bastion of filmmaking in Hollywood could hardly be relied upon for molding commercial works in the interest of US objectives. Despite press coverage surrounding the meetings between the Hollywood mogul Jack Valenti and the George W. Bush adviser Karl Rove, early efforts at collaboration following 9/11 proved largely futile. There was never to be the kind of flamboyant success of WWII productions like *Wing and a Prayer* (1944) or *The Story of G. I. Joe* (1945). "The bottom line," as the journalist Nina Teicholz observed writing for the *Washington Monthly*, was that "entertainment is a much more competitive business than the big-studio oligopoly that dominated the industry in the 1940s."[11] Even in those instances of cooperation success looked very different from the opposing coasts. Kathryn Bigelow's film *Zero Dark Thirty* (2012), for example, which reportedly drew on closed-door access to the CIA files on the hunt for Osama bin Laden, grossed $132 million at the box office because of, not despite, its controversial depiction of torture. Critics such as the Senate Intelligence Committee member Mark Udall interpreted the film's implied narrative that the CIA's use of waterboarding was effective in achieving its aim as "a form of propaganda" intended to deceive the "general public."[12] But this deception concerned only the American public. Overseas, and in particular the Arab and Muslim world, the film's depiction of torture vindicated the perceived injustices of the war on terror. What a more strategic public diplomacy posture toward the Arab and Muslim world called for—namely, peaceful depictions of American beneficence, the country's tolerance toward different religions, and the goodwill of its citizens—was unlikely to come out of the commercial studios. As Teicholz wrote in 2002, "Shelling out millions to produce foreign-language movies and TV shows that would almost certainly lose money was virtually out of the question."[13] But still, officials understood that help was needed. Finding a middle ground would be the work of Layalina and AAM.

What public diplomacy vehicles like Layalina and AAM lacked in commercial firepower they made up for with political clout. Both organizations could boast major influencers from the highest echelons of the country's political establishment. Layalina's board of directors, according to Shahabian, met three or four times a year and consisted almost entirely of former ambassadors and high-powered Washington lawyers. Richard V. Allen, Brent Scowcroft, Zbigniew Brzeziński, and Henry Kissinger, all former national security advisers, featured among the group's board of counselors, a mostly honorific designation. George H. Bush, former US president and CIA director, was the honorary chairman. (He filmed an advertising announcement for the group in 2015.) In addition to its formidable fundraising base, Layalina benefited from Fairbanks's and Ginsberg's close ties with officials from the Board of Broadcasting Governors (BBG). As a point of historical coincidence, Shahabian claimed, Fairbanks and Norm Pattiz were scheduled to have lunch on 9/11 before their plans abruptly changed. Responding to recommendations from the Djerejian report, Pattiz, then a chairman of the BBG's Middle East Committee, severed official ties with Layalina. (It did not prevent him from attending the annual fundraisers.) However, Bruce Sherman, the long-time head of "strategy, research, and business development" for the BBG and the author of then-Senator Joe Biden's 2004 "Initiative 9/11 Act," which made the case for increased funding and "surge capacity" for the country's international broadcasting programs, joined the board of Layalina in 2016. His appointment was preceded, in 2014, by another key collaborator on BBG programming: the Beirut-based "strat comm specialist" Eli Khoury (see chapter 3).[14]

Like Al-Hurra under the leadership of Mouafac Harb, Layalina was ultimately led by the entrepreneurialism and linguistic wherewithal of yet another bicultural interlocutor from Lebanon who would embrace as his own the Herculean task of salvaging America's image for the Arabic-speaking world. A senior in college at the time of 9/11, Leon Shahabian became the youngest cofounder of Layalina when he joined the company in 2002. By his own account, he was among those in Washington who recognized the limitations of a stand-alone content provider, an initiative Pattiz and the BBG were exploring already with the METN. Shahabian, in contrast, believed the group should direct its energies toward a more economical model of content distribution. The Arab world was already inundated with network providers, so the argument went, but even the most successful outfits in the region were hungry for original content. Layalina, with a little help from Hollywood and the weight of Washington behind it, could fill that niche. It was a bold undertaking but not one without precedent.

WORLDNET

The use of satellite TV in the war of ideas has a rich history in the annals of American public diplomacy. Begun in earnest in the mid-1980s as an attempt to widen the spotlight on the Soviet invasion of Afghanistan, the USIA, through its principal vehicle, Worldnet Television, produced a wide range of original programming—some award-winning—as part of a vigorous campaign by the Reagan administration to mitigate perceived ideological deficiencies in the US commercial market and to counter a massive Soviet apparatus that, by the mid-1980s, was thought to be pumping out propaganda in eighty-two languages for an astonishing seven hundred million dollars per year.[15] As described by Alvin Snyder, director of TV at the USIA under Charles Z. Wick—the Hollywood talent agent Reagan appointed to head his inaugural balls committee and, soon after, to serve as director of the USIA—the first Worldnet broadcast occurred on January 31, 1982. Developed as a response to the so-called "Polish crisis" and billed as a one-night extravaganza featuring celebrity testimonies along with musical interludes and prerecorded video montages of the Soviet-backed crackdown on union-led strikes in Poland, the USIA's film *Let Poland Be Poland* laid the groundwork for a new kind of content in the war of ideas. The variety-style live broadcast put to test the philosophy, championed by Wick, that satellite TV, not radio, was the best medium for compelling hearts and minds; he believed that, unlike film, which was being actively cultivated by state-sponsored studios around the globe, satellite TV, in part through Reagan's Star Wars initiative, was a technology the United States was uniquely poised to dominate. In addition to crystalizing the Reagan administration's unabashedly ideological approach to world affairs, *Let Poland Be Poland* epitomized the kind of private-public collaboration that had long characterized the work of the USIA, an organization that, in Snyder's words, had become, by the end of the Reagan administration, the world's largest PR firm. *Let Poland Be Poland* involved public relations experts from major American companies (Procter & Gamble, Philip Morris, General Motors, Walt Disney, and Exxon, among others) and virtually all of the funding—which was channeled through the National Center for Public Diplomacy, a nonprofit organization set up by the Heritage Foundation—came from private donations.[16] Drawing on their connections with Hollywood, Wick and the show's director, Marty Passeta, the producer of the Grammys and the Academy Awards, who had also worked with Wick on the inaugural balls, maximized the role of the celebrities. The key, as Passeta later told the *Washington Post*, was to make sure the actors (Charleston Heston, Glenda Jackson, Max Von Sydow, Bob Hope, Kirk Douglas, James Michener, Frank Sinatra, Orson Welles, and Henry Fonda) didn't take up more time than the "world leaders" (Ronald Reagan, Margaret Thatcher, Pierre Trudeau, and François Mitterand). "Nobody—not Douglas, not Heston, not Orson Welles, was handed a statement and told 'read this,'" Passeta told the *Washington Post*.[17] Wick, who reportedly reached out himself to Sinatra and Hope, maintained an even lighter touch. His work and that of the USIA was performed mostly off-screen: convening desirable talent, fundraising, training content creators, building the infrastructure, and perhaps even coaxing demand. "Twelve new cable channels were being planned for 1984 in Germany," Snyder wrote, "and our initial discussions with cable operators were promising."[18]

To utilize the new satellite technology, foreign cable providers needed content. USIA officials were more than happy to provide it. Doing so, however, meant not only generating and translating American-made content from within the United States but also championing the voices of content creators and journalists abroad. As Snyder described, the agency's first and perhaps most enduring strategy for involving foreign journalists in American propaganda was the invention of the "interactive press conference," a model presented for the first time during a town hall event devoted to addressing the US invasion of Grenada. "It was clear to us that the most efficient way of getting US policy positions on European TV news programs and into newspapers was by holding interactive press conferences," Snyder wrote. By putting "journalists of several nationalities—their key TV and press players—in by-line on-camera situations," USIA officials created a communications by proxy method whereby US policy could be delivered, in a journalistic format, through third-party providers acting in good faith.[19] There was no telling whether foreign news outlets would ultimately turn the information against its source—i.e., US press officials—or, indeed, whether anyone was watching. But the activity served to foster the kind of industrial democracy John Dewey once imagined: an active exchange of ideas and voices that, in the end, USIA officials believed were more conducive to American interests than those of their authoritarian counterparts. This dynamic—of proxied and collaborative communications in the service of American interests—culminated in the first major information operation of the Reagan administration, the Afghan Media Project.

By the mid-1980s, a time in which Soviet soft power was ramping up across Afghanistan in response to numerous military setbacks and a temporary ceasefire between key factions of the Afghan insurgency, including, notably, Ahmed Shah Massoud and the Northern Alliance, Reagan's officials had grown frustrated that "Moscow's

Vietnam" was unfolding "without reporters."[20] Resulting in part because of the country's rugged and inaccessible terrain and the nonexistent commercial incentives to report on another country's distant war, the major networks devoted "fewer than one story per month to the war in Afghanistan," according to Snyder. For all of 1983, NBC, the country's most-watched news outlet, carried a grand total of just over three minutes of coverage of the Soviets' war in Afghanistan.[21] Turning to their network of Hollywood celebrities, Wick and Snyder assigned a producer from the Motion Picture and Television Service of the USIA, Ash Hawkens, to travel to Pakistan and the border of Afghanistan to shoot a documentary about the war's refugee crisis with Kirk Douglas, a Hollywood icon and reliable ally of the USIA. "The program was intended to condemn the Soviet occupation of Afghanistan and reveal the plight of the 4 million refugees who had fled to neighboring Pakistan," Snyder wrote. But Douglas fell ill and the filming was halted.[22] The final product, which carried little to no public attribution to the USIA, was met "with limited success," in Snyder's view.[23] Still, as Hawkens later wrote, Douglas was proud of the work and he promoted it during his "subsequent public appearances."[24] The USIA translated the film into "multiple languages" and distributed it to seventy countries, according to Hawkens.[25] More importantly, the production helped set in motion several important formulas for US propaganda moving forward.

First, it was clear from Douglas's contribution that USIA officials could count on the firepower of Hollywood even after the cultural debacle of the Vietnam War. *Thanksgiving in Peshawar* also demonstrated that the USIA could execute meaningful propaganda on the frontlines of the struggle with the Soviet Union using little more than logistical coordination (itself a major feat) and outside fundraising. The initiative was followed by an hour-long special featuring foreign reports on the conflict. In January 1983, impressed by the work of Wick and Snyder, Reagan signed National Security Decision Directive 77 to further support such campaigns. As described by Steven R. Galster for the National Security Archive, the policy created, among other things, a "Special Planning Group" and "an inter-agency Afghan Working Group" that "met twice a month to discuss ways of increasing media coverage of the war and generating sympathy and support for the mujahidin." By 1985, the USIA had expanded its operations to include grants to the Hearst Corporation and Boston University for the purpose of training Afghan journalists in neighboring Pakistan and helping them to establish new networks of content distribution across Afghanistan.[26] As Snyder later wrote in his memoir, "The war in Afghanistan was the American government's 'made-for-TV' movie. It was the first war in which both AK-47s and video minicams were standard infantry issue. It was a war in which media coverage was purchased from a mail order catalogue, and Uncle Sam owned the warehouse."[27]

Despite its best efforts, Worldnet programming found limited traction in Washington. In 1988, lawmakers voted to cut funding by fifteen million dollars in response to "greatly exaggerated claims about viewership."[28] The freewheeling independence of the enterprise was ultimately absorbed into the bureaucracy of the State Department. By the time Worldnet was officially absolved and its offices incorporated into the VOA, the pioneering satellite news network had made inroads into over a hundred local markets around the world.[29] Worldnet's African Network (AFNET) was competing with Agence France-Presse (AFP) and the Russian-state wire service TASS across much of sub-Saharan Africa; its first salvos were a Washington-based news conference on "famine-relief efforts" and a series of fact-checking reports on the Russian line; the latter were first promulgated through a KGB publication in India, the *Patriot*, and exposed by the State Department's Active Measures Working Group, which stated that the AIDS epidemic had been started as an American plot.[30] By 1987, the Reagan administration was using Worldnet to broadcast interactive news conferences from Washington to Iraq in which journalists based in Kuwait could pose questions. And an agreement had been brokered between the Palestinian Authority and the USIA to air Worldnet and VOA content in exchange for two satellite dishes and training support for journalists in Gaza and the

West Bank.[31] By the end of the Reagan administration, through an "extended service" agreement with the Brazilian-owned satellite company EMBRATEL, Worldnet content became available throughout Latin America and the Caribbean.[32] And in one of the Clinton administration's final public diplomacy relays to the Middle East, the president used Worldnet to send a message of "reconciliation" to the people of Iran.[33]

Gone with the disaggregation of the USIA, however, was much of the independence of the Motion Picture and Television Service, which, through Worldnet, had become one of the agency's most expensive endeavors. Still, it was clear that Snyder and Wick's vision, along with later innovations in the realm of digital content distribution, had become integral to the government's greater communications strategy. Moreover, the institutional memory of their television and film division survived. The VOA adapted the use of satellite feeds for the dissemination of television content to key markets in the global South. And through private and professional networks, Washington's Hollywood dreams lived on. In Layalina and AAM, the model of partnering with foreign-based networks continued unabated and without the additional burden of congressional oversight or public scrutiny. The companies' nonprofit model more closely resembled the early Cold War days and the CIA's "Mighty Wurlitzer" experiment wherein 501(c)(3) organizations such as the National Student Association, American Friends of the Middle East, and others became bastions of subtle influence. Different, however, from those earlier times and much closer to the so-called "Hollywood consortium" of the 1950s, the circles of influence compelled by the nonprofit enterprises assembled knowingly, in most instances, and in good conscience for the singular purpose of ideological gamesmanship. Shahabian would say, "The CVE community didn't fund us, they found us." It was a partially true maxim but also a description of Layalina's own unique game. As with AAM and its use of the DoD-backed Tolo TV in Afghanistan for content distribution, Layalina did not buy or coerce its way onto primetime television in the Middle East. Rather, the company understood the terrain as it existed and found a way to fit in.

TRACK ONE-AND-A-HALF

"Everywhere I went," Shahabian reflected, "people asked me to be the square peg." As one of the few people involved with Layalina who spoke fluent Arabic, Shahabian's role centered on talking to "partners in the Arab world." Finding and creating broadcast opportunities for company-made content became the company's first order of business. It was work that hinged on Shahabian fulfilling his "square peg" function.[34]

"Track Two" or "Track One-and-a-Half" diplomacy was how Shahabian described this vital aspect of Layalina's mission: an exchange of views, confidence, and information with "current and future leaders" in a nonofficial capacity. The most important outcome of Shahabian's Track Two efforts was an agreement to air Layalina content on the "oldest and leading pan-Arab free-to-air satellite broadcaster" in the world, MBC.[35]

With Fairbanks and Ginsberg opening doors, Layalina and Shahabian filmed intercultural town halls at the Dubai headquarters of MBC, managed tours of visiting delegations, and introduced American broadcasting personalities—including the founder of *60 Minutes*, Don Hewitt—to Arab media moguls looking to expand their range. Shahabian's first production with Layalina—a conversation filmed in the Reuters studios on H Street between the Washington bureau chief for MBC's Al-Arabiya, Hisham Melhem, and the *New York Times* columnist Thomas Friedman provided a glimpse of what was to come. Abdulrahman al-Rashed, a critical partner for the American nonprofit and the general manager of Al-Arabiya, MBC's 24-hour Arabic-language cable-news network, reflected on the kind of Track Two diplomacy Shahabian and Layalina were pursuing in an interview for PBS's *Frontline* documentary "War of Ideas" in 2007.

"Personal relations, one-on-one kind of meetings, are extremely useful," al-Rashed said in response to a question about American public diplomacy. "It might not change the views, but at least it helps provide people with information. That's important. Americans are very much far away from the region; they are different from the Europeans. They come here as two groups. Either they are business people that come to do business and walk out, so they don't mingle, really, and talk and convince or change minds. And the second group, the politicians, they stick to the official line. And official lines are not good enough to convince anyone."[36] Setting up the distribution side of Layalina, however, was just part of the equation. Equally important was enlisting qualified filmmakers, soliciting stories, and auditioning actors, as well as all of the ingredients that go into the creation of a made-for-primetime television show in Arabic or any other language. To realize this critical supply side of the production chain, Layalina looked to where American public diplomacy has always turned for creative guidance: Hollywood—or at least nearby at the University of Southern California (USC) and the Institute of Creative Technologies (ICT).

THE CREATIVES

Established in 1999 with a forty-fivemillion-dollar contract from the US Army and the Department of Defense and renewed for another hundred million in 2004, the ICT at USC had identified early on that its mission was "harnessing Hollywood-derived creativity with academic innovation and military-domain expertise."[37] Boasting a wide range of R&D applications—from the use of virtual reality technology for soldier training and rehabilitation to "robotic 'mules' capable of carrying soldiers' equipment and sensing 'enemy movement'"—the ICT, by the end of the second Bush administration, had established itself as an important hub of "futurist" thinking within the defense-intelligence complex.[38] For Layalina, the ICT, with its proximity to Hollywood, presented a different kind of opportunity. Through the introduction of Jane Harman—the long-standing Congresswoman from California whose district also included Marina del Rey's Information Sciences Institute—Layalina pitched to several directors the idea of creating cross-cultural programming for distribution on primetime Arab TV. Jerome Gary's proposal to make a reality TV show based on the hit MTV show *Road Rules* was the "least bad option."[39]

But Gary, in fact, was more than just a former Hollywood director. By the time he took the lead on the Layalina pilot in 2004, he had served as the strategic director at the ICT for over four years. Among his self-reported accomplishments was a "counterterrorism role-playing game" and "wargames" exercise—including "technologies and narratives"—for the CIA. According to Gary's public resume the intelligence agency provided four million dollars a year in funding for ICT activities between 2000 and 2006. Among his own contributions were some two dozen "three-day screenwriting, scenario planning, and storytelling intensives" for CIA personnel, a function he also performed at the Esalen Institute at Big Sur in northern California. It was a fitting tribute to the long war of ideas that the site of the Esalen Soviet-American Exchange Program of the late 1980s, a much-touted site of Track Two diplomacy, would serve as the final destination of the first season of *On the Road in America*.[40]

Most outstanding from Gary's resume was the relative economy with which shows like *On the Road in America* unfolded. Ostensibly, three seasons of it were produced for under five million dollars.[41] State Department grants ranging from four hundred thousand to one million dollars funded shows such as *Life After Death* (*al-Hayat ba'd al-mut*, 2018), which, according to Shahabian, continued to air on Al-Arabiya every year on 9/11 for more than a decade after its first release. *Arab Muslim Women* (2007), an obscure state-funded, six-part series that featured among its promotional material a scantily clad Lara Abu Saifan, star of *On the Road in America*, as well as two one-hour pilots of a show called "Trading Places" and "American Caravan," a Middle East–based follow up to *On the Road in America*, followed suit.[42]

In 2013, working independently of Gary and largely under the direction of Shahabian, Layalina released *Jil al-Injaz* (Generation Entrepreneur), a short-lived series that broadcast on Al-Hurra and the Orbit Showtime Network (OSN). As Shahabian explained for a talk at the Middle East Institute, the show was produced in part as the "implementation of a subcontract" from the Middle East Partnership Initiative (MEPI), a State Department mechanism then steered by Liz Cheney, the deputy assistant secretary of state for Near Eastern affairs and an early confidante of Layalina's management. Launched in 2002 under the direction of Colin Powell, then secretary of state, MEPI became a critical source of soft-power development in the war of ideas. Nearly half a billion dollars flowed through MEPI grants by the end of the second Bush administration. As seen with *Generation Entrepreneur*, a reality show based on the INJAZ al-Arab competitions, MEPI funding also helped to generate the supply side of the State Department's content operations.[43] Created as an expression of US public diplomacy, about public diplomacy, and with public diplomacy funding, *Generation Entrepreneur* in this way represented a closed-circle campaign. The unique tactic of distributing the production through neutral players like MBC or OSN (and perhaps less so, Al-Hurra), and without clear attribution of funding, allowed the program to shuck the stigma of government funding and to hit the streets running, so to speak, as a seemingly organic expression of industrial-like democracy.[44]

THE QUANGO GAME

There were seven reality shows on the MBC docket by the time the second season of *On the Road in America* aired in 2009. When the pilot was launched in 2004, it was among the first Arabic-language satellite productions of its kind. As the Arab media scholar Marwan Kraidy observed, since the outset, reality TV served as "a laboratory for the Arab television industry" insofar as the genre enabled new "business models" and was capable of integrating "television with the Internet and mobile phones"—a triad Kraidy refers to as "*hypermedia space*" (Kraidy's emphasis).[45] Notably, the genre emerged in direct relation to the perceived dominance of Al-Jazeera, a phenomenon that also helped to define the American public diplomacy enterprise. In speaking with Abdulrahman al-Rashed, Kraidy took note of Al-Arabiya's promotional slogan from 2005: "Closer to the Truth." "I asked 'Abdelrahman al-Rashed [sic], the channel's general manager, if 'Closer to the Truth' reflected recognition that the truth always eluded media institutions—whose aim therefore should be to come as close as possible to the truth—or whether the slogan meant that Al-Arabiya was closer to the truth than Al-Jazeera. He smiled, seemingly acknowledging that it was a bit of both."[46] The early synergy between producers at Layalina and Al-Arabiya pivoted in part on the perceived antagonism of Al-Jazeera and what al-Rashed, with Kraidy, described as the Qatari station's emphasis on "'big' pan-Arab causes like Iraq and Palestine.'" Al-Arabiya and MBC in contrast wanted to highlight "practical issues like 'health, education, livelihoods.'" In coordination with subsidiaries like O3 Productions, which also partnered with Layalina for *On the Road*, MBC sought to corner the Arab market for human interest stories. Reality TV that purported to illustrate the "ordinariness" of Arab life ranked highly on the station's docket, as did shows that mirrored existent programming in the West.[47] Shahabian was well aware of these tendencies as he pitched Layalina's new Washington-backed series to al-Rashed and MBC management in 2004.[48]

The adaptability of Layalina's productions to the existent media ecosystem of MBC was important to the group's success insofar as MBC imagined itself as a commercial enterprise with viable market expectations. But there was no denying the synergy between the satellite giant and US public diplomacy.

Originally licensed in London through the British Independent Television Commission in 1991, MBC saw itself as unique compared to the region's multiple state-run satellite channels since it was not beholden to any government entity or agenda. However, this did not prevent the channel from working with certain state entities and agendas—the Kingdom of Saudi Arabia, naturally, but also the United States. In one of its earliest talk-show news programs, MBC partnered with Worldnet and VOA to create *Dialogue with the West*, which, as Nicholas Cull observed, included interviews with high-ranking US officials and featured discussions on topics drawn from the traditional repertoire of US public diplomacy, including women's rights and democracy. Perhaps not without irony, one of the sharpest voices of dissent to this gray exercise in US propaganda came from Mouafac Harb, the future director of Al-Hurra and then a reporter with Compass Media, a private wire service based in DC. Following an article that ran in the *Washington Times* in which Harb claimed the VOA was "aiding a pro-Saudi broadcast" and had "ceded" editorial control of the program to MBC, Geoffrey Cowan, the director of VOA, responded to Harb's critique with the observation that the "compass media reporter" had failed to "interview anyone at VOA or Worldnet about *Dialogue with the West*" and made no mention of the VOA charter that "mandates that our news broadcasts must be accurate, comprehensive, objective and balanced."[49] The MBC bureau chief Aziz Fahmy also responded to Harb's critique by noting that its decision to not cover the deportation from the UK to Saudi Arabia of a proto-Islamist Saudi dissident could hardly be described as toeing the American line. The ferocity of the response to his critique, however, only reenforced the salience of Harb's position, which, in the end, gained evident vindication through his elevation to the directorship of Al-Hurra.[50]

Politics aside, the proverbial battle for hearts and minds struck home for many at MBC. As described by the company's CEO, Sam Barnett, MBC had started as a multinational media enterprise that sought to articulate to and for Arab society a global aesthetic palate (its original slogan was "the world through Arab eyes").[51] The company had been extraordinarily successful in its mission, and many of its most important stars, notably Nasser al-Qasabi, saw their work as both a personal cause célèbre and an act of social reform within Saudi and Gulf Arab society. Al-Qasabi, who has lived under the veil of death threats for most of the past two decades, rose to fame in the 1990s for creating what was considered to be the first Arab counterpart to *Saturday Night Live* with his sketch comedy show *Tash ma Tash* (No Biggie.) Apart from his contribution to the rich history of Arab film and television, he was in many ways a pioneer in the Arab world for his biting satire and criticism of Saudi Arabia's stringent,

Wahhabi-inflected cultural practices. In 2000, the show, then shown on Saudi 1 (now *Al-Saudiyya*) of the Saudi Broadcasting Authority, faced a *fatwa* from the Kingdom's powerful Council of Senior Scholars, who demanded the show be pulled from the air and its distribution prohibited. As noted by al-Qasabi's wife, the writer and television personality Badria al-Bashir, the ban at the time was only partially imposed. Still, the act of censorship served as an indicator of the country's social divisions.[52]

After MBC acquired the rights to *Tash ma Tash* in 2005, the show became a point of pride not only for the cast and its audience but for major stakeholders in the company, including from within the Saudi government. For them, al-Qasabi's liberal form of cultural expressionism afforded a degree of letting off steam in a manner comparable to artists under other authoritarian regimes around the region.[53] But it also allowed for a certain political currency with the West. MBC aired al-Qasabi's show for another six years as a Ramadan special and, then, in 2015, helped al-Qasabi launch a new iteration of the satirical program aimed at taking on ISIS. That show, *Selfie*, the name a double entendre for digital consumer culture and the Salafist dogma of the extremist group, captured headlines after ISIS publicly threatened to kill al-Qasabi. MBC also challenged the status quo through major serial dramas. In 2007, the Arabic-dubbed version of the Turkish drama *Gümüş* (or *Noor*), which celebrated the independence of women in the workplace, depicted premarital sex, and featured in its plot a woman having an abortion, reportedly attracted some eighty-five million viewers for its final episode in 2008. The "Muhannad Effect," as the scholar Christa Salamandra observed of the influence of the principal male character who supports his wife's professional aspirations, drew particular fury among conservatives who saw the androgynous lead as a kind of affront to the social expectations of normative masculinity.[54]

For officials at MBC, the impact of shows like *Selfie* could be measured by the "strength of reaction against us." Barnett observed that such reformist programming did "not start out as propaganda," but the effect of the reactionism at times reinforced Western tropes in the emergent canon of countering violent extremism (CVE).⁵⁵ MBC's most notorious show in this regard was the 2017 Ramadan series *Ghadabeeb Soud* (Black Crows). Airing for just one season (that was cut short) at a reported cost of ten million dollars, the show depicted the recruitment of women into ISIS's self-declared caliphate as it assumed control of the eastern Syrian city of Raqqa. Replicating many of the group's violent social pathologies, the plot aspired toward a kind of "edutainment," in Heather Jaber and Marwan Kraidy's words, wherein the women are shown the errors of their ways, and their deliverance serves as vindication of the group's implied ideological foil, i.e., Western enlightenment.⁵⁶ Although details surrounding the origins of the show remained murky, Ali Jaber, the director of Television at MBC, made little effort to disguise the station's working relationship with the State Department. Following Jaber's remarks as the keynote speaker for the State Department–hosted Ministerial Plenary for the Global Coalition Working to Defeat ISIS in March 2017, Cynthia Schneider, a former ambassador to the Netherlands and codirector of the NGO Muslims on Screen and Television (MOST), described how a partnership with the Sunnylands Retreat of the Annenberg Estate and MBC helped bring Hollywood writers to Dubai for workshops and to embed one of the writers for *Black Crows* within the production crew of the *The Last Tycoon*, an Amazon series produced by Christopher Keyser, who Schneider had advised during the third season of *The Tyrant*, which was shot in Egypt.⁵⁷ The utilization of such established centers of Track Two diplomacy like Sunnylands signaled the arrival of MBC and its formidable talent pool as a preeminent vehicle of collaborative content creation in the war of ideas. But the increased visibility was not without consequences. Critics assailed *Black Crows* as a "gloomy product, which seems to go against the channel's own audience base" and one that 'toed the line' of "Western counterterrorism talk."⁵⁸ Despite such criticisms—which unfolded most visibly across the content feed of MBC's principal antagonist in Al-Jazeera—the open embrace of state-private collaboration as a "back-to-the-future" model of content generation in the war of ideas was a fait accompli by the end of the second Obama administration.[59]

Similar to the convergence of the USIA's cultural exchange and information programs in the pages of *Al-Sadaqah* during the Cold War, government-fueled, nonprofit media organizations like Layalina and AAM piggy-backed on other federally funded public diplomacy programs that in turn provided talent for the companies' productions and PR material for new lines of funding. Distinct from earlier models of collaboration, however, the content of a Layalina-INJAZ production or AAM's town halls was auspiciously void of the ideological didacticism that once colored the USIA's Cold War productions. Where AFNET featured interactive press conferences refuting Soviet disinformation around AIDS in Africa or USIA documentaries about Black integration on US campuses, most of Layalina and AAM's content worked in the vein of what the King's College scholar Mayssoun Sukarieh has described as the "hope crusades," a loosely discernable front of Western-backed PR campaigns aimed at promoting neoliberal market reforms and reinforcing a certain "culturalist ideology" that imagines the world as "being divided into discrete and homogeneous 'cultures.'"[60] Public diplomacy initiatives imagined outside the scope of the traditional "slow" or "fast" channels of propaganda such as the "I Love Life" campaign in Lebanon or the "Culture of Hope" initiative spearheaded by Jordan's Queen Rania and backed by MEPI funding, exemplified the tendency toward ahistoricity in the outsourcing of American public diplomacy following 9/11. But Layalina and AAM could also be seen as guilty in generating content that promoted an artificially inflated worldview, one in which identity formation was imagined against a normative set of broad-based religious or cultural values as opposed to individual life experiences or small group politics. Indeed, both companies' business models were predicated on the promise of bridging the proverbial divide between distinct cultural boundaries. But the degree to which the nonprofits'

programming represented a symptom, rather than a cause of such abstractions, was also apparent.

Reality TV was cheap and documentaries even cheaper. The simple ensemble of a few talking heads, a microphone, a camera, an editor, and a producer with ties to a distribution hub represented the bare minimum for a TV show, but it was enough to deliver on the promise of a grant or donor funding. Informed and guided by seasoned veterans of the American public diplomacy enterprise, including its covert iterations, the organizations' productions illustrated in this way the legacy of Cold War thinking among America's post-9/11 information warriors. Worldnet's interactive press conferences were alive and well in AAM's town halls. The organization's star-studded awards ceremonies that, for the price of entry, paired Defense and State Department officials with Hollywood icons and foreign awardees, recalled Snyder and Wick's Cold War spectaculars. Layalina's only fictional creation in the battle for hearts and minds, the short-lived Jordanian cocreation *Ben wa 'Isam* (Ben and Izzy) tapped into another legacy genre: children's animated fiction. Started in 2004 with a $150,000 grant from the Hewlett Foundation, the cartoon, a time-travel adventure featuring two main characters, "Ben" (an American) and "Isam" (a Jordanian), was an exemplar of Layalina's collaborative approach, connecting animators in Jordan with LA-based writers and soliciting additional support from Jordan's Royal Family.[61] But it was also a rerun of sorts in America's relatively shallow repertoire of propagandistic filmmaking. Similar to the postwar era, *Ben and Izzy*, as a work of fiction, was an exception to the norm. Cold War filmmaking included a remarkable range of productions but nearly all fell within the spectrum of documentary filmmaking or "news and information." The 1954 animated version of George Orwell's political allegory *Animal Farm* (1945) was the first to break the mold. Produced by the CIA "shell corporation" Touchstone, Inc. and distributed to cinemas throughout Africa, Asia, Europe, and Latin America, the adult animation classic, as the historian Hugh Wilford described it, was at once a memorable cinematic accomplishment and a successful example of prudent spending.

To save costs on labor and help throw off the scent of US funding, the film was produced in England rather than Hollywood or New York. Although its primary targets were audiences behind the Iron Curtain, the fact that Orwell's novel allegorized communist elements in the form of pigs and dogs, both considered "unclean animals" in Muslim society, represented, in Wilford's terms, a "happy coincidence" for an agency whose influence operations were increasingly gearing toward third-world targets in the global South, the Middle East in particular.[62] Another more sustained animation project discovered by the National Archives in 2019 attempted a similarly creative approach by repurposing the Arab folktale "*al-Hoja*" (also known as "*Goha*") in the form of a televised puppetry series.[63] Created for the USIA by an independent film studio, Trident Films, and distributed to parts of the Middle East through government partner hubs like the Educational Film, Radio, and Television Center of Turkey, the Hoja project drew inspiration from the heritage turn in postrevolutionary Arabic film and literature wherein artists looked to resuscitate a pre-European sense of aesthetics as a political move toward the decolonization of culture. Layalina's *Ben & Izzy*, through its time-travel schema, also sought to compel local audiences through inferences to cultural and historical oddities from the region. Dissimilar, however, to the Cold War productions, *Ben & Izzy* featured a more ambivalent kind of critique. The show's antagonist, a corrupt Arab businessman, hardly mirrors the mold of the "lazy young radical" who wishes to blow up the coffeehouse where the "beloved old Sheikh" recounts oral tales of Nasr al-Din al-Hoja; in the same vein, Orwell's book was a biting satire of socialism and self-empowerment.[64] In *Ben & Izzy*, rather, not much is wrong at all. The boys and their magical companion, Yasmine, collect treasures as if in a video game. The hunt for personal capital and the joy of shared adventure captures the implied moral messaging of this strange soft power creation.

Like with the reality shows—and unlike their Cold War counterparts—the funding behind these new iterations of American public diplomacy remained occluded beneath layers of deflection and a certain breed of transnationalism built atop a tidal wave of American ingenuity. As discussed, such tactics were nothing new. As far back as 1953, Edward Barrett observed that "by its very nature, international persuasion is *inter*dependent with the other foreign programs and policies of the government."[65] Alberto Fernandez echoed a similar line in 2020, writing: "The biggest contribution that strategic counterterrorism communications make is often not what they produce themselves but rather what, through the convening process, agencies get others (proxies, non-governmental organizations, other government agencies, foreign governments) to produce for them."[66] As with the funding attached to their backs, semiclandestine enterprises such as Layalina, AAM, or the Afghan Media Resource Center before them depended wholly on the vitality of their host partners. More often than not those attachments were short-lived, however, and in some cases left a bitter aftertaste. Diluting the lines yet further between collaboration and co-optation in the new war of ideas would become the critical test for Washington's next generation propagandists.

FIGURE 1 Issa Sabbagh with King Faisal II Al-Hashimi of Iraq on Voice of America Arabic, August 15, 1952. Pictured, from left to right, are Foy D. Kohler, assistant administrator of the International Broadcasting Service; King Faisal II; Prince Abdul-Ilah; and Issa Sabbagh.

Credit: Department of State, Harry S. Truman Library.

FIGURE 2 "The Family of Man," USIS Beirut, 1958. USIS Beirut hosted Edward Steichen and the New York Museum of Modern Art's "The Family of Man" photography exhibition from 1958, one year ahead of the exhibit's eventual display in Moscow. The exhibit was thought to highlight American values such as individualism and freedom of spirit.

Credit: United States Information Agency.

FIGURE 3 "Symbols of change in the American South," *Al-Sadaqah*, July 15, 1965. American propaganda in Arabic regularly featured stories of racial integration.

Credit: United States Information Agency.

FIGURE 4 "Man orbits the earth and a new Islamic center in New York," *Al-Sadaqah*, June 23, 1965.

Credit: United States Information Agency.

FIGURE 5 "*Al-Hayat fi Amrika* / Life in America #35," USIA Beirut. The popular color magazine featured typical scenes of American life with a heavy emphasis on culture, lifestyle, and entertainment.

Credit: United States Information Agency.

FIGURE 6 US Army Major Jeffrey Cantor, commander of Bravo Company, 404th Civil Affairs Battalion (center), answers questions during a televised interview at the Iraq Media Network (IMN) in Kirkuk, Iraq, October 8, 2003. The Coalition Provisional Authority repurposed much of Iraq's existing media infrastructure following the US invasion in March 2003.

Credit: Department of Defense, Office of the Assistant Secretary of Defense (Public Affairs), American Forces Information Service, Defense Visual Information Center.

FIGURE 7 "Radio Information, from 6–11 p.m." Leaflet dropped by the US military during Operation Iraqi Freedom, Library of Congress, 2003. DLC/PP-20031102.

Credit: US Army.

FIGURE 8 "The coalition does not want to destroy the landmarks of your country. The coalition will destroy any military installation." Leaflet dropped by the US military during Operation Iraqi Freedom, Library of Congress, 2003. DLC/PP-20031102.

Credit: US Army.

FIGURE 9 "Greetings from the Arabic department on Voice of America radio." Undated. Beginning on January 1, 1950, from the Voice of America studios in New York and later from Washington, DC, the Voice of America Arabic broadcast news and information throughout the Arabic-speaking world for over half a century. The division was shut down following 9/11 and replaced by the Middle East Radio Network, later Radio Sawa, a mostly pop-music station, on March 23, 2002.

Credit: United States Information Agency.

FIGURE 10 Al-Hurra studios in Springfield, Virginia. In 2018, the main studios of Al-Hurra were overhauled to give the station a younger, sharper look in the style of Sky News and RT.

Credit: USG / MBN / YouTube.

FIGURE 11 Soraya Salti (center), on the set of Layalina's *Generation Entrepreneur* in Doha, Qatar, November 6, 2012. The series premiered in prime time in the Middle East on OSN Yahala Shabab on October 23, 2013. It subsequently aired on Al-Hurra. Photo courtesy of Leon Shahabian.

Credit: © Leon Shahabian

FIGURE 12 Don Hewitt worked with Layalina for the making of *Al-Sa'at* (The Hour), October 18, 2005.

Credit: Courtesy of Leon Shahabian

FIGURE 13 Lara Abu Saifan (center) during the filming of season one of *On the Road in America* (2006), Chicago.

Credit: Courtesy of Leon Shahabian

FIGURE 14 "[ISIS] has displaced them [Yezedis] and slaughtered them." From *The Crimes of Abu-Bakr al-Baghdadi*.

Credit: The Digital Outreach Team, October 29, 2019.

5
SILICON ARMIES

> *We are in a room of industry and sector experts from tech, media, entertainment, brand and civil society. This group is gathered because ISIS isn't just a military enemy; they have proven to be a formidable foe in the communications and culture space.*
>
> —MADISON VALLEYWOOD PROJECT (MVP) BRIEFING,
> U.S. DEPARTMENT OF STATE, 2016

It was late February 2016, and Capitol Hill was abuzz with news from State Department officials that a major joint public-private task force had assembled to "take back the Internet" from online jihadists.[1] The international terrorist organization known as the Islamic State in Iraq and the Levant (ISIL), also known as ISIS, had gained control of an area roughly the size of the United Kingdom and was unleashing a wave of terror on ethnic minorities and secular authorities throughout the region. Around the globe, disparate groups of supporters declared allegiance to the self-proclaimed caliph Abu Bakr al-Baghdadi. They filmed atrocities committed in his name and distributed the content across an estimated ninety thousand Twitter accounts "associated with or sympathetic to ISIL."[2]

Joined now by allies in Iraq, the US government launched an aerial campaign called Operation Inherent Resolve. As in 2003, the campaign was imagined in parallel to a new wave of information operations. "Airstrikes may capture the headlines," Secretary of State John Kerry observed in a December 2014 address to NATO. But "destroying Daesh is going to require defeating the ideology."[3]

Few details escaped the February 24 meeting, dubbed the "Madison Valleywood Project," but news outlets reported participants in the "task force" included a cross-section of federal officials and private sector leaders: public relations experts from Madison Avenue, technology experts from Silicon Valley, and studio representatives from Hollywood. Not surprisingly, the summit had been months in the making. That January, the director of the National Security Agency, Michael Rogers, White House chief of staff Denis McDonough, and FBI director James Comey traveled to Silicon Valley to provide "unclassified background on terrorist use of technology, including encryption" for executives at various software companies, among them Microsoft, Google, Facebook, and Twitter.[4] Kerry went to Los Angeles to field "perspectives & ideas" from Hollywood studio executives on how "to counter #Daesh narrative."[5] John Carlin, Obama's assistant attorney general for national security, was in San Francisco for *Vanity Fair*'s New Establishment Summit in fall 2015.[6] A participant at that event, Bob Jeffrey, a non-executive chairman at J. Walter Thompson, later described his interaction with the federal attorney for an article in the *Atlantic*. "We were talking about the radicalization of youth and terrorism and so on. . . . So I said to John Carlin and his team, 'You know, the ad industry historically used to be helpful to the U.S. in situations like this'. . . . 'John, you know, I think people in the industry would love to figure out a way to contribute.'"[7] At the summit, the Madison Avenue team, including Jeffrey, were shown stories of ISIS defection and discussed online videos used for recruitment. As one participant later remarked, the executives were "astonished" by the quality and "production value" of the filmmaking. "You could hear a pin drop."[8]

A government-made PowerPoint presentation, ultimately disclosed by a request made through the Freedom of Information Act, depicted acts of homegrown violent extremism and laid out the challenge of tailoring information operations to a subset of perceived fence-sitters—individuals who may be persuaded by ISIS propaganda but were not yet alienated from the greater Muslim majority.[9]

The group examined slides depicting ISIS's "extraordinary and charismatic brand," social media posts, and online images that the group's supporters had created to propagate "strength and warmth." For the former, the government presented an image, first published in the UK's *Daily Mail*, of women clad in black niqab, posing with a BMW M5, the ISIS flag, and AK-47s.[10] For the latter—the image thought to convey "warmth"—the government officials showed a photograph, also published in the *Daily Mail*, of a teenager standing in a grocery store (presumably inside the "Caliphate") wearing a balaclava and strapped with an AK-47 while holding to the camera a jar of Nutella.[11]

Adjacent to the summit, at the Institute for Near East Studies, Facebook's head of global policy management, Monika Bickert, described how her company was studying the use of its online platform to combat Islamic State messaging. In the case of England and France, where Facebook had recently analyzed a thousand anti-ISIS pages, Bickert described six best-practice approaches for swaying hearts and minds. Based on numbers of "shares" and a yet undisclosed algorithm for measuring influence, these included pages that featured "ways of responding" to extremist recruitment; illustrated "Islamophobia"; "exposed" Islamic State falsehoods; referenced "national solidarity"; drew differentiations of "Islam from Radical Islam"; or employed "humor and parody."[12] No longer driven by airtime or eyeballs, this new stage in the war of ideas was measured by clicks and likes. The Facebook researchers were also honing in on particular themes: the manner in which information shapes and reconstitutes the aesthetics of group identity or what compels people to action, including taking to the streets, placing a vote, or opening their wallets. Propagandists in Washington—and around the globe—were learning new best practices for their craft.

PEAKS AND VALLEYS

Little more than a blip on the vast timeline of public-private conferences in the service of public diplomacy, the Madison Valleywood summit was nonetheless emblematic of a new phase in the long war of ideas. Technology companies (the silicon arm of Madison Valleywood) were no longer just part of the infrastructure to the war of the ideas; like advertising companies or Hollywood studios, they had become viable sources of content creation.

Similar to WWII with the establishment of the Voice of America (VOA) as an answer to the spread of Nazi propaganda on German radio, the uptake of social media by public diplomacy officials emerged largely in response to the use of the technology by al-Qaeda and other jihadist actors.[13] As articulated by Alberto Fernandez, who (prior to assuming the helm of the Middle East Broadcasting Networks) was director of public diplomacy for the State Department's Near East Bureau from 2005 to 2007, al-Qaeda, by the end of the first decade following 9/11, had "transformed from a global terrorist organization that used the media into a global media organization that uses terrorism."[14] Having evolved beyond their early days of recording video and audiocassettes and distributing them through local vendors, al-Qaeda's principal media organ, Al-Sahab, consisted in essence of a suite of Internet sites and chatrooms, which, fueled by centrally coordinated messages, and branded by al-Qaeda's black flag (*al-uqub*), served as a bridge for the "isolated potential *mujahed* to the global jihad." As the former Foreign Service Officer and psychologist Marc Sageman observed in his 2004 book *Understanding Terror Networks*, al-Qaeda used the Internet to create a "network topology" whereby "small-world networks" or "nodes" linked to and innovated within larger, "well-connected hubs."[15] Al-Sahab's websites or the English-language e-zines *Inspire* and *Resurgence* were also translational, bringing into contact remote actors across time and space and providing material instructions on how to locate targets or to build a bomb. As Sageman noted, these prototypical social media sites were also inherently propagandistic. The interchange of dialogue favored soundbites and abstractions over discussion and reflection, and despite the impression of dynamism as created through the rapid exchange of ideas, the effect of the sites' chatrooms was a kind of static "disembeddedness" that, in the end, offered only reductive symbols of enmity: American hegemony, for example, or the equally abstract target of Zionism.[16]

Al-Qaeda, from early on, also used the Internet to produce and disseminate propaganda in the traditional sense. From hubs in Yemen, Iraq, Algeria, and Somalia, al-Qaeda media foundations (e.g., Al-Malahem Media, al-Basirah Media Foundation, al-Andalus Establishment for Media Production, and Al-Kata'ib Establishment for Media Production) created and disseminated videos documenting the murder of Western hostages, attacks on military infrastructure, guerilla training exercises, or, more simply, audio recordings atop a digital image of the Quran. In addition to the quotation of *surat* (verses of the Quran) and *ahadith* (actions or sayings of the prophet) many of the videos included elaborate soundtracks of *anashid*, or religious chants. The cumulative effect of the digital filmmaking was something of a hypotonic tableau, one that combined remote landscapes and images of fraternalism with unimaginable acts of violence and haunting lamentations in the form of the *anashid*. The videos were edited and annotated with messages of resistance and religious scripture and replayed widely across the Internet. Some also appeared on satellite television and were easily viewed throughout the region. Mishan Jabouri, the former Ba'athist official who, controversially, appeared as an interviewee on Al-Hurra, was among those operating a satellite channel that broadcast early al-Qaeda war footage.

The quantity and quality of jihadist media expanded dramatically following the expansion of al-Qaeda's Islamic State of Iraq branch into Syria in 2013 and its subsequent rebranding as the Islamic State of Iraq and Syria. ISIS's principal organ, *Al-Furqan*, created feature-length documentaries, *ghazawat* or so-called "military expeditions" that included drone footage and scenes of executions shot with high-definition cameras and edited for dramatic effect. *Al-Furqan* added eighty-five dedicated communications experts soon after its establishment in the city of Raqqah, Syria, and two additional media wings, *Al-Hayat* and *Al-Itisam*, soon after that.[17] *Al-Itisam*, which became responsible for some of the most horrific filmmaking during the reign of the self-declared caliph al-Baghdadi, was led by the IT specialist Ahmad Abousamra, who emigrated to Aleppo, Syria, from Massachusetts.[18]

The Internet of course was created with the help of US taxpayer dollars (DARPA famously funded the archetype of the Internet through the creation of ARPANET in the late 1960s as well as the "digital protocols" of the modern Web), and agencies like the United States Information Agency (USIA) were some of the earliest adaptors of the technology.[19] As Nicholas J. Cull observed, the VOA had used the "Gopher protocol" as early as January 1994 to transmit text across the so-called "Information Superhighway." The USIA provided some of the first "World Wide Web materials" on April 12, 1995, through the creation of its dedicated website.[20] But following the collapse of the agency in 1999, American public diplomacy suffered a lapse of nearly ten years in developing an effective online strategy. As William Rugh observed, the slow uptake of the new technology within the State Department, which absorbed the activities of the USIA, was in part cultural and the result of the institution's long-standing emphasis on traditional versus public (read *social media*) diplomacy.[21] But the threat of jihadist communications along with the perceived need to "think in terms of global networks," as laid out in the 2004 report of the Defense Science Board Task Force on Strategic Communication, helped generate a new embrace of digital technology.[22]

Spearheaded by the Department of Defense (DoD) and accompanied by a host of interagency initiatives, the battle for hearts and minds in the war of ideas shifted gradually but decisively toward the digital sphere. Some of the State Department's earliest responses to the war on terror, including a "print and electronic pamphlet," *The Network of Terrorism*, was translated into thirty-six languages and distributed online in an attempt to isolate the networking quality of al-Qaeda propaganda while simultaneously trying to go viral. Along with that pamphlet, the State Department launched the website "Open Dialogue," which aimed to foster exchange between "Muslim American and other Muslims of the world," and it created a series of "electronic pamphlets" on the theme of "Muslim life in America" in reference to the "Shared Values" campaign that was aired on satellite television across the region through paid advertising dollars.[23]

But, as with the news and information side of American propaganda, the online realm quickly became a contested space within the US government itself.

Writing in a study for the US Army War College in 2009, the law historians Daniel Silverberg and Joseph Heimann noted that "finding the appropriate role for the Department of Defense" in the emergent realm of online counter-communications had emerged as one of the stickiest problems, legally and operationally, in the military's new suite of psychological operations. The deputy secretary of defense, Gordon England, had attempted to address the problem as early as June 2007 with the signing of two "policy memoranda" that were intended to "'provide authority and guidance' for conducting communication through the Internet." Known as "interactive Internet activities" (IIA), the memoranda "Policy for Department of Defense (DOD) Interactive Internet Activities" and "Policy for Combatant Command (COCOM) Regional Websites" laid the groundwork for both direct engagement with perceived jihadist influencers on the Internet in the form of online chatroom participation and the creation of covert propaganda to be distributed digitally across the Web.[24] They offered little comfort, however, to traditional information operatives whose turf was increasingly shrinking as a result of the DoD's expansion of public diplomacy beyond the theater of war.

One of the first iterations of this new phenomenon was the online magazine *Magharabia.com*. Launched in 2004 as a joint initiative of USEUCOM (the United States European Command, a military partnership that allowed the United States, among other things, forward operating bases in Africa), the e-zine was ultimately folded into the operations of AFRICOM following the establishment of the US military command for Africa in 2007. It was finally shut down four years later after a review by the Senate Committee on Armed Services found that such operations had become a "significant and costly component" of the military's countering violent extremism (CVE) activities.[25]

Fashioned in the typical style of other US propaganda in Arabic with a masthead approximating an online news site and sections dedicated to arts and culture, sports, politics, science and technology, and business, the e-zine was explicitly tailored to North Africa. It featured dedicated pages for each of the five countries in the region, including Mauritania, and it carried an auspicious emphasis on terrorism. Articles focusing on the "smuggling and financing operations" of al-Qaeda in the Islamic Maghreb (2010), the "presence of jihadist ideology on websites popular among the youth" (2011), and the "killing of Anwar Awlaki" (2011) characterized the e-zine's peculiar mission of producing counter-communications alongside public diplomacy. The publication's interactive feature—"*Zawaya*" (Corners)—echoed the Bush administration's "American Corners" program designed in the spirit of embassy "Reading Rooms" from the Cold War period. Readers were invited to submit comments, share feedback on featured topics, and engage with the editors. Also similar to other US operations, the online magazine featured heavy emphasis on culturally tinted issues such as human rights and the plight of women, and it amplified voices from within the American public diplomacy apparatus. Of particular note, the magazine featured a profile of Lina Ben Mhenni, a Tunisian blogger and cyber-activist who had risen to prominence during the 2010/11 uprising. Her background as a Fulbright exchange student and a participant in the State Department's Alliance of Youth Movements in 2008 was not shared in the article. But like during the Cold War, with the use of foreign exchange students for propaganda purposes, Ben Mhenni's exploitation as an asset reflected another key component to the country's revamped information strategy.

NETWORKING THE MESSAGE

By the end of the second George W. Bush administration, international exchange programs had become a major locus of activity for the country's online information posture. In 2008, under the leadership of James K. Glassman, then under secretary of state for public diplomacy, the outgoing Bush administration set up the State Department's first social media hub—"ExchangesConnect"—where alumni and participants from the myriad exchange programs of the Bureau of Education and Cultural Affairs programs were directed to Facebook and other social media sites "to connect easily, and socially, with the exchange programs and initiatives that are important to you."[26] The modest advancement in virtual networking had been part of what Glassman described fondly as Public Diplomacy 2.0, an idea that culminated in the Alliance of Youth Movements Summit held at Columbia University in December 2008. That event, which included a wide range of private-sector sponsors, from Howcast to Facebook, Google, and AT&T, sent into overdrive the otherwise subtle interplay of fast and slow propaganda in the American tradition of public diplomacy.[27]

Pitched as an effort to "help combat extremism and to use new trends in social networking," the 2008 summit in New York took special aim at the Middle East. In particular, Glassman recalled, the summit included multiple activists from the Egyptian April 6 Youth Movement, a secular-oriented opposition group named for the date of a major labor uprising in the country's industrial heartland. News of the April 6 members' participation generated no shortage of alarm within the Mubarak regime. As Glassman later explained, one participant was especially impacted by the program's fallout. "We invited three members. . . . One was detained at home, another was stopped at the airport, and a third made it to NY. The day before that person was to leave, I summoned the Egyptian ambassador to my office and issued a stern warning that Egypt was not to stop this person and there were not to be reprisals against him when he returned home. That person was Ahmed Salah. . . . He was later arrested and reportedly tortured during the Arab Spring uprising in Cairo."[28] A mostly unknown figure, Saleh's principal violation had been his role in maintaining the Facebook page *Kulluna Khaled Sa'id* (We Are All Khaled Said), which was created by Wael Ghonim, a regional marketing manager at Google's Middle East and North Africa hub in Dubai and one of the predominant voices of the early uprising. "We Are All Khaled Said," named after the young Egyptian blogger who was brutally murdered by police in his hometown, Alexandria, had some three hundred thousand followers at the time of the uprising. The page was widely considered a major source of inspiration and planning for the 2011 revolution. Ghonim said that Saleh continued to administer the page even after his arrest.[29]

The use of social media technology and the redirection of its networking capacity toward information campaigns like "We Are All Khaled Said" had been integral to grassroots activism in the Arab world since the introduction of the Internet in the early 2000s. Concurrently, calls to "leverage private sector capabilities and harness information assets to the Internet revolution" had been flowing through Washington since the early days of the 9/11 response.[30] Officials like Glassman took note of the uncommon crossover potential of social media—between the traditionally slow mode of people-to-people exchanges and the proverbial fast lane of the information programs—and sought to empower the use of the new technology as a kind of catchall mechanism for the production of public diplomacy.

But the risks inherent to this strategy were evident from the outset. WikiLeaks's Julian Assange, who was given his own show on Russia's satellite giant RT shortly after the Arab uprisings, called Facebook an "appalling spy machine."[31] On January 27, the eve of the so-called "Friday of Rage," his organization released a series of stolen State Department cables, mostly from 2008, that framed the uprisings as a US-led conspiracy and implicated many of the self-styled "cyber-dissidents" who attended the Alliance of Youth

Movements Summit in New York. Ahmed Salah and others from the April 6 Youth Movement were among those directly impacted by the exposures. The stunning revelations circulated widely in the Arab press and helped set in motion a brutal crackdown by authoritarian regimes throughout the region. Glassman and the co-organizer of the summit, Jared Cohen, a member of the secretary of state's policy planning staff, were aware of the potential vulnerability of participants, as was expressed during a special briefing on the project in November 2008.

"I would say, you know, for the purposes of those groups' safety and security, you know, right now probably wouldn't be the best time to mention their names," Cohen said in response to a question by a journalist in attendance regarding the identity of the participants from Cuba.

"But their identities will surely be known then, won't they?" the journalist replied.

"Yes," Cohen responded.

The more senior under secretary of state, Glassman, interrupted: "Well, I'm not sure that personal identities of the people who were—"

"No," Cohen interrupted. "The groups that we're thinking about and working to try to get, they have their own methodology for staying anonymous."[32]

Apart from the safety of participants—Glassman confirmed there was no plan in place to counter the potential fallout of the program—the summit also put in jeopardy the long history of US-Egyptian cultural and educational exchange, a practice that dated back to 1949 when an agreement was first established with the British-backed Faruk government and later renewed under the authority of Nasser's United Arab Republic (UAR) a decade later.[33]

A certain blurring of the lines between America's slow and fast propaganda had always existed. The VOA Arabic and *Al-Sadaqah*, for example, regularly featured reports on Egyptians and Americans on exchange in their respective countries. The first such instance of *Al-Sadaqah* highlighting exchanges was a story about the director general of Cairo University Central Library, Hassan Mahmoud, who traveled to the United States on a Fulbright grant to study methods for improving rural literacy, including through the use of mobile libraries. Another prominent example from the Johnson years was the International Field Service program, which worked with the State Department to send American students abroad for immersion experiences and to perform volunteer work. In August 1966, *Al-Sadaqah* featured on its front page a description of the global exchange program that, in the case of Egypt, placed youth from the United States with host families in Egypt for the duration of the summer. "They've swapped out their mothers and their fathers and the families they've known for all of their life in the United States of America," read the headline, "for a new mother, a new father, and a new family . . . in the United Arab Republic."[34]

Advocates of these programs—most famously Senator William Fulbright, who denounced the use of his named award for information purposes—long resisted this tendency and often feared the kind of exposure and backlash made vivid by the case of the 2008 summit. But the use of social media technology, as a method and an objective, was not going away.

In 2015, in an echo of 2008, the White House sponsored a "Global Youth Summit," also held in New York, that brought "hundreds of young people, from 45 countries" to "build digital platforms designed to help keep people off the dark road of radicalization."[35] The new media landscape, in the words of the literary theorist Tarek El-Ariss, was ushering in an era of "anxiety" for the region's "intellectual and ruling class," entities that the State Department was simultaneously propping up and destabilizing through Washington's seemingly insatiable appetite for all things digital. Few viable options for executing such a delicate dance existed beyond the Bureau of Education and Cultural Affairs and its expansive, if scattered, databases. Not surprisingly, irony plagued the enterprise from start to finish.[36]

Despite the forceful analyses of counterterrorism experts like Marc Sageman, who in October 2009 testified before the Committee on Foreign Relations on the inherent utility of social media platforms to the formation of a "leaderless jihad" and "lone wolves," Cohen and Glassman imagined the cultivation of social media by foreign youth would help spur a "new kind of civil society organization." Thanks to the "policies" of "organizations like Facebook and others" that supposedly disallowed extremist content, the State Department, Cohen said, was "driving young leaders towards a methodology that's naturally conducive towards nonviolence—nonviolent movements."[37] Heading into the second decade following 9/11, this parallax view of social media as an inherently positive force in the creation of nonviolent movements permeated nearly every corner of the American public diplomacy enterprise, often at the expense of the more deliberate task of discerning good actors from bad ones. Precipitated by the most momentous political events to befall the Middle East and North Africa since the 1950s, the Arab Spring, the State Department elected to double down on digital diplomacy while reorienting expectations once more toward the war on terror, or what the defense-intelligence establishment was now calling CVE.

THE BLOWBACK MACHINE

It was by sheer force of luck that I was living in downtown Cairo and researching the literary fallout of the 1952 revolution in Egypt when protests erupted in late January 2011. Watching the news of demonstrations in Tunisia and speaking with friends on the phone, it seemed unlikely that what was happening there could spread to Egypt. The demonstrations planned for January 25 went off like many in recent decades. Protesters descended on Midan Tahrir or another neutral site and were met by a sea of police nearly equal their size in number. Some differences were apparent, of course. When I first lived in Cairo in 2003, most of the protests were aimed at US involvement in Iraq, and the government's containment efforts were largely symbolic. In 2007 and 2008, a number of labor protests broke out. Some, including those associated with the April 6 Movement, elicited violent crackdowns. But those mostly occurred in the countryside and one seldom saw any kind of coordinated campaign in the capital. On January 25, 2011, a day of protests that the semi-state-owned news agency *Al-Shorouk* and others were attributing to "Facebook activists," you could hardly discern the demonstrations beyond the traffic circle at Tahrir.[38] From the neighborhood I was living in, Lazoghly, a working-class section of downtown Cairo three blocks to the south of Tahrir, the city lulled along as normal. Three days later, however, on January 28, a radical shift occurred.

The "Friday of Rage," which saw the arrival of the massive and well-organized contingencies of the Muslim Brotherhood who had sat out the first day of protest in recognition of National Police Day, an anniversary that marked the Battle of the Barracks in Ismailia in 1952 when members of the Brotherhood died alongside the military in clashes with British forces, brought more disruption to Cairo than anything in its modern history. As I wrote for the *Seattle Times*, the first several days of protest were met with skepticism by my neighbors. The protesters were seen as "rich kids from Heliopolis." And no one I spoke with was on Facebook. (Or at least no one admitted as much). These protests, in contrast, tore right through the neighborhood. The imam at the giant Sayyida al-Zeinab Mosque, which stood on the opposite end of my block from Tahrir Square and was divided from the latter by the fortress-like Ministry of Justice, broke precedent with the decades' long practice of reciting a *khutba* that had been preapproved by Al-Azhar, the leading Islamic authority in the country, and instead, through an electric sermon that denounced outright the oppressive standards of the government's emergency laws, called over the loudspeakers for an *intifada*, an uprising, that called the people to the streets. It was the beginning of the end for the Mubarak family.

What was not going away, however, was Egypt's military establishment. On Saturday, January 29, the tanks rolled into the city with great fanfare as the cheering masses celebrated their deliverance from the chaos that had engulfed their normally peaceful megalopolis. I documented this eerie repetition of history by walking the streets and photographing the outpouring of support for the troops, who, like in 1952, were welcomed as liberators in the face of a foreign power. Somewhat confoundingly, however, the foreign power in 2011 was in essence the United States and its principal co-conspirator, Facebook.

At first glance that narrative did not look right. Friends and neighbors had warned me that rumors were spreading about American spies behind the chaos. I watched the state news channels and read in the state newspapers about how the US State Department, in 2008, had funded "pro-democracy" groups and online activists in Egypt to the tune of $141 million and was pressured by the minister of international cooperation, Fayza Abu al-Naga, to cut funding for ten organizations on the grounds that they were "not registered NGOs."[39] I had no illusions about the fact that Washington was glomming on to Silicon Valley's digital revolution, but the allegations, which appeared in the January 29 edition of the largest state newspaper, *Al-Ahram*, and came from a translated article in Norway's *Aftenposten*, which had been supplied the information by Wikileaks, did not exactly fit with the dozens of interviews I conducted in Tahrir Square. Young couples, older adults, college students, and just your average drifter—all expressed great disillusionment with the Egyptian state in one way or another: their inability to find housing and to start a family, to find a job despite having college degrees, and to break free from the sense of nepotism and repression that gripped the nation. When I put the question to Glassman, the top official behind the United States' Public Diplomacy 2.0 initiatives from George W. Bush's second term, whether he thought his efforts somehow helped to foster the Arab Spring, he responded, "In a small way, yes." Then he added, "We certainly gave groups of young people, especially, the confidence that the U.S. stood behind them and that there were other groups around the world that were opposing violence and oppression as well." But the idea that the United States had been behind the uprisings in any deliberate way was a "conspiracy theory," in his words, one supported mainly "by right-wingers who supported Mubarak."[40] This narrative did match my findings, and it spoke to a powerful undercurrent in the Middle East that struck right at the heart of the public diplomacy mission. Sadly, however, it was only apparent to public diplomacy officials like Glassman well after the fact. The irony of the Americans' inability to take stock of this new stage in the war of ideas was that the conspiracy theories, in a small way, were correct. The State Department, through campaigns like the Alliance of Youth Movements Summit and Public Diplomacy 2.0, had planted the seed, in Glassman's terms, for organizations to aspire to "work on their own, organically." But there were no plans to "counter the counter-narrative," as he put it.[41] The United States, in this sense, did not seed the revolutionary events of the Arab uprisings. But, rather, through public diplomacy parasitism, the country helped to ignite the counterrevolution or, at least, made no plans to rebut the weaponization of their best intentions by people like Fayza Abu al-Naga, who, fittingly enough, would become the national security adviser to Egypt's next military president, Abdel Fattah al-Sisi.

Apart from the efficacy of Wikileaks in the timing of the disclosures or the expediency with which regimes—from Damascus to Moscow—capitalized on a stolen cache of State Department cables to create fodder for the counterrevolution, the conspiracy theories about Facebook and the US government were simply the latest turn in an ongoing series of authoritarian responses to the well-documented surge in access to (and use of) information and communication technology that occurred throughout the Middle East and North Africa during the second half of the Bush administration and early Obama years.

Between 2008 and 2011, mobile phone subscriptions in Egypt, for example, doubled from 50 percent to 100 percent of the population. Internet use expanded to include a quarter of the population by 2011, up 10 percentage points from just three years before.[42] In response to the explosion of citizen journalism that occurred at this time, the Egyptian government began formulating a defensive containment strategy against the spread of social media. As early as 2007, citing the "fight against terrorism," the Mubarak regime created a "special department" within the Ministry of Interior to monitor Internet traffic.[43] In 2005, the government also purchased a controversial Internet surveillance technology known as deep packet inspection (DPI), giving it license not only to monitor online traffic through keyword searches but also to outsource the technology.[44]

In the months following Mubarak's ouster on February 11, 2011, it appeared Egypt's surveillance state was waning. Competing factions capitalized on the ostensible vacuum of authority to flood the airwaves with a deluge of free expression. State security clearances previously licensed by the General Authority for Investment, an arm of Mubarak's innermost circle, were no longer required. The Ministry of Information was briefly abolished and sixteen new satellite channels appeared, a surge that represented, by one estimate, a 30 percent increase in Egyptian broadcasting overall.[45] But the opening was short-lived. Unlike Tunisia, where legislators famously moved to "neuter" the Tunisian Telecommunications Agency—the country's principal organ of Internet surveillance—the Egyptian government retained much of its footing from before the uprising.[46] In spring 2014, a cache of documents ostensibly leaked from the Ministry of Interior suggested DPI technology was still in use. Published in the staunchly pro-Sisi newspaper *al-Watan*, the leak, which emphasized the Ministry's use of an "iron grip" technology for combating the "security risks" posed by "social networks," was as much a piece of propaganda for the government's populist rhetoric of "law and order" as it was a notice for the public good.[47] Still, it served as a reminder of just how entrenched Egypt's defensive posture had become.

By late 2016, the Egyptian regime had passed legislation allowing, among other things, the revocation of media licenses by a new, all-powerful regulatory body called the Supreme Council for the Administration of the Media. Several months later, the government blocked access to a score of international websites and news organizations, including Al-Jazeera, the *Huffington Post* in Arabic, and *Mada Masr*. The crackdowns occurred despite the Obama administration's continued advocacy for Internet and press freedom, a dynamic that helped set in motion an unprecedented freeze in relations between the two countries. Simultaneously, however, as the administration put pressure on Egypt and others to maintain the brief window of free expression that emerged in the midst of the protests, the State Department was resituating itself for a new decade of conflict in the long war of ideas. Public Diplomacy 2.0 was quickly being redefined as CVE, and the once-generic digital diplomacy of the later Bush years, which focused on youth empowerment and broad civil society reform, was being refocused on the war on terror. Part of this shift, as Nicholas J. Cull wrote, was the result of an internal dynamic between Obama's secretary of state, Hillary Clinton, and his secretary of defense, Robert Gates, who was in favor of redirecting some of the DoD's strategic communications activity back to its natural home in the State Department.[48] But it was also the case, as Fernandez observed during an August 2012 congressional hearing, that the Arab uprisings had reignited the propaganda organs of al- Qaeda while creating space for a more virulent form of recruitment. "One of the most fascinating things which has happened over the last year, which I am sure you are well aware of," Fernandez told the House Subcommittee on Terrorism, Nonproliferation, and Trade of the Committee on Foreign Affairs, "We have had the most dramatic, incredible political events in the Arab world in decades, maybe in centuries ... and al-Qaeda had nothing do with it. . . . You had millions marching, and al-Qaeda was not part of that conversation. This drives them crazy. This drives them crazy in the propaganda, that basically the most important thing that is happening in the Arab world, and al-Qaeda is basically an Arab organization, and they are completely irrelevant to that issue."[49] Across the postrevolutionary Arab world, a new wave of digitally adept al-Qaeda affiliates—most under the banner of the Ansar al-Sharia movement, which, fueled in part by prison breaks and mass amnesties that were spitefully enacted by the outgoing regimes in Tunis, Cairo, and Sanaa, had formed amid the uprisings—were flooding the Internet with a new, embittered kind of propaganda that mixed high-resolution filmmaking with active measures in the streets. It was not lost on the entrenched security regimes in Damascus or Cairo or within the Washington defense-intelligence establishment that the greatest number of foreign fighters to join ISIS in eastern Syria and western Iraq came from Tunisia, the single Arab nation to have sustained some of its revolutionary gains, particularly in the realm of media.

GAMING THE NETWORK

In response to this postrevolutionary landscape where al-Qaeda affiliates were gaining thousands of views on YouTube and Twitter, the Obama administration created its first major vehicle for CVE: the Center for Strategic Counterterrorism Communications (CSCC).

Officially launched in 2011 with a budget of just $6.8 million, the center, as described by Richard Stengel, was the brainchild of Hillary Clinton and CIA director Leon Panetta. The idea, Stengel wrote, was to "combat the communications of a radical terrorist group that was using revolutionary new techniques to get out its message: al-Qaeda."[50] Identifying bad actors in the realm of social media now trumped more benign, if wide-sweeping, efforts to expand access to the Internet or empower civil society actors.

Located within the State Department and drawing on resources and personnel from across the intelligence and defense communities, the center was envisaged from the start as an inter-agency incubator in the war of ideas 2.0. The CSCC coordinator reported to the Office of the Under Secretary for Public Diplomacy and Public Affairs and was responsible for communicating with relevant counterparts from across government, including the Bureau of

Counterterrorism. In his book, *Information Wars: How We Lost the Global Battle Against Disinformation*, Stengel, a former managing editor for *Time* magazine who became Obama's under secretary for public diplomacy in 2014, described a series of failed efforts to staff the leadership role of the new center, which, he wrote, was seen as a "problem child" from the outset. "It was underfunded, its mission was poorly understood, and it became an orphan within the State Department. The National Security Council sought to manage it. The Department of Defense resented it. And Foreign Service Officers avoided it. It was originally seen not as an entity that created content, but one that helped coordinate and inform other entities in government about what al-Qaeda was up to on social media."[51]

Fittingly, the directorship of the center ultimately fell to none other than Fernandez, the storied public diplomacy officer who, not long before, was facing scrutiny for having called US policies in Iraq "arrogant" and "stupid" in an interview with Al-Jazeera.[52] Having expanded to include some forty-five personnel, twenty of whom were native speakers of Arabic, Urdu, and Somali, the CSCC was in essence a "one-stop propaganda shop," in Fernandez's words.[53] Charged with identifying, confronting, and undermining "the communications of Al-Qaeda" through "digital outreach," the CSCC's activity, as he saw it, was threefold: Staff were instructed to conduct "intelligence and academic analysis of the audience" (i.e., understanding what "al-Qaeda was up to on social media," as Stengel wrote); form a "plans and operations team" for the creation of "non-digital CVE communication strategies" (i.e., videos to be disseminated on Al-Hurra or elsewhere); and house the Digital Outreach Team (DOT).[54] The CSCC's motto was "contest the space," and its objective, according to Fernandez, was not simply to observe or inject discourse but to confront jihadist supporters online through mockery and harassment.[55] The tone became most pronounced in the center's heavily scrutinized short video "Welcome to ISIS Land," which, along with graphic images of violence and exploding mosques, taunted viewers to "run ... not walk to ISIS land."⁵⁶ That video, Fernandez wrote, was "mostly mocked" but "widely seen" (some one million viewers found it online); it was the work of the center's most visible tool, the DOT, or "*Fariq al-tawwasul al-Elektroni*" in Arabic.

Initiated in 2006 as a project within the Bureau of International Information Programs (IIP), the game for the DOT was to "educate and raise awareness about the dangers of violent extremist groups like Al-Qaeda and ISIS and to dispel their false narratives."⁵⁷ The group started its outreach, however, through the production and dissemination of a series of innocuous propaganda videos in the aesthetic vein of the "Shared Values" campaign.

"*Amrika—Amerika al-Wilayat al-Mutahada al-Amrikiya Tarahab bikum*" (America, America, the United States Welcomes You), the DOT's first video, was about seven minutes long. It offered a mostly uninspiring stream of stereotypical Americana—a woman watering her flowers, farmhouses, galloping horses, and smiling schoolchildren—over a synthetic soundtrack vaguely reminiscent of the music of Aaron Copland. Over the first fifteen years of sitting on YouTube, its primary venue, the video was viewed just four thousand times. But that video represented a grain of sand in the sea of content that, by 2008, was now flowing across the United States' online propaganda apparatus.

The DOT distributed on YouTube over nine hundred short videos during its twelve-year run. "America, America," like much of the DOT's early fare, reflected content similar to what could be found in Al-Hurra's promotional videos. As a testament to the State Department's ultimate indifference to the campaign at the time, the video attracted only three oblique comments; one read, in Arabic, "Welcome to the United States of America, which killed more than 7 million Red Indians, two million Vietnamese, 140 Japanese, one and a quarter [million] Iraqis, and half a million Afghans. Welcome to the land of human rights ^___^ Greetings from George W. Bush."⁵⁸ Subsequent videos over the first year included Ramadan greetings from American imams, a simulated video illustrating the collapse of the Twin Towers, and dozens of curated messages from American officials. Just fourteen of the nine hundred videos garnered over one hundred thousand views, most of which likely came from a much smaller group of users.

As an act of public diplomacy, the project remained largely under the radar. The few commentators who took note of the work emphasized the group's online engagement activity. In 2009, Al-Jazeera described the effort as an attempt by the United States to supply "counter-misinformation" online.[59] The few outside researchers who looked at the project also concentrated on this aspect of the group's work. As observed by Lina Khatib, William Dutton, and Michael Thelwall in a 2012 case study of the DOT's online engagement surrounding Obama's Cairo speech in 2009, the group's focus on "countering negativity and misrepresentation" meant that its work was more reactive than proactive. The project's emphasis on "contesting the space" became even further pronounced following the Arab uprisings.[60]

As noted by Fernandez, the nature of DOT's output underwent a significant shift in focus following the outbreak of protests in late December 2010. The Arabic wing of the organization was repurposed under the direction of the CSCC, in February 2011, for the specific task of countering terrorism rather than "generally defending US policy in the Middle Eastern social media space."[61] And the volume of output was increased dramatically. In 2011, according to Fernandez, the Arabic unit of the DOT published twenty-one separate videos; it did twenty-seven the following year and nearly triple that amount over the next three years.[62] Generated through the remixing of open-source content, most of the DOT's output was derivative. Beginning in 2011 and continuing through its final post in 2019 (*"Jira'im Abu Bakr al-Baghdadi fi satawwar,"* [The Crimes of Abu Bakr al-Baghdadi by the Books]), footage from al-Qaeda and ISIS's own propaganda videos, including the latter's filmed execution of a Jordanian pilot, and the displacement of Yezedi minorities in Iraq, featured heavily in DOT productions. The overarching message of "The Crimes of Abu Bakr al-Baghdadi"—the group's last video—was that ISIS was fundamentally anti-Islamic and, in the end, al-Baghdadi, the group's leader, could not escape "the hand of justice."[63] An earlier video, one of the group's most popular, depicted the killing of Osama bin Laden through a montage of footage from news outlets around the world. The video implied that Muslim populations around the world were rejoicing over the news of bin Laden's death and that al-Qaeda was auspiciously absent from the Arab Spring. Spliced together with samples of commentary from outlets like Russia's RT, China's NTDTV, or the Saudi-backed Al-Arabiya, the key function of the video appeared to be the deployment of a series of "narrative landmines," small samples of information that, regardless of context or veracity, could be used to direct the flow of public opinion in much the same manner as a rumor.[64] In just three and a half minutes, viewers learn that bin Laden's location was exposed by Ayman al-Zawahari, al-Qaeda's number two; that he used "herbal Viagra supplements"; and that he encouraged his children to live comfortable lives in the West.[65] Recorded sound bites and interviews with the proverbial "man on the street" paint bin Laden as a thug and a cancer on Muslim society. Spliced through third-party sources, and tactfully separated from the fact that the United States was so concerned about the perceived martyrdom of bin Laden that his body was buried at sea, the video became the group's most viewed work, attracting some 155,000 views on YouTube by the end of the year.[66]

Focusing on the divisions in Arab society and separating al-Qaeda from the people for whom the organization purported to fight, the anniversary video of bin Laden's death provided a useful blueprint for future DOT productions. Short, fast, and tactfully edited, the video helped to establish, among other things, what Fernandez described as the *"fitna"* or "sectarian strife" narrative of DOT productions. The emphasis on division and the implicit contradictions of a *takfiri*, or excommunication movement such as ISIS or al-Qaeda gaining influence amid mostly devout Muslim societies was a hypocrisy that information warriors like Fernandez could not resist. The emergent "civil war" between al-Qaeda and ISIS in 2014 fed neatly into the *fitna* narrative that the DOT deployed to maximal effect throughout the bloody days of Operation Inherent Resolve.[67]

Integral to this strategy was the notion that in the pursuit of narratives, the rest would follow. "*Fitna* is an Arabic word meaning 'strife,' temptation, or sedition but has a heavy politico-religious context based on its use in the Qur'an and Islamic history," wrote Fernandez.[68] For the government's self-described "propagandist-in-chief"' and overt crusader of the Western cause, there was no denying the appeal of one-upping the jihadists by way of their own rhetorical fantasies. Drawing a distinction between Islam and radical Islam closely followed suit, as did parody; while it was often artless, it peppered the fringes of many DOT missives. For Fernandez, however, "Measuring the Unmeasurable"—meaning what was classified from public view—was a fruitless cause. Moreover, as he cautioned in an article for the 2020 *Sage Handbook of Propaganda*, "Large numbers of views do not necessarily translate into influence." It was an understatement, to be certain, and not least in the case of the DOT, which produced its missives overtly.[69]

WHITE TO GRAY

On the heels of the DOT, another campaign was unfolding across the Potomac at the Springfield offices of the Middle East Broadcasting Networks (MBN), an organization that Fernandez would also soon lead. In 2015, MBN began its first full-scale online media hub. Replete with social media links, television programming, a radio component, "call in/social media segments," and a bouquet of Iraqi-centered content mostly concerning Islamic extremism and "positive, alternative narratives" to the jihadist paradigm, *Irfaa Sawtak* assumed a light gray posture in the war of ideas: its Facebook and About Us pages assigned attribution to MBN; its stories and posts did not. Its website and Facebook page were organized around weekly themes. A documentary series, "Delusional Paradise," featured testimonials of families impacted by terrorism;

another featured videos on "how to protect children from extremist ideology"; and yet another emphasized "how the lack of reforms in Arab countries" contributed to the growth of extremism.[70] The Iraqi hub was followed shortly thereafter by *Elsaha*—a dynamic, Egypt-based platform that featured stories mainly about arts and culture in Egypt—and *Aswat Magharabia* (Maghreb Voices), a CVE-oriented news website focused on North Africa (Algeria, Libya, Tunisia, Morocco, and Mauritania). Its emphasis was social movements and "humanitarian stories" and like earlier iterations of American propaganda the site doubled as a curatorial hub for other public diplomacy messaging—from *Share America* posts on US history to *Al-Hurra* reports on the conflicts in Libya or the migration crises in the Sahel.

As with the CSCC, Broadcasting Board of Governors (BBG) officials measured the impact of the new media hubs by tracking the number of people who viewed the content. The mantra, as Under Secretary of State for Public Diplomacy Judith McHale articulated of the government's initial forays into social media, was "We need to be in the marketplace."[71] The higher the number of views, the rationale went, the greater the return on investments. BBG's *Fiscal Year 2017 Performance and Accountability Report* noted that *Maghreb Voices* generated "nearly 5 million reactions, 800,000 comments, and more than 440,000 shares" during its first year.[72] "One Alhurra TV video contradicting ISIL's ideology received more than 300,000 views on its Facebook page," reported the Office of Inspector General. A video mash-up "compiling the views of and interpretation of Islam was viewed 160,000 times, shared by 1,400 people, and 'liked' 3,900 times," according to the OIG.[73] While the online hubs represented an innovative and visually compelling space for the distribution of American propaganda, the relevance of such metrics with the aim of 'countering violent extremism,' or the psychology of those viewers who chose to share the material they encountered, remained uncertain. When the Facebook page of *Irfaa Sawtak* first launched in summer 2015, a commentator from Bani Suef in Egypt wrote these words on its home-page banner (which showed a digital animation of a man spray-painting the words "*Irfaa sawtak*" on the side of a destroyed stone building):

> Peace be upon you. I am a disabled young man, and I have a sister who has the same disability. She and I were a heavy burden for our father until he died last October. My name is Ali Muhammad Mabrouk. I hold a BA in Law with a good grade, from 2013.
> I want a job opportunity that I can live from. Doesn't a disabled person have the right to have a family? And if he has the right, how can he provide for this family?
> Therefore, I appeal to every person with a compassionate heart to convey my voice to the officials, so that God may provide happiness for the entirety of his [earthly] family.[74]

Eight years later, the sole comment attached to the home-page image, now a collage of modern-looking Arabs (a man smiling while playing the guitar, a young woman with a large froth of hair, armed men in camouflage gear, and children at a refugee camp), read "The cells that manage this page: were they trained in Israel or within the American embassy?"[75]

Such markedly disparate discourse—an empathetic plea for human rights on one hand and a conspiratorial lament about US/Israeli ties on the other—has long accompanied the reception of American propaganda. The new media hubs accelerated the energizing, yet often polarizing effect of American intervention into foreign media spheres.

"A CONSTANT AND CREATIVE PRESENCE"

The tinted lens of "intersubjective communication," in Habermasian terms, is inevitable to the formation of any public sphere—digital or otherwise. But the public world envisioned by US influence operators in the war on terror was ubiquitously burdened by the pretense of an objective "truth," in the first instance, and, in the second, the often-occluded politics of its information interlocutors. Quantum Communications, one of several firms that helped shape the de facto sympathies of Al-Hurra's Shiite aligned early days (see chapter 3), entered the fray of CVE research with a white paper declaring the top two reasons for an individual's radicalization into ISIS were the group's "defense of Sunnis against apostate and cruel Shias [sic]" and its capacity to wage jihad as "a defensive form against predatory Shia rulers in Damascus and Baghdad."[76] As alternatives to ISIS, the Shiite authorities in Damascus and Baghdad, through the lens of Quantum Communications, were welcome alternatives. Myriad think tanks, lobbyist firms, industry experts, and academics glommed on to the arms race for countering violent extremism. Oftentimes, the solution to the problem reinforced the relevance of the resolver. For Monika Bickert and Facebook, the solution to radicalization on Facebook was more Facebook. Proprietary tools emerged to capture a percentage of the proverbial "firehose" and reams of government-contracted white papers proliferated across government-shared drives. From 2015 to 2017, USAID and the State Department's Bureau of Counterterrorism and Countering Violent Extremism allocated $497 million in funding to overseas providers for the purpose of countering violent extremism.[77] As shown in a government audit from 2019, approximately 33 percent of that funding was directed toward public diplomacy initiatives, which included things like two million dollars in foreign assistance for the creation of an "animated '1001 Nights' television show in Dari/Pashtun" for the purpose of promoting "literacy and civic values among youths"; $2.5 million for the production of season six of *Baghch-e-Simsim* (Sesame Street); and numerous "online media" platforms intended to "amplify credible voices" and highlight "alternative narratives."[78] While effectively continuing the Bush-era legacy of outsourcing public diplomacy, it was unclear, for example, how children's television programming in Afghanistan or a youth club in Lebanon reversed the pull of radicalization. Or, why, exactly, children watching television in Afghanistan—or youth going to clubs in Lebanon—were considered more susceptible to radicalization than any other group. As with the solicitation of documentary proposals for the gray space of satellite content distribution, public diplomacy grant-making, writ large, tended toward the adaptation of the "least bad option." Nowhere was this paradigm more striking than the freewheeling and cash-incentivized universe of Gulf-led CVE initiatives.

Started in 2012 as an outgrowth of the Global Counterterrorism Forum, the United Arab Emirates' Hedayah Center represented a lucid register of the Gulf Arab monarchies' response to the 2011 uprisings and a symbolic sort of endgame in the United States' long war of ideas. Little more than a lavishly funded seminar series for Middle East policy experts and practitioners in the fields of counterterrorism and public diplomacy, the center helped set in motion a new normal in Washington, one in which the US government provided credibility and political cover for the UAE's entrenched authoritarian regime that in turn bankrolled the Obama administration's increasingly bloated CVE agenda. The initial results were underwhelming by most accounts. Thinly drafted policy papers were printed and distributed among participants who shuffled about the marbled interiors of Abu Dhabi's glimmering hotels and office spaces. DC-based "experts" trotted out platitudes on "credible voices" and "strategic narratives," and UAE web designers collected glossy blurbs for the website. The UAE's Washington Embassy home page featured glowing praise about the Emiratis' prowess in CVE from the likes of General Anthony Zinni and General Joseph Votel—both former commanders of US Central Command. General James Mattis, the secretary of defense during the first Trump administration, was also featured on the embassy's home page endorsing the "strategic relationship" of the two countries ("very broad, very deep and very strong").[79] The *Washington Post* later revealed that Mattis also "secretly" advised the UAE on its war in Yemen. Cooperation between the countries in the theater of war dated back to the first Gulf War, according to him.[80] The UAE's role in the second front on the war on terror emerged more gradually, but by the end of the 2020 it had become an all-encompassing force. The UAE was America's indispensable partner in the battle for hearts and minds. The inverse was not always apparent.

In 2015, with personnel and "shepherd guidance" provided by the US State Department and the intelligence community, the UAE launched *Merkaz Sawab* (the Sawab Center). It was a larger, more expensive, and slightly grayer iteration of the DOT.[81] Larry Schwartz, then deputy assistant secretary of state for public diplomacy in the Bureau of Near Eastern Affairs, was among those who brokered the creation of the center, which, as he recalled, was started with about a $20 million contribution from the UAE. The effort was "tangible" in his words and a direct extension of the Obama administration's gripping consternation over the rise of the so-called "ISIS Twittersphere" and the government's seeming paralysis in the face of the mighty tech giants that controlled its fate.[82] Using Twitter and Facebook, the Sawab Center, based out of Abu Dhabi, hired scores of contractors that in turn generated a relentless stream of social media in the name of CVE. The Emirati state-media organ *Al-'Ain* reported that the center's posts had attracted "over 280 million views during its first five months."[83] By its fifth anniversary, the UAE's Washington embassy was claiming its posts still received on average half a million views a day.

The strange irony behind this operation—apart from the neat symmetry of its numbers (half a million views a day, with "over 50 campaigns exposing DAESH lies," in five years; "8 million followers from over 80 countries!") was that the Emiratis were simultaneously deploying a more covert campaign—also based in Abu Dhabi and built on the back of US expertise—that effectively worked against the interests of US policy.[84] In 2016, Jenna McLaughlin, writing for *The Intercept*, reported on an Abu Dhabi-based firm, DarkMatter, that, beginning in 2015, had begun hiring scores of international cyber experts, including from the United States, for a range of hacking and espionage activities across the Emirates and throughout the region. As one former employee described for McLaughlin, the tools being deployed, including those developed by US firms, could "track, locate, and hack basically any person at any time in the UAE."[85] A later report noted that, in addition to suspected ISIS targets, employees hacked into the accounts of "human rights activists, journalists and political rivals" to the Emirati regime.[86] Comparable to the technology and objectives of other governments throughout the region, the UAE operation stood apart in its apparent level of cooperation with Western intelligence services, particularly from the United States. The reporters Christopher Bing and Joel Schectman, writing for *Reuters* in January 2019, and with the assistance of a former intelligence analyst for the National Security Agency who became a whistleblower on the operation known originally as "Project Raven," described how former US intelligence officers working on the project believed they were "on the right side of the law because . . . supervisors told them the mission was blessed by the U.S. government."[87] The employees—including at least two former DoD officials and "a senior technical adviser to the NSA"—were correct to a certain extent.[88] A 2022 notice issued by the State Department indicated that the former US officials hired by DarkMatter had effectively violated the Arms Export Control Act by "furnishing defense services," including "electronic systems, equipment, or software that were specially designed for intelligence purposes that collect, survey, monitor, exploit, analyze, or produce information from the electromagnetic spectrum," to a foreign-owned company.[89] The violation occurred, however, in late 2015 and early 2016 when the UAE's contract for services was transferred from a Maryland-based recruitment firm, CyberPoint, to DarkMatter, which, according to the State Department notice, was not operating pursuant to International Traffic in Arms Regulations (ITAR). The company denied any direct connection to the UAE government but, as McLaughlin reported, its offices were located "two floors away from the country's intelligence agency, the National Electronic Security Authority [NESA]," and its senior vice president was a former official of NESA.[90] Whether Project Raven was officially sanctioned by the US government is uncertain; however, the State Department's notice effectively acknowledged that former officials in possession of ITAR-regulated "computer network exploitation (CNE) expertise" were indeed authorized to furnish "cyber services" to the UAE government via CyberPoint.[91] Also unclear is whether the State Department's collaboration with the Sawab Center was also subject to ITAR regulations or had any overlap with Project Raven. The continuation of the partnership for another four years, despite fallout from the cyber-espionage campaign, seemed indicative of the United States' seemingly unshakable reliance on a Gulf country whose respective dependence on US support was surface level at best.

Sawab Center posts, like much of the digital aesthetics produced by third-party providers in the name of the US government and in the service of countering violent extremism, reflected a narrative gloss similar to other iterations of American public diplomacy. Scenes of ethnic and cultural pluralism, religious tolerance, and human rights flowed across its pages. But the core of its dossier remained a series of triumphant nodes from within the canon of the war of ideas. Here were "former radicals and Muslim victims of terrorism," the "Islamic response to extremists," and "de-glamorized" images of ISIS in abundance. The objective, similar to the output of the DOT, was the inversion of ISIS messaging and the creation of ostensibly "positive narratives" atop the deconstructed aesthetics of ISIS's Dantean tableau.[92] Images of violence and weaponry proliferated across the center's Facebook and Twitter accounts. Women and children, often tearful and grieving, featured heavily, as did overt symbols of sectarian identity—a glowing "mosque of the week" flashed across its feed for all fifty-two weeks of the year. Ancient churches and monasteries, including some destroyed by ISIS, were also a common motif. Meanwhile, artistically rendered portraits alongside words of wisdom from Sheikh Zayed bin Sultan, the former ruler of Abu Dhabi and father of the current royal cohort, wove seamlessly amid stock images of US and Western icons such as Martin Luther King Jr., Albert Einstein, and Picasso's dove of peace. The effect was a "constant and creative presence," in the language of President Obama's former special envoy for strategic counterterrorism communications, one drawn from and seemingly destined for an infinite web of automated diplomacy.[93]

6
ENDGAMES

Libya, site of the largest oil reserve in Africa, point of departure and brutal detention for hundreds-of-thousands of migrants seeking passage to Europe: the country carried a light footprint in US foreign policy, its relevance next to nonexistent in American public discourse. Not so in Europe. In France, the rise of a far-right ideologue and his principal vehicle CNews had buoyed Libya to prominence. "*Vous devriez bénir Poutine*" (You should praise Putin), exclaimed Eric Zemmour in reference to the conflict in Libya, "because he's the only one that will truly take on the Turks."[1] In the years following the collapse of the Gaddafi regime in 2011 and amid descent into civil war, the North African country became a rhetorical black box for populist bombast in the West, a litmus test for one's hostility (or not) to Islamism (read "the Turks") and support (or not) of the far-right cause (read "Poutine"). The public discourse in Europe created an opening for American diplomacy, and for a brief moment the country's portfolio rose in Washington. Calls of support by the Biden administration for an UN-backed ceasefire, in October 2020, and demand for an end to foreign military interventions helped lay the groundwork for a joint military agreement between the country's divided factions.² A so-called "5+5 Action Plan" brought together members of the Russian, French, Emirati, and Egyptian-backed Libyan National Army (LNA) in the East. UN and Turkish-backed forces under the Government of National Accord (GNA) in Tripoli were to help usher in the country's safe political passage and to secure a presidential vote scheduled for December 2021. The ceasefire held but a more elusive battle raged. Libya's nebulous media ecosystem and the foreign-based actors that fueled it had sowed the seeds of chaos and doubt. The will of the country's feeble judiciary to implement election laws was crushed. Indefinite postponement became the only solution.

Virtually from the moment of its ruler's demise, dragged bleeding and unconscious across the hood of a car, Libya became the site of a proxy communications war. The Arab uprisings of 2011 unleashed an unprecedented boom in foreign and domestic mediatization, narrativization, and politicization. As Marc Lynch observed, "The wide-open Libyan arena created too many opportunities for outside powers to ignore."³ The country became ground zero for a new breed of information warfare. Most of the new media outlets to appear in Libya were created by entrepreneurs; some had political aspirations and some had a vested interest in shaping the country's new power struggle.⁴ But the country was an attractive site for a range of actors. Hundreds of print, radio, and television broadcasts appeared where previously only a handful existed.⁵ Cell-phone technology, combined with the lifting of restrictions on access, production, and distribution helped catapult Internet use tenfold between 2011 and 2017.⁶ From near silence to sheer cacophony, the country's information ecosystem descended into anarchy. As former National Transitional Council member and CEO of the ascendant Libyan media group Al-Wasat, Mahmud Shammam, described for the *New York Times*, the country's most "deadly war" was being fought with "lying, falsifying, misleading and mixing facts" and being waged by "electronic armies . . . owned by everyone and used by everyone, without exception."⁷

It was Vladislav Surkov's "fifth world war" in Shammam's eyes: a "non-linear war of all against all" in which the winner writes history as it happens.[8]

Social media became especially fertile ground for such warfare. As reported by Meta (formerly Facebook), Libya became the target of multiple coordinated inauthentic behavior (CIB) campaigns. In August and October 2019 and again in January 2021, the social media company released information describing operations in which individuals disguised as local news organizations, public figures, and average citizens disseminated a barrage of information designed to demonize the UN-backed GNA in Tripoli while reinforcing the image of the rival LNA and its leader, Khalifa Hifter, in the East. The LNA, which launched a full-scale invasion of Tripoli in an attempt to unseat the Islamist-led government there, enjoyed the support of multiple outside parties, namely Russia, the UAE, Saudi Arabia, and France. When Donald Trump came to power, he signaled his support for Hifter despite the official and ultimately prevailing position of his own State Department. It recognized the GNA.[9]

Meta traced the 2019 CIB operation to individuals in Saudi Arabia associated with the Saudi government and two self-described private media groups located in Cairo and Abu Dhabi, respectively.[10] As reported by the *New York Times*, the Egyptian company New Waves was run by a retired military officer and operated "from a military-owned housing project in eastern Cairo."[11] Two months later it was revealed that Russia was also conducting an extensive digital interference campaign across many of the same platforms and to much the same end. According to researchers at the Stanford Internet Observatory, all of the Facebook and Instagram accounts used in Russia's Libya operation were administered from Egypt.[12] In 2020, an ostensibly separate operation in which scores of faux-Facebook accounts pushed pro-Muslim Brotherhood information was attributed to operators in Morocco, Turkey, and an individual in Egypt, who, quizzically, maintained a LinkedIn account advertising his skills in digital marketing.[13]

THE WEIGHT OF CONSENSUS

The use of Facebook in Libya's information war was significant not least because the social media network was the third most popular website in the country, following Google and YouTube. Moreover, it had quickly become a predominant source for news consumption. The three most visited Facebook pages in Libya over spring and summer 2021 were news and information sites, two of which were part of a single conglomerate, *218TV* and *218NEWS*.[14] Based out of Jordan and broadcasting over Nilesat, *218* appeared functionally separate from the most obvious poles of the conflict. Its broadcasters struck a liberal demeanor, and the commentators often included members of American think tanks who expounded on geopolitics in mostly neutral terms. Yet the organization remained inextricable from the country's proxy communications war, a minor star in a rapidly expanding universe.

Both *218TV* and *218NEWS*—named in reference to the anniversary of the 2011 uprising—were part of a network of sites that featured news and information almost exclusively about Libya. The network also included the Jordan-based satellite channel *Libya's Channel* (libyaschannel.com), the Jordan-based online news site *Al-Marsad* (almarsad.co), the Egypt-based websites *Al-Wasat* (alwasat.ly) and *Bawaba Africa* (afrigatenews.net), and *Akhbar Libya* (libyaakhbar.com), a news aggregator site whose Facebook managers were based in Yemen and three other undisclosed locations. Like *218*, each of these media sites were located outside of Libya and their funding sources remained undisclosed. The network was highly synchronic; the five sites posted and reposted near identical stories in rapid succession. However, the ideological slant of some was more pronounced than others. *Bawaba Africa*, or *Afrigatenews*, for example, carried an unapologetically Russian slant. The website was run by a Libyan editor in chief who, citing Kremlin state media, claimed Russia was the key player for "balancing" Libya and that Saif al-Islam al-Gaddafi, the Kremlin's preferred candidate who was wanted for war crimes by the International Criminal Court in the Hague, was the answer for "stabilization."[15] The website promulgated stories that the president of Turkey, Recep Erdoğan, was on a mission to Turkify Libya through Islamist proxies and that along with Western allies, Turkey would make Libya into the next Syria, that is, a scene of mass carnage. This latter claim was promulgated by an adjacent heavyweight to the obscure network of offshore media channels, the Emirati satellite giant Sky News Arabia. There, the obscure editor in chief of *Afrigatenews* was featured, on-air, in an interview that was subsequently reposted on the Russian state-media outlet Sputnik with the title " 'Idlib, Libya' . . . Turkey is following the lead of ISIS in the west of the country." The Sputnik article in turn was reposted on *Afrigatenews* and on Sky News Arabia, too; neither provided attribution.[16]

The term that emerged to describe this circle of myth-making was "information laundering." Much like the criminal technique used to hide money, narratives in this game were repurposed and proxied through obscure online sources. The effect was that of a nail in the coffin of the proverbial truth, a musty corpse of an idea lying buried beneath the weight of an ostensible consensus.

While more discernable than covert CIB operations, these loosely disguised networks of common affinity became invaluable to the soft power objectives of the same foreign actors who were forced to curtail their hard-power operations in advance of the elections. Russia's largest satellite news producer, RT, frequently amplified the reporting of channels such as *218*, which gained legitimacy when quoted and reprinted by outlets like *Al-Wasat*.[17] The UAE used myriad online proxies (*Al-Marsad* and *Libya's Channel*, among others) to disguise their position. Once directed toward a critical flashpoint, networks like these became more than capable of impacting the tenor of the conflict.

A LIBYAN BLOCKBUSTER

Consider Tarhuna. The town in Western Libya, which became the subject of a UN fact-finding mission for possible war crimes after mass graves were discovered in 2020, fell into the crosshairs of the network's web in July 2021 as the phrase *"muqatala Mohamed al-Kani"* (The Killing of Mohamed al-Kani) catapulted to the top of *Al-Wasat*'s "keyword gap," a designation used by Alexa Analytics (the once preeminent tool for mapping online traffic) that meant *Al-Wasat*'s competitors (*Al-Marsad*, *218*, and *Afrigate*) were gaining traffic from use of the phrase. The network, in effect, had been activated to corner a narrative. Anyone searching Google for information on the topic in Arabic would likely be directed to one of its sites.

But the BBC and other media outlets were on the ground covering the situation as well. As reported by the journalist Tim Whewell, al-Kani had been the leader of an infamous clan that controlled the remote Libyan town for well over a decade. He was suspected of switching sides in the 2018 battle for Tripoli by supporting Hifter and the LNA.[18] The latter ultimately recognized the Kaniyat clan as a "regular component" of its military, and Russia, via its satellite and online news giant RT, referred to the group by their own designation: the "9th Brigade."[19] The largest "share of voice" for the phrase, after Facebook, was owned by the aggregator site *Akhbar Libya* (libyaakhbar.com), another satellite in the *218* orbit whose top stories were from *218NEWS*, *Afrigatenews*, *Al-Marsad*, and a website called *Al-Mashhad al-Libi* (almashhadlibya.com), which, operating out of Egypt, shared direct audience overlap with the obscure website *Al-Jamahiriyya*, the former state flagship during the rule of Muammar al-Qadhafi that had been taken over by a Russian-linked firm in 2019.[20] RT reposted the *Al-Mashhad al-Libi* article verbatim, making it go viral. *Afrigatenews* also replicated it for good measure. As for the story itself, the claim was that al-Kani, according to Mahmoud al-Misrati ("a source close to the LNA"), was killed in Benghazi after LNA commanders attempted to serve an arrest warrant based on "crimes he had committed during his affiliation with the Sarraj government and the GNA."[21] Unbeknownst to readers, al-Misrati was also editor in chief of the LNA organ *Al-Hadath*. The "Killing of Mohamed al-Kani" story was therefore a closed-circle operation between Russian, Emirati, and Egyptian influencers in the service of the LNA cause.

If anyone missed the original article concerning al-Kani and the mystery surrounding the massacre at Tarhuna, they could have found the same narrative by tuning in to the Russian movie franchise *Shugalei* (also spelled *Shugaley*). Based on the clandestine maneuvers of the real-life Russian "sociologist" Maxim Shugalei, who was imprisoned for eighteen months in Libya after interviewing and polling on behalf of Saif al-Qadhafi, the franchise crystalized the strategic objectives of the real-world Wagner group, a shadowy Russian militia with whom Shugalei had been associated.[22] *Shugalei 2*, which premiered on RT and YouTube in September 2020, opened with a depiction of the mass grave site at Tarhuna before flashing to a golf course where three Americans discuss pinning the blame for the massacre on Hifter and the LNA. ("Same strategy we used in Kosovo," remarks one of the Americans.) The film goes on to implicate Fathi Bashagha, interior minister of the Tripoli-based GNA and a hostile enemy of the LNA.[23] With sweeping vistas of Tripoli and shadow-drenched dungeons, *Shugalei* helped situate the Libyan paradigm within the aesthetic logos of a distinctly violent and increasingly prolific anti-Islamist and anti-Western imaginary. RT billed the movie as a documentary and produced it on-site in next to real time. Its depiction of a brutal Muslim Brotherhood government in Tripoli operating out of a hotel and collaborating with Sadistic Salafi jailors and nefarious American agents was as much geared toward an Arab audience as a Russian one. An advance headline from the UAE's Sky News Arabia described it as a "film that tells the suffering of the Libyan people under the weight of terrorism."[24]

THE AFRICAN BARGAIN

Robust as the Libyan campaign was, many of the techniques deployed to execute the strategy of denigrating one side to prop up another had been in play for decades and were hardly unique to the Russian, or now Egyptian, Turkish, Emirati, Saudi, or French playbook. Like a bloodier *On the Road in America*, Shugalei and his exploits in Libya were the work of an independent company, "Aurum LLC."[25] That its CEO was none other than Yevgeny Prigozhin, founder of the Wagner group and a prime mover in the Kremlin's covert influence industry, was of little interest to the show's mass audience that watched its opening night in primetime. The *Shugalei* production also tapped into another time-honored tactic in information warfare by recruiting a small cohort of Hollywood actors to record short testimonials calling for Shugalei's release. As described by *Business Insider*, the actors, including Charlie Sheen and Dolph Lundgren, seemed to stumble over the pronunciation of the Russian's name, suggesting the scripts they were reading had been just lightly rehearsed.[26]

Film and TV had long been central to the Kremlin's playbook.[27] In the 1980s, the Soviet's predominant vehicle for the germination of disinformation abroad was the TASS news agency, a transnational organization that dominated the Russian media sphere as well as its overseas markets for decades. The former United States Information Agency (USIA) official Alvin Snyder noted that TASS, along with Novosti, a "so-called 'unofficial' news agency" that "served up the most blatant Soviet pap to the developing world," had offices in 126 countries by the mid-1980s. The organization was publishing "books and pamphlets in more than fifty languages," and it sponsored the travels of "thousands of journalists and government officials to the Soviet Union each year." But the signature tactic of TASS and Novosti was the cultivation of client networks that reproduced TASS stories for a fraction of the syndication price coming from Western counterparts. As Snyder wrote, "The authoritative voice of the Soviet government could boast over six hundred clients—newspapers, radio and TV stations—many of which were in cash-starved developing countries."[28] US officials were so alarmed about Soviet disinformation that the USIA established a dedicated "public relations group"—in Snyder's words—to study the problem and to "gauge the impact of Soviet propaganda around the world."[29] What became known as the Active Measures Working Group (AMWG) represented the first organized effort on the part of the US government to alert targeted communities to the presence of disinformation while also exposing some of the underlying tactics of Soviet influence operations. Little more than a "weekly meeting,"[30] the objective of the interagency group, which was led by the USIA officials Herbert Romerstein and Todd Levanthal, was quixotic at best, not least because the disinformation they sought to expose was being fueled by a Kremlin propaganda machine that by the end of the Reagan administration was estimated to be running on a budget of three to four billion dollars, "conservatively put."[31]

America's post-9/11 public diplomacy reboot inspired a new generation of Russian pap. As with the United States' resurrection of its postwar posture, Russian active measures gained new life in the war on terror. The proximity of the countries' information playbooks provided a foil for one another, but still key differences remained. From the Cairo Packaging Center to the offices of Al-Hurra in northern Virginia, American propaganda relied on proxied locals to filter the information through their own outlets and their own languages. Like Sputnik or RT, VOA and other syndicates sponsored by the Broadcasting Board of Governors replayed quota-driven stories and buried attribution beneath the small print. But while American attacks on Soviet policies during the Cold War centered on instances of human rights abuse, or other peculiarities of the totalitarian system, TASS and Novosti operations in the global South amplified false claims about American use of the AIDS epidemic as an "ethnic weapon" or "toy bombs" being sent to Afghanistan to "maim children."[32] The United States Agency for Global Media (formerly the BBG), the State Department, and other American public diplomacy outfits had been propping up social media networks for nearly a decade by the time Libya's proxy war came around. But the revelations of CIB and its deployment by foreign powers—Egypt, Russia, Saudi Arabia, the UAE, and France, most vividly—were distinct from US campaigns in the sense that the sites backed by the United States Agency for Global Media disclosed, however obliquely, their connection to a foreign government. American-backed networks such as the Sawab Center were presumably operated in good faith by humans as opposed to bots. But bots were indeed present within US information operations (see "WebOps"), and the use of proxy sites for the dissemination of ideologically biased or outrightly fabricated information was also not alien to the American playbook. As the career Foreign Service Officer (FSO) Larry Schwartz explained candidly, "We've been interfering in people's elections for a generation . . . placing stories in people's papers, this is not new stuff."[33] The United States pioneered many of the tactics on display in Libya. Still, the equivalences were mainly false.

RT RISING

Consider RT. Launched in 2005 with an investment of approximately thirty million dollars, Russia Today, as it was initially called, emerged as part of a suite of public diplomacy initiatives designed to reestablish Russia's footprint on a global stage and to challenge the perceived ubiquity of the Anglophone media sphere.[34] In 2009, following Russia's disastrous invasion of Georgia, the Kremlin rebranded the network in an apparent bid to obscure its ties to the Kremlin and to enhance its ability to propagate the Russian line on a global stage.[35] The rebranding of Russia Today to RT preceded an expansion of its broadcasting languages to include Spanish (2009), followed by Russian, German, and French (2012, 2014, and 2017). The creation of new offices in Washington, DC (2010), the UK (2012), and other undetermined locations followed suit, as did new broadcasting mechanisms including a dedicated "documentary" channel in 2011, and, in 2013, the video production unit Ruptly, which the Global Engagement Center described as "a full-service global video news agency."[36]

Similar to the Americans' reboot, the Arabic-speaking world was at the center of the Kremlin's new posture. RT Arabic, just the second channel to be created after English, in 2007, was by many measures the largest player in RT's bouquet of foreign-language networks. Where Al-Jazeera and Al-Hurra, by 2020, were transmitting across five satellites, RT Arabic was on eight, including in war-torn Yemen. As reported in a 2017 Intelligence Community Assessment and described by Mona Elswah and Philip Howard of the Oxford Internet Institute, the Kremlin was thought to be spending some $190 million per year on "distribution of the channel in hotels and via satellite and cable broadcasting."[37] The effort corresponded with a massive push to influence print media in the Arab world through the establishment of Sputnik in 2013. This latter initiative, according to the Washington Institute of Near East Policy researchers Anna Borshchevskaya and Catherine Cleveland, grew exponentially over its first few years of operation, adding "more than eighty native-speaking Arabic writers" across some fifty odd countries. Sputnik's newswire service, Borshchevskaya and Cleveland noted, provided "multiple delivery channels through an FTP server, an online news terminal, and email."[38]

Far from arbitrary, the Kremlin's Arabic-language propaganda apparatus emerged in direct response to the presence of American media in the region, including state-funded initiatives such as Al-Hurra and Radio Sawa. As part of the launch of Russya Segodnya in 2013, Vladimir Putin described the new investments—already exponentially larger with RT being allocated a reported three hundred million dollars in 2011 and fielding some twenty-two bureaus around the globe—as an attempt to "break the Anglo-Saxon monopoly on the global information streams."[39] The Kremlin's doubling down in investment on its overseas propaganda corresponded to the global surge of pro-democracy protests following the outset of the Arab uprisings in late 2010 and would increase over the years ahead. The nature of its expansion, however, reflected the persistence of a simmering arms race over new avenues of technology in the long war of ideas.

Traditional satellite news media—no great prize by the end of 2020—was swamped already in the Arabic context with a superabundance of stations competing for eyes. The much-coveted youth audience had shifted decisively to online consumption and the satellite technologies once pioneered by Worldnet were rapidly being replaced by more efficient and cost-effective terrestrial circuits.[40] Amid this context, a large survey conducted by Gallup on behalf of the BBG in December 2013 showed RT commanded just 1.4 percent of audience share among the adult population in Egypt—the region's largest audience—compared to the 14.9 percent reportedly enjoyed by BBC Arabic and the 4.7 percent and 2.2 percent controlled by Al-Hurra and Sky News Arabia, espectively.[41] Even in the absence of Al-Jazeera which Egypt had banned in the wake of the uprisings, the rival propagandists were barely skimming the surface of the region's largest television audience. The Americans seemed to perform better on satellite TV in Egypt as well as Iraq, the most populous country in the *Mashriq* (or Arab east) where Al-Hurra was actively competing with Al-Jazeera and BBC Arabic as the most watched foreign network in the country.[42] But the battlefield was shifting and with it the tactics necessary to reach hearts and minds.

In 2015, on the sidelines of Putin's first post–Arab Spring visit to Cairo, Dimitry Kiselev, the director general of Russiya Segodyna, the parent company of Sputnik, signed a memorandum of understanding with the chairman of the board of directors at *Al-Ahram*, Egypt's oldest state-run newspaper and still the flagship organ of the Egyptian state, which laid out the principles of a new content-sharing agreement.[43] While details were never reported, it was clear the arrangement involved the placement of Russian state media on Egyptian state and semistate media platforms. The material included both original content from Russian outlets—Sputnik primarily—and reproductions of Western media including Reuters, the *New York Times*, and Agence France-Presse, as translated and provided by Sputnik. The initiative corresponded with a surge of Russian-Egyptian cooperation that included everything from Russian investment in Egypt's offshore gas complex, Zohr, to the construction of a five-million-square-meter industrial zone near the Suez Canal. Deals were reportedly made for the construction of Russian-built nuclear reactors, and joint sorties were conducted near the border with Libya.[44]

Also similar to the Cold War, the new media agreements accompanied stepped-up programming across the board in the realm of public and cultural exchange. By 2020, Russia was sponsoring about a hundred Egyptians to study in Russia, a significant uptick from the previous decade but a gesture fully comparable to the Soviet era.[45] Similar patterns extended across the Middle East and Africa where such exchanges often precipitated material cooperation between key sectors of the economy. In Syria, where Russia had intervened in the country's civil war on the behalf of the al-Assad regime in Damascus, "Russian linked NGOs" were setting up Russian-language training centers and summer camps in Moscow for the families of regime loyalists.[46] As part of the much-touted second Russia-Africa Summit (i.e., the Russia-Africa Economic and Humanitarian Forum) in 2023, Putin claimed that thirty-five thousand students from across Africa were studying in Russia and that another 4,700 would join in 2024.[47] The objective, he explained, was the creation of a " 'Russian-African' consortium of technical universities" dubbed "Africa's Mineral Reserves" that, led by Saint Petersburg University, would develop "joint training of specialists" as part of a perceived push to harness Africa's "natural resources sector."[48] Free Russian classes administered through university-affiliated "Open Education Centers" saw a tenfold increase in enrollment in places such as Côte d'Ivoire, Ghana, and Nigeria. As reported by Martin K. N. Siele for *Semafor*, approximately nine hundred people enrolled in the state-sponsored language classes in Kenya alone. By the mid-2020s, the Kremlin promised to have launched Russian-language centers across twenty-eight countries in Africa.[49] In reporting on the phenomenon, Siele drew comparisons to the rise in popularity of Chinese classes across Africa through the Confucius Institute, but a more tangible point of reference was the American paradigm of public diplomacy. Here again was the Kremlin's answer to the Department of State's American Spaces (also called American Corners or Binational Centers) with their "open internet access," "American English language courses," the "debate clubs," "cultural events," and "professional skills training."[50] As with the Glasnost years, when "thousands of journalists and government officials" traveled to the Soviet Union, when "Third World journalists" (in Alvin Snyder's words) passed through "media training centers in Russian and Eastern bloc countries" and learned "print media journalism" at the Werner Lamberz Institute in Berlin and "radio and TV skills" at the Center of Professional Education of Journalists in Budapest or the Julius Fucik School of Solidarity in Prague, the Kremlin, through its Ministry of Foreign Affairs and state-media apparatus sought to mirror what the United States was doing by providing more of the same.[51] But the reciprocity was both more and less than a proverbial "taste of the West's own medicine." To the naked eye, Russian soft power evinced a parallax view of American public diplomacy. Where the State Department's public diplomacy grants, its resilience building, or media training prioritized "truth" in reporting, Kremlin state-media practices championed "doubt." "Question More" read RT's slogan. Apposition to the truth as reported from the West was the only sure sign of objectivity.

The *Al-Ahram*-Sputnik agreement, the first in a wave of similar partnerships across Africa, the Middle East, and Asia epitomized the Kremlin's new posture. On *Bawaba al-Ahram* (or *Ahramgate*), the online platform of the Egyptian state news giant, about seven hundred articles from Sputnik had appeared by late 2019. At first the Egyptian outlet attributed the articles to its Russian supplier, but it discontinued the practice after the first four years. Like many of the content-sharing arrangements brokered by Kiselev and colleagues across the global South, Egypt's mighty *Al-Ahram* was now effectively an information laundering device for a foreign state power. For Egypt, through a Cold War lens, counterbalancing its relationship with the Americans—including its peace treaty with Israel—naturally spoke of a certain level of engagement with the Kremlin. The ideological prerogatives of the Cold War had changed, but the financial imperatives driving Egyptian cooperation had not. News production in Egypt was dying by the time President El-Sisi came to power. The inordinate requisites of the twenty-four-hour news cycle, the endless streams of competition, the mobile revolution, and the sheer indifference of the average citizen to news in general created a perfect storm for the country's storied newsrooms. RT and

Sputnik aptly exploited the crisis by providing a lifeline to editors in the form of instantly available and linguistically sound content. Although editors were unaware the translations were usually doctored, Russia's supply chain, with Western items included, promised increased traffic to the host country's website.[52]

Across many of these countries, but most notably in Africa, Russian paramilitary forces were also gaining a greater foothold. In Libya, some two thousand mercenaries contracted by the Wagner group were thought to be fighting alongside Hifter's LNA by September 2019.[53] Major deployments of Wagner forces appeared in the Central African Republic, Republic of the Congo, Burkina Faso, Mali, and Mozambique. In Sudan, a country described by Russia's chairman for the Committee on International Affairs of the State Duma as occupying "the most important geographical position on the African continent and in the Arab world," about five hundred mercenaries from the Wagner Group, many flown directly from Crimea and on flights operated by Russia's 223rd detachment, were thought to be operating from a camp in southern Darfur.[54] Russian disinformation operations, exposed through a 2021 Meta report on CIB, played heavily in the favor of the ousted Omar al-Bashir's brutal Rapid Support Forces (RSF) and in particular its leader and UAE-backed warlord Mohamed Hamdan Dagalo ("Hemedti").[55] RT Arabic, as well as Sputnik and RIA Novosti, lionized Hemedti and amplified ancient regime organs like the Sudanese News Agency by reposting their reports and driving traffic to their social media accounts.[56] Along with reinforcing Hemedti's counterrevolutionary drive for power through disinformation, the Wagner Group's primary function in the country was support for mineral extraction in the form of security and logistics for the Russian companies Meroe Gold and Kush, both of which maintained large gold-mining operations in Sudan. (The Russian head of security for Meroe Gold was apprehended by a local police unit in the town of Atabara as he tried to illegally smuggle seven kilograms of gold out of the country.)[57]

While the details of the relationship between RT, Sputnik, or other major Russian state-news operations and Wagner remained murky, the coinciding activities of the overt and clandestine entities echoed earlier Cold War practices. According to Snyder, upwards of 70 percent of TASS correspondents were believed to be KGB agents.[58] Covert disinformation operations tied to Russian media-sharing agreements also ran rampant during the Cold War. In the 1980s, USIS officials in Nigeria detected 1,250 articles containing Soviet disinformation. Local writers contracted for the operation later told US officials that most often they simply added their names to "ghost-written" articles in exchange for "bonuses."[59] Flash forward to the second decade of the twenty-first century and we find Yevgeniy Prigozhin, head of Russia's preeminent vehicle for the coordination of Russia's covert disinformation in the Internet Research Agency (IRA), now leading Wagner and spearheading a host of disinformation operations around the globe. After the exposure of the IRA's most audacious campaign, the so-called "Translator Project" of 2016 in which Russian information operatives, or "trolls," flooded the American social media sphere with a tsunami of false and misleading information, Kremlin strategists shifted their center of operations from St. Petersburg to Africa and elsewhere. In a nod to its Cold War blueprint, two major hubs used to target the 2020 electionwere cash-incentivized offices in English-speaking West Africa, Ghana and Nigeria.[60] Both countries were also major hubs of investment for US public diplomacy. In 2020, the latter received nearly five million dollars in public diplomacy spending, much of it geared toward digital media initiatives and cultural programs.[61] The topsoil looked similar but the fauna was distinct. From one seed came white papers and seminars on human rights violations, women's health, and democracy. The other, strange fruit, bore embellishment, hyperbole, and what one dissident RT reporter described as "hate preaching," a tool of persuasion already cornered in the American market by commercial operators.[62]

The effect in the aggregate of Russia's expanding web of proxied and covert mouthpieces was a dramatic uptick in traffic to Russian-backed channels and the ideologically infused worldview they inevitably carried.

By 2018, RT Arabic's Facebook page boasted "14.9 million followers" and was functioning as part of a network of "themed pages, including *RT Play Arabic* (video), *RT Arabic Knowledge*, and *RT Arabic Sport*," all designed to mimic the effect of consensus and to push the Kremlin's worldview. The massive number of followers, as Borshchevskaya and Cleveland pointed out, could easily have been "padded" by "fake accounts."[63] But the outcome was the same. By July 2020, according to Alexa Analytics, which ranked websites comparatively and based on a site's total number of visits, RT Arabic was the second-highest-ranked news site in the Arab Middle East. In Egypt, its website ranked slightly ahead of Sky News Arabia and trailed only the viral news outlet *Youm 7*, an Egyptian site closely aligned with the government that frequently reposted material from RT. Al-Jazeera.net, the website of the once-dominant Qatari satellite station, trailed RT Arabic online in every Arab country but Algeria. This trend followed RT's already heavy presence on the world's most visited Internet site, YouTube. There RT became the first channel to reach one billion views in 2013. By fall 2020, the channel could boast more than ten billion views. RT Arabic, which launched its YouTube channel in 2008, quickly gained the highest number of dedicated subscribers (5.11 million) of all of the RT subsidiaries, including RT Español (4.33 million) and RT English (4.07 million). Of the major Arabic-language news stations, including Al-Arabiya, Sky News Arabia, BBC Arabic, Al-Jazeera, and France 24, RT Arabic's number of subscribers trailed only BBC Arabic (7.47 million) and Al-Jazeera (7.7 million), both of which started on YouTube before RT Arabic, in 2005 and 2007, respectively.[64]

CAT AND MOUSE

Among the entities tracking the resurgence of Russian propaganda around the globe was the United States' Global Engagement Center (GEC), an analytical offshoot of the bygone battle for hearts and minds and a new central player in the war of ideas. In 2016, on the heels of the opening of the Sawab Center and in the wake of the country's tumultuous presidential election, US Congress formalized the GEC through bipartisan legislation—a rarity in itself—and situated the mostly defense-funded organization within the State Department, which was a nod to its relevance to public diplomacy and to the closing of the books on America's longest wars in Iraq and Afghanistan.

Launched with an approximate budget of twenty million dollars (quickly to be tripled) and drawn together by a staff of over eighty FSOs, civil service employees, former VOA editors, and defense-intelligence specialists detailed from the Pentagon, the GEC was designed to address the new breed of disinformation, or "state-sponsored manipulation of information," that, somewhat ironically, was now flowing across many of the same platforms the United States had once championed.[65] Unlike its predecessor, the Center for Strategic Counterterrorism Communications (CSCC), whose target was primarily nonstate actors, the GEC's focus from the outset was China and Russia. But the mandate was expansive. By 2021, the group's budget had grown to nearly $140 million and its personnel base had increased by 40 percent. As a public diplomacy offshoot, the GEC was charged with the development of "resilience," among other things, an emergent category of civil society preparedness, that, like countering violent extremism (CVE) before it, became a loosely defined organizing principal for confronting "malign influence and propaganda"—the sort that helped shape the 2016 presidential election in the United States and was now cascading across much of the globe.[66] As noted by the researcher Alina Polyakova of the Center of European Policy Analysis before a hearing of the Senate Committee on Foreign Relations, Prigozhin's IRA was thought to have reached "as many as 126 million people" in the United States through its network of faux and autonomized Facebook and Instagram accounts.[67] Cynical by design, the preferred modus operandi of the St. Petersburg group was the impersonation of American citizens and movements—Black Lives Matter especially—with the aim of imploding civil society from the inside out through hyperbole, instigation, and active measures in the form of calls to protest, vandalism, and violence. Data analytics was considered the GEC's principal tool for building resilience (also described at times as media literacy or, later, "pre-bunking") to such campaigns, but the mostly career FSOs charged with executing the mission, as well as those like Polyakova whose Center for European Policy Analysis was a subgrantee of the GEC, were ultimately reliant on the goodwill of the social media companies that controlled the open-source information used to generate the data they discovered.[68] None had expertise in hermeneutics, and few among the subject matter experts were trained beyond a generalist background in political science, anthropology, or other social science fields unrelated to the study of propaganda. The result, in the end, was little more than a cat and mouse game between GEC analysts and other entities in the resilience sphere who watched and recorded as malign influencers multiplied and technologies evolved. It became a vicious cycle of propagation, in the form of faux data, and escalation by way of data accumulation. The war zone of ideas became flooded. The battle for hearts and minds no longer required hearts or minds—only battle.

The National Security Council had identified the GEC as the lead organization on the government's CVE strategy and, indeed, many of its original personnel cut their teeth challenging ISIS and al-Qaeda propaganda online through initiatives like the Digital Outreach Team. As first articulated by former Under Secretary for Public Diplomacy and Public Affairs Richard Stengel, the goal of the GEC was to amplify "credible voices"—the preferred jargon of the State Department's CVE posture—and to empower "a global network of partners" as a kind of carbon copy of the coalition countering ISIS: NGOs, foreign governments, and "religious leaders" that could pose as "credible messengers to target audiences."[69] But emerging amid the early days of the Trump administration with its explicit vitriol toward all things soft power (the position of under secretary of state for public diplomacy sat vacant for 316 days in the first Trump administration), the GEC's mandate as a mechanism for countering ISIS appeared equal parts smoke screen and substance.[70]

Aware of the group's potential impact on their own field of operations, Trump's first secretary of state, Rex Tillerson, and his heavily bloated front-office staff stalled on signing the required memoranda that would unlock the GEC's initial funding while rewriting the directives for the group "ad nauseam."[71] Fittingly, among the GEC's first initiatives under the Trump administration was the Iran Disinformation Project, which quickly gained headlines and was ultimately shut down after reports surfaced that it was spreading its own disinformation and trolling American human rights workers and journalists—a regular target of the Trump administration. In a cynical twist of fate, the trolling also included the *Washington Post*'s Jason Rezaian, a former political prisoner in Iran and a fierce critic of the Ayatollah's regime.[72]

The elected officials who drafted the legislation behind the GEC, however, were focused on the purpose of the interagency group and the impetus behind its creation. "Here in the United States, we have extensive documentation that Russia conducted a coordinated interference campaign in our 2016 elections," said Senator Rob Portman, a long-standing Republican member of Congress and one of the architects of the 2016 legislation. "It is the central nexus of our work to create this effective shield against the falsehoods that threaten the integrity of our democracy and other democracies."[73]

Following the impeachment of Donald Trump and his defeat in 2020 to Joe Biden, the GEC hardened its mission's original intent, establishing dedicated "teams" for China, Iran, and Russia as well as units focused on Africa, Latin America, and the Near East. In 2022, Congress appointed James P. Rubin as the GEC's special envoy and coordinator. It was a somewhat ironic testament to the GEC's throwback posture. A former assistant secretary of state for public affairs under the Clinton administration, Rubin had been an early advocate for concentrating the myriad iterations of public diplomacy that had blossomed during the Gulf War under the singular umbrella of the State Department. That move, which included, as Nicholas Cull observed, the dissolution of the Active Measures Working Group and the eventual return of the group's sole expert on disinformation,

Todd Levanthal, to the Voice of America, set in motion the disaggregation of the USIA in 1999.[74] Yet the GEC, with its myriad regional teams and mixed emphasis on the analysis and exposure of Russian disinformation—while significantly smaller in scope and lacking the capacity to activate its discoveries through Worldnet or other channels of distribution—had become the closest thing the government had to an International Information Committee since the bygone days of the USIA. Its creation was not without cause.

"BLACK LIVES" BY RT

On June 30, 2020, in Utah, a small group of purported Black Lives Matter protesters stood across the street from armed counterprotesters for an event in the State's capital, Provo. Sometime in the late afternoon, a SUV drove slowly through the crowd on the protesters' side of the street. A white male wearing a mask and carrying a weapon approached the vehicle before firing two rounds through the passenger-side window, prompting the car to speed away. The following morning, at 3:26, a Twitter account associated with the online website *Deseret* posted footage of the incident with a description of the shooter as a BLM "protester/rioter."[75] Later that day, at 5:26 P.M., RT posted the tweet on its TweetDeck (now X Pro) and quickly thereafter produced a microstory highlighting the group's Twitter feed. The video posted by *Deseret* arrived first on RT Arabic's YouTube channel, which, along with an ocean of auxiliary websites, rocketed the post into viral orbit before finally arriving at primetime, on July 2, on Fox News' Tucker Carlson show. Mystery surrounded the motivations of the alleged assailant and the origins of the protest and counterprotest (a local news outlet in Provo reported that the protest had not been organized by Black Lives Matter Utah).[76] But the scene, which worked to invert the weaponization of vehicles as an act of domestic terrorism by framing the driver as a victim, was compelling enough to fuel the narrative that "violent criminals [were] being used as a militia by the Democratic Party to seize power."[77]

A similar dynamic unfolded in Portland, Oregon, just a month later. On August 1, a group of protesters set fire to the American flag using a Bible. The Russian-backed video unit Ruptly filmed the incident and disseminated it through social media, where it was eventually picked up by the US senator Ted Cruz and Donald Trump Jr., who tweeted the video as proof of the protesters' belligerence. RT vigorously refuted a report in the *New York Times* that described the video and its viral spread as an example of "disinformation," noting that the footage was unaltered and the story's title, "'Peaceful' Portland Protesters Burn Bible & Flag, 24 Hours After Torching Pig's Head in Cop Hat," was "merely a straightforward description of the video's contents."[78] Whereas the English-language article described an ambiguous number of "protesters" setting fire to "bibles" and "flags," however, the Arabic-language rerun of the story explicitly claimed that demonstrators had burned "dozens of copies of the Bible and the American flag" and that they had done so out of anger that "Christ was White."[79] For the station's global audience, including, notably, those in the Middle East and North Africa, such reporting bolstered existing bias that democratic activism provided a cover for organized chaos. As one commentator remarked on the *Deseret* footage posted on RT Arabic's YouTube channel, "This is how the so-called Arab Spring began with self-declared demonstrators calling for freedom before they begin shooting civilians and police officers."[80]

For anyone who missed RT's coverage of the Black Lives Matter protests, the station's documentary channel provided an alternative means of consumption. Launched in April 2019, and later subtitled and rebroadcast in Arabic under the title *Hayat al-soud mohema* (Black Lives Matter), RT's *Black Lives* series offered a master study in long-form propaganda. Fashioned in the tradition of the infamous Soviet-era film *Man from Fifth Avenue*, written by the Communist Party spokesperson Leonid M. Zamyatin, in which the New Yorker Joseph Mauri leads audiences on a panoply of American homelessness and poverty, *Black Lives* complemented the aesthetic universe of the *Shugalei* franchise and helped crystalize the worldview of RT's current cineastes.[81] Through dense urban shadows, heavy musical background, and emotive lighting, the series presents itself as a raw documentary. But it features no shortage of artistic intervention. Free of voice overlays or omniscient narration, the documentary is told through a series of interlocutors (a "KKK member," a "barber," a "street musician"); most of whom are Black and with the exception of several pastors, an obscure defense attorney in Baltimore, and a social media influencer in Philadelphia, none of whom have any public stature or notable expertise. As with RT's tendency to hire untrained journalists for its news broadcast and B-list stars for its publicity, the use of unknown witnesses afforded the filmmakers the blank slate they needed to create the Black America RT wanted.

Unambiguous but mostly implied, the underlying message of the series is that the American political system is a failure and the country is collapsing in on itself, bit by bit. Like all good propaganda, the series is based on a grain of truth. Crime, poverty, and incarceration—the three predominant themes of the series—indeed disproportionately impact the Black community in the United States. But projected overseas, through its network of social amplifiers, the analogical value of the film supported the Kremlin's narrative of law and order in the face of democratic anarchy. Unlike the overt propaganda flowing from the Trump White House (one thinks of the staged event in front of St. John's Episcopal Church in Washington, DC, in which Trump appeared silent before cameras and displayed a copy of the Bible), law and order are absent signifiers in RT's *Black Lives* series. In the place of the state, one finds armed Black men patrolling unnamed streets; housing blocks bordered and shuttered; drug addicts clamoring for money; and Black bodies lying in the streets of an unnamed city. Speeches by President Obama or an image of his profile stenciled on a subway wall are deployed against scenes of hopelessness and despair. Similar to the operation that unfolded in Libya, where operations on the ground combined with filmmaking and coordinated online media campaigns to bolster the law-and-order narrative of Khalifa Hifter and the LNA, the Kremlin's American canvas promulgated a mostly pragmatic line. Rather than

Islamist extremists, the American condition is the primary antagonist in *Black Lives* by RT. The absent signifier of law and order is delineated by a series of false dichotomies, as the series' titles make plain: "Black Lives Matter Versus the KKK"; "Failing Schools Versus Community Education"; and "Choosing Between Good and Bad in Black U.S. Neighborhoods."[82] Hyperbolic and polarizing yet ostensibly "real," RT's *Black Lives* evinces an apocalyptic vision of America, a world of "carnage" as Trump ominously described in his 2016 inaugural address, or the "bloodbath" he promised in advance of his 2024 campaign.[83] The final episode, which was shown in July 2020, elucidated the global aspirations of the series' propaganda. In lengthy interviews with Imam Abdul Musa—a little-known but controversial American figure who, among other things, was banned from entering the United Kingdom for his advocacy of "terrorist violence"—and the Virginia-based pastor Steve Parson, who has been a vocal supporter of Donald Trump, the final episode, titled "Black Lives: Trap. Why Civil Rights Aren't Enough to Make the American Dream Come True," evokes a burgeoning civil war in the United States. The source of the strife, as Parson explains, is political: "The Democratic party uses it [the label of racism] to keep Black people voting for them," Parson says amid images of a BLM march in New York. He explains, "Actually, it's the Democratic platform that I call the slave master today, meaning what? We're going to provide for you [Black Americans], we're going to be the ones who help you. We'll give you this, we'll give you that. . . . It's just to keep control over them [Black Americans]."[84] Musa also invokes the Democratic Party, and Obama in particular, for having secretly instrumentalized the subjugation of Black Americans. His testimony serves an overt function. Speaking off-camera amid a sequence of images depicting inner-city misery, decay, and armed resistance, he proclaims, in response to Obama's early message of hope, that the "American people have already lost hope but they haven't lost the kind of hope to rebel." Fear, then, of the democratic experience but greater resentment still over the kind of anarchy it may welcome is a promise foretold by the Islamist, and *criminel utile*, Musa.[85]

Appearing amid the Trump campaigns of 2016 and 2020, there was no shortage of irony to the Kremlin's deployment of such timeworn themes. For more than half a century American propagandists had been trying to reframe the Black experience as a story of deliverance. And for more than half a century the Kremlin had been countering the narrative through proxied voices within the Black community and soft sympathizers abroad.[86] Neither the GEC nor any other federal body in the United States possessed the mandate required to confront the generation of foreign interference on domestic soil—an arcane effect of the Smith-Mundt Act, perhaps, or the expression of a certain political will—but there were no such limitations to the exercise of American counter-communications overseas, or, at least, the bygone spaces of the "non-aligned" world where RT's depiction of the United States was primarily directed.[87] This was useful, in the Internet age, and even more so than in the past. What happens in Vegas seldom stays in Vegas anymore, a phenomenon America's next generation of public diplomats will have to embrace.

CONCLUSION: ZELENSKY'S VILLA

The Kremlin's cynical use of not just the US democratic experience but US-made social media tools to reverse the global tide of democratization found a natural habitat in the wilds of the Middle East's online ecosystem. Russian-backed conspiracy theories surrounding the origins of the coronavirus, American support for terrorism, Nazism in the Ukraine, or American plots to destabilize the Middle East through food insecurity or radical Islam found footing in the Middle East before gaining traction elsewhere around the world, including in the United States itself.

Such was the curious case of "Mohammad al-Alwai" and "Zelensky's Villa." According to the former, a "journalist," the Ukrainian president's mother had purchased a luxurious villa somewhere in Egypt, the fruit of her son's spoils, no doubt, from the war with Russia.

After young Mohammad's story first shown on YouTube went viral, morphing along the way into other villas and also yachts, the semi-state Egyptian news sites *Muhtawa +* and *Al-Mustaqabal*, where the stories first appeared, began reporting on Mohammad's own "mysterious" disappearance—or murder even—by a vindicative Zelensky regime that regularly deployed "physical violence against journalists and public figures with oppositional tendencies."[88] As discovered by reporters for Sweden's national public television broadcaster, SVT, not only was the villa a fabrication, but there existed no record of "Mohammad al-Alawi."[89] When questioned about this curious factoid, the *Muhtawa +* and *Al-Mustaqabal* editor-in-chief Mohammad Bakry apologized for the discrepancy and told SVT one of his young reporters had discovered the story on Facebook. It was a reasonable mistake and the story was taken down. But the fantasy, now circulating across the vast and myriad echo chambers of the RT ecosystem, had found a host of new adherents, including the soon-to-be Republican nominee for vice president, J. D. Vance, speaking on the alt-right podcast the *War Room* and embellishing the story of Zelensky and his "yachts" as part of a larger diatribe against US support for Ukraine's defenses.[90]

Such anecdotes, concocted in part through a host of European and US-backed initiatives, paid testament, ironically, to the overall flat-footedness of government in addressing the spread of disinformation. They also reflected the tendency, as Thomas Rid observed, of mainstream media to perpetuate the "actual effect of a disinformation operation" by attempting to expose it.[91] Other countermeasures were underway, of course, but so was Russian reciprocity. By summer 2018, most of RT's broadcasting frequencies in the United States, which had limited viewership to begin with, were shut down following a directive by the Justice Department that the station registers as a "foreign agent."[92] RT's YouTube channels were assigned the designation, implemented by Google since 2018, of being funded by the Russian government. The RT presenter and Wikileaks founder Julian Assange was detained in London and held for extradition to the United States on charges relating to espionage. And in 2024, the Justice Department indicted two RT employees for "conspiracy to violate the Foreign Agents Registration Act" by attempting to "create and distribute content to U.S. audiences with hidden Russian government messaging."[93] Meanwhile, Maria Butina, a suspected Russian influence operative arrested in the United States who was also charged with acting as an unregistered foreign agent, was given her own show on RT. The American journalists Evan Gershkovich and Alsu Kurmasheva were arrested in Russia on charges similar to Assange and Butina while working for the *Wall Street Journal* and RFE/RL, respectively. The latter, a remnant of America's ideological victory in the Cold War, had been limited to online distribution in Russia since 2012 when the Kremlin disallowed the station the license necessary to broadcast on air. A total ban was imposed, in 2017, after the Russian Ministry of Justice designated RFE/RL and VOA as "foreign agents" of the United States.[94]

CONCLUSION
Eyes and Ears, Hearts and Minds

Much had changed in the two decades since 9/11. Yet the past, it seemed, was never far behind. A far cry from the battle for hearts and minds, the emergent competition with Russia and China in Africa and the Near East was old hat for American propagandists. Gone was the "segmentary lineage system" of the wars in Iraq and Afghanistan—the acute competition for talent and resources that splintered America's voice across agencies and continents. But back was the proverbial battle for the global South, the increasingly less remote reaches of the planet where American access to trade routes and resources still gripped the imagination of policy makers, entrepreneurs, and information warriors alike.

The patronage of credible voices during the Cold War through covert mechanisms such as the Congress for Cultural Freedom (CCF) or the Franklin Book Program, as well as overt vehicles of public diplomacy like the Voice of America or the Fulbright exchange, favored the endorsement of leading luminaries, major artists and scientists, and business tycoons whose proximity to the vanguard spaces of their respective societies helped to fashion a certain global zeitgeist that trended in the aggregate toward American aspirations of self-empowerment, individualism, and freedom of thought. Remnants of this tradition have held on through initiatives like the International Visitor Leadership Program (IVLP) of the Bureau of Education and Cultural Affairs (ECA) or, more poignantly, the International Military Education and Training (IMET) program that is coordinated jointly by the State Department and the Department of Defense (DoD). For nearly half a century IVLP and IMET have sponsored civilian and military leaders on nationwide excursions, speaking tours, or study abroad opportunities on the campuses of the US Army War College, the US Naval War College, or the National Defense University. But like richly planted gardens abandoned by time, failures to sustain the cultivation of these programs and their alumni have created a hotbed of historical weeds: Media leaders who attended a series of talks on countering disinformation through the IVLP only to return home and use their platforms to spread disinformation (see Muhtawa + and "Zelensky's Villa"). Or graduates of IMET who rose to power through military coups before driving their countries toward political chaos (see: Amadou Sanogo in Mali) or the open embrace of Vladimir Putin (see: Abdel Fattah el-Sisi in Egypt).[1] Public diplomacy in the Arab context has a long history of providing an exception to the norm. Sayyid Qutb, the intellectual forefather of the radical al-Gama'a al-Islamiyya and a relatively obscure ideologue in postwar Egypt, embodied the notion, expressed by Ambassador Jefferson Caffery in 1951 just months before the launch of *Al-Sadaqah*, that the "urban masses, militant orthodox religious groups and the fellahin" were as much an asset to American interests in bolstering the region against communism as the country's slim segment of educated elites.[2] But the post-9/11 period suggested this Arab exception had become the norm, as a yet more literalist interpretation of direct engagement with Caffery's urban masses, zealots, and peasants dominated the portfolios of American public diplomacy in Arabic following 9/11. At the risk of oversimplifying, it could be argued that the Arab Spring, as one case in point, epitomized the mostly haphazard and often contradictory continuities of an American propaganda playbook. Emboldened alumni of America's youth empowerment campaigns join in the effort to tear down the walls of dictatorship, while other, new authoritarians, including some also touched by American public diplomacy, emerge to erect more immobile ramparts in their place. Less a segmentary lineage system than an expression of Roosevelt's grapeshot tactic agencies and departments, with limited expertise in their target populations and personnel drawn from no particular pool of linguistic or professional experience, throw spaghetti at the wall to see what sticks, not just for talent and resources but for the philosophical soul of American foreign policy.

The Global Engagement Center (GEC) carried the torch of another troubled legacy in the long war of ideas, namely analytical abstraction in the discernment of foreign public opinion and the prioritization of such abstractions as a point of departure for strategic intervention. "Deploying data analytics to provide early warnings of foreign disinformation to our Allies, partners, and domestic stakeholders" was the GEC's first mechanism for responding to Russian and Chinese propaganda, explained Lea Gabrielle in her testimony before Congress in 2020.[3] A dedicated Analytics and Research Team, as well as a Technology Engagement Team to develop natural language processing tools and many of the same aspirational methods once pursued by the DoD in the global war on terror, grew atop the GEC's ecosystem like fungi. As with previous public diplomacy operations, the GEC created a liaison with Silicon Valley and helped facilitate transnational collaborations aimed at achieving much the same goal: data analytics for the purpose of early warnings. Unlike meteorology, however, the government remained well behind private industry in creating the tools it needed to pursue its aims. In some best-case scenarios, the efforts of the latter were folded into the work of government and redirected toward a more targeted end. Other times, industry simply lost interest or stepped away for lack of commercial gain.

Where the State Department through the GEC, in theory, possessed the capacity to coordinate the country's response to the tsunami of propaganda—Russian, Chinese, or other—now flowing across the news feeds of the world's contested publics, its own engines of content creation remained woefully behind.

Voice of America, RFE/RL, and Al-Hurra—the largest assets in the country's propaganda arsenal—barely scratched the surface of their target countries' public discourse. This was the concern within Congress at least, which, in early September 2024, mandated the Middle East Broadcasting Networks (MBN) to reduce costs at Al-Hurra by twenty million dollars. The company announced a 20 percent reduction in staff, a shrinking of its headquarters in Virginia, and the closure of its principal wartime vehicle, Al-Hurra Iraq.

American influence was no less present than it always was—through culture, film, commerce, and sports—and no less imperfect in its impact on world opinion. Christopher Nolan's *Oppenheimer*, with its apocalyptic vision of American genius, won the Academy Award for Best Picture in 2024; upon its opening in Japan one moviegoer interviewed by the *New York Times* described the film as celebrating "a tiny group of white male scientists who really enjoyed their privilege and their love of political power." Others saw the depiction of scientists celebrating the detonation of the bomb over Hiroshima while waving American flags as "shocking."[4] Yet the once-promising strategy of placing specially designed Arabic-language programming on regional networks as a way to compete with Hollywood's dark angels appeared stuck in neutral as funding vehicles such as the MENA Media Fund from the Middle East Partnership Initiative (MEPI) became tethered to sole providers like Jerome Gary's Visionaire Media whose public portfolio included repackaged fare by Layalina (see: *Confessions from a War*) and a handful of culturally patronizing docudramas filtered mostly through the lens of cosmopolitan Beirut.[5] American politics also stumbled toward farcical repetition as two (near) octogenarian presidents competed for the presidency (a repeat disrupted by the sudden nomination and subsequent failed campaign of Kamala Harris). The ever-powerful influence of political symbolism meanwhile continued to define the government's posture in the Middle East: an unmitigated embrace of the Israeli president Benjamin Netanyahu by President Joe Biden following that country's brutal terrorist attack on October 7, 2023, and US warships in the Red Sea and the eastern Mediterranean.

From a president once described as the "guardian angel of public diplomacy" for his defense of RFE/RL amid the breakup of the United States Information Agency (USIA), an echo of Cold War creativity a la Hajji Airlift of 1952 seemed to break the dark clouds that had settled.[6] With public opinion of the United States in the Arab world plummeting to an all-time low, the Biden administration announced that a "bridge to Gaza," figuratively and literally, would be constructed by the United States and its allies to provide food aid and assistance to the besieged Palestinian population.[7] Al-Hurra, along with the ever-reliable Al-Arabiya, carried news of the announcement along with an AI-generated image of American marines, unarmed, wearing life preservers and standing atop an highway-like platform jutting into the sea. Al-Jazeera posted a story featuring the opposite perspective: Palestinians gazing toward a chaotic shoreline with no sight of *"al-mina' al-Amriki"* in view. RT Arabic used news of the port to further the narrative that behind the war in Gaza was a US plot to relocate Palestinians to Egypt's Sinai Peninsula.[8]

In reality, the humanitarian pier, hastily built and damaged by open waters, was abandoned soon after it started. Meanwhile, the violence in Gaza escalated and the United States' key ally in the region, Israel, faced broad accusations of genocide for its seemingly careless slaughter of innocent civilians. Unchecked foreign influence operations related to the war in Gaza distracted the public gaze from other conflicts, including Russia's invasion of Ukraine, and fueled the tides of social unrest on American campuses where self-inflicted wounds on the left of the country's political spectrum threatened to shape the outcome of the presidential election in places like Michigan and Georgia.[9]

October 7 and the wars that followed were poised to dominate American foreign policy toward the Middle East for the foreseeable future. Yet after two decades of supporting the self-determination of Arab publics, and despite some promising endeavors by the GEC and others to collaborate with allies in the space of media literacy and resiliency, the government had no viable means of communicating its position on the emergent wars or at least refuting some of the more rampant misinformation underpinning a new, global wave of anti-Americanism.

So what was the future of American public diplomacy in Arabic two decades after 9/11? I put this question to Larry Schwartz when I reached out to him once more in September 2024. It was not hard to see why the former USIA official and long-time Foreign Service Officer had risen to the highest ranks of his profession. Akin in some ways to a car salesman—smart, jocular, and mostly convincing—the man could talk. With just a few prompts he naturally carried on for well over an hour, stopping only once his stream of thought was exhausted. Al-Hurra, he posited, was a waste of money and had only made sense at a particular moment in time. Arab viewers, like the rest of the world, he argued, mostly gave up watching satellite news broadcasting long ago, and when they did watch TV, it was hardly Al-Hurra they turned to. Like others I had spoken with for this book, Schwartz was deeply skeptical not only of the United States' multimillion-dollar Arabic language apparatus but also the very premise of US-backed broadcasting. Leadership of the United States Agency for Global Media (USAGM) almost always emerged through political calculations, he noted, and the cultural tone of the studios came to reflect the peculiar worldviews of its executive officers. Some of the journalists I spoke with from Al-Hurra and Radio Sawa expressed similar concerns. Under the leadership of Nart Bouran, one told me, business meetings were held during prayer sessions. Women were expected to wear a hijab in some circumstances, and at other times—as shown in a lawsuit from 2020—they were prevented from doing so while on camera.[10]

There were other, less pessimistic perspectives. Ammar Abdulhamid, whose program on Al-Hurra became one of the "signature" shows of Alberto Fernandez's reboot of the channel following the election of Donald Trump in 2016, expressed his hope that the "restructuring" of Al-Hurra, "the umpteenth" in its "short history," would allow it to "live up to its true potential as well as the expectations of its founders: to become the voice of Arab liberal reformers and to cover developments in the U.S. and around the world in an objective non-partisan non-ideological manner."[11] This latter entreaty, of course, as Schwartz and others also described, suggested the opposite was more often the case.

What distinguished American public diplomacy in Arabic from the work of the proverbial car salesman was precisely its ideological manner, its pitting of subjects supposedly empowered by American investment against those implicitly suppressed by it and the subsequent broadcasting of such liberatory funding as an expression of goodwill. Or the more discrete, less secular prioritization of religion (like Obama's 2009 Cairo speech) as an organizing principal through which to view the Arab world and to communicate the country's values. Such ideological conviction seemed appropriate for the sudden repurposing of the country's peacetime public diplomacy for a wartime posture. Yet little discernable research informed which ideological convictions to prioritize or why some should be considered more effective in shaping public opinion.

During the Cold War, support of the region's rising religious identity movements was conceived in juxtaposition to the ideological counterpoint of communist Russia. In the post-9/11 environment the prioritization of themes such as women's empowerment, human rights, or the protection of religious minorities—topics perceived as antithetical to the ideology of groups like al-Qaeda and ISIS— emerged as building blocks to the war of ideas and were projected toward broad Arab publics that, on the whole, marginalized such extremist currents and would hardly disagree with the value-laden messaging emanating from the State Department. In other words, who was the United States trying to convince in the war on terror and to what end?

Whether one accepts the premise that a war of ideas needed to be waged, the simple fact is that millions of federal research dollars were directed at some of the top scientists in the world for the purpose of understanding the social psychologies of Arab and Muslim societies. Yet the degree to which any of the major findings from Minerva-backed neuroimaging research or any other significant DoD-funded research found its way into American information operations—including the military's psychological warfare campaigns or the State Department's public diplomacy programming—remains uncertain, if doubtful. Of the studies that did appear to inform US broadcasting initiatives, mostly interest group polling in the vein of market analyses and consumer reports, none that I reviewed for this study—including those directly commissioned and overseen by the Board of Broadcasting Governors (BBG) (later the USAGM)—reflected awareness of the government's many studies into specific target populations or the methods of communication that had emerged from those studies as best practice for the mitigation of radicalization. But why should they, one may argue, if US-backed media operations like Voice of America and Al-Hurra were intended simply to function as independent journalism in the tradition of the BBC? Conversely, however, one might ask, why should they not? In 2010, for example, the BBG commissioned a focus group study in Egypt, Morocco, and the Palestinian territories to gauge audience reception to Al-Hurra. The report elicited "several content-related strategies Alhurra [sic] might adopt to increase its visibility across countries and attract new viewers." These included "highlighting Alhurra coverage of the Israel-Palestinian crisis," "increasing the promotion of programs such as Al-Youm and Free Hour and downplaying straight news," "offering more programs that challenge U.S. or local government officials or engage them in debates," "helping viewers solve challenges presented in the news," and "providing more religious and documentary programs."[12] Future Al-Hurra programming appeared to absorb some of these recommendations but with little rationale beyond the singular objective of gaining more of an audience. The war of ideas was waged presumably to tell America's story and to win the proverbial battle for hearts and minds. In practice, however, many of the strategies adopted to meet this mission were geared toward winning eyeballs and ears, which are not the same thing.

Leon Shahabian, a keen observer of American public diplomacy, touched on this problem when we last exchanged emails for this book, in fall 2024. "Commercial broadcasters in the Middle East are at a crossroads," he told me. "They must reinvent themselves for the platform agnostic digital-first media environment where qualitative storytelling will earn them younger viewers across platforms, or they will languish when their advertisers chase the viewers they lose for clinging to legacy programming and systems."[13] MBN's loosely affiliated networks in the region offered the possibility for a more "agile" focus, as the company's new CEO, Jeffrey Gedmin, wrote in his public memorandum to employees announcing the cuts. The "move away from brick-and-mortar," along with investment in AI technologies and "multimedia correspondents," would allow the company to develop its "networks across North Africa and the Middle East," a tantalizing nod to the regionally grounded output of the United States Information Service of old and an echo of what the company's nemeses in the region—Al-Jazeera and RT—had been doing for the past two decades.[14] But it was also a contradiction in terms. Empowering regional hubs promised more narrowcast programming, whereas investment in AI technologies, at least in their current shape, seemed to guarantee the opposite: more soulless digital aesthetics scrapped from existent online sources. While the evolution of American broadcasting in Arabic, precipitated by "congressional unhappiness,"[15] seemed to adopt the notion that more is not necessarily better when trying to build bridges between the world's vast and myriad publics, leadership appeared unprepared to embrace the idea, insisting that less content could still be more if artificially designed and automatically augmented.

A more promising horizon for the future of American public diplomacy in Arabic rests in the available model of the education and exchange programs that have historically garnered greater appreciation among foreign publics and naturally reflect already the philosophy of less is more.

The simple things can feel important for the right people at the right time. That was the idea that occurred to me as I set out to write this book.

It was August 2022, and a late summer downpour raged above the Dulles Corridor as I drove to meet our newest Fulbright fellow: a secondary school teacher from an impoverished industrial city outside of Amman, Jordan. My department hosts half a dozen Fulbright teaching assistants in any given year. They are always, without fail, motivated and inspiring individuals from diverse backgrounds. We mostly leave them to their own devices throughout the year, but they invariably strike up meaningful relationships with students, other faculty, or the strangers who rent them a room. I tended to cover the basics with our Fulbright fellows—teaching plans and sometimes strategy for which graduate programs to consider—but on this stormy afternoon, creeping along Highway 50 with lightning crashing down, this first-time traveler to the United States and I veered toward another subject. We both had lost a parent in the previous year. Both of hers were gone, she told me. Her father had passed suddenly. His last words to her, she said, were الله يرضي عليك (God is satisfied with you). I may have heard the phrase before but never grasped its depth. I was in the habit of disguising my agnosticism while traveling in the Arab world, but as we pulled into the parking lot of a Walmart where I would help her buy a phone, I touched on my own spirituality. Would she take this interaction back to her students in Jordan? Would our exchange help shape hearts and minds in some way? Would it build empathy across cultures? Build bridges for the ephemeral future? I sensed not. Not that she would not try to describe the cultural and spiritual diversity of America but that my story was not really made for mass association, and mass association is what the Fulbright, and American public diplomacy in general, has always tried to generate. Americans are good at science but they believe in God, too. This is the basic message that American public diplomacy started out with. The early practitioners conceived of lots of convoluted and complicated ways of communicating it, but this was always the takeaway. The question of whether the projection of a wholesome America, a glossy, AI-enhanced America, or a righteous America has served Americans well in building bridges with foreign publics remains unresolved and probably always will. No polling can capture such a vast and complex kind of politics. But on that rainy afternoon as we labored over her new cell phone and picked out some groceries and flowers for her to bring to her new hosts, I felt certain that the mission of American public diplomacy was accomplishing some good.

In any given year, a small handful of individuals may travel from a country like Jordan, Iraq, Yemen, Tunisia, or Egypt. Those fully funded scholarships are better than gold, but too often our government forsakes their value.

It is critical to provide for that individual and the community hosting them the knowledge and resources necessary to make the exchange meaningful and to ensure that its impact is sustaining. Stories to the opposite (see note 2) are legend, and at present this occurs only by chance: the arbitrary goodwill of an unsuspecting landlord who rents to a visiting scholar without requiring a year's lease or the Walmart employee who helps a customer set up their cell phone. My colleagues and I have witnessed and experienced such random acts of kindness toward Fulbright fellows from the Arab world for over a decade. Every year, and without fail, I am astounded by the possibilities for true mutual understanding that emerge from such exchanges and the near total neglect of the exchange recipient and their communities once the papers have been signed. This is not the fault of the hardworking employees of the Fulbright Commission or other exchange offices but of an institutional culture in the State Department that values numbers over individuals and consistently undervalues the human-to-human labor of translingual and transnational friendship building.

As with the possibilities inherent to a new, more hands-on mode of narrowcast news, American exchange programs should invest at the granular level in the relatively few individuals we can reach in an intimate way and preserve those relationships like a rare and precious gem. Alumni networks and their management should be elevated to the top of our country's public diplomacy and strategic communications portfolios. Talent management, of exchange recipients and of the communities that step up to support them, or of the journalists and interlocutors who tell America's story on the taxpayers' behalf, should be operated by only the most exceptional leaders who in turn should be handsomely incentivized to excel. It is not a job to be contracted out but a career, and an ideology, to be cultivated from the ground up.

NOTES

PREFACE

1. Jean Baudrillard, "L'esprit du terrorisme," *South Atlantic Quarterly* 101, no. 2 (2002): 403–15.

INTRODUCTION

1. Larry Schwartz, personal interview with the author, September 11, 2020.
2. For figures on the war on terror, see the Costs of War Project of the Watson Institute for International and Public Affairs at Brown University, available online at https://watson.brown.edu/costsofwar/.
3. Nicholas J. Cull has determined that the coining of the phrase "public diplomacy" came from an FSO assigned to the Sprague Committee in 1962, in *The Cold War and the United States Information Agency* (Cambridge University Press, 2008), 180. The terms "psychological warfare" and "propaganda" were regularly employed by the United States Advisory Commission on Information throughout the 1950s.
4. Evan Osnos, David Remnick, and Joshua Yaffa, "Trump, Putin, and the New Cold War," *New Yorker*, March 6, 2017, https://www.newyorker.com/magazine/2017/03/06/trump-putin-and-the-new-cold-war.
5. United States Advisory Commission on Information, *Semiannual Report to the Congress*, April 1949, 42.

6. United States Advisory Commission on Information, *Semiannual Report to the Congress*, April 1949, 42. On the Fulbright Awards and its origins, see Sam Lebovic, *A Righteous Smokescreen: Postwar America and the Politics of Cultural Globalization* (University of Chicago Press, 2022), 42.
7. United States Information Agency, "الاسلام جدار روحي مينع لا تستطيع الشيوعية اختراقه" [Islam Is a Spiritual Wall That Communism Cannot Penetrate], Al-Sadaqah, March 19, 1953.
8. Institute for International Public Opinion and Market Research, "Media Survey in Lebanon: Prepared for the United States Information Agency, May-June 1963," Research Data Collection Project Files, 1958–1976, RG 306, Box 11, National Archives II. See also Arab Research and Advertising Centre, "A Study of the Demographic Characteristics of Readers of *Al-Hayat fi Amrika* in the U.A.R. [United Arab Republic]: Prepared for the United States Information Service, June 1966," Research Data Collection Project Files, 1958–1976, RG 306, Box 11, National Archives II.
9. R. S. Zaharna provides an excellent survey of the many policy papers that emerged after 9/11 calling for a reboot of American public diplomacy. She writes, "With each new report, the criticism grew bolder and the recommendations more urgent." But the reports—which included studies by the US Advisory Commission on Public Diplomacy, the US Government Accounting Office, the Heritage Foundation, Brookings, the Djerejian Commission, the Council on Foreign Relations, and many more—shared common blind spots in Zaharna's view. Many evaded the question of policy in favor of basic reorganization and budgeting demands. Others focused largely on the question of countering or combating jihadist messaging at the expense of engaging "publics" more broadly. Zaharna's discussion can be found in her *Battles to Bridges: US Strategic Communication and Public Diplomacy After 9/11* (Palgrave Macmillan, 2010), 55–70. A useful, quantified assessment of many of the same reports' findings can be found in Christopher Paul, "Whither Strategic Communication? A Survey of Current Proposals and Recommendations," RAND, February 13, 2009, 6–7.
10. In Christopher Simpson, *Science of Coercion: Communication Research and Psychological Warfare, 1945-1960* (Oxford University Press, 1994), 38. A description of NSC4-A can be found in Department of State Briefing Memorandum, December 17, 1947, https://history.state.gov/historicaldocuments/frus1945-50Intel/d256.
11. John Prados, *Presidents' Secret Wars: CIA and Pentagon Covert Operations from World War II Through the Persian Gulf* (I. R. Dee, 1996), 29.
12. Prados, *Presidents' Secret Wars*, 29.

13. Other examples of recent studies examining CIA patronage for Arab literary artists in particular during the Cold War include Elizabeth M. Holt, "'Bread or Freedom': The Congress for Cultural Freedom, the CIA, and the Arabic Literary Journal 'Ḥiwār' (1962–67)," *Journal of Arabic Literature* 44, no. 1 (2013); Robyn Cresswell, *City of Beginnings: Poetic Modernism in Beirut* (Princeton University Press, 2019).
14. See Patricia G. Greene, "Building Community Through Entrepreneurship Education (Innovations Case Discussion: INJAZ)," *Innovations* 3, no. 4 (2008): 99–104.
15. Nicholas J. Cull, *Cold War*, 74.
16. Peter Kovach, "Religion and Public Diplomacy," American Diplomacy, March 2014, http://americandiplomacy.web.unc.edu.
17. Allen C. Hansen takes note of the cultural homogeneity within the US government's information services in his volume *USIA: Public Diplomacy in the Computer Age* (Praeger, 1984). While earlier statistics are difficult to come by, he notes, by 1974, just 9 percent of the 4,285 employees at the United States Information Agency were Black women. Two were cultural affairs officers, but the great majority held clerical positions in the Washington office (62).
18. Steven C. Rockefeller, *John Dewey: Religious Faith and Democratic Humanism* (Columbia University Press, 1991), 241.
19. Edward P. Djerejian, et al., *Changing Minds Winning Peace: A New Strategic Direction for U.S. Public Diplomacy in the Arab and Muslim World*, report of the Advisory Group on Public Diplomacy for the Arab and Muslim World, October 1, 2003.
20. See James R. Vaughan, *The Failure of American and British Propaganda in the Arab Middle East, 1945-57: Unconquerable Minds* (Palgrave Macmillan, 2005), 37.
21. United States Advisory Commission on Information, *Tenth Semiannual Report*, US Department of State. Rep. No. 87–84 at 2 (1955).
22. Wilbur Eveland, *Ropes of Sand: America's Failure in the Middle East* (Norton, 1980), 103n.
23. United States Advisory Commission on Information, *Semiannual Report to the Congress*, US Department of State. Rep. No. 348Sa at 107 (1949).
24. *The Future of United States Public Diplomacy: Hearings Before the Subcommittee on International Organizations and Movements of the Committee on Foreign Affairs: Part XI, Winning the Cold War: The U.S. Ideological Offensive*, House of Representatives, 19th Cong. 3 (July 22, 1968) (statement of Edward L. Bernays, president, Edward L. Bernays Foundation). Bernays became recognized, among other things, for the devastating success of his pro-smoking campaign on

behalf of the tobacco industry in the late 1920s. His most famous work was *Crystalizing Public Opinion, Engineering Consent, and Propaganda* (Boni and Liveright, 1923). See Nancy Snow, *Propaganda, Incorporated: Selling America's Culture to the World* (Seven Stories, 1998), 18.

25. Edward W. Barrett, *Truth Is Our Weapon* (Funk & Wagnalls, 1953), 5.
26. Barrett, *Truth*, 6.
27. *The Future of United States Public Diplomacy* (statement of George Gallup, Jr., president, American Institute of Public Opinion).
28. Mark Haeffele attributes the quote to Kennedy's deputy special assistant Walt Rostow. In Mark Haeffele, "John F. Kennedy, USIA, and World Public Opinion," *Diplomatic History* 25, no. 1 (2001): 63–84.
29. John M. Crewdson and Joseph G. Treaster, "Worldwide Propaganda Network Built by CIA," *New York Times*, December 26, 1977. See also J. Michael Sproule, *Propaganda and Democracy: The American Experience of Media and Mass Persuasion* (Cambridge University Press, 1997), 215.
30. Scott Atran, email correspondence with the author, June 14, 2020.
31. The designation of a University Affiliated Research Center (UARC) requires at least $6 million in annual funding from a single federal source.
32. The terms "dynamics," "dimensions," "deterrence," "ideologies," "organizations," and "national security" are among the most frequently found within the Minerva research announcements between 2008 and 2018. See National Academies of Sciences, Engineering, and Medicine, *Evaluation of the Minerva Research Initiative* (National Academies, 2020), 103. The notion of "defense intelligence" in the modern American context can be traced to the establishment of the eponymous Defense Intelligence Agency (DIA) in 1961. See, for example, "'Intelligence' Conformity," *New York Times*, August 9, 1961, 32.
33. Jacob Kipp, Lester Grau, Karl Prinslow, and Don Smith, *The Human Terrain System: A CORDS for the 21st Century* (Foreign Military Studies Office [Army], 2006), 9.
34. Tom Vanden Brook, "Army Kills Controversial Social Science Program," *USA Today*, June 29, 2015, https://www.usatoday.com/story/news/nation/2015/06/29/human-terrain-system-afghanistan/29476409/.
35. The Office of Special Plans was a much maligned and short-lived enterprise established under the auspices of the Pentagon's Office of the Under Secretary of Defense for Policy in the wake of 9/11. In 2007, the office, which was led by Douglas Feith, was accused by members of Congress, with research by the United States' Inspector General's office, of creating "an alternative intelligence analysis of the alleged relationship between Iraq and al-Qaeda in order to help make the case to go to war against Iraq."

See *Briefing on the Department of Defense Inspector General's Report on the Activities of the Office of Special Plans Prior to the War in Iraq: Hearing Before the Committee on Armed Services, United States Senate*, 110th Congress, First Session (February 9, 2007) (statement of Senator Carl Levin, chairman).

The TALON Reporting System, created shortly after the Office of Special Plans in 2002, was in essence a database used to track "suspicious incidents possibly linked to foreign terrorist threats to DoD Resources," including US military bases overseas. In 2005, NBC News reported that the system was being used to track "anti-War activists." Internal investigations found such incidents to be minimal and were relative to overseas demonstrations targeting US military bases. See *Requesting the President and Directing the Secretary of Defense to Transmit to the House of Representatives All Information in the Possession of the President or the Secretary of Defense Relating to the Collection of Intelligence Information Pertaining to Persons Inside the United States Without Obtaining Court-Ordered Warrants Authorizing the Collection of Such Information and Relating to the Policy of the United States with Respect to the Gathering of Counterterrorism Intelligence Within the United States: Adverse Report of the Committee on Armed Services, House of Representatives, on H. R. 645. 15051*, 109th Cong. 55 (March 7, 2006) (statement of Stephen A. Cambone, Under Secretary of Defense).

The Total Information Awareness Program or TIP, was a DARPA-funded "ultra large" data-mining project launched from DARPA's Total Information Awareness office in 2003. The first call for proposals promised $137.5 million in R&D funding and an additional $10 million for "system integration." As described by Newton Lee in his 2013 study devoted to the program, the aim of the project was not data collection technology but rather information processing and analysis. Its principal aims were "Collaborative Reasoning and Decision Support Technologies," "Language Translation Technologies," "Pattern Recognition and Predictive Modeling Technologies," "Data Search and Privacy Protection Technologies," and "Biometric Technologies," which, included among other things, "automated, multimodal, biometric technologies" capable of detecting, recognizing, and identifying "humans, alone or grouped, in disguise or not, at a distance, day or night, and in all weather conditions." Newton Lee, *Counterterrorism and Cybersecurity: Total Information Awareness* (Springer, 2013). Jeffrey Rosen described the program for the *New York Times* as "the most sweeping effort to monitor the activity of Americans since the 1960's." See Jeffrey Rosen, "The Year in Ideas; Total Information Awareness," *New York Times*, December 15, 2002, https://www.nytimes.com/2002/12/15/magazine/the-year-in-ideas-total-information-awareness.html.

36. See Robert M. Gates, "Speech Before the Association of American Universities," (Washington, DC), April 14, 2008, https://archive.defense.gov. Also Michael W. Mosser, "Puzzles Versus Problems: The Alleged Disconnect Between Academics and Military Practitioners," *Perspectives on Politics* 8, no. 4 (2010): 1077–86.
37. On the generation of the phrase "defense intellectuals," see Daniel Bessner, *Democracy in Exile: Hans Speier and the Rise of the Defense Intellectual* (Cornell University Press, 2018).
38. See National Academies of Sciences, Engineering, and Medicine, *Evaluation of the Minerva*, Appendix B.
39. National Academies of Sciences, Engineering, and Medicine, *Evaluation of the Minerva*, 10. On the dearth of US foreign-language expertise, see *U.S. Public Diplomacy: Actions Needed to Improve Strategic Use and Coordination of Research: Report to the Ranking Member, Committee on Foreign Relations, U.S. Senate* (2007), GAO-07-904, July 2007, https://www.gao.gov/assets/a264084.html.
40. Djerejian et al., *Changing Minds Winning Peace*, 68.
41. Djerejian et al., *Changing Minds Winning Peace*, 68.
42. The military saw a near 30 percent increase of Arabic speakers within the first five years after 9/11, from just 4,384 speakers before September 11, to 5,703 by 2005. In Robert D. Kaplan, "What Rumsfeld Got Right," *Atlantic*, August 15, 2008, https://www.theatlantic.com/magazine/archive/2008/07/what-rumsfeld-got-right/306870/.
43. See Thomas H. Kean and Lee Hamilton, *The 9/11 Commission Report: Final Report of the National Commission on Terrorist Attacks Upon the United States* (United States Government Printing Office, 2004), 92.
44. United States General Accounting Office, *U.S. Public Diplomacy: State Department Expands Efforts but Faces Significant Challenges* (GAO, 2003), 27.
45. Quoted in John W. Riley and Leonard S. Cottrell, "Research for Psychological Warfare," *Public Opinion Quarterly* 21, no. 1 (1957): 52.
46. Shibley Telhami, *The Stakes: America and the Middle East: The Consequence of Power and the Choice for Peace* (Basic Books, 2002), 68.
47. Simpson, *Science of Coercion*, 110.
48. Alexander Kendrick, *Prime Time: The Life of Edward R. Murrow* (Little, Brown, 1969), 490. Also quoted in Nicholas J. Cull, "Preface: Evaluation and the History of U.S. Public Diplomacy," in *Data-Driven Public Diplomacy Progress Towards Measuring the Impact of Public Diplomacy and International Broadcasting*. Ed. Katherine Brown and Chris Hensman. American Council on Public Diplomacy, September 16, 2014. https://www.state.gov/wp-content/uploads/2024/02/2014_ACPD_Special_Report_Data-Driven_Public_Diplomacy.pdf.

49. See "BBG Research Series: Contemporary Media Usage in Egypt" (video), US Agency for Global Media, March 13, 2014, https://www.usagm.gov/2014/03/13/bbg-research-series-contemporary-media-use-in-egypt/, quote at 21:25.
50. United States Advisory Commission on Public Diplomacy, *Comprehensive Annual Report on Public Diplomacy and International Broadcasting*, US Dept. of State at 25 (2021).
51. Joseph Nye, *Soft Power: The Means to Success in World Politics* (Public Affairs, 2004), 111.
52. United States General Accountability Office, *U.S. Public Diplomacy: State Department Expands Efforts but Faces Significant Challenges: Report to the Committee on International Relations*, H.R. Rep. No. GAO-03-951 at 12 (September 4, 2003).
53. The Open Technology Fund also receives funding under the USAGM's budget. The 2021 *Comprehensive Annual Report on Public Diplomacy and International Broadcasting* by the US Advisory Commission on Public Diplomacy provides a comprehensive summary of US spending on public diplomacy between 2016 and 2020. It is available online at https://www.state.gov/wp-content/uploads/2022/02/2021_ACPD_Annual_Report.pdf.
54. Larry Pintak, *Reflections in a Bloodshot Lens: America, Islam and the War of Ideas* (Pluto, 2006), 269.
55. Nicholas J. Cull, "How We Got Here," in *Toward a New Public Diplomacy*, ed. Philip Seib (Palgrave, 2009), 35. On the size of the USIA in 1988, see Alvin A. Snyder, *Warriors of Disinformation: American Propaganda, Soviet Lies, and the Winning of the Cold War: An Insider's Account* (Arcade, 1995), xi–xiii.
56. *The Role of Public Diplomacy in Support of the Anti-Terrorism Campaign: Hearing Before the Committee on International Relations, House of Representatives*, 117th Cong. 59 (October 10, 2001) (prepared statement of Ambassador Kenton Keith, senior vice president for programming, Meridian International Center).
57. Krishna Kumar, *Promoting Independent Media: Strategies for Democracy Assistance* (Lynne Rienner, 2006), 8.
58. Wilson P. Dizard, *Inventing Public Diplomacy: The Story of the U.S. Information Agency* (Lynne Rienner, 2004), 227.
59. Barrett, *Truth*, 284.
60. W. P. Davison, "Voices of America," in *Public Opinion and Foreign Policy*, ed. Lester Markel (Harper, 1949), 170.
61. Thomas C. Sorensen, *The Word War: The Story of American Propaganda* (Harper and Row, 1968), 51. C. D. Jackson, also a member of the Office of Strategic Services, helped generate from the Jackson Commission the Operations Coordinating Board, which was imagined as an overview body to replace the Truman-era Psychological Strategy Board. See Cull, *Cold War*, 94–95.

62. United States Advisory Commission on Information, *Tenth Semiannual Report*, US Department of State Rep. No. 87–84 at 2 (1955).
63. Hansen, *USIA*, 92.
64. United States Objectives and Programs for National Security, National Security Council report, April 14, 1950.
65. See Scott Lucas, "'Total Culture' and the State-Private Network: A Commentary," chap. 11 in *Culture and International History* (Berghahn, 2022),
66. Sorensen, *The Word War*, 59.
67. Sorensen, *The Word War*, 59.
68. Sorensen, *The Word War*, 57.
69. Rick Lyman, "A Nation Challenged: The Entertainment Industry; Hollywood Discusses Role in War Effort," *New York Times*, November 12, 2001, https://www.nytimes.com/2001/11/11/us/nation-challenged-film-industry-white-house-takes-steps-renew-tie-hollywood.html.
70. Lyman, "A Nation Challenged."
71. Snyder, *Warriors*, 176.
72. Norm Pattiz, "Radio Sawa and Alhurra TV," in *Engaging the Arab and Islamic Worlds Through Public Diplomacy*, ed. William Rugh (Public Diplomacy Council, 2004), 75.
73. Carnes Lord, *Losing Hearts and Minds? Public Diplomacy and Strategic Influence in the Age of Terror* (Praeger Security International, 2006), 86.
74. Vaughan, *Failure of American and British Propaganda*, 23.
75. Alberto Fernandez, email correspondence with the author, August 18, 2020. See also Alberto Fernandez, "Providence Social Hour Conversation with Alberto M. Fernandez," Facebook, April 16, 2020, https://www.facebook.com/watch/?v=252154415933150.
76. The tenuous safety of collaborators became particularly vivid with the exposure of certain Arab bloggers caught up in the rumored machinations of the State Department's Public Diplomacy 2.0 initiative. See Nathaniel Greenberg, *How Information Warfare Shaped the Arab Spring* (Edinburgh University Press, 2019), 99–119.
77. See Committee to Project Journalists, "Journalists and Media Workers Killed in Iraq," December 12, 2022, https://cpj.org/reports/2008/07/journalists-killed-in-iraq/. Thirty-one journalists or media workers associated with US-backed media were killed or murdered by the end of the US occupation in 2011.
78. See "Under Secretary Charlotte Beers" (video transcript), PBS, January 3, 2003, https://www.pbs.org/newshour/show/under-secretary-charlotte-beers.
79. Nina Teicholz, "Privatizing Propaganda," *Washington Monthly* 34, no. 12 (2002).

80. Antony Blinken, "Now the U.S Needs to Win the Global War of Ideas," *New York Times*, December 8, 2001, https://www.nytimes.com/2001/12/08/opinion/IHT-now-the-us-needs-to-win-the-global-war-of-ideas.html.
81. See C-SPAN, "Bin Laden Videotape," November 8, 2001, https://www.c-span.org/video/?167830-1/bin-laden-videotape.
82. See Al-Jazeera, "البنتاغون يعرض شريط فيديو لبن لادن عن الهجمات" [The Pentagon Shows bin Laden's Video of the Attacks], December 13, 2001, https://web.archive.org/web/20240418195909/https://www.aljazeera.net/news/2001/12/13/البنتاغون-يعرض-شريط-فيديو-لبن-لادن-عن.
83. Karen DeYoung, "Bush to Create Formal Office to Shape U.S. Image Abroad," *Washington Post*, July 3, 2002, https://www.washingtonpost.com/archive/politics/2002/07/30/bush-to-create-formal-office-to-shape-us-image-abroad/fd3b6b54-5cf6-4610-acf5-e8f0e84fe1ee/.
84. Rashad Hussain, "A Strategy for Countering Terrorist Propaganda in the Digital Age," Australia Summit on Countering Violent Extremism, June 12, 2015, https://2009-2017.state.gov/r/cscc/releases/243877.htm.
85. *Countering the Virtual Caliphate: The State Department's Performance*, hearing before the Committee on Foreign Affairs, House of Representatives, 114th Cong. (July 13, 2016) (statement of Richard A. Stengel, under secretary for public diplomacy and public affairs, US Department of State).
86. United States Advisory Commission on Information, *Semiannual Report to the Congress*, US Department of State. Rep. No. 348Sa at 42 (1949).
87. See Paul J. Braisted and Kenneth W. Thompson, *Reconstituting the Human Community*, a report of Colloquium III, Bellagio, Italy, July 27–23, 1972, for the Program of Inquiries, Cultural Relations for the Future, sponsored by the Hazen Foundation, 1973.
88. Cull, *Cold War*, 209.
89. My emphasis. In Richard Dyer MacCann, "Film and Foreign Policy: The USIA, 1962–67," *Cinema Journal* 9, no. 1 (1969): 27.
90. Jean Baudrillard, "L'esprit du terrorisme," *South Atlantic Quarterly* 101, no. 2 (2002): 403–15.
91. W. J. T. Mitchell, *Cloning Terror: The War of Images, 9/11 to the Present* (University of Chicago Press, 2011), 57.

1. PUBLIC DIPLOMACY AND THE ARAB WORLD

1. Wallace Murray, assistant secretary of state for Near Eastern, South Asian and African Affairs, to Archibald MacLeish, "Letter from Colonel Harold B. Hoskins," March 21, 1945, *Documentation on Early Cold War U.S. Propaganda Activities in the Middle East*, National Security Archive Electronic Briefing Book No. 78, ed. Joyce Battle (National Security Archive, December 13, 2002),

https://nsarchive2.gwu.edu/NSAEBB/NSAEBB78/docs.htm. On Hoskins, see Hugh Wilford, *The Mighty Wurlitzer: How the CIA Played America* (Harvard University Press, 2008), 34.
2. See Thomas C. Sorensen, *The Word War: The Story of American Propaganda* (Harper and Row, 1968), 62–63.
3. Quoted in James R. Vaughan, *The Failure of American and British Propaganda in the Arab Middle East, 1945-57: Unconquerable Minds* (Palgrave Macmillan, 2005), 87.
4. The title of MacLeish's inaugural position went through several iterations. MacLeish's successor, William B. Benton, was the "assistant secretary of state for public affairs." According to Nicholas J. Cull, Benton thought the previous title was propagandist (Nicholas J. Cull, *The Cold War and the United States Information Agency* [Cambridge University Press, 2008], 26). Today the position is assistant secretary of state for global public affairs. MacLeish was a cowriter on Hemingway's film, which was made in support of the Republican government in Madrid at the outset of the Spanish Civil War.
5. "Statement by Archibald MacLeish Before the Senate Committee on Foreign Relations," *American Scientist* 33, no. 2 (1945): 118. For more on MacLeish and his early philosophy of public diplomacy, see Justin Hart, *Empire of Ideas: The Origins of Public Diplomacy and the Transformation of US Foreign Policy* (Oxford University Press, 2013), 10.
6. United States Advisory Commission on Information, *Semiannual Report to the Congress*, U.S. Dept. of State. Rep. No. 348Sa at 42 (1949).
7. United States Advisory Commission on Information, *Semiannual Report to the Congress*, U.S. Dept. of State. Rep. No. 348Sa at 42 (1949). On the revamped CU, see Charles Frankel, *The Neglected Aspect of Foreign Affairs: American Educational and Cultural Policy Abroad* (Brookings Institution, 1966), 78. On the "Campaign of Truth," see Cull, *Cold War*, 55–56; and Hart, *Empire*, 117.
8. Lester Markel, "Introduction," in *Public Opinion and Foreign Policy*, ed. Lester Markel Harper, 1949), 7. On the State Department's Division of Cultural Relations, see Frankel, *The Neglected Aspect of Foreign Affairs*, 25; Allen L. Heil, *Voice of America: A History* (Columbia University Press, 2003), 32–33.
9. Wilson P. Dizard, *Inventing Public Diplomacy: The Story of the U.S. Information Agency* (Lynne Rienner, 2004), 2. On the "twin forces of technological inconsistency . . . and enemy jamming" as both obstacles and motivators to the establishment of US foreign broadcasting, see Hart, *Empire*, 85; Hugh Wilford, *America's Great Game: The CIA's Secret Arabists and the Shaping of the Modern Middle East* (Basic Books, 2013), 34.
10. Quoted in "VOA Through the Years," April 3, 2017, VOA, https://www.insidevoa.com/a/3794247.

11. Harold Callender, "The Voice of America Echoes Widely," *New York Times*, November 15, 1942.
12. See Callender, "The Voice of America."
13. Edward W. Barrett, *Truth Is Our Weapon* (Funk & Wagnalls, 1953), 27.
14. Cull, *Cold War*, 17; Dizard, *Inventing Public Diplomacy*, 25.
15. Barrett, *Truth*, 27.
16. A great deal of institutional overhaul and redesign occurred in the years following WWII. Prior to the creation of the USIA the State Department assumed direction of the Office of International Information (OII) and the Office of Educational Exchange (OEX), both established soon after the Smith-Mundt Act in 1948. A year later, the two offices were combined into the United States Information and Education Exchange Program (USIE), which was later consolidated into the International Information Administration (IIA). The IIA was the most immediate predecessor to the USIA.
17. United States Advisory Commission on Information, *Semiannual Report to the Congress*, U.S. Dept. of State. Rep. No. 348Sa at 108 (1949).
18. United States Advisory Commission on Information, *Eleventh Semiannual Report of the United States Advisory Commission on Information*, U.S. Dept. of State. Rep. No. 376–84 at 11 (1956).
19. Barrett, *Truth*, 332.
20. Cable from Henry F. Grady (United States ambassador to Iran) to the Department of State, September 19, 1950, *Documentation on Early Cold War U.S. Propaganda Activities in the Middle East*.
21. See, for example, Dean Acheson, secretary of state, airgram to certain American diplomatic and consular offices, "Anti-Americanism in the Arab World," May 1, 1950, *Documentation on Early Cold War U.S. Propaganda Activities in the Middle East*.

    See also cable from Alan G. Kirk (United States ambassador to Soviet Union) to Department of State, August 19, 1950, *Documentation on Early Cold War U.S. Propaganda Activities in the Middle East*; and cable from Edward S. Crocker II (United States ambassador to Iraq) to the Department of State, "Anti-Communist Poster Material Prepared by USIS Baghdad," March 10, 1951, *Documentation on Early Cold War U.S. Propaganda Activities in the Middle East*.
22. Heil, *Voice of America*, 49.
23. Barrett, *Truth*, 332.
24. On the expansion of the VOA's foreign language broadcasting, see Hulen D. Bertrand, "Information Post Slated for Allen," *New York Times*, January 8, 1948; Nicholas J. Cull, "How We Got Here," in *Toward a New Public Diplomacy: Redirecting U.S. Foreign Policy*, ed. Phillip M. Seib (Palgrave Macmillan, 2009), 29; Vaughan, *Failure of American and British Propaganda in the Arab Middle*

East, 37; United States Advisory Commission on Public Diplomacy, *2017 Comprehensive Annual Report on Public Diplomacy and International Broadcasting* (U.S. Dept. of State, 2017), 30; and Barrett, *Truth*, 332.

25. Julio Antonio, "El impacto de la voz de América," *El Mundo*, March 20, 1951, 3.
26. "3 'Voice' Officials Deny Red Leanings," *New York Times*, February 21, 1953, 7.
27. See, for example, Heil, *Voice of America*, 67.
28. In 2022 the Rare Books and Special Collections Library at the American University in Cairo began digitalizing their holdings of VOA Arabic. A number of segments from the 1970s and 1980s are available online at https://digitalcollections.aucegypt.edu/digital/.
29. Isa Khalil Sabbagh, "من بين أوراقي: ٥٠ عامًا من الإعلام والسياسة" [From My Papers: 50 Years in Media and Politics] (Dar Al-Hani, 1991), 213.
30. See Abd al-Rahman al-Shabili. "أمير المايكروفون: عيسى خليل صبّاغ" [Prince of the Microphone: 'Isa Khalil Sabbagh], Al-Jazeera, June 4, 2000, https://www.al-jazirah.com/2000/20000604/ar8.htm. See also Charles Stuart Kennedy and Isa K. Sabbagh, *Interview with Isa K. Sabbagh*, November 9, 1989, https://www.loc.gov/item/mfdipbib001010/; Isa Khalil Sabbagh, [From My Papers: 50 Years in Media and Politics], 213.
31. See Emad Abdul Latif, "Ahmed Zaki Abu Shadi," in *Dictionary of African Biography*, ed. Henry Louis Gates, Emmanuel Akyeampong, and Steven J. Niven (Oxford University Press, 2012).
32. Ahmed Zaki Abu Shadi, "The Secrets of Life," interview by Edward R. Murrow, *This I Believe*, accessed February 1, 2024, https://thisibelieve.org/essay/16317/.
33. Abu Philip. "منبر الاصلاح" [Posts from Al-Islah]. *Al-Islah*, January 19, 1955. https://gpa.eastview.com/crl/mena/newspapers/islh19550119-01.1.1.

    On *Al-Islah* and the Arabic periodical scene in New York, post-WWII, see William Geerhold, "The Rear Guard Press," Aramco World, January/February 1967, https://archive.aramcoworld.com/issue/196701/the.rear.guard.press.htm.
34. The VOA program guide was published weekly in *Al-Sadaqah*.
35. Barrett, *Truth*, 207; "Moslem Pilgrims Swamp US Airlift," *New York Times*, August 27, 1952, 5; "Early Reaction Pleases," *New York Times*, August 27, 1952, 5.
36. On the "Magic Carpet" airlift and the dissemination of its news, see Vaughan, *Failure of American and British Propaganda in the Arab Middle East*, 21; James T. Currie, "Operation Hajji Baba," *Air Power History* 50, no. 2 (2003): 4–15; Esther Meir-Glitzenstein, "Operation Magic Carpet: Constructing the Myth of the Magical Immigration of Yemenite Jews to Israel," *Israel Studies* 16, no. 3 (2011): 156.

37. For more on Roosevelt and the American Friends of the Middle East (AFME), see Wilford, *America's Great Game*.
38. See Vaughan, *Failure of American and British Propaganda in the Arab Middle East*, 39; see also John Hogan, "Interview with John Hogan," interview by Claude Groce, *Frontline Diplomacy: The Foreign Affairs Oral History Collection of the Association for Diplomatic Studies and Training*, Library of Congress, September 21, 1987, https://www.loc.gov/item/mfdipbib000518/.
39. United States Advisory Commission on Information, *Semiannual Report to the Congress*, January 1958, 26. For more on Edward Steichen and "The Family of Man" exhibition, see Eric J. Sandeen, *Picturing an Exhibition: The Family of Man and 1950s America* (University of New Mexico Press, 1995).
40. Cull, *The Cold War*, 74.
41. Edward S. Crocker II, United States Embassy, Iraq, to the Department of State, "Foreign Leader Grants for Iraqis," March 26, 1951, *Documentation on Early Cold War U.S. Propaganda Activities in the Middle East*,
42. On the colloquium, see Wilson S. Compton to David K. E. Bruce, "Colloquium on Islamic Culture to be held in September, 1953, under the joint sponsorship of the Library of Congress and Princeton University," January 13, 1953, *Documentation on Early Cold War U.S. Propaganda Activities in the Middle East*. See also Jefferson Caffery, ambassador of the United States Embassy in Egypt, to the Department of State, "Colloquium on Islamic Culture and Saeed Ramadhan [sic]," Cairo, July 27, 1953, *Documentation on Early Cold War U.S. Propaganda Activities in the Middle East*. The *New York Times* covered the colloquium, observing that, of the forty Muslim scholars, eighteen came on State Department–funded leadership grants. See "40 Moslem Scholars Meet with 31 from U.S. at Princeton—Sessions to End in Capital," *New York Times*, September 8, 1953, 15.
43. Brent M. Geary, "A Foundation of Sand: United States Public Diplomacy, Egypt, and Arab Nationalism, 1953–1960" (PhD diss., Ohio University, 2007), 111–12.
44. William A. Eddy to Dorothy Thompson, United States Consulate General, Dhahran (Saudi Arabia), June 7, 1951, *Documentation on Early Cold War U.S. Propaganda Activities in the Middle East*.
45. Irene Gendzier, *Dying to Forget: Oil, Power, Palestine, and the Foundations of U.S. Policy in the Middle East* (Columbia University Press, 2015), 11.
46. Eddy to Thompson, *Documentation on Early Cold War U.S. Propaganda Activities in the Middle East*.
47. Memorandum by the director of the Office of Near Eastern and African Affairs (Henderson) to the secretary of state, Washington, August 29, 1945, https://history.state.gov/historicaldocuments/frus1945v08/d13

48. Eddy to Thompson, *Documentation on Early Cold War U.S. Propaganda Activities in the Middle East*.
49. United States Information Agency, "العرب و الدمقراطية" [The Arabs and Democracy], *Al-Sadaqah*, August 6, 1952, 1.
50. USIA, "The Arabs and Democracy."
51. Vaughan, *Failure of American and British Propaganda in the Arab Middle East*, 31.
52. Dizard, *Inventing Public Diplomacy*, 165.
53. Miles Copeland, *The Game of Nations: The Amorality of Power Politics* (Simon and Schuster, 1969), 217.
54. Cable from Edward S. Crocker II (ambassador to Iraq) to the Department of State, February 6, 1952, *Documentation on Early Cold War U.S. Propaganda Activities in the Middle East*.
55. Cable from Burton Berry (ambassador to Iraq), to the Department of State, September 11, 1952, *Documentation on Early Cold War U.S. Propaganda Activities in the Middle East*.
56. Daniel Lerner, *The Passing of Traditional Society: Modernizing the Middle East* (Free Press, 1958), 255. Also quoted in Geary, "A Foundation of Sand," 80. Lerner's study claimed to capture the respective status of three societal "types" (traditional, transitional, and modern). But apart from its focus on the use of foreign media (along with perspectives on international and political affairs) as a partial indicator of the modern type, he offers no indication that the research, as Christopher Simpson asserted some forty years later, had been "conceived and carried out for the specific purpose of advancing U.S. propaganda programs in the Middle East" (Simpson, *Science of Coercion: Communication Research and Psychological Warfare, 1945–1960* [Oxford University Press, 1994], 10). For an excellent discussion of Lerner's typology and its relation to subsequent US media endeavors, see Matt Sienkiewicz, *The Other Air Force: U.S. Efforts to Reshape Middle Eastern Media Since 9/11* (Rutgers University Press, 2016), 30.
57. On the term "defense intellectuals," see Daniel Bessner, *Democracy in Exile: Hans Speier and the Rise of the Defense Intellectual* (Cornell University Press, 2018).
58. John Riley and Leonard S. Cottrell, "Research for Psychological Warfare," *Public Opinion Quarterly* 21, no. 1 (1957): 149.
59. Simpson, *Science of Coercion*, 110.
60. Hadley Cantril, *The Pattern of Human Concerns* (Rutgers University Press, 1965) 7. On Cantril's funding by the CIA, see John M. Crewdson and Joseph G. Treaster, "Worldwide Propaganda Network Built by CIA," *New York Times*, December 26, 1977, 37.
61. As late as 2020, the Broadcasting Board of Governors (BBG) was still using many of the same tactics as those seen during the Cold War. "Omnibus" surveys where BBG media questions are seeded within Gallup World Poll

national surveys had replaced the annual surveys by the end of the first decade following 9/11.

62. See Arab Research and Advertising Centre, "A Study of the Demographic Characteristics of Readers of *Al-Hayat fi Amrika* in the U.A.R. [United Arab Republic]: Prepared for the United States Information Service, June 1966," Research Data Collection Project Files, 1958–1976, RG 306, Box 11, National Archives II. Such careful attention to methodology—including deliberate efforts to obstruct the participants' knowledge of the sponsor or the actual target of the survey—was indicative of US propaganda research writ large during the Cold War. As observed by Sig Mickelson, the former director of Radio Free Europe (RFE) and Radio Liberty (RL), the use of "established research institutes . . . comparable to Gallups, Ropers, Harrises, Nielsens, ARBs and the like" allowed researchers to merge their questionnaires with those of "other clients," thereby obscuring any association between the questions and the sponsor. In Sig Mickelson, *America's Other Voice: The Story of Radio Free Europe and Radio Liberty* (Praeger, 1983), 209.
63. United States Advisory Commission on Information, *Semiannual Report to the Congress*, April 1949, 107.
64. *A Preliminary Survey of Tehran University Students' Attitudes*, National Institute of Psychology, Tehran, Marketing and Public Opinion Research Division, August 1963, RG 306 Entry UD-UP 4 Series Title: Research Data Collection Project files, 1958–1976, Box 11, National Archives II.
65. *Media Survey in Lebanon*, a report prepared for the USIA by the Institute for International Public Opinion and Market Research (EMNID), RG 306 Entry UD-UP 4, Series Title: Research Data Collection Project files, 1958–1976, Box 11, National Archives II.
66. *Media Survey in Tunisia*, a report prepared for the USIA by the Institute for International Public Opinion and Market Research (EMNID), RG 306 Entry UD-UP 4, Series Title: Research Data Collection Project files, 1958–1976, Box 11, National Archives II.
67. Sorensen, *The Word War*, 78.
68. Sorensen, *The Word War*, 77.
69. Sorensen, *The Word War*, 211. In the case of RL, which broadcast from the Iberian Peninsula and targeted Russian speakers within the Soviet Union, the audience surveys could not rely on travelers passing through European ports of transit, as was the case with the Eastern European listeners of RFE. As a result, the number of respondents was thought too small to provide reliable results. To work around this problem, researchers at RL explored alternative methods, including one tack that involved "lengthy and casual conversations in restraurants, coffee shops, or bars, with no notes taken" (Mickelson, *America's Other Voice*, 209).

70. In Cull, *Cold War*, 51.
71. See Geary, "A Foundation of Sand," 109.
72. Holger Lutz Kern and Jens Hainmueller found in a previously classified Cold War survey of East German audiences whose exposure to West German media—which included VOA and RFE/RL programming—"increased support for the East German regime." Somewhat counterintuitively, the authors suggest the "net effect" of exposure to West German television was greater tolerance toward the East German regime. The authors posit some theories for this result, including the possibility that the relatively joyful fare on West German TV made life more bearable in East Germany. See Kern and Hainmueller, "Opium for the Masses: How Foreign Media Can Stabilize Authoritarian Regimes," *Political Analysis* 17, no. 4 (2009): 377–99.
73. Cable from Philip W. Ireland (chargé d'affaires, United States Embassy of Iraq) to the Department of State, "When the Communists Came," July 8, 1953, *Documentation on Early Cold War U.S. Propaganda Activities in the Middle East*. See also Sue Curry Jansen, "Selling America to the World," in *Bring 'Em On: Media and Politics in the Iraq War*, ed. Lee Artz and Yaya R. Kamalipour (Rowman & Littlefield, 2005), 56.
74. Copeland, *Game of Nations*, 113.
75. Muhammad Abd al-Kader Hatem, *Information and the Arab Cause* (Longman, 1974), 144.
76. *Final Report of the Select Committee to Study Governmental Operations with Respect to Intelligence Activities*, United States Senate (U.S. Government Printing Office, 1976), 534.
77. See Cull, *The Cold War*, 73; also William R. Daughtery, *A Psychological Warfare Casebook* (Johns Hopkins University Press, 1958), 762.
78. Victor Weybright to Edward W. Barrett, "New American Library of World Literature, Inc.," November 6, 1951, *Documentation on Early Cold War U.S. Propaganda Activities in the Middle East*.
79. Crewdson and Treaster, "Worldwide," 1.
80. On the early relationship between Praeger and the CIA, see David H. Price, *Cold War Anthropology: The CIA, the Pentagon, and the Growth of Dual Use Anthropology* (Duke University Press, 2016).
81. Joyce Battle, "U.S. Propaganda in the Middle East—the Early Cold War version," *National Security Archive Electronic Briefing Book* no. 78, December 13, 2002.
82. Gamal al-Ghitany, "Social Significance of Obama's Election," Carnegie Endowment for International Peace, December 5, 2008, https://carnegieendowment.org/2008/12/05/social-significance-of-obama-s-election-pub-22510.
83. United States Advisory Commission on Information, *Tenth Semiannual Report of the United States Advisory Commission on Information*, U.S. Dept. of State. Rep. No. 87–84 at 6 (1955).

84. Ian Spector, "Soviet Cultural Propaganda in the Near and Middle East," in *The Middle East: Studies in Contemporary History*, ed. Walter Z. Laqueur (Routledge, 1958), 384.
85. "مشروع بريطاني امريكي مشترك" [Joint British-American Operation], *Al-Misri*, May 22, 1950, 2, https://gpa.eastview.com/crl/mena/newspapers/almi 19500522-01.1.1.
86. Quoted in Amanda Laugesen, *Taking Books to the World: American Publishers and the Cultural Cold War* (University of Massachusetts Press, 2017), 53.
87. Stephen Penrose to Department of State, "Comment on 'The Soviet Challenge in the Near East'—Princeton," Beirut, June 2, 1951, *Documentation on Early Cold War U.S. Propaganda Activities in the Middle East*.
88. "محطة صوت أسرائيل" [The Station "Voice of Israel"], *Al-Muqattam*, April 25, 1946, https://gpa.eastview.com/crl/mena/newspapers/amam19460425 -01.1.1.
89. Hatem, *Information and the Arab Cause* (Longman, 1974), 192.
90. Copeland, *Game of Nations*, 35. See also Gary Davis (director), "Frank Kearns: Foreign Correspondent," PBS, 2013, https://www.pbs.org/video/frank-kearns -american-correspondent-kemsdc/; Wilford, *America's Great Game*, 148.
91. In Davis, *Frank Kearns*, 24:15.
92. Owen Sirrs notes that Mohamed Hassanein Heikal saw Copeland as an "advertising man." Owen L. Sirrs, *A History of the Egyptian Intelligence Service: A History of the Mukhabarat, 1910–2009* (Routledge, 2010), 32.
93. Copeland, *Game of Nations*, 187. In *Ropes of Sand*, the former CIA officer Wilbur Eveland repeated Copeland's apparent disclosure regarding the tower (Wilbur Eveland, *Ropes of Sand: America's Failure in the Middle East* [Norton, 1980]). See also Vaughan, *Failure of American and British Propaganda in the Arab Middle East*, 39.
94. "We combed files of these Germans in a search for talent which could be put to good use, in some cases in the United States itself (Wernher von Braun, the space scientist at Hunstville, Alabama, is the best-known example) but mostly in other countries," Copeland wrote. "In 1953, it became apparent that Nasser needed outside help for his intelligence and security services and our Government found it highly impolitic to help him directly" (Copeland, *Game of Nations*, 103–4); Copeland, *Game of Nations*, 87.
95. Copeland, *Game of Nations*, 100.
96. Copeland, *Game of Nations*, 21.
97. Copeland, *Game of Nations*, 27; Gamal Abdel Nasser, *The Philosophy of the Revolution* (Smith, Keynes & Marshall, 1959), 61.
98. Copeland, *Game of Nations*, 102.
99. Copeland, *Game of Nations*, 60.
100. Copeland, *Game of Nations*, 58.

101. Copeland, *Game of Nations*, 62.
102. See Mohammad Hassanein Heikal, *The Cairo Documents: The Inside Story of Nasser and His Relationship with World Leaders, Rebels, and Statesmen* (Doubleday, 1973), 45.
103. Muhammad Jalal Kishk, كلمتي للمغفلين [My Word to the Fools] (Al-Zahara l-il-'Ilam al-Arabi, 1985), 15.
104. Steven C. Rockefeller, *John Dewey: Religious Faith and Democratic Humanism* (Columbia University Press, 1991), 241. Philippe-Joseph Salazar articulates the notion that there is no "inherently democratic destiny" to the use of communications technology in his masterful study of ISIS communications, *Words Are Weapons: Inside ISIS's Rhetoric of Terror* (Yale University Press, 2017), 87.

2. FREE PLAY

1. President George W. Bush signed the Authorization for Use of Military Force on September 18, 2001. The Senate resolution that preceded it was unanimously passed on September 14. See David Abramowitz, "The President, the Congress, and Use of Force: Legal and Political Considerations in Authorizing Use of Force Against International Terrorism," *Harvard International Law Journal* 43, no. 1 (2002): 71–81.
2. Jacques Chirac, "*Un combat complexe et sans merci*" [A Complex and Merciless Fight], *Le Figaro*, October 8, 2001.
3. Jean-Jacques Mevel, "*L'Amérique frappe en Afghanistan*," *Le Figaro*, October 8, 2001.
4. "*La nouvelle amitié russo-américaine*" [The New Russo-American Friendship], *Le Monde*, October 8, 2001, https://www.lemonde.fr/archives/article/2001/10/07/la-nouvelle-amitie-russo-americaine_4195747_1819218.html.
5. Ignacio Ramonet, "An Enemy at Last," *Le Monde diplomatique*, October 2001, https://mondediplo.com/2001/10/01leader.
6. See "EC-130J," US Air Force, accessed February 1, 2024, https://www.af.mil/About-Us/Fact-Sheets/Display/Article/104535/ec-130j-commando-solo/. See also Arturo Muñoz, *U.S. Military Information Operations in Afghanistan: Effectiveness of Psychological Operations 2001–2010* (RAND, 2012).
7. Arturo Muñoz, personal interview with the author, August 16, 2023. At the outset of the war, the Army's field manual for information operations was the only guiding document for carrying out such campaigns, according to Muñoz. Emma Briant discusses other aspects of the psychological operation approval process in "Pentagon Ju-Jitsu—Reshaping the Field of Propaganda," *Critical Sociology* 45, no. 3 (2019): 371. See also Sultan Faizy and

Shashank Bengali, "U.S. Military Apologizes for 'Highly Offensive' Leaflets It Distributed in Afghanistan," *Los Angeles Times*, September 6, 2017, https://www.latimes.com/world/asia/la-fg-afghanistan-usmilitary-apology-20170906-story.html.

8. Robert D. McFadden, "From New York to Melbourne, Cries for Peace," *New York Times*, February 16, 2003, https://www.nytimes.com/2003/02/16/nyregion/threats-and-responses-overview-from-new-york-to-melbourne-cries-for-peace.html.

9. House of Commons Defence Committee (UK), *Lessons of Iraq*, Third Report, March 3, 2004, 174, https://publications.parliament.uk/pa/cm200304/cmselect/cmdfence/57/5702.htm. See also Steven Collins, "Mind Games," NATO Review, June 1, 2003, https://www.nato.int/docu/review/articles/2003/06/01/mind-games/index.html. The author reviewed several dozen leaflets held by the JFK Special Warfare Museum at Fort Bragg (now Fort Liberty), which were given to the Library of Congress in 2003.

10. House of Commons Defence Committee, *Lessons of Iraq*, 175. See also Matt Sienkiewicz, *The Other Air Force: U.S. Efforts to Reshape Middle Eastern Media Since 9/11* (Rutgers University Press, 2016), 35.

11. "Commando Solo Radio Messages Over Iraq," Psywarrior.com, accessed January 15, 2024, https://www.psywarrior.com/%2FCommandoSoloIraqScripts.html.

12. On overt radio operations in the First Gulf War, see, for example, US Air Force, "EC-130J Commando Solo"; "PSYOP Leaflets of Operation Desert Fox," ed. SGM Herbert A. Friedman (Ret.), Psywarrior.com, accessed January 15, 2024, https://www.psywarrior.com/DesertFoxHerb.html; Christopher Lamb, *Review of Psychological Operations Lessons Learned from Recent Operational Experience* (National Defense University Press, 2005).

13. Stephen T. Hosmer, *Psychological Effects of U.S. Air Operations in Four Wars, 1941–1991: Lessons for U.S. Commanders*, Rand Corporation, 1996.

14. See "Radio Free Iraq Signs Off After 17 Years of Service, RFE/RL, July 30, 2015, https://about.rferl.org/article/radio-free-iraq-signs-off-after-17-years-of-service. The US-established Radio Free Iraq should not be confused with the Cold War broadcast by Radio al-Iraq al-Hurr, which was thought to be based out of Egypt and pushed an anticolonial, Nasserite line of propaganda.

15. Inter Media, "International Broadcasting in Iraq (Preliminary) Report for the BBG," January 2010, 11. The report was made available to the author by the US Agency for Global Media through a Freedom of Information Act request in 2023.

16. See Whitaker, B. (2003); House of Commons Defence Committee (UK), *Lessons of Iraq*, 175.

17. "Broadcast to Iraq," C-SPAN, April 12, 2003, https://www.c-span.org/video/?176127-1/broadcast-iraq.
18. C-SPAN, "Broadcast to Iraq."
19. The *Al-Zaman* (Azzaman) newspaper began in London in the late 1990s. The newspaper's founder, Sa'ad Barzzaz, was the former head of Saddam Hussein's national news agency. During the first Gulf War he sought exile in London where he remained before reportedly returning, along with his newspaper, to Baghdad after the US invasion. According to the *Guardian*, Barzzaz was accused of using the paper as part of a covert propaganda campaign targeting the Qatari Sheikha Moza bint Nasser, on behalf of Saudi Arabia. The announcement regarding *Al-Zaman* on Towards Freedom TV appeared to obscure its origins. See David Pallister, "Media Mogul Accused of Running Saudi-Funded Propaganda Campaign, *Guardian*, January 26, 2005, https://www.theguardian.com/world/2005/jan/26/pressandpublishing.media.

    See also Michael J. Barker, "Democracy or Polyarchy? US-Funded Media Developments in Afghanistan and Iraq Post 9/11," *Media, Culture & Society* 30, no. 1 (2008): 109–30.
20. Department of Defense (DoD), *Information Operations Roadmap*, October 30, 2003, https://nsarchive.gwu.edu/document/16822-department-defense-information-operations.
21. DoD, *Information Operations Roadmap*, 6.
22. DoD, *Information Operations Roadmap*, 6.
23. Larry Schwartz, personal interview with the author, September 11, 2020. The military's *Information Operations Roadmap* attempted to delineate some of the "distinguishing tasks" between Public Affairs, Public Diplomacy, and Psychological Operations—describing for the first two (civilian) offices all "strategic" or long-term applications and, for the last, more near-term or tactical goals. The primary function of units like the 4th Psychological Operations Group was to "directly modify behavior" (through the use of "Radio/TV/Print/Web") within the active theater of war. Its second charge was to "support public diplomacy," and the third to "assist friendly forces in developing PSYOP programs," which would include "foreign language products disseminated in support of local commanders in non- or semi-permissive areas" (DoD, *Information Operations Roadmap*, 71).
24. "US Envoys Confer on Middle East Outlook," *New York Times*, February 15, 1951, 10.
25. Department of State Report, "Conference of Middle East Chiefs of Mission (Istanbul, February 14–21, 1951): Agreed Conclusions and Recommendations," February 21, 1951, *Documentation on Early Cold War U.S. Propaganda Activities in the Middle East*, National Security Archive Electronic Briefing

Book No. 78, ed. Joyce Battle (National Security Archive, December 13, 2002), https://nsarchive2.gwu.edu/NSAEBB/NSAEBB78/docs.htm.
26. Nicholas J. Cull, *The Cold War and the United States Information Agency* (Cambridge University Press, 2008), 73.
27. The archives of the Franklin Book program are available at the Library of Congress in the Rare Book and Special Collections Reading Room. Indexes of the various languages are also available online: See https://www.loc.gov/rr/rarebook/coll/franklinbookprogram.html.
28. Department of State Report, "Conference of Middle East Chiefs."
29. Wilbur Eveland, *Ropes of Sand: America's Failure in the Middle East* (Norton, 1980), 47.
30. Eveland, *Ropes of Sand*, 47.
31. See "Iraq Seizes Arms Cache," *New York Times*, June 18, 1951, 14.
32. Department of State Report, "Conference of Middle East Chiefs."
33. Eveland, *Ropes of Sand*, 46.
34. Samir Farid, تاريخ الرقابة على السينما في مصر [The History of Film Censorship in Egypt], (Al-Maktab al-Misri li-Tawzi' al-Matbu'at, 2002), 58–59. Also quoted in Nathaniel Greenberg, *The Aesthetic of Revolution in the Film and Literature of Naguib Mahfouz (1952-1967)* (Lexington, 2014), 4.
35. Hana Batatu, *The Old Social Classes and the Revolutionary Movements of Iraq: A Study of Iraq's Old Landed and Commercial Classes and of Its Communists, Ba'thists, and Free Officers* (Princeton University Press, 1978), 668.
36. Eveland, *Ropes of Sand*, 55; "U.S. Unit in Iraq Hit by Grenade," *New York Times*, March 20, 1951, 15.
37. Cable from Edward S. Crocker II (ambassador to Iraq) to the Department of State, "Proposed Information Program for Iraq," May 16, 1952, *Documentation on Early Cold War U.S. Propaganda Activities in the Middle East*.
38. Cable from Crocker to the Department of State, "Proposed Information Program for Iraq."
39. Cable from Crocker to the Department of State, "Proposed Information Program for Iraq."
40. James R. Vaughan, *The Failure of American and British Propaganda in the Arab Middle East, 1945–57: Unconquerable Minds* (Palgrave Macmillan, 2005), 40.
41. Vaughan, *Failure of American and British Propaganda in the Arab Middle East*, 40.
42. "Radiotelegraph Circuit to Iraq," *New York Times*, February 20, 1951, 37.
43. "الملك فيصل يفتح معرض الصناعات البريطانية أمس في بغداد" [King Faisal Opens the British Industries Exhibit Yesterday in Baghdad], *Alif baa*, October 26, 1954, https://gpa.eastview.com/crl/mena/newspapers/abab19541026-01.1.4.
44. Sam Pope Brewer, "TV MAGIC CARPET REACHES BAGHDAD: Programs of Entertainment Will Be Supplemented by Ones for Schools," *The New York Times*, September 2, 1956, 7.

45. In Nicholas J. Cull, "'The Perfect War': US Public Diplomacy and International Broadcasting During Desert Shield and Desert Storm, 1990/1991," *Arab Media and Society*, September 5, 2005. As described in the *Information Operations Roadmap*, the military provided only a "support" role for "bringing to theater public diplomacy (DoD, *Information Operations Roadmap*, 71).
46. Richard T. Arndt, a long-time cultural diplomacy officer in the USIA, highlights instances of military-led cultural outreach in Latin America, following the Spanish-American War, and in Germany and Japan in the wake of WWII. Led by the American Council on Education and articulated principally by Archibald MacLeish, the education "reorientation" of post–Nazi Germany represented the "first major postwar miracle," in Arndt's words, and a "triumph of cultural diplomacy." See Richard T. Arndt, *The First Resort of Kings: American Cultural Diplomacy in the Twentieth Century* (Potomac, 2005).
47. Cull, *Cold War*, 158.
48. David. W. Gray, "The U.S. Intervention in Lebanon, 1958: A Commander's Reminiscence," Combat Studies Institute (U.S. Army Command and General Staff College, July 1, 1984), 25, https://apps.dtic.mil/sti/citations/ADA450232.
49. Gray, "The U.S. Intervention in Lebanon," 25.
50. Christopher Paul and James J. Kim, *Reporters on the Battlefield: The Embedded Press System in Historical Context* (RAND, 2004), 1.
51. Robert M. Gates, "Balanced Strategy: Reprogramming the Pentagon for New Age, *Foreign Affairs* 88, no. 1 (2009): 28–40.
52. Tom Mitchell and Xinning Liu, "The America Hawks Circling Beijing," *Financial Times*, December 7, 2018, https://www.ft.com/content/d425ee0a-f9bf-11e8-8b7c-6fa24bd5409c.
53. Robert M. Gates, "Speech Before the Association of American Universities," (Washington, DC), April 14, 2008, https://archive.defense.gov.
54. See "China-Made Artillery Seized in Afghanistan," *Washington Times*, April 12, 2002, https://www.washingtontimes.com/news/2002/apr/12/20020412-041857-7139r/.
55. *Unrestricted Warfare Symposium 2006: Proceedings on Strategy, Analysis, and Technology*, March 14–15, 2006, https://apps.dtic.mil/sti/citations/ADA597396.2006, 254.
56. *Unrestricted Warfare Symposium*, 254.
57. Robert M. Gates, "Speech Before the Association of American Universities."
58. United States Advisory Commission on Public Diplomacy, *Public Diplomacy in the 1990s*, U.S. Dept. of State at 14 (1991).
59. *Report of the Defense Science Board Task Force on Managed Information Dissemination*, Office of the Under Secretary of Defense for Acquisition, Technology, and Logistics, 2001, 51.

60. Cull, "The Perfect War."
61. Pierre Darle, *Saddam Hussein maître des mots : Du langage de la tyrannie à la tyrannie du langage*. [Saddam Hussein Master of Words: From the Language of Tyranny to the Tyranny of Language] (L'Harmattan, 2003), 57.
62. Karl Greenberg and Jim Edwards, "Saatchi's Roberts Advised DOD on Rebranding 'War,'" *Brandweek* 46, no. 33 (2005): 5.
63. Commission on Wartime Contracting, *Transforming Wartime Contracting: Controlling Costs, Reducing Risks*, July 1, 2011, 22, https://apps.dtic.mil/sti/citations/ADA549381.
64. Jeff Gerth, "Military's Information War Is Vast and Often Secretive," *New York Times*, December 11, 2005, http://www.nytimes.com/2005/12/11/politics/militarys-information-war-is-vast-and-often-secretive.html?_r=0.
65. BBC Media Action polled audiences on their reception of programming by Al-Iraqiyya over the course of the 2014–2015 season. While patterns of division among different sects were apparent, researchers noted a prevailing sense of unease toward *Dawlat al-Khurafah*. As one woman responded, "If I had suffered the worst by ISIS, displaced, had my daughter raped or sold, this show would be mocking me" (quoted in Nathaniel Greenberg, "Mythical State: The Aesthetics and Counter-Aesthetics of the Islamic State in Iraq and Syria," *Middle East Journal of Culture and Communication* 10, no. 2–3 (2017): 264. Satirical responses to violence typically generate a certain level of distaste among audiences. Inspired by Allied humor projected toward Axis powers during WWII, American propagandists attempted to distribute to Arab audiences a "Book of Jokes" in 1956, followed by a second edition in 1972. The books were adapted to Egyptian circumstances and events. But as described by Nasser's deputy prime minister, Muhammad Abd al-Kader Hatem, both were received as "enemy propaganda," inspiring a countercampaign from "Voice of the Arabs" in 1956 (Hatem, *Information*, 198). Regarding ISIS satire, even *Saturday Night Live*'s sketch that critiqued American naivete generated a storm of criticism for disregarding the gravity of the conflict (See: Obeidallah). More striking from audience responses to *Dawlat al-Khurafah*, however, was the level of aesthetic disjunction, the sense that regardless of whether or not the show was appropriate it was poorly executed, confused, and "tacky." Quoted in Greenberg, "Mythical State,"255–71.
66. Donald L. Barlett and James B. Steele, "Washington's $8 Billion Shadow," *Vanity Fair*, February 6, 2007, https://www.vanityfair.com/news/2007/03/spyagency200703.
67. Barlett and Steele, "Washington's $8 Billion Shadow." See also Cora Sol Goldstein, "A Strategic Failure: American Information Control Policy in Occupied Iraq," *Military Review* 88, no. 2 (2008): 58–65.

68. "International: A Chance Missed; Iraq's Television," *Economist* 369, no. 8354 (2003): 56.
69. Commission on Wartime Contracting, *Transforming Wartime Contracting*, 1.
70. Commission on Wartime Contracting, *Transforming Wartime Contracting*, 22.
71. Commission on Wartime Contracting, *Transforming Wartime Contracting*, 68.
72. *Coalition Provisional Authority Order Number 65: Iraqi Communications and Media Commission*, March 20, 2004, 4, https://archive.org/details/imn-cpaord-65; *Coalition Provisional Authority Order Number 66: Iraqi Communications and Media Commission*, March 20, 2004, 2, https://archive.org/details/imn-cpaord-66.
73. *Coalition Provisional Authority Order Number 65: Iraqi Communications and Media Commission*, 4; *Coalition Provisional Authority Order Number 66: Iraqi Communications and Media Commission*, 2.
74. In Goldstein, "A Strategic Failure," 61.
75. Wathaq Abbas 'Abd al-Razzaq, "الصفحات العراقية و القيم المجتمع المدني: دراسة تحليلية لصفحة الرأي في جريدة الصباح للفترة من 1-1-2004 الى 31-6-2004" [Societal Values and the Iraqi Press: Analytical Studies of the Opinion Pages in the Newspaper Al-Sabah from 1/1/2004 to 6/31/2004], *Majalat al-jama'at al-Iraqiyya* [Journal of Iraqi Society] 2 no. 30 (2013): 491.
76. See R'ad Jassim Hamza, "مشكلات اعداد البرامج الاذاعية والتلفزيونية في العراق شبكة الاعلام العراقي - دراسة حالة" [Problems of Preparing Radio and Television Programs in Iraq, Iraqi Media Network—a Case Study]. *Al-Adab Journal* 86 (2022), 495.
77. See 'Abd al-Razzaq, "Societal Values and the Iraqi Press."
78. "Journalists and Media Workers Killed in Iraq," Committee to Protect Journalists, December 12, 2022, https://cpj.org/reports/2008/07/journalists-killed-in-iraq/.
79. For an excellent discussion of LIWC and its use in the global war on terror, see Flagg Miller, "Terrorist Violence and the Enrollment of Psychology in Predicting Muslim Extremism: Critical Terrorism Studies Meets Critical Algorithm Studies," *Critical Studies on Terrorism* 12, no. 2 (2019): 185–209. As a point of personal disclosure, I had the honor of receiving a CLS award for Arabic, in 2010, and I was later a principal investigator (PI) for a Project GO grant. Both awards, one a language immersion scholarship and the other a language training administration award, were concluded well before I started my work on this book. Neither provided funding for my research on this topic nor any other topic of my research.
80. Desmond Butler and Richard Lardner, "Congress Probes Islamic State Counter-Propaganda Operations," *AP*, March 9, 2017, https://apnews.com/article/fd18db778953497e8cb531a6f5770f82.

81. Desmond Butler and Richard Lardner, "US Misfires in Online Fight Against Islamic State," *AP*, January 31, 2017, https://apnews.com/article/lifestyle-middle-east-africa-business-islamic-state-group-b3fd7213bb0e41b3b02eb15265e9d292.
82. According to a study by the Brookings Institute, ISIS had no more than five hundred to two thousand dedicated Twitter users in 2014. The vast majority of its interactions were generated by bots. See J. M. Berger and Jonathon Morgan, "The ISIS Twitter Census Defining and Describing the Population of ISIS Supporters on Twitter," Brookings, March 5, 2015, https://www.brookings.edu/articles/the-isis-twitter-census-defining-and-describing-the-population-of-isis-supporters-on-twitter/.
83. Hadley Cantril, *The Pattern of Human Concerns* (Rutgers University Press, 1965), 6.
84. Edward P. Djerejian, et al., *Changing Minds Winning Peace: A New Strategic Direction for U.S. Public Diplomacy in the Arab and Muslim World*, report of the Advisory Group on Public Diplomacy for the Arab and Muslim World, October 1, 2003, 30. The propensity for scientific abstraction in American propaganda research dated back to the 1940s and the early forays of Daniel Lerner, whose seminal text, *The Passing of Traditional Society: Modernizing the Middle East* (Free Press, 1958), presented a series of sweeping generalities on the geographies, colonial history, and religious composition of the Middle East: Lebanon was the "most modern" and an "entrepôt" of influence, Egypt "a population whose birth rate quickly engulfs every gain of modern technique within a swollen tide of ancient needs." In Lerner, *The Passing*, 170.
85. Slavoj Žižek and Frank Wynne, *Violence: Six Sideways Reflections* (Profile, 2010), 83.
86. Djerejian et al., *Changing Minds Winning Peace*, 30.
87. Karl Marx and Friedrich Engels, *The 18th Brumaire of Louis Bonaparte* (London: Electric Book Co., 2001), 7.

3. IRAQ AND THE WORLD

1. Department of Defense, *Information Operations Roadmap*, October 30, 2003, https://nsarchive.gwu.edu/document/16822-department-defense-information-operations, 71.
2. Office of Inspector General (OIG), *Review of Radio Sawa Support to the Transition in Post-Saddam Iraq*, Dept. of State, Rep. No. IBO/IQO-A-05-02 (October 2004), 2, 5.

3. Josh Getlin, "U.S. Nightly News Shows to Make Their Iraqi Television Debut; Some Fear the White House-Backed Program Espousing a Free Press Will Create a Backlash," *Los Angeles Times*, April 15, 2003, https://www.latimes.com/archives/la-xpm-2003-apr-15-war-iraqtv15-story.html.
4. Other notable figures included the Iraqi writer and historian Hassan Al-Alawi; the Egyptian scholar Mamoun Fendi; and the deputy secretary of state during the first George W. Bush administration, Richard Armitage.
5. "ما رأي المفكرين والاعلاميين العرب بتأثير سقوط نظام صدام حسين على مستقبل الديمقراطية العربية؟" [What Do Arab Thinkers and Media Figures Think about the Impact of the Fall of Saddam Hussein's Regime on the Future of Arab Democracy?], *Al-Alaf*, August 6, 2003, https://elaph.com/Web/Archive/1060192313530560200.htm.
6. For more on Fahs and the Association of Muslim 'Ulama' in Lebanon, see Mohammad Ataie, "Exporting the Iranian Revolution: Ecumenical Clerics in Lebanon," *International Journal of Middle East Studies* 53, no. 4 (2021): 672–90.
7. "What Do Arab Thinkers and Media Figures Think?"
8. "What Do Arab Thinkers and Media Figures Think." On Fahs and his role in the Syrian opposition, see Ataie, "Exporting the Iranian Revolution," 672–90.
9. Harb was empowered early on by the Washington Institute for Near East Policy; its long-time executive director, Robert Satloff, gained a near permanent slot as an on-air commentor for Al-Hurra despite his overtly partisan positions on Israel, which routinely polled as the most divisive issue in the greater Arab world. On his testimony before Congress, see *Broadcasting Board of Governors and Alhurra Television: Hearing Before the Subcommittee on Oversight and Investigations of the Committee on International Relations*, House of Representatives, 119th Cong. 18 (November 10, 2005) (statement of Mouafac Harb, news director, Alhurra Television Network).
10. See United States General Accountability Office, Rep. to Chairman of the Subcommittee on National Security, Emerging Threats, and International Relations, Committee on Government Reform, H.R.: *U.S. International Broadcasting Management of Middle East Broadcasting Services Could Be Improved*. H.R. Rep. No. GAO-06-762 (August 2006). The stamp of approval for Al-Hurra broadcasting was made vivid on May 5, 2004, when President George W. Bush concluded an on-screen interview with Harb by remarking "good job." See "President Bush Meets with Alhurra Television on Wednesday," The White House, May 4, 2004, https://georgewbush-whitehouse.archives.gov.
11. Al-Hurra officially went live February 14, 2004. Following the successful construction of two new "in-country" television transmitters and satellite

uplink facilities, Al-Hurra Iraq followed suit in April of that year. See H.R. Rep. No. GAO-06-762 (August 2006).

12. Kami Aseel, "World's Bravest Orchestra Plays On in Iraq," *Reuters*, October 29, 2007, https://www.reuters.com/article/world/worlds-bravest-orchestra-plays-on-in-iraq-idUSNOA931278/.

13. Saad Mohan's letter of resignation can be found in Dafna Lizner, "Alhurra's Baghdad Bureau Mired in Controversy," *ProPublica*, July 8, 2008, https://www.propublica.org/article/alhurras-baghdad-bureau-mired-in-controversy-708.

14. BBG/InterMedia, "International Broadcasting in Iraq (Preliminary)," Media Market Report, January 2010. The survey, which consisted of two thousand respondents and was considered nationally representative, was combined with findings from a 2008-09 poll that had failed to capture enough responses from several provinces, including Basrah, Qadisiyah, Babylon, Maysan, and Wasit. The International Audience Research Program (IARP) of the BBG commissioned the survey on behalf of the Office of Research of the International Broadcasting Bureau (IBB). The survey was provided to the author through a Freedom of Information Act request in 2023.

15. BBG/Gallup, "Analytical Report for Iraq Media Use Survey," January 2018. Gallup carried out the study as part of the BBG's International Audience Research Program (IARP) on behalf of the IBB's Office of Research and Assessment (ORA). The report was made available to the author by Freedom of Information Act request in 2023.

16. Lizner, "Alhurra's Baghdad Bureau."

17. OIG, *Review of the Broadcasting Board of Governors' Middle East Radio Network Launch and Broadcast Initiatives*, Dept. of State, Rep. No. IBO-A-04-12 (November 2004), 22.

18. Jeff Stein, "Bay of Piglets: How the Freemasons Got Caught in a Plot to Topple the Castros," *Newsweek*, April 7, 2014, https://www.newsweek.com/2014/04/18/bay-piglets-how-freemasons-got-caught-plot-topple-castros-248099.html.

19. See Art Levine, "Bad Reception," *American Prospect*, November 8, 2005. https://prospect.org/article/bad-reception/.

20. Salem Mashkour, "حسن نصر الله ...... المنتصر بلا غرور" [Hassan al-Nasrallah: Victory Without Pride], Islam Online, November 18, 2002, https://web.archive.org/web/20250808182005/https://www.yahosein.com/vb/node/10852#post10852.

21. Dafna Lizner, "Lost in Translation: Alhurra—America's Troubled Effort to Win Middle East Hearts and Minds," *ProPublica*, June 22, 2008, https://www.propublica.org/article/alhurra-middle-east-hearts-and-minds-622.

3. IRAQ AND THE WORLD

In 1993, Nassif testified before the Senate Appropriations Subcommittee on Foreign Operations as a "representative" of the Council of Lebanese Organizations requesting a sixty-million-dollar aid package for NGOs and private corporations to alleviate "hunger and homelessness" within the country and for the creation of a "provisional government of national salvation that would be charged with organizing free and fair elections under the United Nations supervision." See "1993 Humanitarian Aid Appropriations," June 9, 1992, C-SPAN, https://www.c-span.org/video/?26511-1/1993-humanitarian-aid-appropriations.

22. Magdi Khalil, "لماذا فشلت قناة الحرة؟" [Why Did Al-Hurra Fail?], *Watani*, October 3, 2005, http://www.mafhoum.com/press9/264C33.htm.
23. Marwan Kraidy observed that by the company's own estimate, Lebanese employees accounted for some 50 percent of the staff at MBC—the largest satellite station in the region. Marwan M. Kraidy, *Reality Television and Arab Politics: Contention in Public Life* (Cambridge University Press, 2010), 79.
24. Quoted in Lizner, "Lost in Translation."
25. *Broadcasting Board of Governors and Alhurra Television*, House of Representatives, 119th Cong. 2, 53 (November 10, 2005).
26. Lizner, "Lost in Translation."
27. Eli Khoury's biography is available at http://www.layalina.tv/about-us/who-we-are/board-of-directors/, Accessed February 1, 2024.
28. Bamo Nouri, "Iraq's Rushed and Divisive Constitution Was Always Doomed to Fail," *The Conversation*, October 31, 2017, https://theconversation.com/iraqs-rushed-and-divisive-constitution-was-always-doomed-to-fail-85026.
29. Eli Khoury, interview with Nadia Michel, *Hakawati Podcasts*, October 17, 2019, https://www.youtube.com/watch?v=ZS_36AvLfDw, 2:13–2:55.
30. Alex Ben Block, "Alhurra Gallops into Mideast Media Mix," *Television Week* 23, no. 7 (2004): 1–37.
31. Leon Shahabian, personal interview with the author, September 8, 2023. According to a former managing editor of Radio Sawa in Dubai, Harb described Khoury as "my best friend in Beirut." The relationship generated clear quid pro quo and was heavily scrutinized during congressional hearings in 2005. In particular, Harb was challenged for awarding no-bid contracts to Khoury's companies, a description Harb rejected. See Art Levine, "Bad Reception, Part II: Did Cronies of Mouafac Harb, the Executive Who Runs America's Arabic-Language Networks, Get Sweetheart Contracts?" American Prospect, November 10, 2005, https://prospect.org/article/bad-reception-part-ii/. And: *Broadcasting Board of Governors and Alhurra Television*, House of Representatives, 119th Cong. 53–54 (November 10, 2005).

32. The tacky graphics of Al-Hurra's opening montage were created by the New York–based marketing firm Lambie-Nairn, according to a *Television Week* cover story in 2004 (See Block, "Alhurra Gallops").
33. Van Ham, Peter. "Opinion Piece: Branding European Power." *Place Branding*, no. 1, 2 (2005): 123.
34. Josh Wood, "The Balance Shifts in Lebanese Politics." *New York Times*, February 16, 2011, https://www.nytimes.com/2011/02/17/world/middleeast/17iht-lebanon.html.
35. See Sharmine Narwani, "An Obituary on Lebanon's 'Cedar Revolution,'" *Mideast Shuffle* (blog), March 13, 2005, https://mideastshuffle.com/2015/03/18/an-obituary-on-lebanons-cedar-revolution/. See also Eli Khoury, interview with Nadia Michel, 19:06.
36. See "Boos for Al-Hurra," *Wall Street Journal*, May 11, 2007, https://www.wsj.com/articles/SB117884907316599493.
37. See Sean Powers and Ahmed El-Gody, "Lessons of Al-Hurra Television," in *Toward a New Public Diplomacy*, ed. Philip Seib (Palgrave, 2009), 53.
38. Linzer, "Lost in Translation."
39. *ProPublica* reported additionally that while in Syria Jabouri had "set up his own regional television network which airs images of attacks on U.S. troops." The US Treasury Department had recently sanctioned Jabouri at the time of his appearance on Al-Hurra Iraq (Linzer, "Lost in Translation."). On the al-Sadr report see Levine, "Bad Reception."
40. Levine, "Bad Reception, Part II."
41. Thomas Dine, the former president for RFE/RL, told Art Levine that that broadcast's "simultaneous translation costs" in "twenty-eight languages" were "zero" and were produced as part of the typical job description of the station's editors and staff (Levine, "Bad Reception, Part II.").
42. See Levine, "Bad Reception, Part II."
43. Linzer, "Lost in Translation.".
44. Khalil, "Why Did Al-Hurra Fail?".
45. See Mamoun Fandy, *(Un)Civil War of Words: Media and Politics in the Arab World* (Praeger Security International, 2007), 109.
46. Khalil, "Why Did Al-Hurra Fail?".
47. See Block, "Alhurra Gallops." On Tomlinson and the State Department's findings of his embezzlement activities, see Stephen Labaton, "Broadcast Chief Misused Office, Inquiry Reports," *New York Times*, August 30, 2006, https://www.nytimes.com/2006/08/30/washington/30broadcast.html?hp&ex=1156996800&en=8590fa5730300061&ei=5094&partner=homepage.
48. Al-Hurra has kept no traceable record of its broadcasts from this period. As such, the claim as reported in the BBG's 2008 budget request that the

station switched to 24/7 news coverage of the Israeli-Hizballah conflict in 2006, cannot be verified.

49. The BBG's total budget request for the MBN in 2008 was $101,764 million, according to its Fiscal Year 2008 budget request. It is available online at https://permanent.fdlp.gov/FDLP1036/index.htm.

50. "FY 2013 Budget Request," BBG, 2013, 42, https://permanent.fdlp.gov/FDLP1036/FY-2013-BBG-Congressional-Budget-Request-FINAL-2-9-12-Small.pdf.

51. A description of "نبض الشارع" (Street Pulse) is available on YouTube. See https://www.youtube.com/user/streetpulseshow.

52. *Eye on Democracy*'s feature length-documentaries from 2012 included "تونس: ثورة الكرامة" (Tunisia: The Revolution of Dignity) and "تونس: الجمهرية" (Tunis: The Republic).

53. See "الأميرتان سحر وجواهر: أبونا ملك السعودية ونحن معتقلتان في قصرنا بالجوع" [Princesses Sahar and Jawaher: Our Father Is the King of Saudi Arabia, and We Are Detained in Our Palace Due to Hunger], Al-Hurra, April 11, 2014. https://web.archive.org/web/20230307205046/https://www.alhurra.com/choice-alhurra/2014/04/11/ملك-أبونا-وجواهر-سحر-الأميرتان-السعودية-ونحن-معتقلتان-في-قصرنا-بالجوع.

54. The author acquired a large sample of BBG-commissioned audience surveys through a Freedom of Information Act request in fall 2023.

55. BBG, FY 2017 Performance and Accountability Report, 2017, 34, https://archive.org/details/usagm-reports/bbg-fy-2017-par/.

56. OIG, Inspection of the Broadcasting Board of Governors' Middle East Broadcasting Networks, Dept. of State, Rep. No. ISP-IB-17-09 (February 2017), 3. The report singled out the success of the live three-hour news magazine show *Al-Youm*, as well *Rayheen 'ala Feen*, which focused on pressing societal issues in Egypt, including "sexual harassment, women's rights, jobs, and education." The report also noted important innovations in the realms of new media—in particular the shows *Maghreb Voices* and *Raise Your Voice* (*Irfaa Sawta*).

57. Other key personnel under Bouran included Jafer al-Zoubi, who, according to his LinkedIn page in 2023 became acting vice president for news in 2020 and was executive producer charged with managing the Dubai office in 2018. For seven years before that, he worked under Bouran at Sky News and then, like Bouran, returned to the Emirati media world as the head of news for Al-Mashad, another UAE-funded start-up. Thaer Soukar was Bouran's head of digital strategy at Sky News Arabia for the same period (2011–2018). He remained at Al-Hurra following Bouran's departure, becoming vice president of digital platforms and strategy. His information was also available on LinkedIn as of October 2023.

58. Seth Frantzman, "The New Face of Al-Hurra: An Interview with Alberto Fernandez," Middle East Center for Reporting and Analysis, November 11, 2018. https://www.mideastcenter.org/post/the-new-face-of-al-hurra-an-interview-with-alberto-fernandez.
59. Author discussion with Ambassador Alberto M. Fernandez, George Mason University, November 12, 2020.
60. Tarek Ali Ahmad, "US-Backed Alhurra TV Relaunches Amid New Iran Sanctions," Arab News, November 6, 2018, https://www.arabnews.com/node/1399901/%7B%7B.
61. Alberto Fernandez, email correspondence with the author, August 18, 2020.
62. See Chris Walsh, "New on the Freedom Collection: Ammar Abdulhamid Updates," George W. Bush Presidential Center, February 25, 2013, https://www.bushcenter.org/publications/new-on-the-freedom-collection-ammar-abdulhamid-updates.
63. Alberto Fernandez, email correspondence with the author, August 18, 2020.
64. See Patricia R. Blanco, "Ni España existía ni la Reconquista es tal y como la cuenta Vox" [Neither Spain nor the Inquisition Existed as Vox Imagines], El País, April 12, 2019, https://elpais.com/elpais/2019/04/11/hechos/1554980000_022524.html. The leader of Vox described Muslim students studying in Spain as a "Trojan horse" through which radicalism in the country was spreading. See Pedro De Pena, "Los caballos de Troya de la España democrática" [The Trojan Horses of Democratic Spain], Libertad digital, December 14, 2014, https://www.libertaddigital.com/opinion/2018-08-26/pedro-de-tena-los-caballos-de-troya-de-la-espana-democratica-6421279/.
65. The description is available on Providence's "About" page at https://providencemag.com/about/.
66. Founded by former Israeli military intelligence officers, MEMRI has been accused of bias in its "selective" coverage of extremism in the Arab world. See Brian Whitaker, "Selective Memri," Guardian, August 12, 2002, https://www.theguardian.com/world/2002/aug/12/worlddispatch.brianwhitaker.
67. See Ann M. Simmons, "Putin Meets with Saudi, UAE Rulers," Wall Street Journal, December 7, 2023, https://www.wsj.com/world/russia/putin-meets-with-saudi-u-a-e-rulers-in-bid-to-refresh-alliances-df321626.
68. On the UAE's connection to coordinated inauthentic behavior operations, see "Removing Coordinated Inauthentic Behavior in UAE, Egypt and Saudi Arabia," Meta, August 1, 2019, https://about.fb.com/news/2019/08/cib-uae-egypt-saudi-arabia/. See also "Removing Coordinated Inauthentic Behavior in UAE, Nigeria, Indonesia and Egypt," Meta, October 3, 2019, https://about.fb.com/news/2019/10/removing-coordinated-inauthentic-behavior-in-uae-nigeria-indonesia-and-egypt/.

250 3. IRAQ AND THE WORLD

69. See Mike Pompeo, "Press Statement: U.S. Approves Advanced Defense Capabilities for the United Arab Emirates," Department of State, November 10, 2020, https://2017-2021.state.gov/u-s-approves-advanced-defense-capabilities-for-the-united-arab-emirates/.

4. GRAY IS THE NEW BLACK

1. A clip of the video, "On the Road in America' on Glenn Beck'" is provided on the Layalina website. See https://web.archive.org/web/20240520081554/https://vimeo.com/7783960, accessed February 8, 2024.
2. Ray Richmond, "On the Road in America," *Hollywood Reporter*, June 1, 2008, https://www.hollywoodreporter.com/movies/movie-reviews/road-america-126081/.
3. Leon Shahabian, personal interview with the author, February 23, 2022.
4. Marc Ginsberg, "Experience," LinkedIn. https://www.linkedin.com/in/marc-ginsberg-3674b017/details/experience/, accessed December 17, 2023.
5. Edward P. Djerejian, *Changing Minds Winning Peace: A New Strategic Direction for U.S. Public Diplomacy in the Arab and Muslim World*, report of the Advisory Group on Public Diplomacy for the Arab and Muslim World, October 1, 2003, 32.
6. See Layalina Productions Inc., "Nonprofit Explorer," ProPublica, https://projects.propublica.org/nonprofits/display_990/300019501/2004_07_EO%2F30-0019501_990_200312, accessed January 23 2024.
7. According to Shahabian, the State Department provided funding for the second and third seasons of *On the Road in America* with grants of a little more than one million dollars for each season. In 2008, the company was anticipating funding through a Senate appropriations bill, but the funds were ultimately diverted through the State Department, which issued a request for proposals (RFP) and ultimately slashed the proposed funding for Layalina by half. According to Shahabian, the author of the State Department's RFP was subsequently hired by AAM, the company's primary competitor in the space of gray propaganda. I was unable to independently verify this claim. Leon Shahabian, personal interview with the author, March 23, 2023.
8. Jordy Yager, "Prejudice in America, Reality-Style," The Hill, June 3, 2008. https://thehill.com/capital-living/20848-prejudice-in-america-reality-style/.
9. A copy of the MBC Ipsos poll commissioned by MBC for March and April 2010 was shared with the author by the show's producer, Leon Shahabian.
10. See Nicholas J. Cull, *The Cold War and the United States Information Agency* (Cambridge University Press, 2008), 31; Wilson P. Dizard, *Inventing Public Diplomacy: The Story of the U.S. Information Agency* (Lynne Rienner, 2004),

66; and Hugh Wilford, *The Mighty Wurlitzer: How the CIA Played America* (Harvard University Press, 2008), 117–19. Also, on the Congress for Cultural Freedom, see Frances Stonor Saunders, *The Cultural Cold War: The CIA and the World of Arts and Letters* (New Press, 2000).
11. Nina Teicholz, "Privatizing Propaganda," *Washington Monthly* 34, no. 12 (2002).
12. Michael Kirk (director), "Secrets, Politics, and Torture," *Frontline*, May 19, 2015, PBS, https://www.pbs.org/wgbh/frontline/documentary/secrets-politics-and-torture/, 1:46–2:20.
13. Teicholz, "Privatizing Propadanda."
14. Information on Layalina's board members can be found on the organization's website. See http://www.layalina.tv/about-us/who-we-are/board-of-directors/. For "Initiative 9/11," see Susan B. Epstein, *U.S. Public Diplomacy: Background and the 9/11 Commission Recommendations*, Congressional Research Service, 2018, and 108th Congress S. 2874, *Initiative 911 Act, Bill Profile*, 2004. For more on Layalina, see Martha Bayles, *Through a Screen Darkly: Popular Culture, Public Diplomacy, and America's Image Abroad* (Yale University Press, 2014).
15. Alvin A. Snyder, *Warriors of Disinformation: American Propaganda, Soviet Lies, and the Winning of the Cold War: An Insider's Account* (Arcade, 1995), 38.
16. Snyder, *Warriors*, 8.
17. Peter W. Kaplan, "Let Poland Be Poland," *Washington Post*, January 28, 1982, https://www.washingtonpost.com/archive/lifestyle/1982/01/28/let-poland-be-poland/f1aaf3c2-6c86-4f50-a14e-702b1a7d7dac/.
18. Snyder, *Warriors*, 40.
19. Snyder, *Warriors*, 40.
20. D. Barboza and N. Nandoe. "The Afghan War at Boston University," *Daily Free Press*, November 5, 1986. Quoted in Snyder, *Warriors*, 40.
21. Snyder, *Warriors*, 204. See also Zalmay Khalilzad, "Afghanistan: Anatomy of a Soviet Failure," *National Interest* 12, no. 12 (National Affairs, 1988), 101–8.
22. Snyder, *Warriors*, 204. Most other estimates of the impact of the conflict refer to three million refugees.
23. Snyder, *Warriors*, 204.
24. Ash Hawkens, "Thanksgiving in Peshawar with Kirk Douglas," *Ash Hawkens: Ideas in Words and Images* (blog), December 29, 2020, https://ashhawken.com/thanksgiving-peshawar-kirk-douglas/.
25. See Hawkens, "Thanksgiving in Peshawar." See also Cull, *Cold War*, 428.
26. Steven Galster, "Afghanistan: The Making of U.S. Policy, 1973–1990," in *Volume II: Afghanistan: Lessons from the Last War*, National Security Archive, October 9, 2001, https://nsarchive2.gwu.edu/NSAEBB/NSAEBB57/essay.html#1.

27. Snyder, *Warriors*, 204.
28. "Washington Talk: United States Information Agency; At $30 Million Is Anyone Watching?" *New York Times*, July 14, 1987, https://www.nytimes.com/1987/07/14/us/washington-talk-united-states-information-agency-30-million-anyone-watching.html.
29. Donna Marie Vincent, *Worldnet: Propaganda and Public Diplomacy* (ProQuest Dissertations & Theses, 1993), 114.
30. Todd Levanthal, "Soviet vs. Post-Soviet Russian Disinformation," *American Diplomacy*, February 1, 2024, https://americandiplomacy.web.unc.edu/2024/02/soviet-vs-post-soviet-russian-disinformation/; Snyder, *Warriors*, 106. On the story of the *Patriot* newspaper and the spread of Soviet disinformation surrounding the AIDS epidemic, see Thomas Rid, *Active Measures: The Secret History of Disinformation and Political Warfare* (Farrar, Straus and Giroux, 2020), 303–7.
31. Nicholas J. Cull, *The Decline and Fall of the United States Information Agency: American Public Diplomacy, 1989–2001* (Palgrave Macmillan, 2012), 136.
32. Vincent, *Worldnet*, 114.
33. "Clinton Sends Conciliatory Message to Iran," *New York Times*, January 30, 1998, https://www.nytimes.com/1998/01/30/world/clinton-sends-conciliatory-message-to-iran.html.
34. Shahabian, personal interview with the author, February 23, 2022.
35. Layalina Productions, "OTR II Is a Hit," *The Layalina Chronicle*, 2010, https://web.archive.org/web/20141119150107/http://www.layalina.tv/publications/the-layalina-chronicle/.
36. "Interview with Abdul Rahman al-Rashed, General Manager, Al-Arabiya," *Frontline*, accessed May 1, 2024, transcript, https://www.pbs.org/frontlineworld/stories/newswar/war_rashed.html.
37. See Adi Robertson, "Inside USC's Crazy Experimental VR Lab," *The Verge*, September 17, 2015, https://www.theverge.com/2015/9/17/9333633/usc-institute-for-creative-technologies-virtual-reality-lab.
38. Sharon Waxman, "Thinking Outside the Tank," *Washington Post*, March 7, 2003, https://www.washingtonpost.com/archive/lifestyle/2003/03/07/thinking-outside-the-tank/1a25372a-e258-484f-acae-5dfbc2585fd1/.
39. Shahabian, personal interview with the author, February 23, 2022.
40. Jerome D. Gary, curriculum vitae, https://web.archive.org/web/20190819091953/https://www.visionairemedia.com/wp-content/uploads/2019/04/PResume6_22_18p.pdf. In 2004, the Esalen Soviet-American Exchange Program was renamed Track Two" and evolved into an institute focused on citizen diplomacy. See "About" at https://www.trackii.com.
41. According to Shahabian, the first season of *On the Road in America* launched with a $1.5 million grant from the Fairbanks Foundation; subsequent years

included grants from the State Department for approximately one million per season. Shahabian, personal interview with the author, February 23, 2022.

42. As late as 2024, Gary, through his company Visionaire Media, continued to attribute to State Department funding a scattering of glossy but mostly undeveloped films crafted in the mold of American neo-orientalism. With funding attributed to the MENA Media Fund, Visionaire Media repackaged the decade-old Layalina production *Yemeniettes* as part of a "MENA Smartphone Festival" in Rabat and promoted a series of mostly Lebanese-based human-interest stories, including some, like *Confessions of a War* (a testimonial documentary about Lebanon's Civil War), which had been made almost a decade before. More peculiar among Visionaire's later slate of propaganda films was a promised "historical epic narrative series in the tradition of *Vikings* and *Game Thrones*" called *The Phoenicians*. It remained unclear whether the filmmakers, or its State Department backers, were aware that the intellectual currency of the Phoenician era in the Arabic tradition, unlike other parts of the Mediterranean, carried a divisive bent, being long associated with the ethno-fascist leanings of Antoun Saadeh, founder of the Syrian Social Nationalist Party, and the mostly Christian imaginings of a pre-Islamic, Levantine past.

43. Shahabian, personal interview with the author, February 23, 2022. On MEPI and its funding history, see Oz Hassan, *Constructing America's Freedom Agenda for the Middle East: Democracy or Domination* (Routledge, 2013). Hassan identifies MEPI as the brainchild of Senator Liz Cheney, who saw the funding line as a "method of pushing for institutional reform in the region" (128).

44. In 2015, the founder of INJAZ al-Arab, Soraya Salti, an outspoken critic of Salafist and other antiwomen viewpoints in Jordanian society, was reported dead along with her sister after being discovered at the foot of a tall building in a run-down part of Jwiedeh, Amman (Suha Maayeh, "Mysterious Deaths of Prominent Sisters Shock Jordan," *The National*, November 8, 2015, https://www.thenationalnews.com/world/mysterious-deaths-of-prominent-sisters-shock-jordan-1.46034). Jordanian police suggested the sisters' death had been a suicide pact, but suspicions of foul play ran high. Salti's death followed an alarming pattern wherein multiple, prominent youth activists associated with the Arab uprisings were reported dead or missing under unusual or violent circumstances. A short list includes the Tunisians Lina Ben Mhenni, who was reported to have died of kidney disease, Sofiene Chourabi, who disappeared in Libya, and Yasmine Ryan, a young reporter on Al-Jazeera's media desk who was among the first to write about the protests in Sidi Bouzid, Tunisia. Ryan was also said to have died by falling off a building in Istanbul.

45. Marwan M. Kraidy, *Reality Television and Arab Politics: Contention in Public Life* (Cambridge University Press, 2010), 11.
46. Kraidy, *Reality Television*, 11.
47. Kraidy, *Reality Television*, 11.
48. Shahabian, personal interview with the author, February 23, 2022.
49. See Geoffrey Cowan, "Voice of America Has Not Ceded Editorial Control to Foreign Broadcasters" (letter), *Washington Times*, January 23, 1996, 16. Cowan's response to Harb was eerily predicative of the criticisms that would follow Harb and his operating practices throughout his tenure as director of Radio Sawa and Al-Hurra during the Bush administration.
50. Aziz Fahmy, "The Story Is the Agenda of the Reporter, Not the Content of Our Show," *Washington Times*, January 26, 1996, 18.
51. Sam Barnett, personal interview with author, February 15, 2021. See also Muhammad Ayish, "Arab Television Goes Commercial: A Case Study of the Middle East Broadcasting Centre," *Gazette (Leiden, Netherlands)* 59, no. 6 (1997): 473–94.
52. "بدرية البشر للعربية.نت: الفتوى ضد طاش ما طاش لم تجد صدى بالسعودية" [Badria al-Bashir: The Fatwa Against Tash ma Tash Will Not Find Support in Saudi], Al-Arabiya, September 10, 2007, https://www.alarabiya.net/articles/2007%2F09%2F10%2F38960.
53. See, for example, Rebecca Joubin, *The Politics of Love: Sexuality, Gender, and Marriage in Syrian Television Drama* (Lexington, 2013), 10.
54. Christa Salamandra, "The Muhannad Effect: Media Panic, Melodrama, and the Arab Female Gaze," *Anthropological Quarterly* 85, no. 1 (2012): 45–77.
55. Barnett, personal interview with author, February 15, 2021.
56. Heather Jaber and Marwan M. Kraidy, "The Geopolitics of Television Drama and the 'Global War on Terror': Gharabeeb Soud Against Islamic State," *International Journal of Communication* (2020): 1868–87.
57. See Cynthia Schneider, "Can Good Television Beat the Islamic State?" *Foreign Policy*, April 7, 2017, https://foreignpolicy.com/2017/04/07/can-good-television-beat-the-islamic-state-mbc/.
58. Jamil Khader, "On ISIL, Arab TV and Post-Ideological Politics," Al-Jazeera, June 22, 2017, https://www.aljazeera.com/opinions/2017/6/22/on-isil-arab-tv-and-post-ideological-politics.

    In her critique, Donatella Della Rata provides a short list of MBC's "antiterrorism" shows including the 2005 series *Hur al-Ayn* (The Maidens of Paradise); *Irhab Academy* (Terrorist Academy), and *Sina'at al-Mawt* (Death Industry). As she notes, much of MBC's CVE programming was shaped by Abdullah Bjiad al-Otibi, a reformed al-Qaeda sympathizer who advised the Kingdom of Saudi

Arabia, as well as the United States, on a range of CVE activities. See Donatella Della Rata, "Fighting ISIL Through TV Drama: The Case of Black Crows", Al-Jazeera, June 19, 2017, https://www.aljazeera.com/features/2017/6/19/fighting-isil-through-tv-drama-the-case-of-black-crows.

59. Joseph Braude, who joined AAM as an adviser in 2012, accredits that organization, led then by its founder Aaron Lobel and Paula Dobriansky, George W. Bush's first under secretary of state for global affairs, with having pioneered the kind of model exemplified by the Sunnylands arrangement, including "educational workshops in which Hollywood screenwriters and producers mentor Arabs in the respective skills, together with government and private investment in the region's entertainment productions." As it were, Layalina had begun developing the relationship with MBC the previous decade. But Braude was correct in associating the Sunnylands agreement with AAM in the sense that the company, which featured Arab and MBC talent, including Nasser al-Qasabi, as part of its annual awards gala, had become a powerful vector for the privatization of public diplomacy. See Joseph Braude, *Broadcasting Change: Arabic Media as a Catalyst for Liberalism* (Rowman & Littlefield, 2017), 114.

60. Mayssoun Sukarieh, "The Hope Crusades: Culturalism and Reform in the Arab World," *Political and Legal Anthropology Review* 35, no. 1 (2012): 115–34.

61. Queen Rania championed the show's launch, and the series gained additional support from the Kingdom of Jordan as part of its sustainable development strategy. Control of the content has since changed hands multiple times. Shahabian, personal interview with author, February 23, 2022.

62. Wilford, *Mighty Wurlitzer*, 118.

63. On the Hoja project, see Aysehan Jülide Etem: "A Transnational Communication Network Promoting Film Diplomacy: The Case of Turkey and the USA, 1950–86," *Historical Journal of Film, Radio, and Television* 41, no. 2 (2021): 292–316.

64. See the United States Information Agency, *The Hoja's Strange Ways*, Video, US National Archives, Motion Picture Films from the "Hoja" Program Series, 1952–1974, Record Group 306: Records of the U.S. Information Agency, 1900–2003, https://catalog.archives.gov/id/140135788.

65. Edward W. Barrett, *Truth Is Our Weapon* (Funk & Wagnalls, 1953), 242.

66. Alberto Fernandez, "Measuring the Unmeasurable: Evaluating the Effectiveness of US Strategic Counterterrorism Communications," *The SAGE Handbook of Propaganda*, ed. by Nancy Snow, Paul Baines, and Nicholas O'Shaughnessy (SAGE, 2020), 324.

5. SILICON ARMIES

1. Monika Bickert, "Internet Security and Privacy in the Age of the Islamic State: The View from Facebook," Washington Institute of Near East Policy, March 2, 2016, https://www.washingtoninstitute.org/policy-analysis/internet-security-and-privacy-age-islamic-state-view-facebook.
2. Lisa Monaco, "Remarks by Lisa O. Monaco at the Council on Foreign Relations," Kenneth A. Moskow Memorial Lecture, March 7, 2016, https://obamawhitehouse.archives.gov. For more on the Islamic State group, including the genealogy of the group's name, see Nathaniel Greenberg, "Islamic State War Documentaries," *International Journal of Communication* 14 (2020): 1808–28.
3. See John Kerry, press availability in Brussels, Belgium, transcript, December 3, 2013, https://2009-2017.state.gov.
4. Danny Yadron, "Silicon Valley Appears Open to Helping US Spy Agencies After Terrorism Summit," *Guardian*, January 8, 2016, https://www.theguardian.com/technology/2016/jan/08/technology-executives-white-house-isis-terrorism-meeting-silicon-valley-facebook-apple-twitter-microsoft.
5. John Kerry, Twitter, February 17, 2016, https://twitter.com/JohnKerry/status/699746890271715328.
6. The involvement of Facebook, Google, Twitter, Instagram, Snapchat, Tumblr, and Microsoft provoked a Freedom of Information Act (FOIA) request by the Electronic Privacy Information Center (EPIC), which claimed the tech companies' involvement had "privacy and constitutional implications." The FOIA request and documents are available at https://epic.org/foia/EPIC-16-03-02-DOJ-FOIA-20160302-Request.pdf.
7. Kaveh Waddell, "How New York's Top Advertisers Are Fighting Terrorist Propaganda," *Atlantic*, March 15, 2016, https://www.theatlantic.com/technology/archive/2016/03/how-new-yorks-top-advertisers-are-helping-fight-terrorist-propaganda/473805/.
8. Waddell, "How New York's Top Advertisers Are Fighting Terrorist Propaganda."
9. "Remarks by Assistant Attorney General John Carlin," opening of Madison Valleywood Project, Department of Justice, February 24, 2016, https://epic.org/foia/MadisonValleywood_2.pdf.
10. The image was published by the UK's *Daily Mail* in March 2015 with this headline: "EXCLUSIVE: 'We're thirsty for your blood': Playboy jihadi's widow poses with her gun-toting 'clique' of female fanatics in front of flash BMW and boasts of 'five-star jihad' lifestyle in Syria."
11. Chris Pleasance, "Trip Advisor for Terrorists: Where to Buy Nutella in the War Zone, What Kind of Trainers to Wear, and How It Feels to Chop

Off Infidels' Heads Revealed in Twisted Chatrooms," *Daily Mail*, August 15, 2014, https://www.dailymail.co.uk/news/article-2726407/Trip-Advisor-terrorists-Where-buy-Nutella-war-zone-kind-trainers-wear-feels-chop-infidels-heads-revealed-twisted-chatrooms.html.

12. Bickert, "Internet Security."
13. See Gabriel Weimann, "Al-Qa'ida's Extensive Use of the Internet," *CTC Sentinel* 2 no. 1 (2008).
14. Alberto Fernandez, email correspondence with the author, August 18, 2020.
15. Marc Sageman, *Understanding Terror Networks* (University of Pennsylvania Press, 2004), 164.
16. Sageman, *Understanding Terror Networks*, 161.
17. Shufan, Nabil, "وزارة إعلام داعش.. منظومة الترويج الفني والحرب النفسية" [ISIS Ministry of Information: A System of Artistic Intimidation and Psychological Warfare]. *Al-'Arabi al-Jadid*, March 29, 2015, https://www.alaraby.co.uk/وزارة-إعلام-داعش-منظومة-الترويج-الفني-والحرب-النفسية/.
18. Abdel Bari Atwan, *Islamic State: The Digital Caliphate* (University of California Press, 2015), 15. See also Greenberg, "Islamic State War Documentaries".
19. See "Paving the Way to the Modern Internet," DARPA, accessed November 15, 2023, https://www.darpa.mil/about-us/timeline/modern-internet.
20. Nicholas J. Cull, *The Decline and Fall of the United States Information Agency: American Public Diplomacy, 1989–2001* (Palgrave Macmillan, 2012), 74.
21. William Rugh, *Frontline Public Diplomacy* (Palgrave, 2014), 96.
22. *Report of the Defense Science Board Task Force on Strategic Communication*, Office of the Under Secretary of Defense for Acquisition, Technology, and Logistics, September 2004, 2.
23. H.R. Rep. No. GAO-03-951 at 12 (September 4, 2003).
24. Daniel Silverberg and Joseph Heimann, "An Ever-Expanding War: Legal Aspects of Online Strategic Communication," *Parameters* 39, no. 2 (2009): 81.
25. Walter Pincus, "A Speed Bump for Pentagon's Information Ops," *Washington Post*, December 6, 2011, https://www.washingtonpost.com/blogs/checkpoint-washington/post/a-speed-bump-for-pentagons-information-ops/2011/12/06/gIQAbxF7YO_blog.html.
26. A description of ExchangesConnect is available at https://exchanges.state.gov/us/connect.
27. A second Alliance of Youth Movements Summit was staged in Mexico City in October 2009. It included many of the same corporate contributors as the first summit.
28. James K. Glassman, email correspondence with the author. August 15, 2020.

29. See Wael Ghonim, *Revolution 2.0: The Power of the People Is Greater than the People in Power: A Memoir* (Houghton Mifflin Harcourt, 2013), 41; and Nathaniel Greenberg, *How Information Warfare Shaped the Arab Spring* (Edinburgh University Press, 2019), 45. For more on the Alliance of Youth Movements Summit and the impact of bloggers on the Arab uprisings, see Linda Herrera, *Revolution in the Age of Social Media: The Egyptian Popular Insurrection and the Internet* (Verso), 2014. Like Ghonim, Salah wrote a memoir about his experience. See Ahmed Salah, *You Are Under Arrest for Masterminding the Egyptian Revolution* (Spark, 2016).
30. *Report of the Defense Science Board Task Force on Strategic Communication*, Office of the Under Secretary of Defense for Acquisition, Technology, and Logistics, 2004, 14.
31. Nicholas Jackson, "Wikileaks' Assange: Facebook Is an Appalling Spy Machine," *Atlantic*, May 2, 2011, https://www.theatlantic.com/technology/archive/2011/05/wikileaks-assange-facebook-is-appalling-spying-machine/238225/.
32. James K. Glassman and Jared Cohen, "Special Briefing to Announce the Alliance of Youth Movement," Department of State, November 24, 2008, https://2001-2009.state.gov/r/us/2008/112310.htm. For more on Wikileaks's exposure of the State Department cables, see Greenberg, *How Information Warfare Shaped the Arab Spring*, 20–21.
33. Board of Foreign Scholarships, *International Educational Exchange: The Opening Decades, 1946-1966* (US Government Printing Office, 1966), 34.
34. United States Information Agency, "المكتبات العامة و النشئ" [Public Libraries and Publications], *Al-Sadaqah*, November 6, 1952, 5. On the International Field Service program, see United States Information Agency, "التجربة المثيرة: ثلاث فتيات امريكيات تعيش كل منهن ابنه لاسرة مصرية" [An Exciting Experience: Three American Girls Live as Daughters in Egyptian Families], *Al-Sadaqah*, August 18, 1966, 1.
35. Monaco, "Remarks by Lisa O. Monaco."
36. Tarek El-Ariss, *Leaks, Hacks, and Scandals: Arab Culture in the Digital Age* (Princeton University Press, 2019), 11.
37. Glassman and Cohen, "Special Briefing." For Sageman's testimony, see *Confronting al-Qaeda: Understanding the Threat in Afghanistan and Beyond, Before the Committee on Foreign Relations*, US Senate, 11th Congress, 16 (2009) (statement of Marc Sageman, senior fellow, Foreign Policy Research Institute).
38. See "يوم الغدب" [The Day of Rage], *Al-Shorouk*, January 25, 2011, 1.
39. "بورقيات الديلومسية" [Wikileaks's Diplomatic Cables], *Al-Ahram*, January 29, 2011, 1.

40. Glassman, email correspondence with the author, August 15, 2020.
41. Glassman, email correspondence with the author, August 15, 2020.
42. World Bank, "Individuals Using the Internet (Percent of Population)," 2017, https://data.worldbank.org/indicator/IT.NET.USER.ZS?locations=EG.
43. "L'Egypte, autre 'ennemi d'Internet' " [Egypt: Another Enemy of the Internet], *Le Monde*, January 26, 2011, https://www.lemonde.fr/technologies/article/2011/01/26/l-egypte-autre-ennemi-d-internet_1470630_651865.html
44. Rebecca MacKinnon, *Consent of the Networked* (Basic Books, 2013), 4.
45. See Emad Mekay, "TV Stations Multiply as Egyptian Censorship Falls," *New York Times*, July 30, 2011, https://www.nytimes.com/2011/07/14/world/middleeast/14iht-M14B-EGYPT-MEDIA.html. See also Abdallah F. Hassan, *Media, Revolution, and Politics in Egypt* (I. B. Tauris, 2015), 76. Egypt's Ministry of Information was abolished in February 2011 but was reinstated on July 12; "Egypt's Reinstatement of Information Ministry Is a Setback," Committee to Project Journalists, July 12, 2011, https://cpj.org/2011/07/egypts-reinstatement-of-information-ministry-is-ma/.
46. Lilia Blaise, "De l'ATI à l'ATT : Quel avenir pour l'internet en Tunisie?" *Huffpost Maghreb*, March 18, 2014.
47. Magdi Galad, "انفراد: «الداخلية» تفرض «قبضة إلكترونية» على جرائم شبكات التواصل الاجتماعى" [Infared: The Ministry of Interior Imposes an "Electronic Control" on Social Networking Crimes], June 1, 2014, https://www.elwatannews.com/news/details/495659.
48. See Cull (2012), 134.
49. *The State Department's Center for Strategic Counterterrorism Communications: Mission, Operations and Impact: Hearing before the Subcommittee on Terrorism, Nonproliferation, and Trade of the Committee on Foreign Affairs*, House of Representatives, 112th Cong. 12 (August 2, 2012) (statement of Alberto Fernandez, coordinator, Center for Strategic Counterterrorism Communications, US Department of State).
50. Richard Stengel, *Information Wars: How We Lost the Global Battle Against Disinformation and What We Can Do About It* (Atlantic Monthly, 2019), 60.
51. Stengel, *Information Wars*, 60.
52. See Department of State, media note, "Mr. Alberto Fernandez's Comments on Al-Jazeera," October 22, 2006, https://2001-2009.state.gov/r/pa/prs/ps/2006/74893.htm.
53. Fernandez, email correspondence with the author, December 11, 2020.
54. *The State Department's Center for Strategic Counterterrorism Communications: Mission, Operations and Impact* (statement of Alberto Fernandez).
55. Quoted in Stengel, *Information Wars*, 61.

56. Greg Miller and Scott Higham, "In a Propaganda War Against ISIS, the U.S. Tried to Play by the Enemies' Rules," *Washington Post*, May 8, 2015, https://www.washingtonpost.com/world/national-security/in-a-propaganda-war-us-tried-to-play-by-the-enemys-rules/2015/05/08/6eb6b732-e52f-11e4-81ea-0649268f729e_story.html.
57. See: فريق التواصل الإلكتروني [The Digital Outreach Team]. About. https://www.youtube.com/@StateDepartment. Also: Alberto M. Fernandez, "Measuring the Unmeasurable: Evaluating the Effectiveness of US Strategic Counterterrorism Communications," in *The SAGE Handbook of Propaganda*, ed. Nancy Snow, Paul Baines, and Nicholas O'Shaughnessy (SAGE, 2020), 325. Fernandez notes that the DOT began as an "outgrowth" of an Arabic-language media "outreach" center set up by the State Department in London.
58. United States Department of State (November 20, 2007), comments.
59. "فريق التواصل الإلكتروني الأميركي" [The American Digital Outreach Team], September 29, 2009, Al-Jazeera, https://www.aljazeera.net/news/2009/9/29/فريق-التواصل-الإلكتروني-الأميركي.
60. Lina Khatib, William Dutton, and Michael Thelwall, "Public Diplomacy 2.0: A Case Study of the US Digital Outreach Team," *Middle East Journal* 66, no. 3 (2012): 453–72.
61. Fernandez, "Measuring," 325.
62. Fernandez "Measuring," 327.
63. Digital Outreach Team, "جرائم ابو بكر البغدادي في سطور." [The Crimes of Abu Bakr al-Baghdadi by the Books], October 29, 2019, https://www.youtube.com/watch?v=d8gDhI2Xwc4, 00:56.
64. See Daniel Bernardi, *Narrative Landmines: Rumors, Islamist Extremism, and the Struggle for Strategic Influence* (Rutgers University Press, 2012).
65. United States Department of State (2012).
66. Fernandez, "Measuring," 327.
67. Fernandez, "Measuring," 325. For an example of the DOT's "fitna" narrative, see United States Department of State (2014).
68. Fernandez, "Measuring," 328.
69. Fernandez, "Measuring," 331.
70. Office of Inspector General (OIG), Inspection of the Broadcasting Board of Governors' Middle East Broadcasting Networks, February, 2017, https://www.stateoig.gov/report/isp-ib-17-09, 4.
71. "Public Diplomacy in the Obama Administration's Second Term," C-SPAN, November 13, 2012, https://www.c-span.org/video/?309417-1/public-diplomacy-obama-administrations-term.
72. Broadcasting Board of Governors, *FY 2017 Performance and Accountability Report*, https://www.usagm.gov/wp-content/media/2017/11/BBG_FY_2017_PAR.pdf.

73. Office of Inspector General (OIG), Inspection of the Broadcasting Board of Governors' Middle East Broadcasting Networks, (February, 2017) https://www.stateoig.gov/report/isp-ib-17-09, 4.
74. Ali Muhammad Mubarak's comment in Arabic can be found on Facebook at https://www.facebook.com/photo/?fbid=870450159675755&set=a.789894802492104, accessed February 1, 2024.
75. Ali Karkoushi's comment can be found on Facebook at https://www.facebook.com/photo/?fbid=789894845825433&set=a.789894802492104, accessed February 1, 2024.
76. See J. M. Brewer, "The Wisdom to Self-Correct: Appreciating the Significance of ISIS's Putative Caliphate and Refining America's Strategy to Destroy It" (MA thesis, United States Marine Corps Command and Staff College, 2016), 10. Also: Quantum Communications, "Understanding Jihadists: In Their Own Words" has since been removed," The White Papers Issue 2 (March 2015), 9.
77. The State Department's funding schema was synchronized across bureaus with the Bureau of Counterterrorism and Countering Violent Extremism in the lead. The other offices included the Office of US Foreign Assistance Resources; the Bureau of Budget and Planning; and the Policy, Planning, and Resources office of the Under Secretary for Public Diplomacy and Public Affairs. See Office of Audits, *Audit of the Department of State Implementation of Policies Intended to Counter Violent Extremism*, Middle East Region Operations, Dept. of State. Rep. No. AUD-MERO-19-27 at 2 (June 28, 2019), https://www.oversight.gov/report/dos/audit-department-state-implementation-policies-intended-counter-violent-extremism.
78. See Office of Audits, *Audit of the Department of State Implementation of Policies Intended to Counter Violent Extremism*, appendix A.
79. See Embassy of the United Arab Emirates, "Counterterrorism," accessed February 1, 2024, https://www.uae-embassy.org/discover-uae/foreign-policy/counterterrorism.
80. See C. Whitlock and N. Jones, "Mattis Secretly Advised Arab Monarch on Yemen War, Records Show." *Washington Post*, February 6, 2024, https://www.washingtonpost.com/investigations/2024/02/06/mattis-advised-uae-yemen-war/.
81. Larry Schwartz, personal interview with the author, September 11, 2020.
82. Schwartz, personal interview with the author, September 11, 2020.
83. Al-'Ain, "الإمارات.. مركز صواب يطلق حملة ضد محاولات تنظيم داعش لطمس الانتماء الوطني" [UAE "Sawab Center" Launches a Campaign Against ISIS's Attempts to Erase National Belonging], January 28, 2016, https://al-ain.com/article/20916.
84. The Embassy of the United Arab Emirates in Washington featured on its "Counterterrorism" page a short, animated video displaying the metrics of the Sawab Center: "Today We Celebrate Sawab's Fifth Anniversary!

Thanks for Your Support," YouTube, July 8, 2020, https://web.archive.org/save/https://www.youtube.com/watch?v=YbQvhBAhC-g&t=34s.
85. Jenna McLaughlin, "Spies for Hire," *The Intercept*, October 24, 2016. https://theintercept.com/2016/10/24/darkmatter-united-arab-emirates-spies-for-hire/.
86. Christopher Bing and Joe Schectman, "Special Report: Inside the UAE's Secret Hacking Team of U.S. Mercenaries," *Reuters*, January 30, 2019, https://www.reuters.com/article/idUSKCN1PO1CV/.
87. Bing and Schectman "Special Report."
88. McLaughlin, "Spies for Hire."
89. Bureau of Political-Military Affairs, Administrative Debarment Under the International Traffic in Arms Regulations Involving Ryan Adams, Marc Baier, and Daniel Gericke, Dept. of State. Pub. Not. 11842 (August 29, 2022), https://www.federalregister.gov/documents/2022/08/29/2022-18504/bureau-of-political-military-affairs-administrative-debarment-under-the-international-traffic-in.
90. McLaughlin, "Spies for Hire."
91. Bureau of Political-Military Affairs, Administrative Debarment Under the International Traffic in Arms Regulations.
92. Rashad Hussain, "A Strategy for Countering Terrorist Propaganda in the Digital Age," Australia Summit on Countering Violent Extremism, June 12, 2015, https://2009-2017.state.gov/r/cscc/releases/243877.htm.
93. Hussain, "A Strategy."

6. ENDGAMES

1. Christine Kelly, "Le débat Bernard-Henri Lévy et Eric Zemmour Face Bernard-Henri Lévy," interview by Christine Kelly, *Face à l'info*, CNews, June 26, 2020, https://www.youtube.com/watch?v=FiFtl856XQI.
2. Edith M. Lederer, "US Calls on Russia, Turkey, UAE to Halt Libya intervention," *AP*, January 28, 2021, https://apnews.com/article/turkey-libya-elections-united-nations-russia-5dd10a3c818204f5baac7f2ee8e4dfe0. See also Wolfgang Pusztai, "Libya's Fragile Ceasefire: A Lost Opportunity?" *Atlantic Council* (blog), June 4, 2021, https://www.atlanticcouncil.org/blogs/menasource/libyas-fragile-ceasefire-a-lost-opportunity/.
3. Marc Lynch, *The New Arab Wars* (Public Affairs, 2016), 181.
4. Fatima El Issawi, *Transitional Libyan Media: Free at Last?* (Carnegie Endowment for International Peace and POLIS, London School of Economics and Political Science, 2013).

5. Fatima El Issawi, *Libya Media Transition: Heading to the Unknown* (POLIS, London School of Economics and Political Science, 2013).
6. The World Bank's 2017 data on "Individuals Using the Internet (% of Population)" in Libya can be found at https://data.worldbank.org/indicator/IT.NET.USER.ZS?locations=LY.
7. Declan Walsh and Suliman Ali Zway, "A Facebook War: Libyans Battle on the Streets and on Screens," *New York Times*, September 4, 2018, https://www.nytimes.com/2018/09/04/world/middleeast/libya-facebook.html.
8. Peter Pomerantsev, *Nothing Is True and Everything Is Possible* (Public Affairs, 2014), 4.
9. Karen DeYoung and Missy Ryan, "Trump's Call with Renegade Libyan General Could Signal a Shift in U.S. Policy," *Washington Post*, April 1, 2019, https://www.washingtonpost.com/world/national-security/trumps-call-with-renegade-libyan-general-could-signal-a-shift-in-us-policy/2019/04/19/d1428264-62d0-11e9-9ff2-abc984dc9eec_story.html.
10. Nathaniel Gleicher, "Removing More Coordinated Inauthentic Behavior from Russia," Meta, October 30, 2019, https://about.fb.com/news/2019/10/removing-more-coordinated-inauthentic-behavior-from-russia/.
11. Declan Walsh and Nada Rashwan, "'We're at War': A Covert Social Media Campaign Boosts Military Rulers," *New York Times*, September 6, 2019, https://www.nytimes.com/2019/09/06/world/middleeast/sudan-social-media.html.
12. See Shelby Grossman, Daniel Bush, and Renée DiResta, "Evidence of Russia-Linked Influence Operations in Africa," Stanford Internet Observatory, October 29, 2019, https://doi.org/10.25740/yh993mk2487.
13. See Shelby Grossman et al., "Hello from the Other Side: An Investigation into a Musical Pro-Muslim Brotherhood Disinformation Operation," Stanford Internet Observatory, November 5, 2020, https://cyber.fsi.stanford.edu/io/publication/hello-other-side-investigation-musical-pro-muslim-brotherhood-disinformation-operation.
14. YouTube channel Stats on Libya can be found at https://www.socialbakers.com/statistics/youtube/channels/libya. Accessed February 13, 2021.
15. Al-Mayadeen Programs, "حوار الساعة: حسين مفتاح - نائب رئيس تحرير موقع بوابة افريقيا الاخبارية" [Conversation of the Hour: Hussein Moftah—Deputy Editor-in-Chief of the Africa News Portal], YouTube, December 29, 2019, https://www.youtube.com/watch?v=mza1oPHyIGg.
16. "إدلب ليبيا.. تركيا على خطى داعش في غرب البلاد" [Idlib, Libya . . . Turkey Is Following the Lead of ISIS in the West of the Country], Sky News Arabia, January 4, 2021, https://web.archive.org/web/20240418174531/https://www.skynewsarabia.com/middle-east/1404799-إدلب-ليبيا-تركيا-خطى-داعش-غرب-البلاد.

17. See, for example, "القبض على مصريين اثنين متهمين باختطاف ابن دبلوماسي ليبي في أوكرانيا" [Two Egyptians Arrested for Kidnapping the Son of a Libyan Diplomat in Ukraine], *Al-Wasat*, June 28, 2018, http://alwasat.ly/news/libya/210821.
18. See Tim Whewell, "How Six Brothers—and Their Lions—Terrorised a Libyan Town," BBC, January 2, 2021, https://www.bbc.com/news/stories-55564933.
19. For more on the Kaniyat saga and the relationship between the clan and the LNA, see Jalel Harchaoui, "Tarhuna, Mass Graves, and Libya's Internationalized Civil War," War on the Rocks, July 30, 2020, https://warontherocks.com/2020/07/tarhuna-mass-graves-and-libyas-internationalized-civil-war/; "ليبيا.. تفاصيل مقتل آمر اللواء التاسع مشاة في بنغازي" [Libya . . . Details of the Killing of the Commander of the 9th Infantry Brigade in Benghazi]. RT Arabic, July 27, 2021, https://web.archive.org/web/20240531084855/https://arabic.rt.com/middle_east/1255964-ليبيا-تفاصيل-مقتل-محمد-الكاني-آمر-اللواء-التاسع-مشاة-في-بنغازي/.
20. See Shelby Grossman, Khadeja Ramali, and Renée DiResta, "Blurring the Lines of Media Authenticity: Prigozhin-Linked Group Funding Libyan Broadcast Media," Stanford Internet Observatory, March 20, 2020, https://fsi.stanford.edu/news/libya-prigozhin. Gaddafi's name is also transliterated as al-Qadhafi.
21. "Libya . . . Details of the Killing."
22. See Jared Malsin and Thomas Grove. "Researcher or Spy? Maxim Shugaley Saga Points to How Russia Now Builds Influence Abroad," *Wall Street Journal*, October 5, 2021, https://www.wsj.com/articles/researcher-or-spy-maxim-shugaley-saga-points-to-how-russia-now-builds-influence-abroad-11633448407.
23. For an excellence profile of Bashagha, see Frederic Wehrey, "A Minister, a General, & the Militias: Libya's Shifting Balance of Power," *New York Review*, March 9, 2019, https://www.nybooks.com/online/2019/03/19/a-minister-a-general-militias-libyas-shifting-balance-of-power/.
24. "شوغالي: فيلم روسي يحكي معاناة الشعب الليبي تحت وطأة الإرهاب" [Shugalei: A Russian Film that Tells of the Suffering of the Libyan People Under the Weight of Terrorism], Sky News Arabia, May 7, 2020, https://www.skynewsarabia.com/varieties/1342541-شوغالي-فيلم-روسي-يحكي-معاناة-الشعب-الليبي-وطأة-الإرهاب.
25. See Shelby Grossman et al., "Stoking Conflict by Keystroke," Stanford Internet Observatory, December 15, 2020, https://doi.org/10.25740/qg973fs1649.
26. See Kevin Shalvey, "Facebook Posts and Cameo Videos by Charlie Sheen and Dolph Lundgren Were Used by Russian Trolls to Persuade Libya to Release a Suspected Spy," *Business Insider*, December 23, 2020, https://www.businessinsider.com/russian-trolls-used-facebook-cameo-free-alleged-spy-in-libya-2020-12.
27. For good, recent study of the modern use of Russian cinema for propaganda, see A. Rojavin and H. Haft (eds.), *Modern Russian Cinema as a Battleground in Russia's Information War* (Routledge, 2024).

28. Alvin A. Snyder, *Warriors of Disinformation: American Propaganda, Soviet Lies, and the Winning of the Cold War: An Insider's Account* (Arcade, 1995), 101.
29. Snyder, *Warriors*, 103.
30. Todd Levanthal, personal interview with the author, April 30, 2024.
31. See "The Rhythm of Struggle," *Economist* 435, no. 9194: 73–74. As Todd Levanthal and others have noted, the AMWG drew heavily on the expertise of key defectors from within the Soviet Union's active measures apparatus, most notably Ladislav Bittman, the former deputy chief of active measures and disinformation for the Czechoslovak foreign intelligence services in the 1960s, and Stanislav Levchenko, a major in the KGB who, according to Levanthal, had been in charge of the active measures section of the KGB's *rezidentura* of the Soviet embassy in Tokyo. See Todd Levanthal, "The Need to Up Our Game in Countering Disinformation," *Comparative Strategy* 42, no. 2 (2023): 176. See also Fletcher Schoen and Christopher J. Lamb, "Deception, Disinformation, and Strategic Communications: How One Interagency Group Made a Major Difference," *Strategic Perspectives* 11 (2012): 83.
32. Snyder, *Warriors*, 100. Among the most predominant examples of USSR disinformation directed toward countries in Africa and the global South were reportedly stories "that the U.S. kidnapped or illegally adopted South American babies and sold their organs for transplant"; "that a CIA assassination team was assigned to kill the religious madman Jim Jones . . . because Jones was planning to move his cult to the Soviet Union"; "that the U.S. is responsible for an assortment of assassinations overseas"; and that "the U.S. has cultivated a variety of bacteriological weapons designed to kill Cubans and Africans, including the AIDS virus, which the Soviets said was created by the CIA and the Pentagon." See Jack Anderson and Dale Van Atta, "Soviets Back Off Disinformation Drive," *The Washington Post*, Oct. 24, 1989, 1. For a full summary of Soviet disinformation around AIDS and other issues affecting Africa in particular, see "Soviet Influence Activities: A Report on Active Measures and Propaganda, 1986–87," US Dept. of State, August 1987, http://catalog.hathitrust.org/Record/100843917.
33. Larry Schwartz, personal interview with the author, September 11, 2020.
34. Mona Elswah and Philip N. Howard. "'Anything That Causes Chaos': The Organizational Behavior of Russia Today (RT)," *Journal of Communication* 70, no. 5 (2020): 624.
35. Elswah and Howard, "Anything," 624.
36. See GEC Special Report, *Kremlin-Funded Media: RT and Sputnik's Role in Russia's Disinformation and Propaganda Ecosystem*, Dept. of State at p. 21 (January 20, 2022).
37. Elswah and Howard, "Anything," 624.

38. Anna Borshchevskaya and Catherine Cleveland, "Russia's Arabic Propaganda: What It Is, Why It Matters," Washington Institute of Near East Policy, December 19, 2018, https://www.washingtoninstitute.org/policy-analysis/russias-arabic-propaganda-what-it-why-it-matters, 3.
39. Elswah and Howard, "Anything," 624; Todd Helmus et al., *Russian Social Media Influence Understanding Russian Propaganda in Eastern Europe* (RAND, 2019), 15, https://www.rand.org/pubs/research_reports/RR2237.html.
40. On changes in infrastructure, in particular the shift to Multiprotocol Label Switching (MPLS), see Broadcasting Board of Governors, *FY 2017 Performance and Accountability Report*, https://www.usagm.gov/wp-content/media/2017/11/BBG_FY_2017_PAR.pdf, 57–58.
41. Gallup/BBG, *Analytical Report for Egypt Media Use Survey* (March, 2014). The report, conducted by Gallup, was commissioned by the Broadcasting Board of Governors' (BBG) International Audience Research Program (IARP) on behalf of Middle East Broadcasting Networks, Inc. (MBN). A copy of the report was made available to the author through a FOIA request.
42. Gallup/BBG, *Analytical Report for Iraq Media Use Survey* (June, 2016). The report, conducted by Gallup, was commissioned by the Broadcasting Board of Governors' (BBG) International Audience Research Program (IARP) on behalf of Middle East Broadcasting Networks, Inc. (MBN). A copy of the report was made available to the author through a FOIA request.
43. "الوكالة الدولية للأنباء روسية سيغودنية و مؤسسة ألاهرام توعقان مذكرة تعاون" [The International News Agency Russia Segodnya and Al-Ahram Foundation Sign a Memorandum of Cooperation], Sputnik Arabic, November 2, 2015, https://sputnikarabic.ae/20150211/1013393610.html.
44. "Egypt and Russia Sign 50-Year Industrial Zone Agreement," *Reuters*, May 23, 2018, https://www.reuters.com/article/idUSL5N1SU5SI/.
45. See "Russian Ambassador to Cairo: Culture Relations Between Egypt, Russia Flourished in Sisi's Era," *Egypt Today*, November 12, 2020, https://www.egypttoday.com/Article/4/94162/Russian-Ambassador-to-Cairo-Culture-relations-between-Egypt-Russia-flourished.
46. Mohammed Abu Hasan, "Religious Patronage and Clientelism: Russia's Soft Power and Networks of Influence in Syria," *Syria Studies* 15, no. 1 (2023): 51.
47. See "Top Russian Universities to Open Branches in Africa," *Daily News*, August 3, 2023, https://dailynews.co.tz/top-russian-universities-to-open-branches-in-africa. Also Martin K. N. Siele, "Putin's Free Russian Classes Are Taking off in Africa," *Semafor*, January 5, 2024, https://www.semafor.com/article/01/05/2024/free-russian-classes-are-taking-off-in-africa.

48. Daily News, "Top Russian Universities."
49. Siele, "Putin's Free Russian Classes."
50. See United States Department of State Bureau of Educational and Cultural Affairs, "American Spaces" (undated), https://eca.state.gov/programs-and-initiatives/initiatives/office-american-spaces.
51. Snyder, *Warriors*, 103.
52. The Institute for the Study of War has documented many of the content-sharing agreements between Sputnik, RT, and state-media organizations in the global South. In 2015, along with Egypt, Russya Segodnya signed agreements in Cambodia, Indonesia, Mexico, and Serbia. The following year it struck content-sharing agreements with state flagships in Algeria, Italy, Japan, Lebanon, Paraguay, and Syria. In 2017, Bulgaria, China, Cuba, Iran, Malyasia, Mongolia, Myanmar, the Philippines, South Africa, Turkey, and Vietnam jumped on board. In 2018, it was India, Morocco, Palestine, and the UAE. Argentina, the Congo, North Korea, Pakistan, and Saudi Arabia followed suit in 2019. See Nataliya Bugayova and George Barros, "The Kremlin's Expanding Media Conglomerate," Institute for the Study of War, January 15, 2020, https://www.understandingwar.org/backgrounder/kremlin%E2%80%99s-expanding-media-conglomerate.
53. See Lou Osborn and Dimitri Zufferey, *Wagner: Enquête au coeur du système Prgojine* (Faubourg, 2023), 196.
54. "Russian Lawmakers Criticize Sudan Coup as 'Unconstitutional,'" *Moscow Times*, April 11, 2019, https://www.themoscowtimes.com/2019/04/11/russian-lawmakers-criticize-sudan-coup-as-unconstitutional-a65190. On the transport of Wagner mercenaries to and from Ukraine and Africa, see Osborn and Zufferey, *Wagner*, 208.
55. See "September 2021 Coordinated Inauthentic Behavior Report," Meta, September 10, 2021, https://about.fb.com/news/2021/10/september-2021-coordinated-inauthentic-behavior-report/.
56. See, for example, "قوة الدعم السريع من هراوة بيد البشير إلى خنجر في ظهره!" [Rapid Support Force from a Club in the Hand of Bashir to a Dagger in the Back!]. RT Arabic, April 12, 2019, https://web.archive.org/web/20240418181044/https://arabic.rt.com/middle_east/1012945-قوة-الدعم-السريع-المثيرة-للجدل-في-السودان-من-هراوة-بيد-البشير-إلى-خنجر-في-ظهره/.
57. Osborn and Zufferey, *Wagner*, 213.
58. Snyder, *Warriors*, 101.
59. Snyder, *Warriors*, 100.
60. Clarissa Ward et al. "Russian Election Meddling Is Back—via Ghana and Nigeria—and in Your Feeds," CNN, April 11, 2020, https://www.cnn.com/2020/03/12/world/russia-ghana-troll-farms-2020-ward/index.html.

61. See Advisory Commission on Public Diplomacy, *Comprehensive Annual Report on Public Diplomacy and International Broadcasting*, US Department of State, 2021, https://www.state.gov/wp-content/uploads/2022/02/2021_ACPD_Annual_Report.pdf, 137, accessed July 22, 2025.
62. In Misja Pekel, dir., *The World According to Russia Today* (Icarus Films, 2015).
63. Borshchevskaya and Cleveland, "Russia's Arabic Propaganda," 6.
64. See Nathaniel Greenberg, "American Spring: How Russian State Media Translate American Protests for an Arab Audience," *International Journal of Communication* 15 (2021): 2550.
65. *The Global Engagement Center: Leading the United States Government's Fight Against Global Disinformation Threat: Hearings Before the Subcommitte on State Department and USAID Management, International Operations, and Bilateral International Development, Committee on Foreign Relations*, US Senate, 116th Cong. 3 (2020) (opening statement of Senator Rob Portman from Ohio).
66. *The Global Engagement Center: Leading the United States Government's Fight Against Global Disinformation Threat* (prepared statement of Lea Gabrielle, Special Envoy and Coordinator of the Global Engagement Center, US Department of State).
67. *The Global Engagement Center: Leading the United States Government's Fight Against Global Disinformation Threat* (prepared statement of Alina Polyakova, president and CEO, Center for European Policy Analysis).
68. *The Global Engagement Center: Leading the United States Government's Fight Against Global Disinformation Threat* (prepared statement of Lea Gabrielle).
69. *Countering the Virtual Caliphate: The State Department's Performance: Hearing Before the Committee on Foreign Affairs*, House of Representatives. 114th Cong. (July 13, 2016) (statement of Richard A. Stengel, under secretary for public diplomacy and public Affairs, U.S. Department of State).
70. The Trump administration's failure to appoint an under secretary of state for public diplomacy was superseded only by the Biden administration, which left the post vacant for well over a year. Matt Armstrong chronicles the neglect of the under secretary position as well as everything else public diplomacy for his blog *Mountain Runner*.
71. Robbie Gramer, Dan De Luce, and Colum Lynch, "How the Trump Administration Broke the State Department," *Foreign Policy*, July 31, 2017, https://foreignpolicy.com/2017/07/31/how-the-trump-administration-broke-the-state-department/.
72. Julian Borger, "US Cuts Funds for 'Anti-propaganda' Iran Group that Trolled Activists," *Guardian*, May 31, 2019, https://www.theguardian.com/us-news/2019/may/31/us-cuts-funds-for-anti-propaganda-group-that-trolled-activists.

73. *The Global Engagement Center: Leading the United States Government's Fight Against Global Disinformation Threat*, Congressional Hearing, March 5, 2020, 3 (opening statement of Senator Rob Portman from Ohio).
74. Nicholas J. Cull, "'The Perfect War': US Public Diplomacy and International Broadcasting During Desert Shield and Desert Storm, 1990/1991," *Arab Media and Society*, September 5, 2005; see also "Iraqi Disinformation Campaign," C-SPAN, February 1, 1991, https://www.c-span.org/video/?16136-1/iraqi-disinformation-campaign.
75. See W. H. Prophecy, "WE MADE IT TO @TuckerCarlson #DezNat #WeeklyHoss," Twitter, July 2, 2020, https://twitter.com/NiasDiad/status/1278874404601032705.
76. Hayley Crombleholme, "Protests Converge in Provo, with Both Groups Agreeing Violence Is Uncalled For," KJZZ, July 2, 2020, https://kjzz.com/news/protests-converge-in-provo-with-%20both-groups-agreeing-violence-is-uncalled-for.
77. Ian Schwartz, "Tucker Carlson: These Are the Criminals Being Used by the Democratic Party to Destroy Your Country," RealClear Politics, July 3, 2020, https://www.realclearpolitics.com/video/2020/07/03/tucker_carlson_these_are_the_criminals_being_used_by_the_democratic_party_to_destroy_your_country.html.
78. Matthew Rosenberg and Julien E. Barnes, "A Bible Burning, a Russian News Agency and a Story Too Good to Check Out," *New York Times*, August 11, 2020, https://www.nytimes.com/2020/08/11/us/politics/russia-disinformation-election-meddling.html. See also "'Peaceful'" Portland Protesters Burn Bible & Flag, 24 Hours After Torching Pig's Head in Cop Hat," RT, August 1, 2020, https://www.rt.com/usa/496847-portland-protests-burn-bible-flag-pig/.
79. "'Peaceful'" Portland Protesters"; "الكنيسة الروسية: نشطاء 'حياة السود مهمة' أحرقوا سمعتهم بإحراق الإنجيل" [The Russian Church: Black Lives Matter Activists Burned Their Reputation by Burning the Gospel], RT Arabic, August 4, 2020, https://web.archive.org/web/20240531083525/https://arabic.rt.com/world/1141164-مسؤول-في-الكنيسة-الروسية-عن-حركة-حياة-السود-مهمة-بإحراقهم-الإنجيل-أحرقوا-سمعتهم/.
80. See Nathaniel Greenberg, "American Spring: How Russian State Media Translate American Protests for an Arab Audience," *International Journal of Communication* 15 (2021): 2552. As detailed in the Senate intelligence report from 2018, nearly all of the YouTube videos associated with the IRA and published in advance of the 2016 presidential election, some 1,100 videos in total, focused on police violence and Black Lives Matter. Promulgating the videos was a vast web of embellished websites and social media accounts. In one instance, a single Instagram account, @blackstagram_, amassed

"more than 300,000 followers and elicited more than 28 million reactions." See Nicholas Thompson and Issie Lapowsky, "How Russian Trolls Used Meme Warfare to Divide America," *Wired*, December 17, 2018, https://www.wired.com/story/russia-ira-propaganda-senate-report/.

81. On "The Man from Fifth Avenue," see Philip Taubman, "Through Soviet Lens: Gomorrah on Hudson," *New York Times*, April 7, 1986, https://www.nytimes.com/1986/04/07/world/through-a-soviet-lens-gomorrah-on-hudson.html. A Russian version of *Man from Fifth Avenue* is available at https://www.youtube.com/watch?v=oEHhojTH0K4.

82. See "Black Lives: Agents of Change. Failing Schools Versus Community Education in America," video, RT, March 22, 2019, accessed November 10, 2023, https://www.youtube.com/watch?v=-4XXaBgEsfk&list=PLBRLKmBip431NY_yQIbTekXjzr6C8FbM9&index=5; "Black Lives: Deadlock. Black Lives Matter Versus the KKK: Racial Tensions Spark Anger in the USA," video, RT, April 28, 2019, accessed November 10, 2023, https://www.youtube.com/watch?v=NkdGsUxijDU&list=PLBRLKmBip431NY_yQIbTekXjzr6C8FbM9&index=1; and "Black Lives: Doom. Choosing Between Good and Bad in Black U.S. Neighborhoods," video, RT, June 28, 2019, accessed November 12, 2023, https://www.youtube.com/watch?v=Mdbs8rQ1xiY&list=PLBRLKmBip431NY_yQIbTekXjzr6C8FbM9&index=9.

83. Trump's inaugural address and his use of the phrase "American carnage" is available at https://www.pbs.org/newshour/politics/transcript-read-president-trumps-full-inaugural-address. On his 2024 campaign rhetoric, see David Jackson, "Donald Trump Repeats 'Bloodbath' Comment as He Criticizes Joe Biden Border Policy," *USA Today*, April 2, 2024, https://www.usatoday.com/story/news/politics/elections/2024/04/02/trump-bloodbath-biden/73105362007/.

84. "Black Lives: Trap. Why Civil Rights Aren't Enough to Make the American Dream Come True," video, RT, July 25, 2019, accessed November 12, 2023, https://www.youtube.com/watch?v=pw5bg5iLhro&list=PLBRLKmBip431NY_yQIbTekXjzr6C8FbM9&index=10&t=6s.

85. "Black Lives: Trap." For background on Abdul Alim Musa, see BBC, "Who Is on UK 'Least Wanted' List?" BBC, May 5, 2009, http://news.bbc.co.uk/2/hi/uk_news/8033319.stm.

86. Thomas Rid explores the exploitation of Black America by Soviet propagandists at great length in *Active Measures: The Secret History of Disinformation and Political Warfare* (Farrar, Straus and Giroux, 2020).

87. An effort was made to address the perceived scourge of foreign disinformation on American soil through the creation of a Disinformation Governance Board within the Department of Homeland Security in 2022. Its first director, however, Nina Jankowicz, a political appointee, was forced

to resign after an army of right-wing trolls effectively doxed her out of office. See Shannon Bond, "She Joined DHS to Fight Disinformation. She Says She Was Halted by . . . Disinformation," NPR, May 21, 2022, https://www.npr.org/2022/05/21/1100438703/dhs-disinformation-board-nina-jankowicz.

88. Ayman, Aymani, "مقتل مراسل أعلن شراء حماة زيلينسكي لفيلا فاخرة" [A Reporter Who Announced the Purchase of a Luxury Villa by Zelensky's Mother-in-Law Was Killed], Muhtwa +, December 22, 2023, https://web.archive.org/web/20231212052851/https:muhtwaplus.com/485344/2023/11/02/ما-لا-تعرفوه-عن-عبد-السلام-الأسود-قاتل-مشجعي-كرة-القدم-السويدية-المرتزق-السابق/.

89. For an English summary of the SVT report, see "How Pro-Russian Disinformation Is Laundered," SVT, February 3, 2024, https://www.svt.se/special/how-pro-russian-disinformation-is-laundered/.

90. Steven Lee Myers, "From Russia, Elaborate Tales of Fake Journalists, *New York Times*, March 18, 2024, https://www.nytimes.com/2024/03/18/business/media/russia-fake-journalists.html.

91. Quoted in J. E. Leonardson, "Intelligence in Public Media." *Studies in Intelligence* 64, no. 1, 2020. "J. E. Leonardon" is the penname of an American intelligence official. A host of countering disinformation initiatives sprouted across Washington in the wake of Russia's 2016 election interference. Among the most notable was the USAGM's fact-checking website "Polygraph.info." Its findings are frequently replayed across other public diplomacy platforms but rarely get picked up by mainstream media.

92. Amanda Erickson, "If Russia Today Is Moscow's Propaganda Arm, It's Not Very Good at Its Job," *Washington Post*, January 12, 2017, https://www.washingtonpost.com/news/worldviews/wp/2017/01/12/if-russia-today-is-moscows-propaganda-arm-its-not-very-good-at-its-job/.

93. US Department of Justice, "Two RT Employees Indicted for Covertly Funding and Directing U.S. Company that Published Thousands of Videos in Furtherance of Russian Interests" (press release), September 4, 2024, https://www.justice.gov/opa/pr/two-rt-employees-indicted-covertly-funding-and-directing-us-company-published-thousands.

94. "Russia Bans Radio Free Europe/Radio Liberty as 'Undesirable'," Committee to Protect Journalists, February 21, 2024, https://cpj.org/2024/02/russia-bans-radio-free-europe-radio-liberty-as-undesirable/.

CONCLUSION

1. Joshua Kurlantzick identifies the problem of alumni management in his memorandum on policy innovation for the Council on Foreign Relations. The problem continues to plague a number of DoD and State Department

soft power initiatives since 9/11. See Joshua Kurlantzick, "Reforming the U.S. International Military Education and Training Program," Council on Foreign Relations, June 2016, https://www.cfr.org/report/reforming-us-international-military-education-and-training-program.

2. Quoted in Becca Synnestvedt Smith, "Rejecting America's Cold War: Sayyid Qutb's Nationalist-Islamist Agenda and the Failure of U.S. Efforts to Win Over Egyptian Muslims Following World War II" (PhD diss., Georgetown University, 2017), 58.

3. *The Global Engagement Center: Leading the United States Government's Fight Against Global Disinformation Threat*, Congressional Hearing, March 3, 2020, 12 (prepared statement of Lea Gabrielle, Special Envoy and Coordinator of the Global Engagement Center, US Department of State).

4. See Motoko Rich and Kiuko Notoya, "'Oppenheimer' Opens in Nuclear-Scarred Japan, 8 Months After U.S. Premiere," *New York Times*, April 1, 2024, https://www.nytimes.com/2024/04/01/world/asia/oppenheimer-opens-japan.html.

5. A list of Visionaire projects "in development" for MEPI can be found on the MENA Media Fund website at https://menamediafund.com/.

6. See Nicholas J. Cull, *The Decline and Fall of the United States Information Agency: American Public Diplomacy, 1989–2001* (Palgrave Macmillan, 2012), 92.

7. Munqith Dagher and Karl Kaltenthaler, "The United States Is Rapidly Losing Arab Hearts and Minds Through Gaza War, While Competitors Benefit," Fikra Forum, November 21, 2023, https://www.washingtoninstitute.org/policy-analysis/united-states-rapidly-losing-arab-hearts-and-minds-through-gaza-war-while.

8. [Like Lego, What Do We Know About the American Floating Port Off the Coast of Gaza?], Al-Arabiya, March 10, 2024, https://www.alarabiya.net/arab-and-world/2024/03/10/مثل-الليغو-ماذا-نعرف-عن-الميناء-الأميركي-العائم-قبالة-غزة؟; Mahmoud al-'Adam, [The American Port in Gaza. . . . Hunger Redraws the Map of War and Politics], Al-Jazeera, March 9, 2024, https://www.aljazeera.net/politics/2024/3/9/الميناء-الأميركي-بغزة-حين-يرسم-الجوع; "[Amidst killing and starvation, the 'Biden Port' in Gaza raises fears of displacing Gazans]," *RT Arabic*, March 9, 2024. https://arabic.rt.com/middle_east/1545523/.

9. See Joseph Brodsky, "The Truth About Iran's Efforts to Promote Gaza Protests," *Time*, July 30, 2024, https://time.com/7005190/iran-gaza-protests-nuanced-reality/.

10. See "Palestinian Anchor Sues US-Based Channel for Anti-Hijab Discrimination," *New Arab*, May 5, 2020, https://www.newarab.com/news/palestinian-anchor-sues-us-based-channel-anti-hijab-discrimination.

11. Ammar Abdulhamid, email correspondence with the author, September 12, 2024.
12. *Alhurra Broadcasting to Egypt, Morocco, and the Palestinian Territories (A Focus Group Study of Television Viewing Preferences)* (InterMedia, 2010), 2. The report was obtained by the author in 2023 through a Freedom of Information Act request.
13. Leon Shahabian, email correspondence with the author, September 13, 2024.
14. Gedmin's memorandum can be found at https://www.alhurra.com/byanat-shfyt/2024/09/02/reform-layoffs-and-way-forward.
15. Alberto Fernandez, email correspondence with the author, September 13, 2024.

BIBLIOGRAPHY

'Abd al-Razzaq, Wathaq Abbas. "الصفحات العراقية و القيم المجتمع المدني: دراسة تحليلية لصفحة الرأي في جريدة للفترة من 1-1-2004 الى 31-6-2004" [Societal Values and the Iraqi Press: Analytical Studies of the Opinion Pages in the Newspaper Al-Sabah from 1/1/2004 to 6/31/2004]. *Majalat al-jama'at al-Iraqiyya* [Journal of Iraqi Society] 2, no. 30 (2013): 473–510.

Abdallah, Ahsan. "أشهر أقوال الصحاف التاريخية:ماذا تحقق؟؟" [The Sayings of Al-Sahhaf: What Do They Reveal?], Elaph, October 31, 2003. https://elaph.com/Web/Archive/1067608571356542900.htm.

Abdulla, Rasha. "Egypt's Media in the Midst of Revolution." Carnegie Endowment for International Peace, July 15, 2014. https://carnegieendowment.org/2014/07/16/egypt-s-media-in-midst-of-revolution-pub-56164.

Abdul Latif, Emad. "Ahmed Zaki Abu Shadi." In *Dictionary of African Biography*. Ed. Henry Louis Gates, Emmanuel Akyeampong, and Steven J. Niven. Oxford University Press, 2012.

Abramowitz, David. "The President, the Congress, and Use of Force: Legal and Political Considerations in Authorizing Use of Force Against International Terrorism." *Harvard International Law Journal* 43, no. 1 (2002): 71–81.

Abu Hasan, Mohammed. "Religious Patronage and Clientelism: Russia's Soft Power and Networks of Influence in Syria." *Syria Studies* 15, no. 1 (2023): 1–57.

Abu Philip. "منبر الاصلاح" [Posts from Al-Islah]. *Al-Islah*, January 19, 1955. https://gpa.eastview.com/crl/mena/newspapers/islh19550119-01.1.1.

Abu Shadi, Ahmed Zaki. "The Secrets of Life." Interview by Edward R. Murrow. *This I Believe*, CBS Radio, accessed February 1, 2024. https://thisibelieve.org/essay/16317/.

Ahmad, Tarek Ali. "US-Backed Alhurra TV Relaunches Amid New Iran Sanctions." Arab News, November 6, 2018. https://www.arabnews.com/node/1399901/%7B%7B.

Ahmed, Issam. "US Funding for Pakistani Journalists Raises Questions of Transparency." *Christian Science Monitor*, September 2, 2011. https://www.csmonitor.com/World/Asia-South-Central/2011/0902/US-funding-for-Pakistani-journalists-raises-questions-of-transparency.

Al-Ahram. "بورقيات الديبلومسية" [Wikileaks's Diplomatic Cables]. January 29, 2011.

Al-'Ain. "الإمارات.. مركز صواب يطلق حملة ضد محاولات تنظيم داعش لطمس الانتماء الوطني" [UAE "Sawab Center" Launches a Campaign Against ISIS's Attempts to Erase National Belonging]. January 28, 2016. https://al-ain.com/article/20916.

Al-Alaf. "ما رأي المفكرين والاعلاميين العرب بتأثير سقوط نظام صدام حسين على مستقبل الديمقراطية العربية؟" [What Do Arab Thinkers and Media Figures Think About the Impact of the Fall of Saddam Hussein's Regime on the Future of Arab Democracy?]. August 6, 2003. https://elaph.com/Web/Archive/1060192313530560200.htm.

Al-Arabiya. "بدرية البشر للعربية.نت: الفتوى ضد طاش ما طاش لم تجد صدى بالسعودية" [Badria al-Bashir: The Fatwa Against Tash Ma Tash Will Not Find Support in Saudi Arabia]. September 10, 2007. https://www.alarabiya.net/articles/2007%2F09%2F10%2F38960.

Al-Hurra. "الأميرتان سحر وجواهر: أبونا ملك السعودية ونحن معتقلتان في قصرنا بالجوع" [Princesses Sahar and Jawaher: Our Father Is the King of Saudi Arabia, and We Are Detained in Our Palace Due to Hunger]. April 11, 2014. https://web.archive.org/web/20230307205046/https://www.alhurra.com/choice-alhurra/2014/04/11/الأميرتان-سحر-وجواهر-أبونا-ملك-السعودية-ونحن-معتقلتان-في-قصرنا-بالجوع/.

Alif baa. "الملك فيصل يفتح معرض الصناعات البريطانية أمس في بغداد" [King Faisal Opens the British Industries Exhibit Yesterday in Baghdad]. October 26, 1954. https://gpa.eastview.com/crl/mena/newspapers/abab19541026-01.1.4.j.

Al-Galad, Magdi. "انفراد: «الداخلية» تفرض «قبضة إلكترونية» على جرائم شبكات التواصل الاجتماعي" [Infared: The Ministry of Interior Imposes an 'Electronic Control' on Social Networking Crimes]. *Al-Watan*, June 1, 2014. https://www.elwatannews.com/news/details/495659.

Al-Ghitany, Gamal. "Social Significance of Obama's Election." Carnegie Endowment for International Peace, December 5, 2008. https://carnegieendowment.org/2008/12/05/social-significance-of-obama-s-election-pub-22510.

Al-Jazeera. "البنتاغون يعرض شريط فيديو لبن لادن عن الهجمات" [The Pentagon Shows bin Laden's Video of the Attacks]. December 13, 2001. https://web.archive.org/web/20240418195909/https://www.aljazeera.net/news/2001/12/13/البنتاغون-يعرض-شريط-فيديو-لبن-لادن-عن/.

Al-Jazeera. "فريق التواصل الإلكتروني الأميركي" [The American Digital Outreach Team]. September 29, 2009. https://www.aljazeera.net/news/2009/9/29/فريق-التواصل-الإلكتروني-الأميركي.

Al-Mayadeen Programs. "حوار الساعة: حسين مفتاح - نائب رئيس تحرير موقع بوابة افريقيا الاخبارية" [Conversation of the Hour: Hussein Moftah—Deputy Editor-in-Chief of the Africa News Portal]. December 29, 2019. /https://www.youtube.com/watch?v=mza1oPHyIGg.

Al-Misri. "مشروع بريطاني امريكي مشترك" [Joint British-American operation]. May 22, 1950. https://gpa.eastview.com/crl/mena/newspapers/almi19500522-01.1.1.

Al-Muqattam. "محطة "صوت أسرائيل"" [The Station 'Voice of Israel']. April 25, 1946. https://gpa.eastview.com/crl/mena/newspapers/amam19460425-01.1.1.

Al-Shabili, Abd al-Rahman. "أمير المايكروفون: عيسى خليل صبّاغ" [Prince of the Microphone: 'Issa Khalil Sabbagh]. Al-Jazeera, June 4, 2000. https://www.al-jazirah.com/2000/20000604/ar8.htm.

Al-Shorouk. "يوم الغدب" [The Day of Rage]. January 25, 2011.

Anderson, Jack and Dale Van Atta, "Soviets Back Off Disinformation Drive." *The Washington Post*, Oct. 24, 1989.

Antonio, Julio. "El impacto de la voz de América." *El Mundo*, March 20, 1951. https://gpa.eastview.com/crl/elmundo/newspapers/mndo19510320-01.1.1.

Arab Research and Advertising Centre. "A Study of the Demographic Characteristics of Readers of *Al-Hayat fi Amrika* in the U.A.R. [United Arab Republic]: Prepared for the United States Information Service, June 1966." Research Data Collection Project Files, 1958–1976, RG 306, Box 11, National Archives II.

Armstrong, Matt. "Is it Time to Do Away with the Under Secretary for Public Diplomacy?" *Mountain Runner* (blog). January 14, 2022. https://mountainrunner.us/2022/01/abolish-public-diplomacy/.

Arndt, Richard T. *The First Resort of Kings: American Cultural Diplomacy in the Twentieth Century*. Potomac, 2005.

As'ad, Mohammad. "هيئاة جديدة للصحفة و العلام" [New Life for the Press and Media]. *Youm 7*, November 19, 2016. https://web.archive.org/web/20161219210525/http://www.youm7.com/story/2016/11/19/3-2974004/هيئات-جديدة-للصحافة-والإعلام-ننشر-ملامح-تشكيل-المجلس-الأعلى.

Aseel, Kami. "World's Bravest Orchestra Plays on in Iraq." *Reuters*, October 23, 2007. https://www.reuters.com/article/us-iraq-orchestra/worlds-bravest-orchestra-plays-on-in-iraq-idINCOL66319620071029/.

Ataie, Mohammad. "Exporting the Iranian Revolution: Ecumenical Clerics in Lebanon." *International Journal of Middle East Studies* 53, no. 4 (2021): 672–90.

Atwan, Abdel Bari. *Islamic State: The Digital Caliphate*. University of California Press, 2015.

Ayish, Muhammad I. "Arab Television Goes Commercial: A Case Study of the Middle East Broadcasting Centre." *Gazette (Leiden, Netherlands)* 59, no. 6 (1997): 473–94.

Ayman, Aymani (pseudonym). "مقتل مراسل أعلن شراء حماة زيلينسكي لفيلا فاخرة" [A Reporter Who Announced the Purchase of a Luxury Villa by Zelensky's Mother-in-Law Was Killed]. Muhtwa +, December 22, 2023. https://web.archive.org/web/20231212052851/https:/muhtwaplus.com/485344/2023/11/02/ما-لا-تعرفوه-عن-عبد-السلام-الأسود-قاتل-مشجعي-كرة-القدم-السويدية-المرتزق-السابق/.

Ayoub, Betty, and Pete Cobus. "Amid Virtual News Blackout, Lebanese Protests Default to Social Media." Voice of America, January 23, 2020. https://www.voanews.com/a/middle-east_amid-virtual-news-blackout-lebanese-protests-default-social-media/6183060.html.

Barker, Michael J. "Democracy or Polyarchy? US-Funded Media Developments in Afghanistan and Iraq Post 9/11." *Media, Culture & Society* 30, no. 1 (2008): 109–30.

Barlett, Donald L., and James B. Steele. "Washington's $8 Billion Shadow." *Vanity Fair*, February 6, 2007. https://www.vanityfair.com/news/2007/03/spyagency200703.

Barrett, Edward W. *Truth Is Our Weapon*. Funk & Wagnalls, 1953.

Batatu, Hana. *The Old Social Classes and the Revolutionary Movements of Iraq: A Study of Iraq's Old Landed and Commercial Classes and of Its Communists, Ba'thists, and Free Officers*. Princeton University Press, 1978.

Battle, Joyce, ed. "U.S. Propaganda in the Middle East—the Early Cold War Version." *National Security Archive Electronic Briefing Book* 78, December 13, 2002. https://nsarchive2.gwu.edu/NSAEBB/NSAEBB78/essay.htm.

Baudrillard, Jean. "L'esprit du terrorisme." *South Atlantic Quarterly* 101, no. 2 (2002): 403–15.

Bayles, Martha. *Through a Screen Darkly: Popular Culture, Public Diplomacy, and America's Image Abroad*. Yale University Press, 2014.

BBC. "Who Is on UK 'Least Wanted' List?" May 5, 2009. http://news.bbc.co.uk/2/hi/uk_news/8033319.stm.

Berger, J. M., and Jonathon Morgan. "The ISIS Twitter Census Defining and Describing the Population of ISIS Supporters on Twitter." The Brookings Project on U.S. Relations with the Islamic World 20, March 5, 2015. https://www.brookings.edu/articles/the-isis-twitter-census-defining-and-describing-the-population-of-isis-supporters-on-twitter/.

Bernardi, Daniel. *Narrative Landmines: Rumors, Islamist Extremism, and the Struggle for Strategic Influence*. Rutgers University Press, 2012.

Bernays, Edward L. *Crystalizing Public Opinion, Engineering Consent, and Propaganda*. Boni and Liveright, 1923.

Bertrand, Hulen D. "Information Post Slated for Allen." *New York Times*, January 8, 1948.

Bessner, Daniel. *Democracy in Exile: Hans Speier and the Rise of the Defense Intellectual*. Cornell University Press, 2018.

Beydoun, Khaled A. *The New Crusades: Islamophobia and the Global War on Muslims*, University of California Press, 2023.
Bickert, Monika. "Internet Security and Privacy in the Age of the Islamic State: The View from Facebook." Washington Institute of Near East Policy, March 2, 2016. https://www.washingtoninstitute.org/policy-analysis/internet-security-and-privacy-age-islamic-state-view-facebook.
Bing, Christopher, and Joe Schectman. "Special Report: Inside the UAE's Secret Hacking Team of U.S. Mercenaries." *Reuters*, January 30, 2019. https://www.reuters.com/article/idUSKCN1PO1CV/.
Blanco, Patricia R. "Ni España existía ni la Reconquista es tal y como la cuenta Vox" [Neither Spain nor the Inquisition Existed as Vox Imagines]. *El País*, April 12, 2019. https://elpais.com/elpais/2019/04/11/hechos/1554980000_022524.html.
Blinken, Antony. "Now the U.S Needs to Win the Global War of Ideas." *New York Times*, December 8, 2001. https://www.nytimes.com/2001/12/08/opinion/IHT-now-the-us-needs-to-win-the-global-war-of-ideas.html.
Block, Alex Ben. "Alhurra Gallops into Mideast Media Mix." *Television Week* 23, no. 7 (2004): 1–37.
Bond, Shannon. "She Joined DHS to Fight Disinformation. She Says She Was Halted by . . . Disinformation." NPR, May 21, 2022. https://www.npr.org/2022/05/21/1100438703/dhs-disinformation-board-nina-jankowicz.
Borger, Julian. "US Cuts Funds for 'Anti-propaganda' Iran Group that Trolled Activists." *Guardian*, May 31, 2019. https://www.theguardian.com/us-news/2019/may/31/us-cuts-funds-for-anti-propaganda-group-that-trolled-activists.
Borshchevskaya, Anna, and Catherine Cleveland. "Russia's Arabic Propaganda: What It Is, Why It Matters." Washington Institute of Near East Policy, December 19, 2018. https://www.washingtoninstitute.org/policy-analysis/russias-arabic-propaganda-what-it-why-it-matters.
Braisted, Paul J., and Kenneth W. Thompson, *Reconstituting the Human Community: A Report of Colloquium III*, Bellagio, Italy, July 27–23, 1972, for the Program of Inquiries, Cultural Relations for the Future, sponsored by the Hazen Foundation, 1973.
Braude, Joseph. *Broadcasting Change: Arabic Media as a Catalyst for Liberalism*. Rowman & Littlefield, 2017.
Brewer, J. M. "The Wisdom to Self-Correct: Appreciating the Significance of ISIS's Putative Caliphate and Refining America's Strategy to Destroy It." MA thesis. United States Marine Corps Command and Staff College, 2016.
Briant, Emma L. "Pentagon Ju-Jitsu—Reshaping the Field of Propaganda." *Critical Sociology* 45, no. 3 (2019): 361–78.
Bugayova, Nataliya, and George Barros. "The Kremlin's Expanding Media Conglomerate." Institute for the Study of War, January 15, 2020. https://www.understandingwar.org/backgrounder/kremlin%E2%80%99s-expanding-media-conglomerate.

Butler, Desmond, and Richard Lardner. "US Misfires in Online Fight Against Islamic State." *AP*, January 31, 2017. https://apnews.com/article/lifestyle-middle-east-africa-business-islamic-state-group-b3fd7213bb0e41b3b02eb15265e9d292.

Butler, Desmond, and Richard Lardner. "Congress Probes Islamic State Counter-Propaganda Operations." *AP*, March 9, 2017. https://apnews.com/article/fd18db778953497e8cb531a6f5770f82.

Byman, Daniel. "The Social Media War in the Middle East." *Middle East Journal* 75, no. 3 (2021): 449–68.

Cantril, Hadley. *The Pattern of Human Concerns*. Rutgers University Press, 1965.

Callender, Harold. "The Voice of America Echoes Widely." *New York Times*, November 15, 1942.

Chirac, Jacques. "Un combat complexe et sans merci" [A Complex and Merciless Fight]. *Le Figaro*, October 8, 2001.

Coalition Provisional Authority order number 65: Iraqi Communications and Media Commission, 2004. https://archive.org/details/imn-cpaord-65.

Coalition Provisional Authority order number 66: Iraqi Communications and Media Commission, 2004. https://archive.org/details/imn-cpaord-66.

Collins, Steven. "Mind Games." *NATO Review*, June 1, 2003. Retrieved from: https://www.nato.int/docu/review/articles/2003/06/01/mind-games/index.html.

Commission on Wartime Contracting. *Transforming Wartime Contracting: Controlling Costs, Reducing Risks*. July 1, 2011. https://apps.dtic.mil/sti/citations/ADA549381.

Committee to Protect Journalists. "Egypt's Reinstatement of Information Ministry Is a Setback." July 12, 2011. https://cpj.org/2011/07/egypts-reinstatement-of-information-ministry-is-ma/.

Committee to Protect Journalists. "Journalists and Media Workers Killed in Iraq." December 12, 2022. https://cpj.org/reports/2008/07/journalists-killed-in-iraq/.

Committee to Protect Journalists. "Russia Bans Radio Free Europe/Radio Liberty as 'Undesirable.'" February 21, 2024. https://cpj.org/2024/02/russia-bans-radio-free-europe-radio-liberty-as-undesirable/.

Copeland, Miles. *The Game of Nations: The Amorality of Power Politics*. Simon and Schuster, 1969.

Cowan, Geoffrey. "Voice of America Has Not Ceded Editorial Control to Foreign Broadcasters" (letter). *Washington Times*, January 23, 1996.

Cresswell, Robyn. *City of Beginnings: Poetic Modernism in Beirut*. Princeton University Press, 2019.

Crewdson, John M., and Joseph G. Trester. "Worldwide Propaganda Network Built by CIA." *New York Times*, December 26, 1977.

Crombleholme, Hayley. "Protests Converge in Provo, with Both Groups Agreeing Violence Is Uncalled For." KJZZ, July 2, 2020. https://kjzz.com/news/protests-converge-in-provo-with-%20both-groups-agreeing-violence-is-uncalled-for.

C-SPAN. "Bin Laden Videotape." November 8, 2001. https://www.c-span.org/video/?167830-1/bin-laden-videotape.

C-SPAN. "Broadcast to Iraq." April 12, 2003. https://www.c-span.org/video/?176127-1/broadcast-iraq.

C-SPAN. "Public Diplomacy in the Obama Administration's Second Term." November 13, 2012. https://www.c-span.org/video/?309417-1/public-diplomacy-obama-administrations-term.

Cull, Nicholas J. "'The Perfect War': US Public Diplomacy and International Broadcasting During Desert Shield and Desert Storm, 1990/1991." *Arab Media and Society*, September 5, 2005.

Cull, Nicholas J. *The Cold War and the United States Information Agency*. Cambridge University Press, 2008.

Cull, Nicholas J. "How We Got Here." In *Toward a New Public Diplomacy: Redirecting U.S. Foreign Policy*, ed. Phillip M. Seib. Palgrave Macmillan, 2009.

Cull, Nicholas J. *The Decline and Fall of the United States Information Agency: American Public Diplomacy, 1989-2001*. Palgrave Macmillan, 2012.

Cull, Nicholas J. "Preface: Evaluation and the History of U.S. Public Diplomacy," in *Data-Driven Public Diplomacy Progress Towards Measuring the Impact of Public Diplomacy and International Broadcasting*. Ed. Brown, Katherine and Chris Hensman. American Council on Public Diplomacy, September 16, 2014. https://www.state.gov/wp-content/uploads/2024/02/2014_ACPD_Special_Report_Data-Driven_Public_Diplomacy.pdf.

Currie, James T. "Operation Hajji Baba." *Air Power History* 50, no. 2 (2003): 4–15.

Dagher, Munqith and Karl Kaltenthaler. "The United States Is Rapidly Losing Arab Hearts and Minds Through Gaza War, While Competitors Benefit." Fikra Forum, November 21, 2023. https://www.washingtoninstitute.org/policy-analysis/united-states-rapidly-losing-arab-hearts-and-minds-through-gaza-war-while.

Daily Mail. "Exclusive: 'We're Thirsty for Your Blood:' Playboy Jihadi's Widow Poses with her Gun-Toting 'Clique' of Female Fanatics in Front of Flash BMW and Boasts of 'Five-Star Jihad' Lifestyle in Syria." *Daily Mail*, March 17, 2015. https://www.dailymail.co.uk/news/article-2999925/We-thirsty-blood-Playboy-jihadi-s-widow-poses-gun-toting-clique-female-fanatics-flash-BMW-boasts-five-star-jihad-lifestyle-Syria.html.

Darle, Pierre. *Saddam Hussein maître des mots: Du langage de la tyrannie à la tyrannie du langage*. [Saddam Hussein Master of Words: From the Language of Tyranny to the Tyranny of Language]. L'Harmattan, 2003.

Daugherty, William E. *A Psychological Warfare Casebook*. Johns Hopkins University Press, 1958.

Davis, Gary (director). *Frank Kearns: Foreign Correspondent* (video). PBS, 2013. https://www.pbs.org/video/frank-kearns-american-correspondent-kemsdc/.

Davison, W. P. "Voices of America." In *Public Opinion and Foreign Policy*, ed. Lester Markel. Harper, 1949.

Della Rata, Donatella. "Fighting ISIL Through TV Drama: The Case of Black Crows." Al-Jazeera, June 19, 2017. https://www.aljazeera.com/features/2017/6/19/fighting-isil-through-tv-drama-the-case-of-black-crows.

Department of Defense (DoD). *Information Operations Roadmap*, October 30, 2003. https://nsarchive.gwu.edu/document/16822-department-defense-information-operations.

De Pena, Pedro. "Los Caballo de Troya" [The Trojan Horses of Democratic Spain]. *Libertad Digital*, December 14, 2014. https://www.libertaddigital.com/opinion/2018-08-26/pedro-de-tena-los-caballos-de-troya-de-la-espana-democratica-6421279/.

DeYoung, Karen. "Bush to Create Formal Office to Shape U.S. Image Abroad." *Washington Post*, July 3, 2002. https://www.washingtonpost.com/archive/politics/2002/07/30/bush-to-create-formal-office-to-shape-us-image-abroad/fd3b6b54-5cf6-4610-acf5-e8f0e84fe1ee/.

DeYoung, Karen, and Missy Ryan. "Trump's Call with Renegade Libyan General Could Signal a Shift in U.S. Policy." *Washington Post*, April 1, 2019. https://www.washingtonpost.com/world/national-security/trumps-call-with-renegade-libyan-general-could-signal-a-shift-in-us-policy/2019/04/19/d1428264-62d0-11e9-9ff2-abc984dc9eec_story.html.

Dizard, Wilson P. *Inventing Public Diplomacy: The Story of the U.S. Information Agency*. Lynne Rienner, 2004.

Djerejian, Edward P. *Changing Minds Winning Peace: A New Strategic Direction for U.S. Public Diplomacy in the Arab and Muslim World*, report of the Advisory Group on Public Diplomacy for the Arab and Muslim World, October 1, 2003.

Economist. "The Rhythm of Struggle." *Economist* 435, no. 9194 (2020).

El-Ariss, Tarek. *Leaks, Hacks, and Scandals: Arab Culture in the Digital Age*. Princeton University Press, 2019.

El Mundo. "Argentina permite Voz de América" [Argentina Allows Voice of America]. March 30, 1951. https://gpa.eastview.com/crl/elmundo/newspapers/mndo19510330-01.1.1.

El Issawi, Fatima. *Libya Media Transition: Heading to the Unknown*. POLIS, London School of Economics and Political Science, 2013.

El Issawi, Fatima. *Transitional Libyan Media: Free at Last?* Carnegie Endowment for International Peace and POLIS, London School of Economics and Political Science, 2013.

Elswah, Mona, and Philip N. Howard. "'Anything That Causes Chaos': The Organizational Behavior of Russia Today (RT)." *Journal of Communication* 70, no. 5 (2020): 623–45.

Epstein, Susan B. *U.S. Public Diplomacy: Background and the 9/11 Commission Recommendations* [Library of Congress public edition]. Congressional Research Service, 2018.

Erickson, Amanda. "If Russia Today Is Moscow's Propaganda Arm, It's Not Very Good at Its Job." *Washington Post*, January 12, 2017. https://www.washingtonpost.com/news/worldviews/wp/2017/01/12/if-russia-today-is-moscows-propaganda-arm-its-not-very-good-at-its-job/.

Etem, Aysehan Jülide. "A Transnational Communication Network Promoting Film Diplomacy: The Case of Turkey and the USA, 1950–86." *Historical Journal of Film, Radio, and Television* 41, no. 2 (2021): 292–316.

Eveland, Wilbur. *Ropes of Sand: America's Failure in the Middle East*. Norton, 1980.

Fahmy, Aziz. "The Story Is the Agenda of the Reporter, Not the Content of Our Show." *Washington Times*, January 26, 1996, 18. https://link.gale.com/apps/doc/A56857646/OVIC?u=viva_gmu&sid=bookmark-OVIC&xid=1f8ea954.

Faizy, Sultan, and Shashank Bengali. "U.S. Military Apologizes for 'Highly Offensive' Leaflets It Distributed in Afghanistan." *Los Angeles Times*, September 6, 2017. https://www.latimes.com/world/asia/la-fg-afghanistan-usmilitary-apology-20170906-story.html.

Fandy, Mamoun. *(Un)Civil War of Words: Media and Politics in the Arab World*. Praeger Security International, 2007.

Farid, Samir. تاريخ الرقابة على السينما في مصر [The History of Film Censorship in Egypt]. Al-Maktab al-Misri li-Tawziʻ al-Matbuʻat, 2002.

Fernandez, Alberto M. "Measuring the Unmeasurable: Evaluating the Effectiveness of US Strategic Counterterrorism Communications." In *The SAGE Handbook of Propaganda*, ed. Nancy Snow, Paul Baines, and Nicholas O'Shaughnessy, 323–35. SAGE, 2020.

Frankel, Charles. *The Neglected Aspect of Foreign Affairs: American Educational and Cultural Policy Abroad*. Brookings Institution, 1966.

Galster, Steven. "Afghanistan: The Making of U.S. Policy, 1973–1990." In *Volume II: Afghanistan: Lessons from the Last War*. National Security Archive, October 9, 2001. https://nsarchive2.gwu.edu/NSAEBB/NSAEBB57/essay.html#1.

Gates, Robert M. "Speech Before the Association of American Universities." Washington, DC, April 14, 2008. https://archive.defense.gov.

Gates, Robert M. "Balanced Strategy: Reprogramming the Pentagon for New Age," *Foreign Affairs* 88, no. 1 (2009): 28–40.

Geary, Brent M. "A Foundation of Sand: United States Public Diplomacy, Egypt, and Arab Nationalism, 1953–1960." PhD diss., Ohio University, 2007.

Geerhold, William. "The Rear Guard Press." *Saudi Aramco*, January/February, 1967. https://archive.aramcoworld.com/issue/196701/the.rear.guard.press.htm.

Gendzier, Irene L. *Dying to Forget: Oil, Power, Palestine, and the Foundations of U.S. Policy in the Middle East*. Columbia University Press, 2015.

Gerth, Jeff. "Military's Information War Is Vast and Often Secretive." *New York Times*, December 11, 2005. http://www.nytimes.com/2005/12/11/politics/militarys-information-war-is-vast-and-often-secretive.html?_r=0.

Getlin, Josh. "U.S. Nightly News Shows to Make Their Iraqi Television Debut; Some fear the White House-Backed Program Espousing a Free Press Will Create a Backlash." *Los Angeles Times*, April 15, 2003. https://www.latimes.com/archives/la-xpm-2003-apr-15-war-iraqtv15-story.html.

Ghonim, Wael. *Revolution 2.0: The Power of the People Is Greater than the People in Power: A Memoir*. Boston: Houghton Mifflin Harcourt, 2013.

Goldstein, Cora Sol. "A Strategic Failure: American Information Control Policy in Occupied Iraq." *Military Review* 88, no. 2 (2008): 58–65.

Gramer, Robbie, Dan De Luce, and Colum Lynch. "How the Trump Administration Broke the State Department." *Foreign Policy*, July 31, 2017. https://foreignpolicy.com/2017/07/31/how-the-trump-administration-broke-the-state-department/.

Gray, David. W. "The U.S. Intervention in Lebanon, 1958: A Commander's Reminiscence." Combat Studies Institute. U.S. Army Command and General Staff College, July 1, 1984. https://apps.dtic.mil/sti/citations/ADA450232.

Greenberg, Karl, and Jim Edwards. "Saatchi's Roberts Advised DOD on Rebranding 'War.'" *Brandweek* 46, no. 33 (2005).

Greenberg, Nathaniel. *The Aesthetic of Revolution in the Film and Literature of Naguib Mahfouz (1952-1967)*. Lexington, 2014.

Greenberg, Nathaniel. "Mythical State: The Aesthetics and Counter-Aesthetics of the Islamic State in Iraq and Syria." *Middle East Journal of Culture and Communication* 10, no. 2–3 (2017): 255–71.

Greenberg, Nathaniel. *How Information Warfare Shaped the Arab Spring*. Edinburgh University Press, 2019.

Greenberg, Nathaniel. "Islamic State War Documentaries." *International Journal of Communication* 14 (2020): 1808–28.

Greenberg, Nathaniel. "American Spring: How Russian State Media Translate American Protests for an Arab Audience." *International Journal of Communication* 15 (2021): 2547–68.

Greene, Patricia G. "Building Community Through Entrepreneurship Education (Innovations Case Discussion: INJAZ)." *Innovations* 3, no. 4 (2008): 99–104.

Grossman, Shelby, Daniel Bush, and Renée DiResta. "Evidence of Russia-Linked Influence Operations in Africa." Stanford Internet Observatory, October 29, 2019. https://doi.org/10.25740/yh993mk2487.

Grossman, Shelby, Khadeja Ramali, and Renée DiResta. "Blurring the Lines of Media Authenticity: Prigozhin-Linked Group Funding Libyan Broadcast Media." Stanford Internet Observatory, March 20, 2020. https://fsi.stanford.edu/news/libya-prigozhin.

Grossman, Shelby, Khadeja Ramali, Renée DiResta, R., Lucas Beissner, Samantha Bradshaw, William Healzer, and Ira Hubert. "Stoking Conflict by Keystroke." Stanford Internet Observatory, December 15, 2020. https://doi.org/10.25740/qg973fs1649.

Grossman, Shelby, Maria Fernanda Porras, Khadeja Ramali, and David Thiel. "Hello from the Other Side: An Investigation into a Musical Pro-Muslim Brotherhood Disinformation Operation." Stanford Internet Observatory, November 5, 2020. https://cyber.fsi.stanford.edu/io/publication/hello-other-side-investigation-musical-pro-muslim-brotherhood-disinformation-operation.

Haeffele, Mark. "John F. Kennedy, USIA, and World Public Opinion." *Diplomatic History* 25, no.1 (2001): 63–84.

Hamza, Rʿad Jassim. "مشكلات اعداد البرامج الاذاعية والتلفزيونية في العراق شبكة الاعلام العراقي - دراسة حالة" [Problems of Preparing Radio and Television Programs in Iraq, Iraqi Media Network—a Case Study]. *Al-Adab Journal* 86 (2022): 486–517.

Hansen, Allen C. *USIA: Public Diplomacy in the Computer Age.* Praeger, 1984.

Harchaoui, Jalel. "Tarhuna, Mass Graves, and Libya's Internationalized Civil War." War on the Rocks, July 30, 2020. https://warontherocks.com/2020/07/tarhuna-mass-graves-and-libyas-internationalized-civil-war/.

Hart, Justin. *Empire of Ideas: The Origins of Public Diplomacy and the Transformation of US Foreign Policy.* Oxford University Press, 2013.

Hassan, Abdallah F. *Media, Revolution, and Politics in Egypt.* London: I. B. Tauris, 2015.

Hassan, Oz. *Constructing America's Freedom Agenda for the Middle East: Democracy or Domination.* Routledge, 2013.

Hatem, Muhammad Abd al-Qadir. *Information and the Arab Cause.* Longman, 1974.

Hawkens, Ash. "Thanksgiving in Peshawar with Kirk Douglas." *Ash Hawkens: Ideas in Words and Images* (blog), December 29, 2020. https://ashhawken.com/thanksgiving-peshawar-kirk-douglas/.

Heikal, Mohammad Hassanein. *The Cairo Documents: The Inside Story of Nasser and His Relationship with World Leaders, Rebels, and Statesmen.* Doubleday, 1973.

Heil, Allen L. *Voice of America: A History.* Columbia University Press, 2003.

Helmus, Todd C., Elizabeth Bodine-Baron, Andrew Radin, et al. *Russian Social Media Influence Understanding Russian Propaganda in Eastern Europe.* RAND, 2019. https://www.rand.org/pubs/research_reports/RR2237.html.

Herrera, Linda. *Revolution in the Age of Social Media: The Egyptian Popular Insurrection and the Internet.* Verso, 2014.

Hogan, John. "Interview with John Hogan." Interview by Claude Groce. *Frontline Diplomacy: The Foreign Affairs Oral History Collection of the Association for Diplomatic Studies and Training,* Library of Congress, September 21, 1987. https://www.loc.gov/item/mfdipbib000518/.

Holt, Elizabeth M. "'Bread or Freedom': The Congress for Cultural Freedom, the CIA, and the Arabic Literary Journal 'Ḥiwār'" (1962–67). *Journal of Arabic Literature* 44, no. 1 (2013).

Hosmer, Stephen T. *Psychological Effects of U.S. Air Operations in Four Wars, 1941–1991: Lessons for U.S. Commanders.* Rand Corporation, 1996.

House of Commons Defence Committee (UK), *Lessons of Iraq,* Third Report, 2004. https://publications.parliament.uk/pa/cm200304/cmselect/cmdfence/57/5702.htm.

"International: A Chance Missed; Iraq's Television." *Economist* 369, no. 8354 (2003): 56.

Jaber, Heather, and Marwan M. Kraidy. "The Geopolitics of Television Drama and the 'Global War on Terror': Gharabeeb Soud Against Islamic State." *International Journal of Communication* (2020): 1868–87.

Jackson, David. "Donald Trump Repeats 'Bloodbath' Comment as He Criticizes Joe Biden Border Policy." *USA Today,* April 2, 2024. https://www.usatoday.com/story/news/politics/elections/2024/04/02/trump-bloodbath-biden/73105362007/.

Jackson, Nicholas. "Wikileaks' Assange: Facebook Is an Appalling Spy Machine." *Atlantic.* May 2, 2011. https://www.theatlantic.com/technology/archive/2011/05/wikileaks-assange-facebook-is-appalling-spying-machine/238225/.

Jansen, Sue Curry. "Selling America to the World." In *Bring 'Em On: Media and Politics in the Iraq War,* ed. Lee Artz and Yaya R. Kamalipour. Rowman & Littlefield, 2005.

Joubin, Rebecca. *The Politics of Love: Sexuality, Gender, and Marriage in Syrian Television Drama.* Lexington, 2013.

Kaplan, Robert D. "What Rumsfeld Got Right." *Atlantic,* August 15, 2008. https://www.theatlantic.com/magazine/archive/2008/07/what-rumsfeld-got-right/306870/.

Kaplan, Peter W. "'Let Poland Be Poland.'" *Washington Post,* January 28, 1982. https://www.washingtonpost.com/archive/lifestyle/1982/01/28/let-poland-be-poland/f1aaf3c2-6c86-4f50-a14e-702b1a7d7dac/.

Kean, Thomas H., and Lee Hamilton. *The 9/11 Commission Report: Final Report of the National Commission on Terrorist Attacks Upon the United States.* United States Government Printing Office, 2004.

Kelly, Christine. "Le débat Bernard-Henri Lévy et Eric Zemmour." Interview by Christine Kelly. *Face à l'info*, CNews, June 26, 2020. https://www.youtube.com/watch?v=FiFtl856XQI.

Kendrick, Alexander. *Prime Time: The Life of Edward R. Murrow*. Little, Brown, 1969.

Kern, Holger Lutz, and Jens Hainmueller. "Opium for the Masses: How Foreign Media Can Stabilize Authoritarian Regimes." *Political Analysis* 17, no. 4 (2009): 377–99.

Khader, Jamil. "On ISIL, Arab TV and Post-Ideological Politics." Al-Jazeera, June 22, 2017. https://www.aljazeera.com/opinions/2017/6/22/on-isil-arab-tv-and-post-ideological-politics.

Khalil, Magdi. "لماذا فشلت قناة الحرة؟" [Why Did Al-Hurra Fail?]. *Watani*, October 3, 2005. http://www.mafhoum.com/press9/264C33.htm.

Khalilzad, Zalmay. "Afghanistan: Anatomy of a Soviet Failure." *National Interest* 12, no. 12 (National Affairs, 1988), 101–8.

Kipp, Jacob, Lester Grau, Karl Prinslow, and Don Smith. *The Human Terrain System: A CORDS for the 21st Century*. Foreign Military Studies Office (Army), 2006.

Kirk, Michael (director). *Frontline. Secrets, Politics, and Torture. Frontline* (video). PBS, 2015. https://www.pbs.org/wgbh/frontline/documentary/secrets-politics-and-torture/.

Kishk, Muhammad Jalal. كلمتي للمغفلين [My Word to the Fools]. Al-Zahara l-il-'Ilam al-Arabi, 1985.

Kovach, Peter. "Religion and Public Diplomacy." *American Diplomacy*, March 2014. http://americandiplomacy.web.unc.edu.

Kraidy, Marwan M. *Reality Television and Arab Politics: Contention in Public Life*. Cambridge University Press, 2010.

Kumar, Krishna. *Promoting Independent Media: Strategies for Democracy Assistance*. Lynne Rienner, 2006.

Kurlantzick, Joshua. "Reforming the U.S. International Military Education and Training Program." Council on Foreign Relations, June 2016. https://www.cfr.org/report/reforming-us-international-military-education-and-training-program.

Labaton, Stephen. "Broadcast Chief Misused Office, Inquiry Reports," *New York Times*, August 30, 2006. https://www.nytimes.com/2006/08/30/washington/30broadcast.html?hp&ex=1156996800&en=8590fa5730300061&ei=5094&partner=homepage.

Lamb, Christopher J. *Review of Psychological Operations Lessons Learned from Recent Operational Experience*. National Defense University Press, 2005.

Laugesen, Amanda. *Taking Books to the World: American Publishers and the Cultural Cold War*. University of Massachusetts Press, 2017.

Layalina. "The Cast of 'On the Road in America' on Al-Jazeera (2006)." *The Layalina Chronicle*, 2006. http://www.layalina.tv/publications/the-layalina-chronicle/.

Layalina. "OTR II Is a Hit." *The Layalina Chronicle*, 2010. http://www.layalina.tv/publications/the-layalina-chronicle/.

Lebovic, Sam. *A Righteous Smokescreen: Postwar America and the Politics of Cultural Globalization*. University of Chicago Press, 2022.

Lederer, Edith M. "US Calls on Russia, Turkey, UAE to Halt Libya Intervention." AP, January 28, 2021. https://apnews.com/article/turkey-libya-elections-united-nations-russia-5dd10a3c818204f5baac7f2ee8e4dfe0.

Lee, Newton. *Counterterrorism and Cybersecurity: Total Information Awareness*. Springer, 2013.

Le Monde. "La nouvelle amitié russo-américaine" [The New Russo-American Friendship]. October 8, 2001. https://www.lemonde.fr/archives/article/2001/10/07/la-nouvelle-amitie-russo-americaine_4195747_1819218.html.

Le Monde. "L'Egypt: autre 'ennemi d'Internet'" [Egypt: Another Enemy of the Internet]. January 26, 2011. https://www.lemonde.fr/archives/article/2001/10/07/la-nouvelle-amitie-russo-americaine_4195747_1819218.html.

Leonardson, J. E. "Intelligence in Public Media." *Studies in Intelligence* 64, no. 1 (2020).

Lerner, Daniel. *The Passing of Traditional Society: Modernizing the Middle East*. Free Press, 1958.

Levanthal, Todd. "The Need to Up Our Game in Countering Disinformation." *Comparative Strategy* 42, no. 2 (2023): 173–86.

Levanthal, Todd. "Soviet vs. Post-Soviet Russian Disinformation." *American Diplomacy*, 2024. https://americandiplomacy.web.unc.edu/2024/02/soviet-vs-post-soviet-russian-disinformation/.

Levine, Art. "Bad Reception." *American Prospect*, November 8, 2005. https://prospect.org/article/bad-reception/.

Levine, Art. "Bad Reception, Part II: Did Cronies of Mouafac Harb, the Executive Who Runs America's Arabic-Language Networks, Get Sweetheart Contracts?" *American Prospect*, November 10, 2005. https://prospect.org/article/bad-reception-part-ii/.

Lizner, Dafna. "Lost in Translation: Alhurra—America's Troubled Effort to Win Middle East Hearts and Minds." *ProPublica*, June 22, 2008. https://www.propublica.org/article/alhurra-middle-east-hearts-and-minds-622.

Lizner, Dafna. "Alhurra's Baghdad Bureau Mired in Controversy." *ProPublica*, July 8, 2008. https://www.propublica.org/article/alhurras-baghdad-bureau-mired-in-controversy-708.

Lord, Carnes. *Losing Hearts and Minds? Public Diplomacy and Strategic Influence in the Age of Terror*. Praeger Security International, 2006.

Lucas, Scott. "'Total Culture' and the State-Private Network: A Commentary." Chap. 11 in *Culture and International History*. Berghahn, 2022.

Lyman, Rick. "A Nation Challenged: The Entertainment Industry; Hollywood Discusses Role in War Effort." *New York Times*, November 12, 2001. https://www.nytimes.com/2001/11/11/us/nation-challenged-film-industry-white-house-takes-steps-renew-tie-hollywood.html.

Lynch, Marc. *The New Arab Wars*. Public Affairs, 2016.

Maayeh, Suha. "Mysterious Deaths of Prominent Sisters Shock Jordan." *The National*, November 8, 2015. https://www.thenationalnews.com/world/mysterious-deaths-of-prominent-sisters-shock-jordan-1.46034.

MacCann, Richard Dyer. "Film and Foreign Policy: The USIA, 1962–67." *Cinema Journal* 9, no. 1 (1969): 23–42.

MacKinnon, Rebecca. *Consent of the Networked*. Basic Books, 2013.

Malsin, Jared, and Thoms Grove. "Researcher or Spy? Maxim Shugaley Saga Points to How Russia Now Builds Influence Abroad." *Wall Street Journal*, October 5, 2021. https://www.wsj.com/articles/researcher-or-spy-maxim-shugaley-saga-points-to-how-russia-now-builds-influence-abroad-11633448407.

Markel, Lester, ed. *Public Opinion and Foreign Policy*. Harper, 1949.

Mashkour, Salem. "حسن نصر الله ......المنتصر بلا غرور" [Hassan al-Nasrallah: Victory Without Pride]. Islam Online, November 18, 2002. https://www.yahosein.com/vb/node/10852#post10852.

McFadden, Robert D. "From New York to Melbourne, Cries for Peace." *New York Times*, February 16, 2003. https://www.nytimes.com/2003/02/16/nyregion/threats-and-responses-overview-from-new-york-to-melbourne-cries-for-peace.html.

McLaughlin, Jenna. "Spies for Hire." *The Intercept*, October 24, 2016. https://theintercept.com/2016/10/24/darkmatter-united-arab-emirates-spies-for-hire/.

Mekay, Emad. "TV Stations Multiply as Egyptian Censorship Falls." *New York Times*, July 30, 2011. https://www.nytimes.com/2011/07/14/world/middleeast/14iht-M14B-EGYPT-MEDIA.html.

Meir-Glitzenstein, Esther. "Operation Magic Carpet: Constructing the Myth of the Magical Immigration of Yemenite Jews to Israel." *Israel Studies* 16, no. 3 (2011): 149–73.

Mevel, Jean-Jacques. "L'Amérique frappe en Afghanistan" [America Strikes Afghanistan]. *Le Figaro*, October 8, 2001.

Mickelson, Sig. *America's Other Voice: The Story of Radio Free Europe and Radio Liberty*. Praeger, 1983.

Michaelson, Ruth. "Egypt Blocks Access to News Websites Including Al-Jazeera and Mada Masr." *Guardian*, May 25, 2017. https://www.theguardian.com/world/2017/may/25/egypt-blocks-access-news-websites-al-jazeera-mada-masr-press-freedom.

Miller, Flagg. "Terrorist Violence and the Enrollment of Psychology in Predicting Muslim Extremism: Critical Terrorism Studies Meets Critical Algorithm Studies." *Critical Studies on Terrorism* 12, no. 2 (2019): 185–209.

Miller, Greg, and Scott Higham. "In a Propaganda War Against ISIS the US Tried to Play by the Enemies' Rules." *Washington Post*, May 8, 2015. https://www.washingtonpost.com/world/national-security/in-a-propaganda-war-us-tried-to-play-by-the-enemys-rules/2015/05/08/6eb6b732-e52f-11e4-81ea-0649268f729e_story.html.

Mitchell, Tom and Xinning Liu. "The America Hawks Circling Beijing." *Financial Times*, December 7, 2018. https://www.ft.com/content/d425ee0a-f9bf-11e8-8b7c-6fa24bd5409c.

Mitchell, W. J. T. *Cloning Terror: The War of Images, 9/11 to the Present*. University of Chicago Press, 2011.

Mosser, Michael W. "Puzzles Versus Problems: The Alleged Disconnect Between Academics and Military Practitioners." *Perspectives on Politics* 8, no. 4 (2010): 1077–86.

Muñoz, Arturo. *U.S. Military Information Operations in Afghanistan: Effectiveness of Psychological Operations 2001–2010*. RAND, 2012.

Myers, Steven Lee. "From Russia, Elaborate Tales of Fake Journalists." *New York Times*. March 18, 2024. https://www.nytimes.com/2024/03/18/business/media/russia-fake-journalists.html.

Narwani, Sharmine. "An Obituary on Lebanon's 'Cedar Revolution.'" *Mideast Shuffle* (blog), March 13, 2005. https://mideastshuffle.com/2015/03/18/an-obituary-on-lebanons-cedar-revolution/.

Nasser, Gamal Abdel. *The Philosophy of the Revolution*. Smith, Keynes & Marshall, 1959.

National Academies of Sciences, Engineering, and Medicine. *Evaluation of the Minerva Research Initiative*. National Academies Press, 2020.

New York Times. "Radiotelegraph Circuit to Iraq," February 20, 1951.

New York Times. "Turkey's Defense and Aid Decided, Ankara Says." February 27, 1951.

New York Times. "U.S. Unit in Iraq Hit by Grenade," March 20, 1951.

New York Times. "Iraq Seizes Arms Cache." June 18, 1951.

New York Times. "Early Reaction Pleases," August 27, 1952.

New York Times. "Moslem Pilgrims Swamp US Airlift." August 27, 1952.

New York Times. "3 'Voice' Officials Deny Red Leanings." February 21, 1953.

New York Times. "'Intelligence' Conformity." August 9, 1961.

New York Times. "Washington Talk: United States Information Agency; At $30 Million Is Anyone Watching?" July 14, 1987. https://www.nytimes.com/1987/07/14/us/washington-talk-united-states-information-agency-30-million-anyone-watching.html.

New York Times. "Clinton Sends Conciliatory Message to Iran," January 30, 1998. https://www.nytimes.com/1998/01/30/world/clinton-sends-conciliatory-message-to-iran.html.

Nouri, Bamo. "Iraq's Rushed and Divisive Constitution Was Always Doomed to Fail." *The Conversation*, October 31, 2017. https://theconversation.com/iraqs-rushed-and-divisive-constitution-was-always-doomed-to-fail-85026.

Nye, Joseph S. *Soft Power: The Means to Success in World Politics*. Public Affairs, 2004.

Obeidallah, Dean. "Did SNL Isis Skit Cross a Line?" CNN, March, 2015. http://www.cnn.com/2015/03/02/opinion/obeidallah-snl-isis-skit/.

Osborn, Lou, and Dimitri Zufferey. *Wagner : Enquête au coeur du système Prgojine*. Faubourg, 2023.

Osipova-Stocker, Yelena, Eulynn Shiu, Thomas Layou, and Shawn Powers, "Assessing Impact in Global Media: Methods, Innovations, and Challenges." *Place Branding and Public Diplomacy* 18, no. 3 (2022): 287–304.

Osnos, Evan, David Remnick, and Joshua Yaffa. "Trump, Putin, and the New Cold War." *New Yorker*, March 6, 2017. https://www.newyorker.com/magazine/2017/03/06/trump-putin-and-the-new-cold-war.

Pallister, David. "Media Mogul Accused of Running Saudi-Funded Propaganda Campaign." *Guardian*, January 26, 2005. https://www.theguardian.com/world/2005/jan/26/pressandpublishing.media.

Pattiz, Norman. "Radio Sawa and Alhurra TV." In *Engaging the Arab and Islamic Worlds Through Public Diplomacy*, ed. William Rugh. Public Diplomacy Council, 2004.

Paul, Christopher. "Whither Strategic Communication? A Survey of Current Proposals and Recommendations." RAND, 2009.

Paul, Christopher, and James J. Kim. *Reporters on the Battlefield: The Embedded Press System in Historical Context*. RAND, 2004.

Pekel, Misja, dir. *The World According to Russia Today*. Icarus Films, 2015.

Pincus, Walter. "A Speed Bump for Pentagon's Information Ops." *Washington Post*, December 6, 2011. https://www.washingtonpost.com/blogs/checkpoint-washington/post/a-speed-bump-for-pentagons-information-ops/2011/12/06/gIQAbxF7YO_blog.html.

Pintak, Larry. *Reflections in a Bloodshot Lens: America, Islam and the War of Ideas*. Pluto, 2006.

Pleasance, Chris. "Trip Advisor for Terrorists: Where to Buy Nutella in the War Zone, What Kind of Trainers to Wear, and How it Feels to Chop off Infidels' Heads Revealed in Twisted Chatrooms." *Daily Mail*, August 15, 2014. https://www.dailymail.co.uk/news/article-2726407/Trip-Advisor-terrorists-Where-buy-Nutella-war-zone-kind-trainers-wear-feels-chop-infidels-heads-revealed-twisted-chatrooms.html.

Pomerantsev, Peter. *Nothing Is True and Everything Is Possible*. Public Affairs, 2014.

Powers, Sean, and Ahmed El-Gody. "Lessons of Al-Hurra Television." In *Toward a New Public Diplomacy*, ed. Philip Seib. Palgrave, 2009.

Prados, John. *Presidents' Secret Wars: CIA and Pentagon Covert Operations from World War II Through the Persian Gulf*. I. R. Dee, 1996.

Price, David H. *Cold War Anthropology: The CIA, the Pentagon, and the Growth of Dual Use Anthropology*. Duke University Press, 2016.

Pusztai, Wolfgang. "Libya's Fragile Ceasefire: A Lost Opportunity?" *Atlantic Council* (blog), June 4, 2021. https://www.atlanticcouncil.org/blogs/menasource/libyas-fragile-ceasefire-a-lost-opportunity/.

Ramonet, Ignacio. "An Enemy at Last." *Le Monde diplomatique*, October 2001. https://mondediplo.com/2001/10/01leader.

Richmond, Ray. "On the Road in America." *Hollywood Reporter*, June 1, 2008. https://www.hollywoodreporter.com/movies/movie-reviews/road-america-126081/.

Report of the Defense Science Board Task Force on Managed Information Dissemination. Office of the Under Secretary of Defense for Acquisition, Technology and Logistics, 2001.

Report of the Defense Science Board Task Force on Strategic Communication. Office of the Under Secretary of Defense for Acquisition, Technology, and Logistics, 2004.

Revkin, Andrew C. "U.S. Resists New Targets for Curbing Emissions." *New York Times*, December 8, 2005. https://www.nytimes.com/2005/12/08/world/us-resists-new-targets-for-curbing-emissions.html.

Rich, Motoko, and Notoya Kiuko. "'Oppenheimer' Opens in Nuclear-Scarred Japan, 8 Months After U.S. Premiere." *New York Times*, April 1, 2024. https://www.nytimes.com/2024/04/01/world/asia/oppenheimer-opens-japan.html.

Rid, Thomas. *Active Measures: The Secret History of Disinformation and Political Warfare*. Farrar, Straus and Giroux, 2020.

Riley, John W., and Leonard S. Cottrell. "Research for Psychological Warfare." *Public Opinion Quarterly* 21, no. 1 (1957).

Robertson, Adi. "Inside USC's Crazy Experimental VR Lab." *The Verge*, September 17, 2015. https://www.theverge.com/2015/9/17/9333633/usc-institute-for-creative-technologies-virtual-reality-lab.

Rockefeller, Steven C. *John Dewey: Religious Faith and Democratic Humanism*. Columbia University Press, 1991.

Rosen, Jeffrey. "The Year in Ideas; Total Information Awareness." *New York Times*, December 15, 2002. https://www.nytimes.com/2002/12/15/magazine/the-year-in-ideas-total-information-awareness.html.

Rosenberg, Matthew, and Julien E. Barnes. "A Bible Burning, a Russian News Agency and a Story Too Good to Check Out." *New York Times*, August 11, 2020. https://www.nytimes.com/2020/08/11/us/politics/russia-disinformation-election-meddling.html.

RT Arabic. "ليبيا.. تفاصيل مقتل آمر اللواء التاسع مشاة في بنغازي" [Libya . . . Details of the Killing of the Commander of the 9th Infantry Brigade in Benghazi]. July 27, 2021. https://web.archive.org/web/20240531084855/https://arabic.rt.com/middle_east/1255964-ليبيا-تفاصيل-مقتل-محمد-الكاني-آمر-اللواء-التاسع-مشاة-في-بنغازي/.

RT Arabic. "الكنيسة الروسية: نشطاء 'حياة السود مهمة' أحرقوا سمعتهم بإحراق الإنجيل" [The Russian Church: Black Lives Matter Activists Burned Their Reputation by Burning the Gospel]. August 4, 2020. https://web.archive.org/web/20240531083525/https://arabic.rt.com/world/1141164-الكنيسة-مسؤول-في-السود-مهمة-بإحراقهم-الإنجيل-أحرقوا-سمعتهم/.

RT Arabic. "قوة الدعم السريع من هراوة بيد البشير إلى خنجر في ظهره!" [Rapid Support Force from a Club in the Hand of Bashir to a Dagger in the Back!]. April 12, 2019, https://web.archive.org/web/20240418181044/https://arabic.rt.com/middle_east/1012945-قوةالدعم-السريع-المثيرة-للجدل-في-السودان-من-هراوة-بيد-البشير-إلى-خنجر-في-ظهره/.

Rugh, William. *Frontline Public Diplomacy*. Palgrave, 2014.

Sabbagh, Isa Khalil. من بين أوراقي: ٥٠ عامًا من الإعلام والسياسة. [From My Papers: 50 Years in Media and Politics]. Dar Al-Hani, 1991.

Sageman, Marc. *Understanding Terror Networks*. University of Pennsylvania Press, 2004.

Salah, Ahmed. *You Are Under Arrest for Masterminding the Egyptian Revolution*. Spark, 2016.

Salamandra, Christa. "The Muhannad Effect: Media Panic, Melodrama, and the Arab Female Gaze." *Anthropological Quarterly* 85, no. 1 (2012): 45–77.

Salazar, Philippe-Joseph. *Words Are Weapons: Inside ISIS's Rhetoric of Terror*. Yale University Press, 2017.

Sandeen, Eric J. *Picturing an Exhibition: The Family of Man and 1950s America*. University of New Mexico Press, 1995.

Saunders, Frances Stonor. *The Cultural Cold War: The CIA and the World of Arts and Letters*. New Press, 2000.

Schneider, Cynthia. "Can Good Television Beat the Islamic State?" *Foreign Policy*, April 7, 2017. https://foreignpolicy.com/2017/04/07/can-good-television-beat-the-islamic-state-mbc/.

Schoen, Fletcher, and Christopher J. Lamb. "Deception, Disinformation, and Strategic Communications: How One Interagency Group Made a Major Difference." *Strategic Perspectives* 11 (2012).

Schwartz, Ian. "Tucker Carlson: These Are the Criminals Being Used by the Democratic Party to Destroy Your Country." RealClear Politics, July 3, 2020. https://www.realclearpolitics.com/video/2020/07/03/tucker_carlson_these_are_the_criminals_being_used_by_the_democratic_party_to_destroy_your_country.html.

Shalvey, Kevin. "Facebook Posts and Cameo Videos by Charlie Sheen and Dolph Lundgren Were Used by Russian Trolls to Persuade Libya to Release a Suspected Spy." *Business Insider*, December 23, 2020. https://www.businessinsider.com/russian-trolls-used-facebook-cameo-free-alleged-spy-in-libya-2020-12.

Shufan, Nabil. "وزارة إعلام داعش.. منظومة الترويج الفني والحرب النفسية" [ISIS Ministry of Information: A System of Artistic Intimidation and Psychological Warfare]. *Al-'Arabi al-Jadid*, March 29, 2015. https://www.alaraby.co.uk/وزارة-إعلام-داعش-منظومة-الترويج-الفني-والحرب-النفسية/.

Siele, Martin K. N. "Putin's Free Russian Classes Are Taking off in Africa." *Semafor*, January 5, 2024. https://www.semafor.com/article/01/05/2024/free-russian-classes-are-taking-off-in-africa.

Sienkiewicz, Matt. *The Other Air Force: U.S. Efforts to Reshape Middle Eastern Media Since 9/11*. Rutgers University Press, 2016.

Silverberg, Daniel, and Joseph Heimann. "An Ever-Expanding War: Legal Aspects of Online Strategic Communication." *Parameters* 39, no. 2 (2009): 77–93.

Simmons, Ann M. "Putin Meets with Saudi, UAE Rulers." *Wall Street Journal*, December 7, 2023. https://www.wsj.com/world/russia/putin-meets-with-saudi-u-a-e-rulers-in-bid-to-refresh-alliances-df321626.

Simpson, Christopher. *Science of Coercion: Communication Research and Psychological Warfare, 1945–1960*. Oxford University Press, 1994.

Sirrs, Owen L. *A History of the Egyptian Intelligence Service: A History of the Mukhabarat, 1910–2009*. Routledge, 2010.

Sky News Arabia. "شوغالي: فيلم روسي يحكي معاناة الشعب الليبي تحت وطأة الإرهاب" [Shugalei: A Russian Film That Tells of the Suffering of the Libyan People Under the Weight of Terrorism]. May 7, 2020. https://www.skynewsarabia.com/varieties/1342541-شوغالي-فيلم-روسي-يحكي-معاناة-الشعب-الليبي-وطأة-الإرهاب.

Sky News Arabia. "إدلب ليبيا.. تركيا على خطى داعش في غرب البلاد" [Idlib, Libya . . . Turkey Is Following the Lead of ISIS in the West of the Country], January 4, 2021. https://web.archive.org/web/20240418174531/https://www.skynewsarabia.com/middle-east/1404799-إدلب-ليبيا-تركيا-خطى-داعش-غرب-البلاد.

Smith, Becca Synnestvedt. "Rejecting America's Cold War: Sayyid Qutb's Nationalist-Islamist Agenda and the Failure of U.S. Efforts to Win Over Egyptian Muslims Following World War II." PhD diss., Georgetown University, 2017.

Snow, Nancy. *Propaganda, Incorporated: Selling America's Culture to the World*. Seven Stories, 1998.

Snyder, Alvin A. *Warriors of Disinformation: American Propaganda, Soviet Lies, and the Winning of the Cold War: An Insider's Account*. Arcade, 1995.

Sorensen, Thomas C. *The Word War: The Story of American Propaganda*. Harper and Row, 1968.

Soroka, Stuart N. "Media, Public Opinion, and Foreign Policy." *Harvard International Journal of Press/Politics* 8, no. 1, 2003.

Spector, Ian. "Soviet Cultural Propaganda in the Near and Middle East." In *The Middle East: Studies in Contemporary History*, ed. Walter Z. Laqueur. Routledge, 1958.

Sproule, J. Michael. *Propaganda and Democracy: The American Experience of Media and Mass Persuasion*. Cambridge University Press, 1997.

Sputnik Arabic. "الوكالة الدولية للأنباء روسية سيغودنية و مؤسسة ألاهرام توعقان مذكرة تعاون" [The International News Agency Russia Segodnya and Al-Ahram Foundation Sign a Memorandum of Cooperation]. November 2, 2015. https://sputnikarabic.ae/20150211/1013393610.html.

Stein, Jeff. "Bay of Piglets: How the Freemasons Got Caught in a Plot to Topple the Castros." *Newsweek*, April 7, 2014. https://www.newsweek.com/2014/04/18/bay-piglets-how-freemasons-got-caught-plot-topple-castros-248099.html.

Stengel, Richard. *Information Wars: How We Lost the Global Battle Against Disinformation and What We Can Do About It*. Atlantic Monthly, 2019.

Sukarieh, Mayssoun. "The Hope Crusades: Culturalism and Reform in the Arab World." *Political and Legal Anthropology Review* 35, no. 1 (2012): 115–34.

SVT. "How Pro-Russian Disinformation Is Laundered." February 3, 2024. https://www.svt.se/special/how-pro-russian-disinformation-is-laundered/.

Teicholz, Nina. "Privatizing Propaganda." *Washington Monthly* 34, no. 12 (2002).

Telhami, Shibley. *The Stakes: America and the Middle East: The Consequences of Power and the Choice for Peace*. Basic Books, 2002.

Thompson, Nicholas, and Issie Lapowsky, "How Russian Trolls Used Meme Warfare to Divide America." *Wired*, December 17, 2018. https://www.wired.com/story/russia-ira-propaganda-senate-report/.

United States Advisory Commission on Public Diplomacy. *2017 Comprehensive Annual Report on Public Diplomacy and International Broadcasting*. U.S. Dept. of State, 2017.

United States Information Agency. "العرب و الدمقراطية" [The Arabs and Democracy]. *Al-Sadaqah*. Maktab al-Wilayat al-Muttahidah lil-isti'lamat li-ta'ziz al-tafahum al-duwali, August 6, 1952.

United States Information Agency. "المكتبات العامة و النشئ" [Public Libraries and Publications]. *Al-Sadaqah*, November 6, 1952.

United States Information Agency. "الاسلام جدار روحي مينع لا تستطيع الشيوعية اختراقه" [Islam Is a Spiritual Wall That Communism Cannot Penetrate]. *Al-Sadaqah*, March 19, 1953.

United States Information Agency. "التجربة المثيرة: ثلاث فتيات امريكيات تعيش كل منهن ابنه لاسرة مصرية" [An Exciting Experience: Three American Girls Live as Daughters in Egyptian Families]. *Al-Sadaqah*, August 18, 1966.

Vanden Brook, Tom. "Army Kills Controversial Social Science Program." *USA Today*, June 29, 2015. https://www.usatoday.com/story/news/nation/2015/06/29/human-terrain-system-afghanistan/29476409/.

Van Ham, Peter. "Opinion Piece Branding European Power." *Place Branding and Public Diplomacy* no. 1–2 (2005): 122–26.

Vaughan, James R. *The Failure of American and British Propaganda in the Arab Middle East, 1945–57: Unconquerable Minds*. Palgrave Macmillan, 2005.

Vincent, Donna Marie. *Worldnet: Propaganda and Public Diplomacy*. 1993. ProQuest Dissertations and Theses.

Waddell, Kaveh. "How New York's Top Advertisers Are Fighting Terrorist Propaganda," *Atlantic*, March 15, 2016. https://www.theatlantic.com/technology/archive/2016/03/how-new-yorks-top-advertisers-are-helping-fight-terrorist-propaganda/473805/.

Wall Street Journal. "Boos for Al-Hurra." May 11, 2007.

Walsh, Chris. "New on the Freedom Collection: Ammar Abdulhamid Updates." George W. Bush Presidential Center, February 25, 2013. https://www.bushcenter.org/publications/new-on-the-freedom-collection-ammar-abdulhamid-updates.

Walsh, Declan, and Nada Rashwan. "'We're at War': A Covert Social Media Campaign Boosts Military Rulers." *New York Times*, September 6, 2019. https://www.nytimes.com/2019/09/06/world/middleeast/sudan-social-media.html.

Walsh, Declan, and Suliman Ali Zway. "A Facebook War: Libyans Battle on the Streets and on Screens." *New York Times*, September 4, 2018. https://www.nytimes.com/2018/09/04/world/middleeast/libya-facebook.html.

Ward, Clarissa, Katie Polglase, Sebastian Shukla, Gianluca Mezzofiore, and Tim Lister. "Russian Election Meddling Is Back—via Ghana and Nigeria—and in Your Feeds." CNN, April 11, 2020. https://www.cnn.com/2020/03/12/world/russia-ghana-troll-farms-2020-ward/index.html.

Washington Times. "China-Made Artillery Seized in Afghanistan." April 12, 2002. https://www.washingtontimes.com/news/2002/apr/12/20020412-041857-7139r/.

Waxman, Sharon. "Thinking Outside the Tank." *Washington Post*, March 7, 2003. https://www.washingtonpost.com/archive/lifestyle/2003/03/07/thinking-outside-the-tank/1a25372a-e258-484f-acae-5dfbc2585fd1/.

Wehrey, Frederic. "A Minister, a General, & the Militias: Libya's Shifting Balance of Power." *New York Review*, March 9, 2019. https://www.nybooks.com/online/2019/03/19/a-minister-a-general-militias-libyas-shifting-balance-of-power/.

Weimann, Gabriel. "Al-Qa'ida's Extensive Use of the Internet." *CTC Sentinel* 2 no. 1 (2008). https://ctc.westpoint.edu/al-qaidas-extensive-use-of-the-internet/.

Whewell, Tim. "How Six Brothers—and Their Lions—Terrorised a Libyan Town." BBC, January 2, 2021. https://www.bbc.com/news/stories-55564933.

Whitaker, Brian. "Selective Memri." *Guardian*, August 12, 2002. https://www.theguardian.com/world/2002/aug/12/worlddispatch.brianwhitaker.

Whitaker, Brian. "Wargames Open with Clandestine Broadcast." *Guardian*, February 23, 2003. https://www.theguardian.com/world/2003/feb/25/iraq.brianwhitaker.

Whitlock, C., and N. Jones. "Mattis Secretly Advised Arab Monarch on Yemen War, Records Show." *Washington Post*, February 6, 2024. https://www.washingtonpost.com/investigations/2024/02/06/mattis-advised-uae-yemen-war/.

Wilford, Hugh. *The Mighty Wurlitzer: How the CIA Played America*. Harvard University Press, 2008.

Wilford, Hugh. *America's Great Game: The CIA's Secret Arabists and the Shaping of the Modern Middle East*. Basic Books, 2013.

Wood, Josh. "The Balance Shifts in Lebanese Politics." *New York Times*, February 16, 2011. https://www.nytimes.com/2011/02/17/world/middleeast/17iht-lebanon.html.

World Bank. "Individuals Using the Internet (Percent of Population)," 2017. Retrieved from https://data.worldbank.org/indicator/IT.NET.USER.ZS?locations&name_desc=true.

Yadron, Danny. "Silicon Valley Appears Open to Helping US Spy Agencies After Terrorism Summit." *Guardian*, January 8, 2016. https://www.theguardian.com/technology/2016/jan/08/technology-executives-white-house-isis-terrorism-meeting-silicon-valley-facebook-apple-twitter-microsoft.

Yager, Jordy. "Prejudice in America, Reality-Style." The Hill. June 3, 2008. https://thehill.com/capital-living/20848-prejudice-in-america-reality-style/.

Zaharna, R. S. *Battles to Bridges: U.S. Strategic Communication and Public Diplomacy After 9/11*. Palgrave Macmillan, 2010.

Žižek, Slavoj, and Frank Wynne. *Violence: Six Sideways Reflections*. Profile, 2010.

SELECT INTERVIEWS

Scott Atran, Co-founder Artis International (email correspondence)
Sam Barnett, CEO of MBC Group
Ambassador Alberto Fernandez, President of the Middle East Broadcasting Networks 2017–2020 (email correspondence)
James K. Glassman, Undersecretary of State for Public Diplomacy 2008–2009 (email correspondence)

Todd Levanthal, Chief of the Counter-Misinformation Team for the U.S. Department of State (retired)
Aaron Lobel, founder America Abroad Media
Fadoua Massat, Editor, Maghreb Voices USAGM, 2016-2019
Arturo Muñoz, CIA (retired)
Ambassador William Rugh (retired)
Larry Schwartz, Deputy Assistant Secretary for Press and Public Diplomacy Bureau of Near Eastern Affairs, State Department (retired)
Ambassador Margaret Scobey (retired)
Leon Shahabian, founder Layalina, Inc.
Eulynn Shiu, Director of Research, USAGM, 2019–2025

INDEX

Photo insert images are indicated by *p1*, *p2*, *p3*, etc.

AAA. *See* American Anthropological Association
AAM. *See* America Abroad Media
'Abd al-'Aal, Hassan, 45
Abdulhamid, Ammar, 119
Abdul-Ilah (Prince), *p1*
Abdullah (King), 117
Abel, Walter, 42
Abraham Accords, 120–22
Abu Ghaith, Sulaiman, 27
Abu al-Naga, Fayza, 162
Abu Shadi, Ahmed Zaki, 8, 44–46
Acheson, Dean, 54, 70, 229n21
Afghanistan: Al-Hurra coverage in, 106; Operation Enduring Freedom in, 73–80; Soviet Union in, 131–32
Afghanistan (film), 30
Afghan Media Resource Center, 146
AFME. *See* American Friends of the Middle East

AFNET. *See* African Network
AFOSR. *See* Air Force Office of Scientific Research
AFP. *See* Agence France-Presse
Africa, Russia-Africa Summit in, 191. *See also* sub-Saharan Africa; *specific countries*
African Network (AFNET), 133, 143
Afrigatenews, 182–84
Agence France-Presse (AFP), 133
Air Force Office of Scientific Research (AFOSR), 11
Al-Ahram (newspaper), 190, 192–93
Al-Ahram-Sputnik agreement, 192–93
Al-Akhbar, 4, 53, 62
Al-Alawi, Hassan, 244n4
Al-Arabiya network, 107, 139, 210
'Ala tariq fi Amrika. *See On the Road in America*
al-Baghdadi, Abu Bakr, 147
al-Bashir, Badria, 141

al-Bashir, Omar, 193
al-Chadriji, Kamil, 83
Al-Furqan, 151–52
Algeria, Al-Qaeda in, 151
al-Hafiz, Abdel Halim, 42
Al-Haqiqah ("the truth"), 25–26
Al-Hashimi, Faisal II (King), *p1*
Al-Hayat fi Amrika (*Life in America*), 4; as counter-communication vehicle, 53; open engagement with Arab audiences, 62; programming for, 58–59; public opinion polling, 58–59; reader demographics for, 56–61
"*Al-Hayat fi Amrika* / Life in America #35," *p5*
al-Hoja, Nasr al-Din, 145
Al-Hurra: analysis of, 120–22; Arab Spring uprisings, 116; in Baghdad, 107; criticism of, 114–15; *Dakhil Washington*, 115; educational programming on, 106; *Generation Entrepreneur*, *p9*; Harb and, 103, 108–9, 128–29; Hizballah-Israeli coverage, 115–16; international election coverage, 102–7; *Iraq and the World* and, 102; Israeli-Palestine crisis coverage, 213; Khoury and, 111–13; limited effectiveness of, 209; morning programming on, 116; new programming direction for, 119; Pattiz and, 102, 112; public diplomacy and, 109; Quantum Communications and, 173; Radio Sawa and, 107; reboot of, 117–20; Russia Today and, 188–89; Sky News Arabia and, 118–19; studios for, *p9*; targeting of journalists from, 107; during Donald Trump administration, 117–21, 210–12

al-Husseini, Hajji Amin, 51
Ali, al-Faeq al-Sheikh, 103
al-Issa, Shamlan, 103
Al-Jazeera, 27, 71; bombing of, 101; in Iraq, 107; MBC programming in response to, 138–39; al-Qaeda and, 74; Russia Today and, 188, 190; Saifan and, 124
al-Jumaili, Rasim, 107
Al-Karnak Publishing, 64
Allen, George V., 30, 40
Allen, Richard V., 128
Alliance of Youth Movements, 151, 155–57, 257n27; Arab Spring uprisings and, 162; Global Youth Summit, 158
Alliluyeva, Svetlana, 21
Al-Majal, 4, 44
al-Misrati, Mahmoud, 184
Al-Misri, 66
Al-Mustaqbal, 44
Al-Nabulsi, Shaker, 103
Al-Nahar, 21, 104
al-Najjar, Ghanem, 103
al-Qadhafi, Muammar, 184
al-Qadhafi, Saif, 185
Al-Qaeda, 27–28; civil war with ISIS, 169–70; as global media organization, 150–51; Internet use by, 150; Al Jazeera and, 74; rebranding of, 151–52; Al-Sahab and, 150–51; technological use by, 150–51
al-Qasabi, Nasser, 140–41, 255n59
al-Rab'ee, Ahmed, 103
al-Rashed, Abdulrahman, 135–36, 138–39
Al-Raz, Ali, 104
Al-Sa'at (The Hour), *p9–p10*
Al-Sabah (newspaper), 95–97
Al-Sadaqah, 49, *p4*; American propaganda in, *p3*; as

INDEX

counter-communication vehicle, 53; Franklin Book program and, 65; international exchange programs and, 157–58; open engagement with Arab audiences, 62; origins of, 4; photography in, 4; public diplomacy through, 53
al-Sadr, Muqtada, 114
al-Sadr, Musa (Imam), 109
Al-Sahab, 150–51
Al-Sahhaf, Mohammed Saeed, 73
Al Saud, Abdul Aziz (King), 50–51
al-Sehai, Hani, 27
Al-Tahrir, 119
Al-Wasat, 180, 183–84
Alyahyai, Mohammad, 116
al-Za'im, Husni, 68, 70
Al-Zaman, 238n19
al-Zawahiri, Aymin, 27, 169
al-Zoubi, Jafer, 248n57
America Abroad Media (AAM), 25, 125; foreign-based network partnerships with, 134; political clout of, 128
American Anthropological Association (AAA), 91
American Friends of the Middle East (AFME), 47
American Institute on Public Opinion, 10
American propaganda: through CSCC, 165–70; after 9/11 terrorist attacks in U.S., 2, 106, 220n9; Operation Enduring Freedom and, 76–80; Worldnet and, 129–34. *See also* psychological warfare
American propaganda, in Arabic, 1, *p3*; during Cold War era, 3–7; conceptual approach to, 2–3; Franklin Book program and, 81; Hollywood industry and, 33–34; Khoury and, 112–13; after 9/11 terrorist attacks in U.S., 2, 106; process of, 3–4; Voice of America and, 4–5. *See also* "New Cold War"; psychological warfare; public diplomacy; *specific topics*
American Prospect, 114
Amin, Ahmad, 114
Animal Farm (Orwell), 144–45
Ansar al-Sharia movement, 165
Aoun, Michel, 104
Apollo (journal), 44
April 6 Movement, 160
Aqqad, Abbas Mahmud al-, 45
Arabic language, use of: American propaganda in, 2–7, *p3*; in Russian propaganda, 189; in Voice of America broadcasts, 8, 42–46
Arab-Israeli War, 43
Arab League, 4, 43
Arab Muslim Women, 137
Arab nationalism, 61, 70
"Arabs and Democracy, The" (Azzam), 52
Arab Spring uprisings, 207–8; April 6 Movement, 160; in Cairo, 159–65; citizen journalism during, 163; Facebook activists and, 160; "Friday of Rage" and, 160; Al-Hurra coverage of, 116; Muslim Brotherhood and, 160; Obama and, 116; Public Diplomacy 2.0 initiatives, 161–62; Russia Today and, 156; *Al-Sharouk* and, 160; social media and, 160; Tahrir Square and, 159–60; in Tunisia, 159, 163
Armitage, Richard, 244n4
Arms Export Control Act, U.S. (1976), 176
Armstrong, Matt, 268n70
Army Research Office (ARO), 11

Arndt, Richard, 240n46
ARO. *See* Army Research Office
Asia Foundation, 64
Assange, Julian, 156
Association of Muslim 'Ulama, 104
Austin, J. J., 69
Awad, Fadhil, 107
Aziz, Abdul (King), 43
Aziz, Mohammad bin Abdul (Crown Prince), 43
Azzam, Abd al-Rahman, 4, 43, 51–53

Badrakhan, Abdul Wahhab, 104
Baghdad, Iraq, Al-Hurra in, 107
Baghdad Pact, 61, 86
Baker, James, 25
Bakry, Mohammad, 204
Banna, Hassan, 49
Barnett, Sam, 140–42
Barrett, Edward W., 7, 10, 19, 63, 146
Barzzaz, Sa'ad, 238n19
Bashagha, Fathi, 185
Battle of the Barracks, in Egypt, 160
Batutu, Hana, 83
BBC. *See* British Broadcasting Corporation
BBG. *See* Broadcasting Board of Governors
Beers, Charlotte, 17–18, 25, 96
Beirut, Lebanon, 110–13
Ben Mhenni, Lina, 154, 253n44
Benton, William B., 228n4
Berger, Sandy, 25
Bernays, Edward L., 10
Berry, Burton, 54
Bessner, Daniel, 10
Bickert, Monika, 149, 173
Biden, Joe, 210; Global Engagement Center under, 198; "Initiative 9/11 Act," 128; Libya and, 179–80
Bigelow, Kathryn, 127

Bing, Christopher, 176
bin Laden, Osama, 27, 127, 169
bin Sultan, Zayed (Sheikh), 177
bint Nasser, Moza, 238n19
Bittman, Ladislav, 265n31
"black/gray" operations, in public diplomacy, 4, 24–26; *Irfaa Sawtak*, 170–72
Black Lives Matter movement: Global Engagement Center and, 196–97; Russia Today propaganda on, 199–203, 269n80
Blinken, Antony, 26
book translation campaigns, 6
Borshchevskaya, Anna, 189
Bouran, Nart, 118–19, 211, 248n57
Braude, Joseph, 255n59
Braun, Wernher von, 235n94
Bremer, Paul, 93
Breton, André, 41
Brewer, Sam Pope, 86
Brims, Robin, 78
British Broadcasting Corporation (BBC), 107
British Palestine Broadcasting Station, 67
Broadcasting Board of Governors (BBG), 77–78, 213, 232n61; credibility score for, 117; governing statutes of, 106; International Audience Research Program and, 245n14; in Iraq, 17, 102–3; Khoury and, 113; social media use and, 171; television programming and, 102. *See also* United States Agency for Global Media
Brokaw, Tom, 102–3
Brzeziński, Zbigniew, 128
Bureau of Education and Cultural Affairs, 207
Burkina Faso, 193

Bush, George H. W., 18, 25, 128
Bush, George W., 127, 255n59; Authorization for Use of Military Force under, 236n1; Chirac and, 73–74; Gates and, 88; international exchange programs under, 155–59; international law and, 73; Operation Enduring Freedom, 73–74; outsourcing of public diplomacy under, 173; Public Diplomacy 2.0 initiatives under, 161; public diplomacy under, 17; use of media through private sector, 22. *See also* 9/11 terrorist attacks
Butina, Maria, 205
Byrnes, Francis, 50–51

Caffery, Jefferson, 52, 207
Cairo, Egypt: Arab Spring uprisings in, 159–65; crypto-diplomacy in, 68; Radio Cairo, 9, 47–48; Soviet Union partnerships with bookstores in, 65; USIS in, 8, 47–48
Cairo Documents (Copeland), 71
Cairo Packaging Center, 47–48, 56, 85–86
Cairo project, 5
"Campaign of Truth," 35
Camp David Accords, 15
Cantor, Jeffrey, *p6*
Cantril, Hadley, 11, 56, 99
Caribbean region, Worldnet expansion into, 134
Carlin, John, 148
Carlson, Tucker, 199
CCF. *See* Congress for Cultural Freedom
Center for Strategic Counterterrorism Communications (CSCC), 28, 30; as American propaganda machine, 166; H. Clinton and, 165; CVE and, 165–70; Digital Outreach Team, 167–70, 197; Fernandez on, 166–67; ISIS as focus of, 168–69; National Security Council and, 166; origins and establishment of, 165; public diplomacy and, 168; YouTube and, 167
Central African Republic, 193
Central Intelligence Agency (CIA): Cairo project, 5; covert operations by, 5; creation and establishment of, 38; crypto-diplomacy and, 5, 96; Foreign Broadcasting Information Service, 61, 98; Franklin Book program funded by, 64; Nasser and, 71–72. *See also* Office of Strategic Services
Chamoun, Camille, 87
Chaurize, Alphonse Djamil, 45
Chirac, Jacques, 73–74
Chourabi, Sofiene, 253n44
Christian Maronite movement, in Lebanon, 104
Church Committee, 5
Churchill, Charles, 59
CIA. *See* Central Intelligence Agency
CIB campaigns. *See* coordinated inauthentic behavior campaigns
citizen journalism, during Arab Spring uprisings, 163
Civil Operations and the Revolutionary Development Support initiative (CORDS initiative), 90
Cleveland, Catherine, 189
Clinton, Bill: USIA disaggregation under, 18; Worldnet and, 134
Clinton, Hillary, 164–65
CNews, 179
Coalition Provisional Authority, in Iraq, 14, 86, 93, 111

304 INDEX

Cohen, Jared, 157, 159
Cold War: American propaganda during, 3–7; "Campaign of Truth" during, 35; Congress for Cultural Freedom and, 206; FSOs during, 97; Iron Curtain during, 39; Psychological Strategy Board and, 61–62. *See also* "New Cold War"
Colwell, Robert, 96
Comey, James, 148
Congress for Cultural Freedom (CCF), 206
Conniff, Brian, 108
Conover, Willis, 42
coordinated inauthentic behavior campaigns (CIB campaigns), 181
Copeland, Miles: *Cairo Documents*, 71; in Egypt, 68; *The Game of Nations*, 33, 60, 68–69, 71; Nasser and, 53–54, 60–61, 69
CORDS initiative. *See* Civil Operations and the Revolutionary Development Support initiative
Côte d'Ivoire, 191
Cottrell, Leonard S., 55
Council on Foreign Relations (U.S.), 36
countering violent extremism initiatives (CVE), 154; CSCC and, 165–70; defense intelligence establishment and, 159; MBC and, 142; Public Diplomacy 2.0 and, 164; on social media, 165
Cowan, Geoffrey, 140
Crewdson, John M., 63
Crimes of Abu-Bakr al-Baghdadi, The, p12
Crocker, Edward S, 54, 83–85
Cruz, Ted, 200
crypto-diplomacy, 5, 68, 96
CSCC. *See* Center for Strategic Counterterrorism Communications

Cull, Nicholas J., 6, 18, 29, 48, 60–62, 139–40, 164; on dissolution of Active Measure Working Group, 198–99; Gopher protocol and, 152
cultural exchange programs, Fulbright Award, 3
Currie, James T., 47
Cutler, Lloyd, 25
CVE. *See* countering violent extremism initiatives

Dagalo, Mohamed Hamdan, 193
Dakhil Washington, 115, 121
Daoud, Samy, 66
Darle, Pierre, 93
DARPA. *See* Defense Advanced Research Projects Agency
Daugherty, William E., 62
deep packet inspection technology (DPI), 163
Defense Advanced Research Projects Agency (DARPA), 12, 152
defense intellectuals, 55, 92
Defense Intelligence Agency (DIA), 222n32
defense intelligence industry, 11, 222n32; countering violent extremism initiatives and, 159
DeMille, Cecil B., 126
democracy, doctrine of equality and, 52–53. *See also* industrial democracy
democratic fallacy, 15
Democratic Republic of the Congo: Russian-based narrowcast campaigns from, 31
Department of Defense (DoD), U.S.: *Information Operations Roadmap*, 79; interactive Internet activities and, 153; Internet use by, 152–53; Military Education and Training

Program, 207; Minerva initiative, 13–14; Operations Research Division, 62; Radio Sawa and, 102; strategic communications and, 12
Dewey, John, 7, 36
DIA. *See* Defense Intelligence Agency
Digital Outreach Team (DOT), in CSCC, 167–70, 197
Dine, Thomas, 247n41
diplomacy. *See* crypto-diplomacy; public diplomacy
Dizard, Wilson P., 19, 36–37, 53, 228n9
Djerejian, Edward P., 95
"Djerejian Report," 14
Dobriansky, Paula, 255n59
doctrine of equality. *See* equality
DoD. *See* Department of Defense
Doha, Qatar, *Generation Entrepreneur, p9*
DOT. *See* Digital Outreach Team
Douglas, Kirk, 132
DPI. *See* deep packet inspection technology
Dukan, Saad Mohan, 107
Dutton, William, 168

Eddy, William A., 50–52
Educational Exchange Act, U.S. (1948), 35
Egypt: *Al-Ahram* in, 190, 192; Ansar al-Sharia movement in, 165; Arab nationalism in, 61; Battle of the Barracks in, 160; Cairo Packaging Center and, 47–48; cinema in, 64–65; Copeland in, 68; Free Officers' revolution in, 53; intellectual information invasion in, 66–72; Internet use in, 162–63; Al-Karnak Publishing in, 64; news sites in, 204; 1952 revolution in, 159; pro-democracy groups in, 161; publishing houses in, 64; Radio Cairo, 9; revocation of media licenses in, 163–64; Revolutionary Command Council in, 83; Russian-based narrowcast campaigns from, 31; Six Day War and, 53, 68; skepticism towards Americans in, 67; USIA budget in, 8–9; USIS in, 8–9. *See also* Cairo, Egypt; Nasser, Gamal Abdel
Eichelberger, James, 60, 68, 96
Einstein, Albert, 178
Eisa, Ibrahim, 119
Eisenhower, Dwight, 8, 87
El-Ariss, Tarek, 158
El-Mehrabi, Haidar, 117
Elswah, Mona, 189
Emergency Wartime Supplemental Appropriations Act, U.S. (2003), 106
England, Gordon, 153
equality, doctrine of, 52–53
Erdoğan, Recep, 183
Esalen Soviet-American Exchange Program, 137
European colonialism, communications technology and, 39
Evans, Ryan, 91–92
Eveland Wilbur, 68, 81–82, 235n93
Eye on Democracy, 117

Facebook: Arab Spring uprisings and, 160; *Irfaa Sawtak* and, 171–72; *Kulluna Khaled Sa'id*, 156–57; in Libya, 182; Madison Volleywood Project and, 149; radicalization via, 173; RT Arabic and, 195; Salah and, 156–57
Fahmy, Aziz, 140
Fahs, Sayyid Hani, 104–5
Fairbanks, Richard, 25, 125–26, 128, 135
Faisal II (King), 82, 86
"Family of Man, The" (Steichen), *p2*

Fayrouz, 42
Feith, Douglas, 222n35
Fendi, Mamoun, 244n4
Fernandez, Alberto, 110, 118–19, 164, 166–67, 211–12
film and cinema: in Egypt, 64–65; Voice of America use of, 127. *See also* Hollywood industry
FIS. *See* Foreign Information Service
5+5 Action Plan, 180
Ford Foundation, 19
Foreign Affairs, 88
Foreign Affairs Reform And Restructuring Act, U.S. (1998), 18
Foreign Agents Registration Act, U.S. (1938), 205
Foreign Broadcasting Information Service (Open Source Center), 61, 98
Foreign Information Service (FIS), 37
Foreign Service Officers (FSOs), 1, 15, 97
France, Libya and, 179
Franklin Book program, 64–66, 81, 206; Operation Enduring Freedom and, 73–74
Franklin Publications, 62
Free, Lloyd, 11
Freedom of Information Act, U.S. (1967), 149, 256n6
Free Officers' revolution, in Egypt, 53
"Friday of Rage," 160
Friedman, Thomas, 135
Frontline, 135
FSOs. *See* Foreign Service Officers
Fulbright, William, 158

Gabrielle, Lea, 208
Gallup, George, 10. *See also* public opinion polling

Galster, Steven R., 132–33
Game of Nations, The (Copeland), 33, 60, 68–69, 71
Garbo, Greta, 60
Gary, Jerome, 123, 137, 209
Gates, Robert M., 12, 88–90, 92, 164
Geary, Brent, 49
GEC. *See* Global Engagement Center
Gedmin, Jeffrey, 214
Generation Entrepreneur, 6, 26, 137–38, *p9*
Gershkovich, Evan, 205
Ghana, 191
Ghonim, Wael, 156
Ginsberg, Marc, 125
Glassman, James K., 155–59
Global Counterterrorism Forum, 174
Global Engagement Center (GEC), 16, 28, 195, 199; under Biden, 198; Black Lives Matter movement and, 196–97; budget for, 196; congressional formalization of, 196; goal and purpose of, 196–97; ISIS and, 197–98; legacy of, 208; National Security Council and, 197; resilience-building as focus of, 196–97; under Donald Trump, 198
global South: Asia Foundation and, 64; Russian propaganda in, 265n32, 267n52. *See also specific countries*
Government Performance and Results Act (GPRA), U.S. (1993), 16
Grady, Henry F., 39–40
Gray, David W., 87

Haddad, Joumana, 119
Haidar, Sharar, 78

Hainmueller, Jens, 234n72
Harb, Mouafac, 103, 108–9, 128–29, 140, 244n9, 246n31
Hariri, Rafik, 113
Harman, Jane, 136–37
Harris, Kamala, 28, 209
Hart, Justin, 6
Hatem, Muhammad Abd al-Kader, 60–61, 67, 241n65
Hawkens, Ash, 132
Heikal, Mohammad Hassanein, 71
Heil, Alan, 36
Heimann, Joseph, 153
Hewitt, Don, 135, *p10*
Hezbollah/Hizballah, 109, 111
Hifter, Khalifa, 181, 201–2
Hitti, Philip K., 49
Hogan, John, 48
Hollywood industry: American propaganda via, 33–34; political outreach to, 22; USIA and, 126–27
Hoskins, Harold, 33–34
Hour, The. See *Al-Sa'at*
Howard, Philip, 189
HTS initiative. *See* Human Terrain System initiative
Hughes, Karen P., 27, 110
Human Terrain System initiative (HTS initiative), 12, 90–92
Hussain, Rashad, 27
Hussein, Saddam, 93, 95–96, 101, 104, 110, 238n19
Hyde, Henry, 18

I Believe (radio program), 44
Ibrahim, Saad Eddin, 103
ICT. *See* Institute of Creative Technologies
Idris, Youssef, 42

IIA. *See* interactive Internet activities; International Information Administration
IISR. *See* Institute for International Social Research
"I Love Life" campaign, 143
IMN. *See* Iraqi Media Network
Independent Media Foundation, 19
industrial democracy, 7
informational and educational exchange programs, 1. *See also* public diplomacy
Information and Educational Exchange Act of 1948, U.S., 3
information radio. *See* Radio Mu'alamat
information statecraft, 25
information terrain, 90–92
Information Wars (Stengel), 166
"Initiative 9/11 Act," 128
Injaz initiative, 6
Institute for International Social Research (IISR), 11
Institute for the Study of War, 267n52
Institute of Creative Technologies (ICT), 136–38
interactive Internet activities (IIA), 153
International Broadcasting Service, *p1*
international exchange programs: Alliance of Youth Movements, 151, 155–58; models for, 214–15; public diplomacy through, 155–59; Russian sponsorship of, 190–91; *Al-Sadaqah* and, 157–58
international exchange programs under, 155–59
International Information Administration (IIA), 9, 41, 229n16
international law, George W. Bush foreign policies under, 73

308 INDEX

International Traffic in Arms Regulations (ITAR), 176
International Visitor Leadership Program, 207
Internet: DARPA and, 12, 152; deep packet inspection technology, 163; Department of Defense use of, 152–53; in Egypt, 162–63; interactive Internet activities, 153; in Libya, 184; Al-Qaeda use of, 150–51. *See also* social media
intersubjective communication, 172
Iran, Operation "Ajax," 70
Iran Disinformation Project, 198
Iraq: Al Arabiya in, 107; Baghdad Pact, 61, 86; British presence in, 85; Broadcasting Board of Governors in, 17, 102–3; Coalition Provisional Authority in, 14, 86, 93, 111; Communications and Media Commission in, 95; development history of, 93; international media organizations in, 107–8; Al Jazeera in, 107; March 14 Movement in, 113; media networks in, 92–97; *The Old Social Classes and the Revolutionary Movement of Iraq*, 83; Operation Desert Storm in, 88; Operation Enduring Freedom, 73–80; Al-Qaeda in, 151; Radio Baghdad, 85; Radio Free Iraq, 24, 77; *Radio Mu'alamat* in, 76; USAID in, 102; USIA in, 80, 85–86; USIS in, 80; U.S. media operations in, 80–87. *See also* Iraq War; Islamic State of Iraq and Syria; Operation Iraqi Freedom; *specific topics*
Iraq and the World (TV show), 102
Iraqi Media Network (IMN), 86, 92–93; Cantor and, p6; programming on, 94; *Al-Sabah* as part of, 95–97

Iraq News Agency, 95–96, 101
Iraq War (2003): Human Terrain System, 12; media projects during, 24; public diplomacy during, 12
Ireland, Philip, 60
Irfaa Sawtak, 170–72
Iron Curtain, 39
ISIL. *See* Islamic State in Iraq and the Levant
ISIS. *See* Islamic State of Iraq and Syria
Al-Islah, 45
Islamic State in Iraq and the Levant (ISIL), 147
Islamic State of Iraq and Syria (ISIS), 147, 149, 168; civil war with Al-Qaeda, 169–70; *Al-Furqan* and, 151–52; Global Engagement Center and, 197–98; messaging by, 177–78; online activity by, 175–76; rebranding of, 151–52; Twittersphere for, 175
Islamophobia, 149
Israel: Abraham Accords and, 120–21; British Palestine Broadcasting Station, 67; Al-Hurra coverage of, 213; Six Day War and, 53, 68; state creation for, 81–82; U.S. support of, 47; Zionism and, 47
ITAR. *See* International Traffic in Arms Regulations
Izvestia, 41

Jaber, Ali, 142
Jaber, Heather, 142
Jabouri, Mishan, 114, 247n39
Jackson, C. D., 19–20
James, William, 36
Jankowicz, Nina, 270n87
Jeffrey, Bob, 148
Jennings, Peter, 103

INDEX 309

John Dewey (Rockefeller), 7
John S. and James L. Knight Foundation, 19
Johnson, Lyndon B., 34, 90
Jones, Jim, 265n32
Jordan, Six Day War and, 53, 68
journalism, journalists and: embedded press system for, 87–88; *Reporters on the Battlefield*, 88
Jumblatt, Walid, 104–5, 113

Kaplan, Robert, 14
Kearns, Frank, 68
Kennedy, John F., 42
Kern, Holger Lutz, 234n72
Kerry, John, 148
Keyser, Christopher, 142
Khoury, Eli, 111–13, 128
King, Martin Luther, Jr., 178
Kiselev, Dimitry, 190
Kishk, Jalal, 70–71
Kissinger, Henry, 25, 128
Kohler, Foy D., *p1*
Kraidy, Marwan, 138–39, 142, 246n23
Kulluna Khaled Sa'id (We Are All Khaled Said) (Facebook page), 156–57
Kurmasheva, Alsu, 205

Language and Speech Exploitation Resources project (LASER project), 12
Language Flagship program, 14
LASER project. *See* Language and Speech Exploitation Resources project
Lashin, Mahmud Tahir, 65
Laswell, Harold, 10
Latin America, Worldnet expansion into, 134
Layalina Productions, 250n7, 253n42, *p10*; *'Ala tariq fi Amrika* and, 125–29;

Fairbanks and, 125–26; foreign-based network partnerships with, 134; funding of, 143–46; *Generation Entrepreneur*, 6, 26, 137–38, *p9*; ICT and, 136–38; Middle East Broadcasting Company and, *p3*; political clout of, 128; Shahabian and, 123, 128–29; Track Two diplomacy and, 135
Lebanese Broadcasting Corporation International (LBCI), 95
Lebanon, 87; Association of Muslim 'Ulama', 104; Christian Maronite movement in, 104; Druze sect in, 104; "I Love Life" campaign in, 143; Khoury in, 113; media surveys in, 59; Operation Magic Carpet in, 46
Le Corbusier, 64
Lerner, Daniel, 10, 54–55, 59, 232n56
Let Poland Be Poland (film), 30, 130
Levanthal, Todd, 187, 199, 265n31
Levchenko, Stanislav, 265n31
Levine, Art, 114, 247n41
Lévi-Strauss, Claude, 41
Libya: *Afrigatenews* in, 182–84; Biden and, 179–80; CIB campaigns in, 181; CNews and, 179; Facebook in, 182; 5+5 Action Plan and, 180; France and, 179; Internet websites in, 184; media groups in, 180; Meta in, 181; Muslim Brotherhood and, 181, 185; proxy communications war in, 180; Russia in, 181, 185–88; Russian-based narrowcast campaigns from, 31; social media in, 181–82; Tarhuna massacre, 183–85; *218TV/218NEWS*, 182–84. *See also* Tripoli, Libya
Libyan National Army (LNA), 180
Lieberman, Evelyn, 18
Linebarger, Paul, 69

310 INDEX

Linguistic Inquiry and Word Count tool, 98
Lippman, Walter, 10, 59
LNA. *See* Libyan National Army
Lobel, Aaron, 26, 255n59
Lord, Carnes, 23
Losing Hearts and Minds? (Lord), 23
Lundgren, Dolph, 186

MacArthur, Douglas, 62
MacCann, Richard Dyer, 29–30
MacLeish, Archibald, 34, 35, 228n4, 240n46
Madi, Ilya Abu, 43
Madison Volleywood Project: Facebook and, 149; Freedom of Information Act and, 149; ISIL and, 147; ISIS and, 147, 149; Islamophobia and, 149; Operation Inherent Resolve and, 148; origins of, 148; Silicon Valley and, 150–54; social media and, 150; technology companies' role in, 147–54
Magharabia.com, 153–54
Maghreb region, Office of War Information in, 39
Mahfouz, Naguib, 42
Mahmoud, Hassan, 158
Mali, 193
March 14 Movement, in Iraq, 113
Markel, Lester, 36
Marks, Leonard, 59
Mashkour, Salem, 109
Massoud, Ahmed Shah, 131
Mattis, James, 174
Mauri, Joseph, 200
Mauritania, 154
May, Mark, 9, 58, 65
MBC. *See* Middle East Broadcasting Company

MBN. *See* Middle East Broadcasting Network
McCarthy, Joseph, 41–42
McClure, Robert A., 50
McDonough, Denis, 148
McHale, Judith, 171
McKinstry, Arthur, 50
McLaughlin, Jenna, 175
Meet the Press, 21
Melhem, Hisham, 135
MEMRI. *See* Middle East Media Research Institute
MEPI. *See* Middle East Partnership Initiative
MERN. *See* Middle East Radio Network
Meta, 181. *See also* Facebook
METN. *See* Middle East Television Network
Michel, Nadia, 111
Mickelson, Sig, 233n62
Middle East and North Africa region: Middle East Doctrine and, 87; Voice of America broadcasts in, 39–40. *See also* North Africa; *specific countries*
Middle East Broadcasting Company (MBC), 126; British licensing for, 139–40; countering violent extremism initiatives and, 142; hypermedia space and, 138; Al-Jazeera and, 138–39; Layalina Productions and, 139; al-Qasabi and, 140–41; reality TV on, 138; Saudi Broadcasting Authority and, 141; *Selfie*, 141–42; talk shows on, 139–40; *Tash ma Tash*, 140–41. See also *On the Road in America*
Middle East Broadcasting Network (MBN), 17, 30; audience metrics for, 117; creation and origins of,

23, 100; Fernandez and, 110, 118; *Irfaa Sawtak*, 170–72; social media and, 170–72; staff reductions at, 209; structure of, 106
Middle East Doctrine, under Eisenhower, 87
Middle East Media Research Institute (MEMRI), 120
Middle East Partnership Initiative (MEPI), 138, 209
Middle East Radio Network (MERN), 23, 103, *p8*
Middle East Television Network (METN), 125
Military Education and Training Program, 207
Minerva initiative, 13–14
Minerva Project, 89
Mitchell, W. J. T., 31
Monde, Le, 74–75
MOST. See Muslims on Screen and Television
Motion Picture Service, of USIA, 20, 134
Mozambique, 193
Mroueh, Jamil, 104
Mubarak, Hosni, 163
Muhieddin, Zakaria, 69
Muñoz, Arturo, 75, 79–80, 236n7
Murrow, Edward R., 16, 42, 44, 81
Musa, Abdul, 202
Muslim Brotherhood, 49, 160, 181, 185
Muslims on Screen and Television (MOST), 142

Naguib, Mohammed, 69
Nahwa al-huriyya (Towards Freedom TV), 78–79
Nasser, Gamal Abdel, 235n94; anti-imperialism policies under, 67; Arab nationalism and, 61, 70; Baghdad Pact and, 61; CIA and, 71–72; Copeland and, 53–54, 60–61, 69; nonalignment policies under, 61; Radio Cairo and, 55; Voice of the Arabs and, 67
Nassif, Daniel, 110, 245n21
Nassrallah, Hassan, 109–10
National Defense Education Act, U.S. (2008), 13
National Electronic Security Authority, 176
National Institute of Psychology, 59
nationalism, Arab, 61, 70
National Security Agency (U.S.), 61, 176–77
National Security Council (U.S.), 81, 166, 197
Nazi Germany, 36–38
Netanyahu, Benjamin, 210
"New Beginning, A" (Obama), 116
"New Cold War," 3
New York Times, 11, 37–38, 63, 76, 180
Nicholson, Emma, 78
Nigeria, 191
9/11 terrorist attacks, in U.S.: American propaganda apparatus after, 2, 106, 220n9; public diplomacy funding after, 1, 16; Al Qaeda and, 27–28. See also Bush, George W.; war on terror
Nine from Little Rock (film), 30
Nixon, Richard, 21
Nolan, Christopher, 209
North Africa: Maghreb region, 39; Office of War Information in, 8, 79; public diplomacy in, 7–8; USIA operations in, 66. *See also specific countries*
Nunn, Sam, 25

Nusseibeh, Sari, 103
Nye, Joseph, 16, 19

Obama, Barack, 27; Arab Spring uprisings and, 116; CSCC under, 28, 30, 165–70; Gates and, 88; "A New Beginning" speech, 116
Objectives and Programs for National Security, 20
Office of Educational Exchange, 229n16
Office of International Information (OII), 229n16
Office of International Information and Cultural Affairs (OICA), 126
Office of Naval Research (ONR), 11
Office of Strategic Influence (OSI), 93–94
Office of Strategic Services (OSS), 33–34
Office of War Information (OWI): dissolution of, 38; MacLeish and, 35; in Maghreb, 39; in North Africa, 8, 79; F. Roosevelt and, 38; Voice of America and, 37
OICA. See Office of International Information and Cultural Affairs
OII. See Office of International Information
Old Social Classes and the Revolutionary Movement of Iraq, The (Batutu), 83
On the Road in America (*'Ala tariq fi Amrika*), 137, 139, 250n7, p5, p11; inspiration for, 124; Layalina Productions and, 125–29; public diplomacy through, 124–25; Saifan and, 123–25; Shahabian and, 123–25; Soviet influences on, 125
ONR. See Office of Naval Research
Open Source Center. See Foreign Broadcasting Information Service
Open Technology Fund, 225n53

Operation "Ajax," 70
Operation Desert Storm, 88
Operation Enduring Freedom, 73–75; American propaganda during, 76–80; Baghdad Pact, 61, 86; protests against, 76; psychological warfare during, 76–78; Radio Free Iraq, 77; "Voice of the Gulf," 77
Operation Inherent Resolve, 148, 170
Operation Iraqi Freedom, p7. See also Iraq War
Operation Magic Carpet, 46–48
Orwell, George, 144–45
OSI. See Office of Strategic Influence
Osnos, Evan, 2
OSN Yahala Shabab, p9
Outb, Sayyid, 207
OWI. See Office of War Information

Palestine, Al-Hurra coverage of, 213
Panetta, Leon, 165
PAOs. See public affairs officers
Parker, Jason C., 6
Parson, Steve, 202
Pasha, Azzam, 51–52
Passeta, Marty, 130
Passing of Traditional Society, The (Lerner), 54–55
Pattern of Human Concerns, The (Cantril), 56
Pattiz, Norman J., 22–23, 102, 112–13, 115, 128
Pax Britannica, 68
Penrose, Stephen, 66–67
people's radio. See *Volksempfänger*
Picasso, Pablo, 178
Pintak, Lawrence, 18
pluralism, in U.S., 36
"Polish crisis," 129–30
Polk, William R., 54

polling. *See* public opinion polling
Polyakova, Alina, 196
Pompeo, Mike, 122
Portman, Rob, 198
Powell, Colin, 138
Prados, John, 5
Pravda, 41
Price, David H., 10
Prigozhin, Yevgeny, 186, 194
Project Global Officer (Project GO), 98
Project Raven, 176–77
propaganda: hard science approach to, 15–16; public diplomacy as distinct from, 7–8; public opinion polling and, 10; from Russia, 31, 189; from Soviet Union, 40. *See also* American propaganda; Russia; Russia Today
ProPublica, 108, 114, 247n39
Providence (magazine), 120
Psychological Strategy Board (PSB), 61–62
psychological warfare, 1; during Operation Enduring Freedom, 76–78; "Research for Psychological Warfare," 55; Voice of America and, 38. *See also* public diplomacy
public affairs officers (PAOs), 40
public diplomacy: through *'Ala tariq fi Amrika*, 124–25; "black/grey" operations, 4, 24–26, 170–72; during G. H. W. Bush administration, 18; during G. W. Bush administration, 17; conceptual approach to, 1–3; CSCC and, 168; DARPA and, 12; funding for, 1; future of, 214–17; HTS initiative, 12; Al-Hurra and, 109; information statecraft and, 25; through international exchange programs, 155–59; during Iraq War, 12; LASER project, 12; mission of, 16–25; in North Africa, 7–8; outsourcing of, 173; overt examples of, 4; during postwar era, 29–32; propaganda as distinct from, 7–8; public opinion polling on, 8; *Al-Sadaqah* and, 4, 53; social media and, 150; soft power and, 1–2, 9; TIDES initiative, 12, 98; Track One-and-a-Half, 135–36; Track Two, 21, 135, 137, 142; 2.0 initiatives, 161–62, 164; in United Arab Emirates, 120–22; "white" operations, 4. *See also* American propaganda
Public Diplomacy 2.0 initiatives, 161–62; countering violent extremism initiatives and, 164
public opinion polling: American Institute on Public Opinion, 10; American propaganda and, 10; in *Al-Hayat fi Amrika*, 58–59; in Lebanon, 59; on public diplomacy, 8; in West Germany, 59
Public Opinion Quarterly, 11, 56
Pudovkin, V. I., 65
Putin, Vladimir, 189, 207

Qatar, *Generation Entrepreneur*, p9
Qiao Liang, 89, 92
Quantum Communications, 173

Rabatat Minerfah (The Minerva Association) (journal), 44
Radio Baghdad, 85
Radio Cairo, 9, 47–48, 55
Radio Free Asia (RFA), 17
Radio Free Europe/Radio Liberty (RFE/RI), 17, 23, 42, 212, 233n62

Radio Free Iraq, 24, 77
Radio Mu'alamat (information radio), 76
Radio Mustaqbal, 78
Radio Nahrain, 78
Radio Sawa, 100, p8; Department of Defense and, 102; early iterations of, 102; Al-Hurra and, 107; Pattiz and, 22–23, 102; Russia Today and, 189
Radio Tikrit, 77
Rahman, Anwar Abdul, 103
Ramadan, Said, 49
Ramonet, Ignacio, 74
Rania (Queen), 143, 255n61
Rather, Dan, 102
Reagan, Ronald, 129–30
reality TV, 138, 144. See also *On the Road in America*
Register, Larry, 113
Remnick, David, 2
Reorganization Plan No. 8, 41
Reorganization Plan No. 9, 61
Reporters on the Battlefield, 88
Republic of the Congo, 193
"Research for Psychological Warfare" (Riley and Cottrell), 55
Rezaian, Jason, 198
RFA. See Radio Free Asia
RFE/RL. See Radio Free Europe/Radio Liberty
Rid, Thomas, 204, 270n86
Riley, John W., 55
Roberts, Kevin, 112–13
Rockefeller, Steven, 7
Rockefeller Foundation, 19
Rogers, Michael, 148
Rohrabacher, Dana, 106
Romerstein, Herbert, 187
Roosevelt, Eleanor, 33–34
Roosevelt, Franklin D., 38

Roosevelt, Jr., Kermit (Kim), 47, 68, 70
Roosevelt, Theodore, 47
Rove, Karl, 22, 127
RT. See Russia Today
RT Arabic, 119, 188–89, 195
Rubin, James P., 198
Rugh, William, 152
Russia: Arab language propaganda, 189; in global South, 265n32, 265n52; international exchange programs and, 190–91; in Libya, 181, 185–88; media-sharing agreements with, 194; narrowcast campaigns, 31; propaganda from, 31; soft power for, 192; in sub-Saharan Africa, 191–93, 265n32; in Syria, 191; "Translator Project," 194; Ukraine and, 203–5
Russia-Africa Summit, 191
Russia Today (RT): Al-Ahram-Sputnik agreement and, 192–93; Arab Spring uprisings and, 156; audience share for, 190; Black Lives Matter movement propaganda and, 199–203, 269n80; "hate preaching," 194; Al-Hurra and, 188–89; Al Jazeera and, 188, 190; origins of, 188; Radio Sawa and, 189; rebranding of, 188; Sky News Arabia and, 121; subscription rates for, 195; Western media reproduced on, 190; YouTube channels for, 204. *See also specific channels*
Ryan, Yasmine, 253n44

Saadeh, Antoun, 253n42
Saatch & Saatchi Levant, in Beirut, 111–13
Sabbagh, Isa Khalil, 8, 42–44

Sabbagh, Issa, 43, *p1*
Sadaawi, Nawaal, 42
Sage Handbook of Propaganda, 170
Sageman, Marc, 150–51, 159
Saghieh, Hazem, 104
Saifan, Lara Abu, 123–25, *p11*
Salah, Ahmed, 156–57
Salamandra, Christa, 141
Salazar, Philippe-Joseph, 236n104
Salman, Farid, 104
Salti, Soraya, 253n44, *p9*
Satloff, Robert, 121, 244n9
Saudi Arabia, censorship in, 82–83
Saudi Broadcasting Authority, 141
Saunders, Frances Stonor, 6
Sawab Center, 29–30, 175, 177, 187, 196
Sawt al-Arab, 67
Schectman, Joel, 176
Schneider, Cynthia, 142
Schramm, Wilbur, 10
Schultz, George, 25
Schwartz, Larry, 1, 80, 175, 188, 211, 238n23
Scott, Martha, 42
Scowcroft, Brent, 25, 128
Seib, Philip, 6
Seif, Salah Abu, 42
Selfie (TV show), 141–42
Shahabian, Leon, 6, 25–26, 123, 128–29, 214, 246n31, 250n7; Track Two diplomacy and, 135
Shammam, Mahmud, 180
Sheen, Charlie, 186
Sherwood, Robert, 37
Shugalei (film), 31–32, 185–86
Siele, Martin K. N., 191
Silverberg, Daniel, 153
Simpson, Christopher, 5, 10, 232n56
Six Day War, 53, 68
60 Minutes, 108
Sky News Arabia, 118–19, 121

Smith-Mundt Act, U.S. (1948), 35
Snyder, Alvin, 129–30, 132, 134, 144, 186, 191–92
social media: Arab Spring uprisings and, 160; Broadcasting Board of Governors and, 171; countering violent extremism initiatives on, 165; *Kulluna Khaled Sa'id*, 156–57; in Libya, 181–82; Madison Volleywood Project and, 150; MBN presence on, 170–72; media and, 150. *See also* Facebook; Twitter; YouTube
soft power: Gates on, 88; as hard science, 9–16; Nye on, 19; public diplomacy and, 1–2, 9; Russia and, 192; of Soviet Union, 131–32; war on terror and, 1–2
Somalia, Al-Qaeda in, 151
Sorensen, Thomas C., 20–21, 59, 233n69
Soros Foundation, 19
Soukar, Thaer, 248n57
South Asia, language designated positions for, 14–15
Soviet Union: in Afghanistan, 131–32; Cairo bookstore partnerships with, 65; Esalen Soviet-American Exchange Program, 137; propaganda broadcasts from, 40; soft power of, 131–32; TASS news service in, 133, 186–87. *See also* Cold War
Spanish Earth, The (film), 34
Speier, Hans, 10, 15
Sproule, J. Michael, 10
Stakes, The (Telhami), 15
Star Wars initiative, 130
state-private networks, 24
Steichen, Edward, *p2*
Stengel, Richard, 28, 165–66, 197
stereotypes, 10

Stevens, George, 126
Story of G. I. Joe, The, 127
Streibert, Theodore, 29–30
sub-Saharan Africa: Russian involvement in, 191–93, 265n32. *See also specific countries*
Sudan, 31, 193
Sukarieh, Mayssoun, 143
Surkov, Vladislav, 181
Syria, 53, 68, 70, 87, 191. *See also* Islamic State of Iraq and Syria

Tadros, Samuel, 119
Taliban, 26
TALON Reporting System, 222n35
Tarhuna, Libya, massacre in, 183–85
Tash ma Tash (TV show), 140–41
TASS news service, in Soviet Union, 133, 186–87
Taymur, Mahmud, 65
Teicholz, Nina, 127–28
Telhami, Shibley, 15
Thanksgiving in Peshawar (film), 132
Thelwall, Michael, 168
This I Believe (Murrow), 81
Thomson, Dorothy, 51
TIDES initiative. *See* Translingual Information Detection, Extraction, and Summarization initiative
Tikerly, Fuad, 107
Tillerson, Rex, 198
TIP. *See* Total Information Awareness Program
Tomlinson, Kenneth, 101, 115
Total Information Awareness Program (TIP), 222n35
Towards Freedom TV. *See Nahwa al-huriyya*
Track One-and-a-Half diplomacy, 135–36

Track Two diplomacy, 21, 135, 137, 142
"Translator Project," 194
Translingual Information Detection, Extraction, and Summarization initiative (TIDES initiative), 12, 98
Treaster, Joseph R., 63
Tripoli, Libya, invasion of, 181
Truman, Harry, 7, 61, 81
Trump, Donald, 28, 181, 202; Abraham Accords and, 120–22; Global Engagement Center under, 198; Al-Hurra and, 117–21, 211–12; Iran Disinformation Project, 198
Trump, Donald, Jr., 200
Tueni, Gebran, 104, 113
Tunisia, 59, 106; Arab Spring uprisings in, 159, 163
Tunisian Telecommunications Agency, 163
Twitter (X), 175
218TV/218NEWS, 182–84

UAE. *See* United Arab Emirates
Udall, Mark, 127
Ukraine, Russian propaganda in, 203–5
Understanding Terror Networks (Sageman), 150–51
United Arab Emirates (UAE): Abraham Accords and, 120–21; authoritarian regime in, 174; sale of U.S. weapons to, 122; Sawab Center, 29–30, 175, 177, 187, 196; Sky News Arabia and, 118–19; U.S. public diplomacy in, 120–22; war on terror and, 174–75
United States (U.S.): Alliance of Youth Movements program,

151, 155–58, 162, 257n27; Arms Export Control Act, 176; Council on Foreign Relations, 36; Educational Exchange Act, 35; Emergency Wartime Supplemental Appropriations Act, 106; Foreign Affairs Reform And Restructuring Act, 18; Foreign Agents Registration Act, 205; Freedom of Information Act, 149, 256n6; Global Engagement Center, 195–99; Government Performance and Results Act, 16; Information and Educational Exchange Act of 1948, 3; National Defense Education Act, 13; National Electronic Security Authority, 176; National Security Agency, 61, 176–77; National Security Council, 81, 166, 197; Office of Strategic Influence, 93–94; pluralism in, 36; Smith-Mundt Act, 35. *See also* American propaganda; Central Intelligence Agency; Cold War; Department of Defense; 9/11 terrorist attacks; Operation Iraqi Freedom; *specific topics*

United States Agency for Global Media (USAGM), 187–88, 211

United States Agency for International Development (USAID): independent media assistance funding by, 18–19; Injaz initiative, 6; investment in Iraq, 102

United States European Command (USEUCOM), 153–54

United States Information Agency (USIA): under B. Clinton, 18; creation and establishment of, 38; DARPA and, 152; disaggregation of, 7, 18, 210; Egyptian budget, 8–9; foreign-language expansion of, 53–54; Hollywood industry involvement in, 126–27; in Iraq, 80, 85–86; under Johnson, 34; *Let Poland Be Poland*, 30, 130; media surveys by, 58–59; Motion Picture and Television Division, 63; Motion Picture Service, 20, 134; publications produced through, 53; target audience for, 53–56; *Thanksgiving in Peshawar*, 132; Wick and, 129–30; Worldnet and, 130–32. *See also Al-Hayat fi Amrika*; *Al-Sadaqah*; United States Information Service; *specific topics*

United States Information and Education Exchange Program, 229n16

United States Information Service (USIS): in Cairo, 8, 47–48; Cairo Packaging Center and, 47–48, 56; consolidation of, 9; in Iraq, 80; Voice of America and, 38

United States International Information and Educational Exchange Program (USIE), 49

Unrestricted Warfare (Gates), 89–90

U.S. *See* United States

U.S. Agency for Global Media (USAGM), 16–17

USAGM. *See* United States Agency for Global Media

USAID. *See* United States Agency for International Development

USEUCOM. *See* United States European Command

USIA. *See* United States Information Agency

USIA Beirut, *p2, p5*
USIE. *See* United States International Information and Educational Exchange Program
USIS. *See* United States Information Service
U.S. *Military Information Operations in Afghanistan*, 75

Valenti, Jack, 127
Vance, J. D., 204
Vaughn, James R., 24, 85–86
VOA. *See* Voice of America
VOA Arabic, 8, 42–46, 157
Voice of America (VOA): in Arabic, 8, 42–46, 157; book translation campaigns, 6; consolidation of, 9; expansion of languages on, 41; film units in, 127; Foreign Information Service and, 37; Gopher protocol and, 152; Al-Hashimi on, *p1*; limited effectiveness of, 209; MacLeish and, 35; in Middle East and North Africa region, 39–40; in Nazi Germany, 37–38; *New York Times* and, 37–38; Office of War Information takeover of, 37; origins of, 37; overt propaganda through, 4–5; psychological warfare and, 38; Reorganization Plan No. 8, 41; Sabbagh and, 43, *p1*; satellite technology and, 134; scope of international broadcasts, 37–38; studios for, *p8*; USAGM and, 17; USIS and, 38; during WWII, 127. *See also specific channels*
Voice of FreeIraq, 101–2
Voice of Israel, 67
Voice of the Arabs, 67
"Voice of the Gulf," 77

Volksempfänger (people's radio), 36
Votel, Joseph, 174

Wahab, Mohammed Abdel, 42
Wang Xiangsui, 89, 92
war on terror: second front for, 75; soft power and, 1–2; United Arab Emirates' role in, 174–75
War on the Rocks, 91–92
Washington Institute of Near East Studies, 115, 121, 244n9
Washington Post, 27, 87, 130, 174, 198
Washington Times, 90, 140
We Are All Khaled Said. See Kulluna Khaled Sa'id
West Germany, 59, 60, 234n72
Weybright, Victor, 63–64
Whewell, Tim, 184
"white" operations, in public diplomacy, 4
Wick, Charles, 22, 129, 132, 134, 144
Wikileaks, 156, 162
Wilford, Hugh, 6
Wilson, Woodrow, 51
Wing and a Prayer, 127
Wolfe, Bertram, 41
Wolf Pack (film), 31–32
Word War, The (Sorensen), 20–21
Worldnet: AFP and, 133; African Network, 133, 143; American propaganda through, 129–34; B. Clinton and, 134; expansion of, 131; funding reduction for, 133; international competition to, 133; in Latin America and Caribbean, 134; origins of, 129; "Polish crisis" on, 129–30; Reagan and, 129–30; satellite technology and, 131; TASS and, 133; USIA and, 130–32
Wynne, Frank, 99

X. *See* Twitter

Yaffa, Joshua, 3
Yakovlev, Alexandre, 22
Yemen, Al-Qaeda in, 151
Yemenite Jews, migration of, 47
YouTube, 167, 204, 269n80

Zaharna, R. S., 220n9
Zamyatin, Leonid M., 200
Zemmour, Eric, 179
Zero Dark Thirty, 127
Zinni, Anthony, 174
Zionism, Zionist movements and, 43, 47
Žižek, Slavoj, 99

GPSR Authorized Representative: Easy Access System Europe, Mustamäe tee
50, 10621 Tallinn, Estonia, gpsr.requests@easproject.com

www.ingramcontent.com/pod-product-compliance
Lightning Source LLC
Chambersburg PA
CBHW022029290426
44109CB00014B/800